BASIL STREET BLUES and MOSAIC

Michael Holroyd has written the Lives of Augustus John, Bernard Shaw and Lytton Strachey (which was filmed as *Carrington*) as well as a group biography of the Irving–Terry dynasty called *A Strange Eventful History*. His most recent publication is *A Book of Secrets*. He is the first non-fiction writer to have been awarded the British Literature Prize and has been knighted for his services to Literature. He lives in London and Somerset with his wife Margaret Drabble.

ALSO BY MICHAEL HOLROYD

Non Fiction

Hugh Kingsmill

Unreceived Opinions

Lytton Strachey

Augustus John

Bernard Shaw

Works on Paper

A Strange Eventful History

A Book of Secrets

Fiction

A Dog's Life

As Editor

The Best of Hugh Kingsmill

Lytton Strachey by Himself

The Art of Augustus John (with Malcolm Easton)

The Genius of Shaw

The Shorter Strachey (with Paul Levy)

William Gerhardie's God's Fifth Column
(with Robert Skidelsky)

MICHAEL HOLROYD

Basil Street Blues
and
Mosaic

Family Stories

VINTAGE BOOKS
London

Published by Vintage 2010

2 4 6 8 10 9 7 5 3 1

Basil Street Blues copyright © Michael Holroyd 1999
Mosaic copyright © Michael Holroyd 2004

Basil Street Blues first published in Great Britain in 1999 by
Little, Brown and Company
Mosaic first published in 2004 by Little, Brown and Company

Vintage
Random House, 20 Vauxhall Bridge Road,
London SW1V 2SA

www.vintage-books.co.uk

Addresses for companies within The Random House Group Limited can be
found at: www.randomhouse.co.uk/offices.htm

The Random House Group Limited Reg. No. 954009

A CIP catalogue record for this book
is available from the British Library

ISBN 9780099548959

Typeset in Sabon by Palimpsest Book Production Limited,
Falkirk, Stirlingshire
Printed and bound in Great Britain by
CPI Cox & Wyman, Reading RG1 8EX

Contents

Basil Street Blues

PART I

INTERVAL

Mosaic

Acknowledgements

I am indebted to many individuals and organisations in the preparation of *Basil Street Blues*. Among the former are: Margit Andréen, I. V. and A-M. Attwell, David Benedictus, Jeffrey Bowman, Christopher Capron, Anne Chisholm, Anders Clason, Keith Clements, G.C. Frowde, Viola Germain, Hilda Gledhill, Winston Graham, Vicky Hall, Leslie Hodgson, Jennifer Holden, John Holroyd, Sessie Hylander, Jeremy Isaacs, Robert Lescher, Maureen Levenson, Richard Magor, John Mein, Niall McMonagle, Michael Ockenden, Anders Öfverstöm, Roger Packham, Griffy Philipps, Merle Rafferty, Michael and Moussie Sayers, Michael Seifert, Michael Sevenoaks, Ronald Stent, Lena Svanberg, Richard Vickers, Mary Young.

I am most grateful to: Head of Administration, the General Council of the Bar; Mary Stewart, Clinic Secretary, Family & Child Guidance Service, Royal County of Berkshire; County Solicitor, Royal County of Berkshire; R. J. Ewing, Bircham & Co, solicitors; Jonathan Barker and Alastair Niven, Literature Department, the British Council, London; Michelle Appleton, the British Council, France; Clare College Archive, Cambridge; Mark Nicholls, Department of Manuscripts and University

Archives, Cambridge University Library; Timothy H. Duke, Chester Herald, College of Arms; Naomi da Silva, Family Proceedings Department, the Court Service, Somerset House; P. Hatfield, Eton College Archivist; Mike Waller, Gallerie Moderne; P. Berney, Registration Directorate, General Medical Council; R. Simpson, Suprevisor, Glasgow Necropolis; Avril Gordon, Glasgow City Council; Mark Jones, Deputy Librarian, Gray's Inn Library; Nadene Hansen, Company Archivist at Harrods; Peter Hunter, Librarian, Harrow School; the Insolvency Service; Elizabeth Stratton, Assistant Archivist, King's College, Library, Cambridge; T. Shepherd, Regulatory Enquiry Services, the Law Society; Office for National Statistics; N.P. Willmoth, Senior Financial Services Officer, Life & Investment Services, NatWest; Colin Matthew, editor of the *New Dictionary of National Biography*; Jean Rose, Library Manager, Reed Book Services Limited; V.J. Baxter, Local Studies Librarian, London Borough of Richmond upon Thames; Royal Air Force Personnel Management Agency; the Sandhurst Collection; Scottish Record Office; S.J. Berry, Senior Archivist, Somerset County Record Office; Anthony Howard, Obituaries Editor, *The Times*; Jonathan Smith, Manuscripts Cataloguer, Trinity College Library, Cambridge; J.P. Rudman, Archivist, Uppingham School; Le Secrétaire Général délégé, Vernet-les-Bains; Patrick Mclure, Secrtary, Wykehamist Society.

To Sarah Johnson, who is now the only person in the world who can read my handwriting, especially when it appears between the lines of my typing, I owe special thanks for putting everything on to immaculate disks. I am also grateful to Philippa Harrison for her editorial sensitivity and thoroughness, to Caroline North, and to Kate Truman.

Quotations from *Eton Renewed: A History from 1860 to the Present Day* (1994) by Tim Card are reproduced with the permission of the publisher, John Murray. Lines from Nevill

Coghill's translation of Geoffrey Chaucer's *Troilus and Criseyde* are reproduced with the permission of Curtis Brown Ltd, London on behalf of the Estate of Nevill Coghill. Copyright Nevill Coghill 1971. Glass sculptures by René Lalique, photographed by Andrew Stewart: *Perche* (Contents page), *Longchamp* (page 1), *Renard* (page 99), *Tête de Paon* (page 115), *Tête de Coq* (page 301).

Among the many people to whom I am grateful for help with the research for *Mosaic* are Mrs M. S. Adams, Stella Astor, Neil Austin, Michael Barber, Mark Beaumont-Thomas, Lilla Bek, Alan Bell, Anthony Blond, Peter Blond, Pearl Brewis, Carmen Callil, Peter Calvert, Honor Clerk, Sarah Constantine, Diana Dracopoli, Jack Dracopoli, Margaret Dracopoli, Patricia Ellegard, Vicki Feaver, Michael Foss, Sally Gaywood, Mariolina Gent, Myfi Heim, Ann Johnson, Jim Knowlson, Judith Landry, Murray Last, Paul Levy, Linda Lloyd Jones, T. G. Lyttelton, Andrew McCall, Clare Michell, John Michell, Betty Parsons, Eduardo Sant'Anna, Jennifer Scarf, David Shepherd, Robert Skidelsky, Hilary Spurling, David Sutton, Robin Treherne-Thomas.

I have also relied on the expertise of several local historians including Judy Collingwood, Pamela Peskett, Janet Rowarth and J. Derek Skepper, all of whom made vital contributions to my researches.

I would also like to record my thanks to libraries and institutions that have assisted me: Roy Andrews at Andrews, Gwynne and Associates; the Beverley Local Studies Library; the British Racing Drivers Club; Geoffrey J. Crump and the Cheshire Military Museum; Mrs P. Hatfield, archivist at Eton College Library; W. J. B. Meakin and Geoffrey Grant at Grant Saw and Son; the Reference Library at Hull; the Local Studies Centre of the Kensington and Chelsea Central Library; Simon Jones, curator at the King's Regiment; Alfred and Ewart Longhurst;

the National Maritime Museum; the Royal Academy of Arts; the Royal Motor Yacht Club; the Royal Society of Marine Artists; the Royal Solent Yacht Club; the Royal Thames Yacht Club; Daphne Todd, president of the Royal Society of Portrait Painters; and Trinity Hospice.

I owe much, as ever, to Sarah Johnson for deciphering my text and enabling me to present it to my publishers in legible form. At Little, Brown I must thank my editors, Richard Beswick, Caroline North and Viv Redman, and proof-reader Kate Truman for continuing this process for the benefit of readers. I would also like to thank Viv Mullett for drawing the family trees.

Finally I must pay tribute to the patience, generosity and goodwill of my wife, Margaret Drabble, who went with me on many of my travels for *Basil Street Blues* and without whom *Mosaic* would not have come into existence.

For this combined edition of my family stories I am indebted to Clara Farmer, Alison Hennessey and Peter McAdie at Vintage Books.

List of Illustrations

Basil Street Blues

A Family Story

'The past puts a fine edge on our own days. It tells us more of the present than the present can tell us.'

William Gerhardie, 'An Historical Credo'
The Romanovs, An Evocation of the Past as a Mirror for the Present

PART I

1

Two Types of Ambiguity

Towards the end of the nineteen-seventies I asked my parents to let me have some account of their early lives. I had never been interested in my family. My career as a biographer probably arose from my need to escape from family involvements and immerse myself in other people's lives. 'We don't go to Heaven in families any more – but one by one.' I remember how struck I was when I came across this sentence in Gwen John's correspondence. That was certainly how I felt. I also remember quoting in my first biography Hugh Kingsmill's aphorism: 'Friends are God's apology for families,' and feeling a chord of agreement.

My parents, who had long been divorced, and gone through a couple of subsequent marriages, each of them, as well as various additional liaisons, were by the late nineteen-seventies living alone in fragile health and meagre circumstances. They appeared bewildered by the rubble into which everything was collapsing. After all, it had started so promisingly.

The accounts they wrote were very different. This did not surprise me. They had seldom agreed about anything, not even the date of my birth. As a gesture of tact I preserved two birthdays forty-eight hours apart, one for each of them. This had begun as a joke, grew into a habit and finally became a rather ageing conceit which will enable me to claim by the year 2000 the wisdom of a 130-year-old.

My parents' marriage was something of a mystery to me. What did they have in common? After the age of six I seldom saw them together and could imagine few people more dissimilar. What few scraps of memory I retained brought back echoes of reverberating arguments that floated up to me as I lay in a dark bedroom in the north of England – echoes that, to gain popularity, I would later assemble into dramatic stories for the school dormitory. A breadknife flashed in the dark, a line of blood suddenly appeared, and we shivered delightedly in our beds. But I have few actual memories of my very early years, few recollections of my childhood I can trust, and not many of adolescence. There were probably good reasons for this erasure, though I am hoping that some events may stir from their resting place and rise to the surface as I write.

I was born in the summer of 1935. My mother was Swedish, and my father thought of himself as English, though his mother actually came from the south of Ireland and his paternal grandmother was Scottish. All I knew was that my parents had met on a boat in the North Sea, got along fine on water, then fairly soon after striking land, dashed their marriage on the rocks. I had been conceived, my mother once remarked as we were travelling by bus through Knightsbridge, at the Hyde Park Hotel where King Gustav of Sweden (calling himself Colonel Gustaveson) often stayed. I remember her laughing as we swayed into Sloane Street and travelled on. At another time, in a taxi, she pointed to the Basil Street Hotel with a similar laugh before turning into Sloane Street.

I was largely brought up in the Home Counties by my paternal grandparents and a tennis-playing aunt. But there were irregular intervals, sometimes at odd places abroad, with unfamiliar step-parents who, like minor characters in a badly-managed melodrama, would introduce themselves with a flourish, a bray of trumpets, and then inexplicably disappear. Perhaps the peculiar enchantment that sustained and integrated narratives, enriched with involving plots, were to hold for me sprang from my sense of being brought up by so many characters – parental, step-parental and grand-parental characters – who seldom met, showed little interest in one another, and apparently possessed no connecting story.

In some respects my father had a 'good war', or so I believed. But he could not adjust to the peace afterwards. Though increasingly impoverished, he somehow found (I never knew how) the money to send me to Eton College because he had been there himself at the end of the First World War. He spoke of his time at Eton with unconvincing jollity and was evidently looking forward to a second, vicarious, innings there.

My mother didn't mind where I was educated. She did not have an ideology and simply wanted me to be happy, preferably without too much trouble. She never regarded education, which was full of awkward exams, as an obvious route to happiness. But probably such things were different for men.

They certainly appeared different to my father who had the air of a man acting responsibly on my behalf – as, he implied, his own father should have acted for him. By the time I was sixteen, he judged the moment had come to take me to one side and explain the main purpose of my education – which was to retrieve the family fortunes that would otherwise descend on me, he revealed, in the form of serious debts. Eton was providing me with many valuable friendships that could catapult me, he believed, to success. It did not occur to me to ask why Eton had not provided him with such vaulting associations. He gave the impression of someone who had overshot success and landed somewhere else. In the event, I failed comprehensively in this romantic quest he had assigned me (my average income between the mid-nineteen-sixties and mid-nineteen-seventies was to be £1,500 a year). I did not even know how the exotic family fortunes I was to rescue had originated or where they had gone. Was it all a mirage?

Lack of money was very evident in my parents' last years, when my father was living in a rundown flat in Surrey and my mother in a one-room apartment in London. I thought that the exercise of exploring happier years and travelling back to more prosperous times might bring them some release from their difficulties. From being their only child, the sole child from five marriages, I was to become their guardian and a barely-adequate protector. Having, as it were, commissioned them to write for me, I proposed paying them some commission money. After hesitating, my mother accepted the money with eager reluctance. She had always associated men with money, but understandably had not associated me with it, and was worried that I did not have enough. But times were improving for me, as if I were sitting on the opposite end of a seesaw from my descending parents. My *Lytton Strachey* had eventually been brought out as a paperback and after one very good year, when my *Augustus John* was published, I settled down at the end of the nineteen-seventies to annual net income of between four and five thousand pounds. I could afford to hand over a little money. Besides, I explained to my mother, she would not take my request seriously unless it was put on a business basis. Desperately needing the money, she gave me a kiss and took it.

But my father would not take anything. He wanted to give money and receive praise: he found it almost impossible to receive money or give praise. He felt deeply humiliated by his poverty. 'I certainly wouldn't dream of allowing you to pay 1 cent for anything I write about the family,' he notified me. I

remember reading his letter with exasperation. He was so difficult to help. The truth was he felt embarrassed by my offer
which, he wrote, 'made me feel very ashamed of myself. I am not
yet as down and out as you may imagine.' Now, re-reading his
letter after his death, an unexpected sadness spreads through me.
It was true that he had been 'down' many times, 'down' but not
quite 'out'. Cursing the foul blows delivered on him by politicians, he would somehow pick himself up each time – just in
time. But in his late sixties and early seventies, with only a State
pension and a couple of hundred pounds from a mysterious
'Holroyd Settlement', though he would still speak with anima-
tion of things 'turning up', my father had in fact settled into
involuntary retirement. The game was up. 'I find that time is
heavy on my hands,' he had written to me. That was one of the
reasons I had inflicted this homework on him. Nevertheless I
emphasised that it was for my sake rather than his own that I
was asking him to write an account. And perhaps there was
more truth in this than I realised. For after my father and mother
died in the nineteen-eighties I began to feel a need to fill the
space they left with a story. Neither of them were in the front
line of great historical events: their dramas are the dramas of
ordinary lives, each one nevertheless extraordinary. From their
accounts, from various photograph albums and a few clues in
two or three boxes of miscellaneous odds and ends, I want to
recreate the events that would give my own fragmented upbringing a context. Can I stir these few remnants and start a flame, an
illumination? This book is not simply a search for facts, but for
echoes and associations, signs and images, the recovery of a lost
narrative and a sense of continuity: things I seem to miss and
believe I never had.

I had to distance myself from my parents while they were
alive, not out of hostility to them, but from a natural urge to find
my individual identity, my own route. 'When a writer is born
into a family,' wrote Philip Roth, 'the family is finished.'

Inhabiting their worlds as a child and then an adolescent, I felt invisible; after which I traded somewhat in invisibility as a biographer. But following my parents' deaths, when they became invisible and I was seen to have attained my independence, my feelings began to change. I was drawn into the vacancy their deaths created, needing to trace my origins. It is an experience, I believe, that possesses many people in these circumstances: to ask questions when it is apparently too late for answers, and then be forced to discover answers of our own.

The unexamined life, Saul Bellow reminds us, is meaningless. But the examined life, he adds, is full of dangers. I have found wonderful freedom in that maverick condition which can be described as meaningless: a freedom in not being tied to social contexts or engulfed in family chauvinism. My identity was shaped by what I wrote, though this identity was concealed behind the people I wrote about – concealed I think from others, and also from myself. But now I must go back and explore. My parents, my family scattered over time and place, have become my biographical subjects as I search for something of me in them, and them in me. For this is a vicarious autobiography I am writing, a chronicle with a personal subtext, charting my evolution into someone who would never have been recognised by myself when young.

2

With Virginia Woolf
at Sheffield Place

My father wrote with a ballpoint pen on blue Basildon Bond paper. I remember thinking that, his name being Basil, this was almost a pun – especially since he was largely playing the history don in this investigation, the don he occasionally felt he would like to have been. The handwriting, as always, is wonderfully clear: thirty lines to the page, three hundred words, as regular as a marching soldier – quite unlike my own unformed and erratic writing.

He had probably prepared this fair copy from an earlier version. It stops suddenly in mid-sentence, at the foot of the thirty-eighth page, leaving him in his truncated schooldays during the early nineteen-twenties suffering from double pneumonia. But there are a couple of stray white pages, numbered 19 and 20, and a fragment of 21, that contain a variant text. They allude rather tantalisingly to 'the only indiscretion' of his own father, the 'real start of our financial disasters', and a 'Holroyd Settlement'.

There are signs that in his fair copy my father somewhat held back. Perhaps he remembered an attempt I had made to write about the family ten years earlier and the drama it caused. It had been an attempt at using my family to find a career of my own rather than following one of the uninviting professions they were urging on me.

My father started his saga in its first version in the eighteenth century and moved fairly rapidly on to his parents – my grandparents at whose house in Berkshire I had passed much of my childhood and adolescence. But coming across a privately-printed history of the family prepared in 1879 by Thomas Holroyd, High Sheriff of Calcutta, for his son in Australia (later brought up to 1914 by Caroline Holroyd, Thomas Holroyd's daughter, also for her brother who was by then a retired judge of the Supreme Court of Victoria in Melbourne, Sir Edward Dundas Holroyd), my father had been able eventually to reach back into the sixteenth century. That privately-printed history had been largely taken from Burke's *Colonial Gentry* and Foss's *Lives of the Judges*.

My father believed that the 'royd' in Holroyd came from a Yorkshire word meaning stream. I do not know where he picked up this piece of learning. In the opinion of a Yorkshire local historian, Hilda Gledhill, 'royd' was actually a Norse word meaning clearing or place which had been introduced by the Vikings after landing at Durham in the eighth century and making their way south west into northern Wales. When surnames became more common, people were often called after the land where they lived, Holroyd being someone who occupied a hollow place or valley. My father enjoyed history, and had he come across a rare volume, John Lodge's *The Peerage of Ireland*, published by James Moore in 1789, he might have liked to read that the Holroyd family is 'of great antiquity in the West-Riding of the county of York, and derives its name from the hamlet or estate of Holroyd, or Howroyd, as it was pronounced, in Bark-Island six miles from Halifax, which they formerly possessed'. According to John Lodge, who provided a pedigree going back to the thirteenth century, the word Holroyd 'signifies, when applied to land, such as was barren and uncultivated . . . The origin well suits the soil and situation of Holroyd . . . which joins to the mountainous country separating Lancashire from Yorkshire, called Blackstone-edge.' It is spacious country with vast skies and steep valleys full of clinging mists; also deep green fields marked out by granite and millstone walls, and miles of brown windswept moors, dramatic and desolate, round which, in the teeth of the weather, the people of the South Pennines quarried out their lives.

For several centuries Yorkshire seems to have been crammed with these Holroyds – butchers, clergymen, clothiers, farmers, landowners, soldiers, yeoman of all kinds. It was as well my father did not gain access to all this early material or he might never have reached the twentieth century at all.

He began his story with two brothers, George and Isaac Holroyd, in the seventeenth century. From these brothers, he wrote, 'our particular branch of the family is descended'. The elder brother was the great-great-grandfather of the first Earl of Sheffield, now remembered as the friend and patron of Edward Gibbon, or 'Gibbons' as my father rather endearingly called him. This Earl of Sheffield, John Baker Holroyd, is one of only two members of the family to have appeared in the original edition of Leslie Stephen's and Sidney Lee's *Dictionary of National Biography*. There his political career is described, his three marriages noted, and the price paid (£31,000) for the house and grounds at Sheffield Place in Sussex recorded (the purchase of which my father, who was having trouble with his central heating, ascribes to the climate of Sussex being more congenial than Yorkshire 'for his family seat'). There too are listed Sheffield's various Irish and English titles (Baron of Dunamore in the County of Meath, Viscount Pevensey etc.) and a bibliography presented of his observations, reports, and editing of Gibbon's posthumous works. There is scarcely a hint of what Leslie Stephen's daughter Virginia Woolf was to call, in her biographical pastiche *Orlando*, 'that riot and confusion of the passions and emotions which every good biographer detests'.

Virginia Woolf wanted to 'revolutionize biography in a night'. She wanted to free the imagination of the biographer from that tedious parade of dates and battles, that dubious weight of notes, indexes and bibliographies which remove it from the common reader. She wanted to introduce riot and confusion, passion and humour. And then she also wanted to clear those forests of family trees planted from father to son in the colonising territory of male culture. Such dreams lie between the lines of an essay she wrote in 1937 called 'Reflections at Sheffield Place'. At the end of this essay she follows not the male heirs (through the first Lord Sheffield's grandson, an idiosyncratic patron of cricket who in 1891 took an English team, including W.G. Grace, over to Australia and founded the Sheffield Shield competition), but a daughter and then on to her granddaughter Kate Amberley who was the mother of Bertrand Russell. If you hop on to the right line it can take you almost anywhere.

For Virginia Woolf, the great gardens at Sheffield Place, with their series of descending lakes, came to reflect something too intimate to find its way into works of historical reference. 'No place was more like home to him [Edward Gibbon] than Sheffield Place,' she wrote, 'and he looked upon the Holroyds as his own flesh and blood.'

Virginia Woolf hands over the telling of her story to Sheffield's daughter, 'the soft and stately Maria', as Gibbon described her. Only she could bring understanding to this devoted friendship between the Peer and the Historian, or 'the Gib' as she sometimes calls him (my father would have liked that). It was a friendship based on opposites, an attachment that (like biography itself perhaps) enabled them both to live lives each could never have lived simply in his own person. In the headstrong figure of Sheffield, Gibbon found someone caught up in those sorts of political and military affairs that, from the calmness of his study and over great distances of time, he sat composing into the sonorous sentences of his *Decline and Fall*. With his friend Sheffield, he was able to slip off his purple language and become quite racy and colloquial. In matters of the heart, where Gibbon was so ineffectual, Sheffield appeared recklessly extravagant. This emotional extravagance troubled Maria who looked to Gibbon for support. For though he was ridiculously vain and prodigiously fat, over-dressed and top-heavy, a waddling indoor figure of a man, 'rather testy too, an old bachelor, who lived like clockwork and hated to have his plans upset' (this must have brought her friend Lytton Strachey to Virginia Woolf's mind), yet he was also 'le grand Gibbon' whom Maria could not help liking. She saw how only in deference to Gibbon would her father check the self-destructive riot and confusion of his passions, and she felt grateful.

In 'Reflections at Sheffield Place' Virginia Woolf was indicating the change she wanted to see in historical biography, 'changing as the furniture changed in the firelight, as the waters of the lake changed when the night wind swept over them'. It is a turning away from the general narratives of history, with their wheeling armies and splendid processions that pass through the gorgeous tapestry of Gibbon's pages. It is an attempt, in miniature form, to put into practice Samuel Johnson's advice to biographers not to dwell on 'those performances and incidents which produce vulgar greatness, but lead the thoughts into domestic privacies': an eye-level rather than the overall view of our past.

This is what has attracted me to biography: the idea of an 'intimacy between strangers', a closeness growing up during the acts of writing and reading between an author, the reader and their subject, all unknown to one another before the book began coming into existence. For I do not think of biography as being an information-retrieval exercise: information, now the fruit of technology, has little fascination for me unless it takes root in my emotions and grows in my imagination into knowledge. What increasingly absorbs me is the unconscious process of learning. While writing I forget myself, and when I return to my world I sense that I am someone slightly different. The effect of these working holidays is of course cumulative, and perhaps there is significance in my having two birthdays. I was born the son of my parents, the grandson of their parents, and so on; and then, as it were, reborn the child of my writings – for it is they that have taken me round the world and shaped my adult existence. Now I must sit at my desk and see if I can bring together these two people who were consecutively, and who are cumulatively, myself.

3

The Swedish
Experiment

My mother's beginning was dramatic. In 1916 her parents were living at Örebro, 200 kilometres west of Stockholm. They had been married three years, had a two-year-old son Karl-Åke, and my grandmother was over five months pregnant with her second child. On 19 November Karl-Åke was playing in the kitchen where his nurse was cooking – simply boiling water it seems at the fireplace. Some say the child knocked over an oil lamp and started a fire; others that he tipped the boiling saucepan over himself. He was rushed to hospital, lingered there almost three weeks, then died on 9 December. The shock caused my grandmother to give birth prematurely to a tiny daughter on the day after the accident and in the hospital where her son was dying. They called their daughter Ulla. This was my mother.

I knew none of this until my mother wrote it down for me. I am not certain how much she knew of it herself before then – perhaps it is the sort of knowledge we suppress. But while preparing her account she told me that Greta, a neighbour of her mother in Stockholm, 'is trying to pump her without her knowing so, to keep her mind off her health – let's see what we'll get.' In other words Greta was doing what I was doing.

What we got was to be one of the main sources of my mother's rapid narrative. She wrote on lined paper, twenty centimetres long, and with forty-six narrow lines to the page which her fast-flowing handwriting often overlapped. She wrote in pencil, suggesting the impermanence of the past, yet with great speed and dash, almost violence, underlining words – names, dates, countries, towns, as well as words that needed special emphasis such as <u>all</u> and <u>dead</u>. Her writing appears full of activity, as if responding to the urgency of these events which streamed confusingly in and out of each other until they came to an end at the top of the thirteenth page. Then she started again, from somewhere near the middle, ending this time with notes of her various dogs: another fourteen pages. My mother had little time for the past. What absorbed her was the eternal present. Nevertheless, as she wrote, and then as I read, an unusual interest in these events seemed to grow up between us.

She noted that her father, a major in the Swedish army, had died in 1945. That surprised me. I had thought it was very much earlier. Only when I came to write this book did I realise he actually died several years later. I never met him. Nineteen forty-five was the year I began making regular sea-journeys with my mother to visit our Swedish relatives in Borås and Stockholm, Göteborg and a holiday island nearby called Marstrand.

My understanding at the time was that, despite being in one of the country's safest professions, the Swedish army, my grandfather had died young. I imagined him, sword in hand, falling gloriously from a horse during hectic manoeuvres in a northern forest.

From my mother's notes I see that he was the son of Knut

Johansson, a director of the Växjö Match Company in southern Sweden and his wife Amanda Hall who came from a family that ran the Krueger Match Company. On her marriage certificate my mother was to give her maiden name as Ulla Knutsson-Hall. Evidently her father took, or was given, his father's first name, a second syllable to remind us that he was the son of his father, and finally his mother's maiden name. He is Karl Knutsson-Hall.

Karl (or Kalle as he was usually called) had a good voice and had once dreamed of being an opera singer. He did sing in a few amateur productions, but his parents wanted him to take over the family's match empire. Eventually, by way of compromise, he went into the army which was thought to provide a respectable career.

My mother's maternal family had come from southern Germany, and her great-grandfather, Gustav Jagenburg, worked in Moscow early in the nineteenth century before settling down with his wife at Rydboholm, near Borås. He was a textile manufacturer and his son Rudolf was said to have invented a wondrous dye that never faded. In the eighteen-eighties Rudolf married the daughter of the prison priest at the Castle of Varberg. The second of their six children was my grandmother. Her formal name was Karin though we all called her Kaja.

How Karl and Kaja first met I do not know. But I do know that the Jagenburgs considered themselves socially superior to Karl's matchmaking family which was lower-middle class. They strongly opposed the marriage of this handsome couple on the grounds that Kaja could do better for herself. There was no money to be made in the army and Karl's excellent horsemanship did not particularly impress them. But Kaja in those days was a headstrong, passionate girl. A photograph of her in her early twenties among my mother's possessions shows a sweet face, with watchful slanting eyes, a rather sensuous but determined mouth, her expression provocative and full of character. No one was going to tell her whom to marry. She was in love with this charming officer, and that was enough.

So, in 1913, she married Lieutenant Karl Knutsson-Hall and went up to Boden in the north of Sweden where he was stationed. She was twenty-one and could marry without parental consent; he was four years older.

It seems probable that the marriage never recovered from the burning to death of their infant son Karl-Åke at the end of 1916. They had no more children after my mother Ulla and by the nineteen-twenties, when the family moved to Stockholm and my mother was old enough to notice things, Karl was spending more time with his brother officers than with his wife. They seemed to regard him still as a romantic bachelor. 'A more gentlemanly officer than Karl Hall could not be found in 1920s Sweden,' wrote one of his subordinates who recalled this 'idyllic warrior' during their company's 'legendary manoeuvres in Trosa during 1922 . . . and the merry ball in Trosa's grand hotel where Karl Hall reigned over the dusty recruits and young beauties . . . a generous, chivalrous heartbreaker.'

Ulla went first to the Margaretha School in Stockholm and then to Franska Skolan at 9 Döbelnsgatan where she began to learn her many languages. In the holidays she often went to Växjö where the Hall family had a large country house. Her most enduring memory was of twin earth-closets in a red building with white gables where 'I used to sit with my cousin'. Her father being the eldest of nine children, there were plenty of these cousins with whom to play. At the end of the garden stood a lake where they would all swim ('trod on a snake once on the way down the slope', my mother wrote). What she most enjoyed were the children's suppers by this lake in the endless summer evenings – sandwiches made from newly-baked brown bread with delicious fillings. 'I once ate 15!' my mother boasted. 'A record.' She was looked after during those early holidays by

Karin – not her mother (who disliked the Hall family and didn't often go to Växjö) but one of her in-laws whom she thought of as her 'nanny'.

At the age of twelve Ulla was sent to a French family in the Haute Savoie for three months to practise her French. But there was another reason for removing her from Stockholm. Her parents had decided to separate. This was not a friendly arrangement but a stubbornly-fought duel that lasted almost four years and according to the family was to lead to a change in the Swedish divorce laws. Up till that time 'we lived in various nice flats', my mother wrote. But after she returned from France everything changed. Mother and daughter moved rapidly between small apartments and boarding houses pursued by Karl. Sometimes at night there were drunken brawls in the street and on one memorable occasion Karl staggered towards them shouting and waving a revolver.

Kaja was determined to win her divorce. But though Karl was apparently drinking heavily and had, Kaja told her daughter, contracted venereal disease from an extra-marital liaison, there seemed no way for her to obtain a legal divorce unless her husband consented to it. His condition of consent was a million kronor, which he calculated Kaja's father (he of the miraculous unfading dye) could afford to pay him. There was a prolonged and bitter feud that my mother found unnerving. 'I suffered,' she wrote. But what struck me as strange when reading her brief account was that she didn't appear to blame her father for those dreadful years. Perhaps she romanticised him, not knowing him so well, and missing him. Kaja had never been very 'understanding' with her as a child and was, Ulla felt, too 'demanding' with her husband.

Eventually Kaja won the divorce battle largely because one of her uncles was Riksmarskalk of Sweden (equivalent to Lord High Chamberlain in England). After 'Lex versus Hall' was settled in 1932 it became easier for women to get divorced in Sweden.

Following their divorce Karl retreated into a home for alcoholics where he was nursed by the daughter of a priest (the
home was apparently managed by the Church). Then in her
mid-twenties, Marianne was half Karl's age, but 'understanding
and kind which was what he *needed*', my mother insisted. So
they married. As a bonus, she was 'very good-looking', my
mother observed. This suggests that she must have seen
Marianne, but she gets her name wrong (Margareta instead of
Marianne) which suggests she did not actually know her.
Perhaps they met only at Karl's funeral. In my mother's speedy
narrative, the happy couple are disposed of rather brutally: 'My
father died of T.B. and god knows what else,' she wrote. 'He
caught T.B. from his wife who was later killed by being squashed
by a lorry against a wall whilst walking with a girlfriend in
Stockholm – 5 years after Papa died.' This must have been based
on what Kaja was telling her neighbour, Greta. In fact Karl's
cause of death is given as a respectable heart attack ('Infartus
cordis kardiosclerasis').

In her 'teens Kaja had done some sewing and cutting in her
father's textile workshops in Borås. Then, arriving in Stockholm
as a married woman, she persuaded her father to introduce her
to Countess Margareta von Schwerin, known as Marg, who in
1927 was to open the celebrated fashion house Märthaskolan
where elegant ladies had their dresses made. Before long Kaja
became a consultant there and was coming into contact with
Swedish high society. She took her work seriously and, she
would tell her daughter, was never late, not even by five minutes,
for an appointment. 'I can see Kaja entering the salons well
aware of the impression she made, so sure of herself and her
beauty,' a friend of my mother's wrote to me. 'Everyone had to
admire her, and then entered Ulla, pretty, laughing and much
more warm at heart, everybody felt.'

Kaja soon floated free from the disreputable business of her
divorce and settled into her work as a couturier for

Märthaskolan. This was a school of dress as well as a fashion house and in those days the greatest single influence in the creation of Swedish femininity. The Countess Margareta von Schwerin herself was really a fashion reporter with strong opinions as to what would be useful for young girls. She travelled widely and dealt with most of the French couturiers. But she did not promote a single style or confine her interests to high fashion. She was an ambitious woman and wanted to dress all women in Sweden, whatever their age or status. She saw herself as an educator. Her mission was to give Swedish women confidence in the home and at work by the way they presented themselves.

Among the bits and pieces my mother left after her death are a few photographs of our trips together to Sweden from the late nineteen-forties and the nineteen-fifties. There I am sitting on the floor with my pretty cousin Mary. She is smiling, blonde and lively; I, aged nine or ten, am blank-faced and bird-like, decked out in foreign tailoring, with blue and yellow Swedish cufflinks, a frilled handkerchief and bow tie (my God! What would my schoolfriends in Surrey have said?). Behind us, sitting and standing in rows, a contingent of the family has formed up for the photograph. I can recognise my grandmother Kaja, a formidably handsome woman looking frankly at the camera; and I can see my mother, unsmiling, with a similar gingham frock and hair neatly arranged like my grandmother's – she is on her very best behaviour. But I cannot identify anyone else. Which is Elis? Where is Inga?

But with my mother's written account before me I can at last make some sense of this family group. My grandmother was in her mid-fifties at the time these photographs were taken, though she looks younger. And these are her brothers and sisters, their wives and husbands and children, who have lined up before the camera. There is a bank manager, an engineer, a doctor, a businessman: all respectable middle-class people. Of course there are some lapses from respectability. One of the brothers, for example, an import–export manager, imported syphilis from a Hamburg brothel and has never quite recovered. My grandmother believes it must have addled his brain – why else would he have married a waitress from a Borås hotel? My mother likes Kristina, her waitress-aunt, who has always been kind to her. But my grandmother cannot stand her and makes pointed remarks such as, when Kristina comes into the room with some drinks: 'You must be used to carrying trays.'

My grandmother is a snob. Snobbishness is her form of authority. It cows other people, and this suits her. That is why she looks so young in the photographs and my mother so ill-at-ease. My grandmother believes in appearances and, living up to her beliefs, she appears splendidly superior.

Kaja always walked, sat, spoke and generally carried herself with soldierly precision. She had the unquestioning air of an officer – more so than her ex-husband. She assumed the posture of high command, straightened her back, raised her chin, yet somehow retained her attractiveness. This is a determined and successful couturier we see in the photographs.

Kaja revelled in this work and felt proud of being part of the Countess's team at Märthaskolan. She allowed herself one acknowledged admirer, Birger Sandström, a middle-aged gentleman with a brilliant white moustache, whose presence breathed respectability. He escorted her to parties and she employed him almost as a fashion accessory. It was a discreet arrangement which became easier to manage after 1934 when Ulla sailed for England.

4

Links in the Chain

I like to think of Virginia Woolf having used one of my ancestors
to plead the revolution in biography. Unfortunately my father
had not been strictly accurate when claiming that our branch of
the family was directly descended from the two sixteenth-
century brothers George and Isaac Holroyd. The first Earl of
Sheffield's direct ancestor was George, but we succeeded from
the younger brother Isaac. Isaac's most illustrious descendant
was Sir George Sowley Holroyd, a Judge of the King's Bench.
Like Lord Sheffield he was painted by Joshua Reynolds, and
was the second Holroyd to gain entry (a more modest entry) into
the original *Dictionary of National Biography*.

My father used to say that most of our family during the
eighteenth and nineteenth centuries had been lawyers or soldiers, and that the judges were far more deadly than the
generals. I imagined a gallery of hanging judges. But George
Sowley Holroyd appears to have been an exceptionally mild

man. In an essay for the *Edinburgh Review*, Lord Brougham
emphasised his humour and gentleness, the elegance and ingenuity of his arguments, and the lightness with which he employed
his learning. I began to notice as I read this eulogium how I was
beginning to compare my own circumstances with this distinguished forebear and, like the reader of an astrological chart,
take possession of flattering items. 'To whatever branch of investigation he had devoted his life in that he would have eminently
excelled.' What an investigative biographer this special pleader
might have made!

QUEM TE DEUS ESSE JUSSIT ('What God has commanded you to
do'). My father quoted these portentous words at the head of
his narrative (though he did not provide a translation). This
was a family motto which, with Arms showing Five Roses in
Saltire, the Crest a Demi-Griffin, Wings Endorsed and holding
between its claws a Ducal Coronet, appeared as an armorial
bookplate, framed in black, which hung in the lavatory of his
flat in Surrey. On the opposite side of the water-cistern, also
registering my father's reduced position, was suspended another
framed bookplate which, perhaps because of its complexity, he
left without comment. I needed the assistance of the Chester
Herald himself to record these Arms correctly. They are: Five
Pierced Mullets in Saltire impaled on the Arms of Virginie,
daughter of General Mottet de la Fontaine of Compiègne in
Picardy, which should properly be blazoned Argent à Chevron
Azure between in chief Two Roses Gules slipped and leaved
Vert and in base a Mound Sable on a chief of the second
Three Mullets Or. The motto below this paraphernalia was
COMPONERE LEGIBUS ORBEM ('To build a world with laws') which
George Sowley Holroyd had apparently chosen. But the name
beneath this Motto, Arms and Crest is that of his eldest son,
George Chaplin Holroyd, a naval officer who passed most of
his life in India, married Virginie (daughter of the Governor of
Pondicherry), and finally returned to be buried in Exeter. With

this man's third son, my great-grandfather Charles Holroyd who was born in Hyderabad in 1822, the family finally comes into view. For, in a cardboard box marked Six Cod Steaks 24 × 12 oz among my aunt's possessions, there is a photograph of Charles Holroyd with his three children taken at Eastbourne in the late nineteenth century.

Charles Holroyd passed most of his life on the Bengal Military Staff in Assam. During the Indian Mutiny of 1857, he unravelled a plot to massacre the European tea planters in Upper Assam. In heartfelt thanks for saving their lives they presented him with 'a very handsome silver salver', and more significantly perhaps, also gave him an interest in their tea gardens.

Five years after the Mutiny, at the age of forty, Charles married a widow, Mary Hannay, who had two sons by her first marriage. But nine months later, probably when pregnant, she died of apoplexy. Charles, who continued bringing up his stepsons, did not marry again for another nine years. His second wife, Anna Eliza Smith, the daughter of an indigo planter, was Scottish. She gave birth in Calcutta to two boys in 1874 and 1875, Patrick Charles (called Patrick or Pat) and my grandfather Edward Fraser Rochfort (called Fraser); and then a daughter, Norah Palmer, who was born in 1877 at Eastbourne in Sussex, where Charles had retired with the rank of Major-General. According to the privately-printed family tree, Anna died three years later. But I can find no record of her death in London. Then I see in an Eastbourne newspaper that she was buried at the Glasgow Necropolis. So I write to the General Register Office for Scotland in Edinburgh which sends me her death certificate.

Is it possible to be shocked by something that happened over a hundred years ago? I do feel a jolt as I read that Anna Eliza Holroyd, my great-grandmother, committed 'suicide by carbolic acid' at 29 Arlington Street, Glasgow, on 7 January 1880. She was aged thirty, that is twenty-eight years younger than her husband. This Arlington Street address was the home of her uncle, William Smith, an accountant, and his wife. But the 'informant' on the death certificate two days later is Charles Holroyd, her husband. This suggests that she had travelled to Scotland alone and that he went up from Eastbourne on hearing the dreadful news, leaving his two sons, Pat and Fraser, aged five and four, and his daughter Norah, who was a couple of weeks short of her third birthday, at home. Were they ever told of their mother's suicide? No whisper of it reached my father, I am sure, or came down to the rest of the family. There is no photograph of her anywhere.

Carbolic acid was used as a strong domestic disinfectant which cleaned by its caustic action. Anna would have died through internal burning. What can have driven her to do such an unimaginably painful thing, to kill herself when she had three very young children? There is no report of her suicide in the Scottish newspapers (there was a more dramatic suicide in Glasgow that day by an unnamed woman who threw herself from a bridge in Jamaica Street on the stroke of midnight). Nor is there any fatal accident inquiry concerning Anna on record. She left no Will or inventory, no testamentary deeds. There is simply no living memory of this tragedy, simply a trail of speculation.

Having lived most of her life in India, Anna may well have found it difficult to settle at Eastbourne where she knew no one. The prospect of spending the next twenty years or so as the wife of a retired soldier nearly twice her age cannot have been very appealing. By the beginning of 1880, she could well have been pregnant again and she may have been subject to unrecognised post-natal depression, the prospect of which renewed her feelings of guilt. All this is possible and could form a contributory cause of her death. But none of it provides a convincing explanation for killing herself so appallingly. Where no easy explanations were available, many women who did not have a tenacious hold on life and who found it eventually intolerable were considered to be mentally unstable. I have been unable to find evidence of her being in love with another man, or having had any connection with that other woman, with dark brown hair, whose body was recovered by lowering a boat from the Carrick Castle that January night. Nor is there any evidence of her husband having ill-treated her – otherwise her uncle would surely not have summoned him to Glasgow, or her mother, years later, have sent a wreath 'in affectionate remembrance' when Charles Holroyd himself died.

Anna Eliza, 'the Beloved Wife of Major Gen Charles Holroyd', was buried at the Glasgow Necropolis on 10 January 1880. And that must surely be the end of her story. But it is not quite the end. Over seventeen years later a man was buried beside her. His name – one I have never seen before – was John Stewart Paul and he died in June 1897 at the age of sixty-one. Who was this mysterious man? On the grave-stone it is written that he was the 'brother in law of Major Gen Holroyd'. He turns out to be Anna's uncle by marriage (the husband of her mother's sister) who had christened his younger son Charles Holroyd Paul. What can this tell me? It appears that Anna's family wished to retain the connection with her husband Charles, and that no blame was laid on him for her suicide. In 1901, Anna's mother was buried in the same plot, and so in 1914 was her aunt, Janet Stewart Paul. In Lair 59 of the Necropolis, the four of them lie together with their secrets.

The Eastbourne photograph shows the widower and his three children a few years after Anna's death. They are formally grouped as if in a studio conservatory. The father, sitting on a stone bench, is attired in morning clothes; the two boys (one sitting on the ground balancing a tennis racket, the other standing next to the bench) are dressed in Eton jackets and collars, with buttoned waistcoats and sober spotted ties. Norah, their sister, is perched on the back of the bench, aged about ten, wearing a long-sleeved pleated dress with a high lace collar and lace cuffs. What struck me most when first examining this picture is how old the father appears in comparison with his children. He *is* rather old to have a ten-year-old daughter – in his mid- to late-sixties. But, with his bald head and full white beard, half-closed eyes and melancholic expression, he seems nearer eighty. It is as if his wife's terrible death has marked him for ever. The two boys themselves have somewhat wary and solemn expressions matching their father's. Only Norah, from her superior position on the back of the bench, confronts the camera direct. She is not smiling, but she has a modern look. She appears forthright and freer than the boys.

The four of them were living at a large, rather sombre flint house called The Links built in 1869 close to Beachy Head in the Meads district of Eastbourne. The house itself stood in extensive grounds out of sight of the sea and protected by a high flint wall. Behind this wall, on naturally-sloping, partly-levelled grounds shaded by beech and yew trees, ilex, chestnut and Cedar of Lebanon, lay a sunken garden with a large expanse of lawn over which crying seagulls would sail – a good place for games. During his twenty years there, Charles Holroyd enlarged this property considerably. His Will refers to outbuildings, cottages and pleasure grounds as part of his land. He employed a gardener (who lived with his family in a cottage on the grounds), cook, parlourmaid, housemaid, house parlourmaid, coachman and a governess, Mary Easlea, later described as a companion.

The Major-General makes his appearance in the local newspapers as someone who 'took no part in public affairs, for like other residents who have served their country in distant parts of the world, he came to Eastbourne in search of quiet and rest'. He was a Tory and a member of the Church of England, worshipping at St John's on Sundays and going to the Sussex Club twice a day during the rest of the week. The two boys were 'rather in awe of him', my father writes. But as the tennis racket in the photograph suggests, there was an escape through sport. Both boys had guns, made their own cartridges, and would go rough shooting on the Downs. There were also the adventures of bird's-nesting, moth- and butterfly-collecting, and fishing expeditions at sea. Eventually there was the more permanent escape to boarding school.

But none of these escapes was available to Norah. Her chief pastime seems to have been stamp-collecting. Though she did have friends to stay – the 1891 census lists a fourteen-year-old visitor from Paris, Georgette Backellery – Norah's life appears to have been somewhat solitary. She was educated at home under the supervision of Mary Easlea and remained at The Links with this middle-aged companion until after her father's death at the end of the century. Despite her forthright look in that family photograph, she was said to have been delicate. 'How much this state of health was a state of mind it is impossible to say,' my father wrote, adding that he never heard his own father refer to his sister Norah when talking of his boyhood.

Charles Holroyd was educated at the East India Company's college at Addiscombe, and his father and grandfather had been Harrovians. His choice for Pat and Fraser was Uppingham, a tiny, unsalubrious, sixteenth-century grammar school in Rutland which, under its evangelical headmaster, Edward Thring, was recognised as one of the most progressive public schools in the country. Thring was a powerful personality, 'quick and articulate, charismatic, quarrelsome', the school historian describes him. It was he, rather than Dr Arnold of Rugby, who today appears the radical pioneer in mid-nineteenth-century education. Arnold had been at Winchester and Oxford; Thring at Eton (under the brutal regime of Dr Keate) and Cambridge. Arnold emerged a pessimist, Thring an optimist. Thring was also passionately egalitarian, insisting that 'every boy in the school must receive equal and full attention', and that 'ordinary boys needed as much time as the brilliant'. This inclusiveness contrasted strongly with Dr Arnold's regime of public expulsions and private removals founded on the belief that, boys having 'an essential inferiority' as compared with men, 'the first, second and third duty of a schoolmaster is to get rid of unpromising subjects'. In Thring's opinion, Dr Arnold was 'a very great man, but a bad schoolmaster'. It was true that he had added mathematics, modern history and languages to the school course; but so had Thring added them – as well as chemistry, drawing, carpentry and music too. Both were ordained clergymen, driven by a sense of moral purpose, but Thring's temperament was far less morbid than Arnold's. He was a New Testament man and his sermons never lasted longer than ten minutes. Above all he was a genuine innovator, establishing workshops, laboratories, an aviary and gymnasium at Uppingham, emphasising the skill needed even in elementary teaching, discouraging the multiplication of prizes as motives for work, and campaigning on behalf of a liberal education for girls.

When Thring came to Uppingham in the early eighteen-fifties the school contained twenty-five boys. Thirty years later there were over three hundred boarding in eleven houses, and thirty masters. It could have grown still more but, believing that most public schools were too large, Thring restricted the number of boys to a maximum of 320 with no more than thirty in each house.

My great-grandfather was one of the last parents to interview Thring who died in the autumn of 1887. Six months later the Major-General's elder son Pat arrived at Uppingham, and he was followed a year later by his brother (my grandfather) Fraser. Within these eighteen months Uppingham had grown to almost four hundred boys and in one respect at least begun to change. Thring argued that 'organised games received excessive attention'. Though he encouraged games at which masters could play in the teams – this being a good way for everyone to get to know one another better – he disliked the worship of competitive athletics which he considered unfair to the ordinary boys. A year after Thring's death, however, rugby football began to be played at Uppingham and the spirit of Dr Arnold entered the school. The great man there in the late eighteen-eighties and early eighteen-nineties was H.H. Stephenson, the legendary cricket coach, who had captained the first English team to tour Australia.

I occasionally heard my grandfather speak of Stephenson as we drank our cider together in the evenings. His tone was reverential, for we were after all discussing one of the great heroes of the game and 'the best cricket coach at any school'. I loved these stories of my grandfather, but generally he was too barricaded by worries to entertain me with them, though I sometimes pleaded with him and made him smile. Only at moments would he bow down his head, hush his voice, and whisper, 'Ah! Stephenson!' Such an exclamation conveyed more than any inventory of facts. I would stare into the past and nod my understanding. I got the impression that he venerated Stephenson because he had received from him all the attention and encouragement he missed at home. He may even have received special attention on account of being a kinsman of Henry North Holroyd, third Earl of Sheffield, the great cricket patron of those days in whose grounds at Sheffield Place the Australians always opened their tour of England.

As a result of intensive coaching, my grandfather did pretty well at Uppingham. Stephenson noted in 1892 that he was 'developing into a good run-getting bat', though he 'did not punish the loose balls with sufficient severity'. Also, Stephenson added in Fraser's last year, he was perhaps 'rather nervous'. This nervousness, his lack of aggression, and the sad fact that he was 'not a safe pair of hands' may be said to have marked his later life beyond the cricket field.

Nevertheless, my grandfather was one of the stars in the new philathletic era. This was a vintage patch in Uppingham cricket, full of masterly innings, decisive victories, sensational fight-backs, astonishing records (Fraser making his contribution to all this brave achievement with a 75 against Uppingham's deadly rivals Repton). He quite outshone Pat, one of the ordinary boys for whom Thring had been concerned, and immediately took precedence over him in class, *Holroyd mi* being placed in a higher form than *Holroyd ma*. Perhaps it was this paradox that helped to gain for my grandfather a reputation for academic brilliance in the family years later. We would have found it difficult to believe that 'Uncle Pat' was actually a long way below average, that Fraser himself never reached the upper division of the Classical Sixth where the scholars clustered, or that he won no medals, distinctions or prizes. He appears in several photographs of Constable's House, the school praepostors, and the cricket eleven. All the boys look far older than similar groups in the twentieth century, and no boy looks older than my grandfather. I can quite easily recognise the man I knew in his seventies and eighties – indeed he already looks nearly half that age, weighed down with a Johnsonian heaviness. I find these photographs curiously disturbing. No one is smiling. Between this solemn young boy seen with his family at Eastbourne and the prematurely-aged praepostor of Uppingham, did my grandfather have any carefree childhood and adolescence? What I have discovered suggests that his youth was much delayed.

Pat left Uppingham after three years and went on to the Military Academy at Sandhurst. That, at any rate, was what my father understood. But 'Uncle Pat' did not go to Sandhurst and does not turn out to have been the professional soldier who, with five medals blazing on his chest, marches across my father's narrative. He was an amateur soldier in the auxiliary military force called the Militia which was enlisted locally, sometimes paraded for drill and could be called on in wartime. A photograph taken in the mid-eighteen-nineties at Eastbourne shows him in his uniform, a mild and handsome face with a well-designed moustache nicely waxed at its tips.

While Pat was drilling with the Royal Welch Fusiliers, Fraser went to King's College, Cambridge. My father writes enthusiastically of his playing there against the two most brilliant cricketers of the times, C.B. Fry and Ranjitsinhji. In fact he seems to have given up cricket and did not get a Blue. My father also believed that 'he was an excellent mathematician, worked hard, finally taking a First'. The printed register of King's admissions records him as having been awarded a Third in the History Tripos of 1897. As something starts going wrong, so the gap between ascertainable fact and family legend widens.

Though my father liked to picture Fraser making lifelong friendships in the glamorous atmosphere of Cambridge, he suspected there had been some setback and attributed it to varicose veins (which he himself had), brought on by the 'tight elastic garters' Fraser was obliged to wear. This rumour of illness took many forms and I remember hearing how my grandfather's brilliant prospects as an oarsman had been blighted by his hernia. The truth appears to have been more complicated.

Towards the end of 1894 Fraser was given what the Major-General indignantly describes as an 'arbitrary order, compelling him to give up Classics and take up History' by his college tutor, Alfred Cooke. Cooke was an Old Etonian Classics scholar with a bewildering medley of occupations – he was a priest, a famous versifier, a conchologist and a talented footballer. Early in 1895, Fraser is asking his friend Oscar Browning for advice as to what he should do. The prolonged difficulty in getting tuition lost him 'a full year'.

This friendship with Oscar Browning is surprising. A hugely fat socialite and friend of Oscar Wilde, he had been dismissed as an assistant-master at Eton 'on unsubstantiated charges of misconduct' and then returned to King's as a lecturer in history. A notorious 'character' and (in the words of E.F. Benson) a 'genius flawed by abysmal fatuity', Browning inhabited a world I had never remotely associated with my grandfather.

By the summer of 1896 my grandfather, having crammed two years' work into one, seems to have had some kind of breakdown, raising in the examiners' minds a question of whether he should be allowed to stay on and complete his studies. While they were deliberating, his father sent him out to Cape Town with his brother Pat (the two of them were good friends) 'in the hope the entire change would keep him from brooding over his misfortunes'. But 'the wound still rankles', he reported. What was this wound? The Major-General wrote in confidence to Oscar Browning with some attempt at an explanation.

> He was not well at the time of the examination: shortly
> before it commenced he heard of the sudden death of his
> Godfather who was his best friend, and a great help to
> him. He was working 8 to 9 hours a day, & at night
> unable to sleep brooding over his loss . . . He is not of a
> nature to confide in others, & keeps his feelings to
> himself. I am about the only one he confides in. I do not
> think Mr Cook [*sic*] understands him in the slightest, & I
> do not imagine he would take the trouble to do so . . . he
> has not met with much consideration since he has been at
> the university, excepting from yourself, of whom he
> always speaks in the warmest praise.

It is obvious that Fraser was unhappy at Cambridge and not prospering there. The contrast with those simple sunlit days at Uppingham must have been dismaying. He had entered a far more ambiguous world.

When the decision was made to allow my grandfather to stay on for his third year, the Major-General wired the happy news to Cape Town. So that autumn, Fraser returned to King's, dividing his vacations between Eastbourne and an apartment in London at 22 Montague Place, near the Reading Room of the British Museum.

But it was a gloomy time. In a letter sent from The Links shortly before Christmas 1896, the Major-General wrote that 'it would have been a great pleasure' to invite Oscar Browning to lunch or dine (he had apparently tried to invite himself), 'but my Daughter is so poorly I regret I cannot ask anyone to the House'. So the family rumour of her illness had been based on fact. But what was wrong with her? Had she found out about her mother's suicide? Was she suspected of having inherited through the female line some mental instability? There were whispers of a scandal that my own father picked up when a child on the only occasion he saw her. He refers to 'some story the details of which I never heard, about some awful experience that Norah had at the hands of some man . . . whom she was visiting'.

During 1897 and 1898 The Links became something of a sanatorium. 'Progress is very slow, almost imperceptible, & it will take a long time before, if ever, I am myself again,' the Major-General wrote in a very shaky hand shortly before Norah's twentieth birthday and when he himself was in his seventy-fifth year. According to the *Eastbourne Chronicle*, he had suffered a stroke and was partly paralysed. As for Fraser, 'I hope he has prospered,' the old man wrote to Oscar Browning: 'it will be a crushing blow to him if he has not for he has . . . I know done his best.'

In February 1897 my great-grandfather made his Will. He leaves The Links, its grounds and contents ('furniture plated goods linen glass china books ornaments manuscripts pictures prints statuary musical instruments and articles of vertu . . . and all wines liquors and consumable stores and all my plants and garden tools') in trust to his elder son Patrick. The property is given to him under the condition that, until he reaches the age of twenty-five (when it becomes his own absolutely), he allows his brother and sister to live there if they wish, so that The Links can 'be maintained as a home for my family'.

'The watches jewels trinkets and personal ornaments belonging to me at the time of my death', many of which must have once belonged to Norah's mother, he leaves to Norah herself. The residuary estate is to be divided equally in trust between his three children.

There are pages of instruction designed to protect his daughter from fortune-hunting men. Her third part in the estate is to be retained by trustees 'for as long as she shall remain unmarried and whether she shall be competent or incompetent to give legal discharge'. In the event of her marriage, this Holroyd money shall be for 'her separate use free from marital control and without power of alienation'. The one-third interest in the estate then becomes vested in her and the capital eventually passes to her children after they come of age. It is evident that her father had given much thought to these provisions, considerably more than to his second son who is bequeathed nothing beyond his one-third share of the residuary estate. But after Fraser was awarded his degree in the autumn of 1897, his father added a codicil to the Will leaving him various exotic Indian debentures and securities, including 92,500 rupees at the Bank of Bengal and a thousand shares in the fabulous Rajmai Tea Company, the sound and substance of which were to echo down the years – and were still echoing strangely through my childhood, more sound than substance then.

A second codicil Charles Holroyd signed on 14 July 1898 leaves all his staff an extra year's wages because of the burden placed on them by his long illness.

Six weeks later Patrick marries. His wife Coral is the daughter of another Major-General, and the wedding takes place on 7 September 1898 at the parish church of St Mary's in Bath. Fraser is present, but no one else from Patrick's family. The husband and wife then go off for their honeymoon, and Fraser returns to

The Links. His father was now dying. The cause of his death was given as thirty-two hours of cerebral haemorrhaging with convulsions leading to a coma and eventually culminating in respiratory paralysis. My grandfather was present during this final agony of illness and he is named as 'informant' on the death certificate, dated 19 September.

The funeral was held four days later at St John's Church, and the body was interred at Ocklynge cemetery. Fraser was there, also Pat and his wife Coral with her father, Major-General Montague. Colonel and Mrs Hannay were listed among the mourners. A friend from India, Richard Magor, connected with the Rajmai tea plantations, came to the service; so did numerous nephews, nieces and in-laws, as well as Mary Easlea, but not Norah Holroyd, the dead man's daughter. There were special wreaths from the coachman, gardeners and indoor servants, as well as from his late wife's family. There was none from Norah. But there is one 'in ever loving memory of my dear father, from his heart-broken Fraser'.

Probate was granted at the end of October, and the Major-General's estate was valued at £80,913 8s 10d. A hundred years later such a sum would be roughly equivalent to four-and-a-half million pounds.

On 4 June 1899 Patrick was twenty-five and The Links became his absolute property. He immediately sold the house which was converted into an expensive 'Ladies School' – among its pupils were to be Edwina Ashley, god-daughter of Edward VII, later to gain fame as Lady Mountbatten; and the Marchioness of Bath who, as Daphne Fielding, was to write a celebrated autobiography, *Mercury Presides*. Later, The Links was bought by the Methodist Guild, and became a Christian Holiday Centre, its interior partitioned and sub-divided by the tortured geometry of fire regulations.

The Militia was to do good service in the Boer War and Lieutenant Patrick Holroyd was one of those who volunteered to embark for South Africa. He took his wife Coral, and there, in the summer of 1900, their son Ivor was born. Fraser, who accurately described his occupation as being 'of independent means', had meanwhile fallen in love, a complaint that was to carry him off to Ireland. But while the two brothers were abroad what became of Norah? There was a family rumour that she died young. But my father wrote of having seen her once when he was aged about six – 'someone lying down who was very gentle to a little boy' and who (my aunt recalled) had 'beautiful hair'. That must have been approximately in 1913. So I went in search of a death certificate.

Birth, death and marriage certificates were still held in 1996 at St Catherine's House in the Aldwych. The National Statistics Public Search Room there looked like a medieval place of torment. I joined the panting crowds of fellow-researchers, sweating, glazed, cursing as we bumped against one another, jostling with decades of unwieldy volumes and staring at the lists, and more lists, of the dead. All of us apparently were hunting for our family stories. But I could find no death certificate for Norah Palmer Holroyd. Had she secretly married? She seemed to have vanished.

I had no other information about her, except a whisper my father had picked up from among the grown-ups that she lived with a Dr Macnamara. The family whispers had it that he was a Svengali, with an uncanny hold over this unmarried girl, plotting to get her money. There appeared to be no way of checking this. The trail had ended.

Then I had an idea. Maybe Norah made a Will. Wills and certificates of divorce were then lodged at Somerset House which was just the other side of the Aldwych from St Catherine's House. The crowds are less dense there and the torture more refined. No one who searches for a Will was allowed to take off his or her overcoat in winter lest it contain high explosives. The central heating was kept high, very high, and all the staff worked in shirtsleeves. In this unbalanced atmosphere I began my hot pursuit. I started in the year 1913, tracking backwards and forwards, and came across a Will Norah had made in 1907. This revealed that she died, aged thirty-six, on 22 October 1913. There had been no death certificate because she died at Vernet-les-Bains, a spa town in the far south west of France that was popular among British travellers in the late nineteenth century. Evidently she had visited her brother Fraser, and met her nephews and niece, shortly before setting out on that last journey.

Norah's Will fills a few of the empty spaces in her life and plants some signposts over this lost territory. Whatever immediately happened to her when The Links was sold late in 1899, she was according to the Census living at Beaufort House at Ham in Surrey at the beginning of 1901. The house was occupied by a Dr William Simpson Craig who was replaced as its occupant by his son-in-law Dr Macnamara in 1907, the year Norah made her Will.

When probate was granted in the summer of 1914, Norah's estate was valued at £11,992 16s, which would be equivalent to approximately half-a-million pounds at the end of the century. The chief beneficiaries were indeed Dr and Mrs Macnamara who continued living at Beaufort House until 1920. But Norah's Will gives a good reason for allowing what money she controlled to pass out of the Holroyd family. For fifteen years she had been able to 'enjoy the income' of a one-third share in her father's residuary estate. But because she was dying unmarried, her capital would pass to Pat and Fraser. For this reason 'I do not consider it necessary,' she writes, 'to bequeath to my said brothers or either of them any portion of the savings accrued or which may accrue in my lifetime in respect of the income of the said share and I have for that reason made the dispositions hereinafter contained without reference to my said brothers.'

But there is no malice against Pat and Fraser whose sons and daughter are each left a specific gift – for one nephew 'my gilt Empire clock'; for another 'my sleevelinks and tie clips'; and for her niece 'my gold watch and chain'. All of them receive £100 on their twenty-first birthdays. But my father, who was born four days before his aunt made her Will, is not mentioned; and, since there was to be no codicil, nor did Pat's daughter born in 1908 receive anything. The implication is that Norah's contact with her brothers' families had grown more distant during the last six years of her life.

Her largest legacy of all – £1,400 – goes to 'my friend Frances Mary Macnamara wife of the said Eric Danvers Macnamara' who is himself merely given 'my gold ring set with two diamonds and my crescent scarf pin'. Unless Norah's solicitor had advised against the impropriety of leaving the bulk of her estate to a married man, the conclusion any reader of this testament reaches is that the special friend of this woman with the watch chain, tie and cufflinks, was not the doctor but his wife.

Dr Macnamara was a well-known psychiatrist who practised in Harley Street. He 'devoted his life to mental disease', his obituary in the *British Medical Journal* states, '. . . even his domestic life had many associations with his special study'. Norah Palmer Holroyd was almost certainly the subject of one of the papers he published in medical journals and encyclopaedias on neurological and psychopathological matters – on paralysis, insomnia, the use of morphine and what was called 'functional insanity'.

Whatever he believed her to be suffering from, her death certificate at the Marie de Vernet-les-Bains in the Pyrenees provides no cause of death. It is as if she simply gave up living. She died at four o'clock in the afternoon of 22 October 1913 at the Hôtel du Parc, an 'établissement thermal'. There appear to have been no friends with her. The note of death is of a life unlived, 'célibataire', 'sans profession', signed at ten o'clock the following morning by two local Frenchmen and the mayor. There is no more.

After his sister's death, Fraser increased his holding in Rajmai Tea to 1,752 shares, and continued to hold this special number, with a nominal value of £10 a share, until the decline and fall of his own fortunes.

5

The Breves Process:
Tea into Glass

In the late eighteen-nineties my grandfather fell into the company of a large, noisy, ramshackle Irish family. The Corbets had been brought up in the Sunday's Well district of Cork and were utterly unlike Fraser's own family – indeed that was probably their principal charm. There were eleven Corbet sisters and one brother who, to compensate for his solitary condition, had been blessed with fifteen Christian names which his sisters were obliged to learn by heart: Roland, Hudson, Sands, De Courcy, Blennerhassett . . . He sailed away to the United States, built up a chain of garages and eventually perished under a car.

The sheer femininity of these vivacious Corbet girls, with their waspwaists and prominent busts, their bright eyes and lilting voices, seems to have bewitched Fraser after the invalidism of The Links, the heavy male world of Uppingham and his worrying time at Cambridge. Though apparently penniless, these

Corbets were always laughing. My grandfather was enchanted by their happy-go-lucky ways.

He had been introduced to them by a new friend Stephen (nicknamed 'Nipper') Anderson who was to become a partner in the Magor family's tea merchant company. 'Nipper' Anderson was on the verge of being engaged to the beautiful Alice Corbet and would take several years advancing to the verge of marrying her. When Alice came over from Ireland to see him, she brought with her a selection of her sisters: Iley, who played the piano so delightfully; Ida, who had escaped from a convent and gone on the music hall stage; Lizzie, the jolliest of the lot of them, famous for her punctuality (she once turned up for a train half-a-day early, fell asleep in the waiting-room, and missed it); Lannie, who would one day emigrate to Australia; and the very pretty and petite Adeline.

Their parents were both dead. If you spoke to Ida she would tell you that their father Michael Augustus Corbet had been a dedicated physician, and how her mother had died transporting medicines on horseback through the snows of winter. If you questioned Adeline, she would whisper of their father's unmitigated brilliance as a poor professor at Cork University. Each sister had her own story; and all relished the others' repertory of stories. On Adeline's birth certificate – she was born at 6 Lower Janemount in Cork on 13 July 1876 – her father's profession is given as 'Traveller' which means neither gypsy nor hedge scholar, but commercial traveller.

The eldest of these Corbet girls is Minnie. She has married the huge and friendly Tom White, director of a pharmaceutical company, and lives in Bray, County Wicklow. They have no family of their own but act *in loco parentis* to Minnie's unmarried sisters, the delicate Atty, the mysterious Sloper and others. But these sisters are rapidly getting married. When 'Nipper' Anderson hurried over to Ireland soon after Fraser's father's death to meet the rest of Alice's family, he took Fraser along with him. It was a holiday he needed. There were picnics by the sea and sunny days at the races, trips up to Dublin, walks around the magical waters of Glendaloch, and always the congenial company of this tumultuous family teeming with enjoyment.

Alice, as we know, is to be engaged to 'Nipper' Anderson. Lizzie has recently married and, as Mrs Parsons, gone to live in Bristol. Ida's career as a singer in the music halls is being brought to an end by some passionate love letters from an older man, William Temple, whom (despite the disapproval of his mother, 'old Lady Temple of Leeswood') she suddenly marries. Even the youngest sister of all, Lannie, will soon be engaged to a champion cyclist and billiards player. Romance is in the air and there seems no time to lose. Fraser's attention is caught by the next youngest sister, Adeline, a slip of a girl with a sensuous curving mouth and elaborate, altitudinous hair. She is called 'Bang' by her sisters: Fraser they call 'Josh'.

Bang and Josh were married on 4 April 1899 from Lizzie's new home in Bristol (her husband acting as one of the witnesses). Bang took only one year off her age (making herself a romantic twenty-one instead of twenty-two) on the marriage certificate, and gave her late father's profession innocuously as 'Gentleman'. There is no evidence that she went to Eastbourne and saw The Links which was being sold that summer. She was soon pregnant and living in her new home, the Red House, at Datchet, near Windsor in Buckinghamshire. They had chosen Datchet because her sister Ida now lived there.

On 7 January 1900 Bang and Josh's first child was born – a son whom they named Desmond Sowley Holroyd. But after sixteen weeks he was to die of bronchial pneumonia. Fraser, who was with his son when he died, was once again the 'informant' and signed the death certificate.

Two years later Adeline gave birth to a daughter. She and Fraser had gone down to stay with Bang's sister Lizzie at Bristol for the birth, and Yolande Phyllis was born at Lizzie's home in

Victoria Square, Clifton, on 22 April 1902. The house was alive with Corbet sisters, and Alice won the contest to sign Yolande's birth certificate as one of the many 'present at the birth'.

Everyone agreed that it was 'unfair' to have only one child. Lizzie had three; so did Lannie; and also Ida. Adeline's next child, a son whom they christened Kenneth De Courcy, was born at the Red House on 16 December 1903. And that, Adeline decided, was enough. Of course married women were expected to have children – it was their duty. But Bang was in many ways hardly out of childhood herself and never really would be. She was not naturally a loving mother. Her children got so much in the way of the exciting social life she was beginning to enjoy in England. She employed a young Welsh nurse, Kate Griffin (whom the children called 'Nan'), to look after Yolande and Kenneth; and in 1906 the family left the Red House and moved nearby to Meadowcroft, a house in Bolton Avenue, New Windsor, not far from the castle. But then something unexpected happened. 'It was here that I was born in 1907,' writes my father, '– an evident mishap.' The date of his birth was 20 October 1907, and after some debate they named him Basil De Courcy Fraser. What comes through a close reading of my father's account, written near the end of his life, is his sense of being unwanted: an outsider at home, a reject at school, an exile during later life, and inferior to his elder brother and sister. 'I was a sickly infant with a pidgeon [*sic*] chest and a frail hold on life,' he wrote. 'Nan sat up night after night looking after me, and there is no doubt that I owed my continued presence in the world to her. I saw little of my mother.'

The photographs of him at Windsor from infancy through childhood show him more ill-at-ease than ill. Aged one month he lies awkwardly on a cushion between Yolande and Kenneth who are more interested in the photographer than their new sibling. Later he is being held in place on a pony between the others' smarter horses; and later still he perches precariously on a *chaise-longue* to make a pretty threesome. For these are studio portraits which the proud parents will pass round their friends. Kenneth puts up with this business quite well – he is like someone holding his breath until the ordeal is over, yet still in command of himself. Basil's round face looks vulnerable and bewildered – but then he is the youngest. It is Yolande who appears in her element. She 'makes eyes' at the camera, puts an arm round her younger brother, sits elegantly on her horse. Or she poses alone, bare feet dangling from a podium. And there she is again, reclining on a sofa, studying a flower, standing small and defiant on a bench in the garden. Like her Aunt Norah she focuses, she comes alive, while her brothers look rather wooden or lost.

The children saw a good deal of their mother's sisters and their husbands over these early years, but little of Uncle Pat and his family. He had come back from South Africa with his wife Coral and their son Ivor, been appointed a captain in the Militia in 1903 and gone to live in Hampshire. Here, on 17 November 1908, his daughter Verity was born. My father could not remember going to Ropley Manor, his Uncle Pat's home in Hampshire, and he believed that his Aunt Coral disapproved of Fraser's marriage. The two brothers maintained a rather furtive friendship despite the gap that was appearing between their two families and that would widen over the years.

However, there were plenty of Corbet aunts to entertain the children. Aunt Iley, the pianist, was living not far away at Reigate in Surrey; and jolly punctual Aunt Lizzie they would sometimes visit in Bristol. But my father remembered most vividly going to play at Datchet where his Aunt Ida, the ex-music hall singer, and her husband from the zoo lived. Were the paddocks there really 'full of Zebras, Giraffes and Wildebeasts' as he imagined? 'There was an awful lot to see if one was lucky,' he insisted. There were those bright birds flying in the aviary and animals at the end of the garden ('small ones of course and I've forgotten what they were now'), and a big pond flashing with red and yellow fish in the sunlight. 'Halycon days!' he exclaimed, recovering with his childhood excitement his authentic childhood spelling.

There were three Temple daughters with whom my father sometimes played at Datchet. One, prim and religious, later married a man connected with cigarettes ('Passing Clouds' they were called) and had numerous daughters herself; another took after her father and devoted her life to horses and dogs; while a third, reviving memories of her mother's music hall days, travelled far, gambled long and had, we were told, a child by Rex Harrison. Not a bad family record.

Fraser and Adeline would occasionally leave Nan in charge of the children and go to Ireland where they became 'Josh' and 'Bang' again. There are some exuberant pictures of these holidays with the Corbet sisters, showing them on bridges and rocks against a waterfall or the sea, then in woods with their bicycles and in jaunting carts with horses. And there is one of Josh in his three-piece suit and watch chain, a pipe in his mouth, jumping high in the air. He loved these trips to Ireland and was thinking of buying a house called Greystones near Minnie and Tom White at Bray.

The family sometimes kept photographs but never letters and seldom postcards unless the pictures took their fancy. There is one postcard from this period, kept because the picture was drawn and coloured in by my Aunt Yolande. Written from Brocket, a large, newly-built house at Maidenhead into which the family moved in 1912, it was posted to her mother in Ireland. It tells of an air balloon which 'came right over our house. Nanny was so excited and called Yolande so many times that I thought the house was on fire.' The card is addressed to 8 Prince of Wales Terrace, Bray, and was probably written early in 1914 when Josh still had ideas of moving to Ireland. But the

Great War changed his plans, and a little later Tom and Minnie White came instead to live near Maidenhead.

They came with one of Minnie's sisters, Lannie (my father's favourite aunt) whose husband went off to Australia to make his fortune. He took with him their second son who prospered there and before long was employing his father; but he left in Ireland their elder son who did rather well in the IRA before, things getting too hot for him, he joined his father as a fellow-employee in his brother's Australian business. Lannie's daughter Joan, the youngest child, went with her to Maidenhead and was my father's chief companion in these war years. 'She was certainly closer to me than my own brother and sister,' he writes. One thing they had in common was a lack of confidence. Waiting for the fortune her father never made in Australia and for the call to join him that never seemed to arrive, Joan grew up as a poor relation wearing the cast-off clothes of her cousins, all of whom she hated 'except perhaps myself', my father adds.

The happiest days of my father's life 'were certainly those between the ages of five and eight – before I was sent to school', he wrote. 'I was spoilt by the old Nurse, had a small companion to play with and few worries. Exciting things happened too.' On good days he and Joan would play together among the flashing birds, amazing fish and small animals at Datchet. On bad days the two of them used to be dragged out from their hiding places and sent together to dancing class, Basil shamefully dressed in black velveteen knickers 'which showed every mark if one slid around on the floor for a few happy minutes', Joan in some frock that Yolande or one of her other cousins had discarded. Basil knew how she felt as he had inherited his brother's rotten toys.

Far better were their games outdoors such as drinking a special brew from an old tin and being tremendously sick. Joan often came to play at Brocket. The gardens there were 'the nicest part of all', my father wrote. They were laid out in three tiers with a drop of six feet between them, like a giant's staircase, and made a magical playground. Along the back of the house ran a stone-paved terrace and against its wall were apricots, nectarines and peaches facing southwards to the sun. The top level of the garden next to the house was the adults' play area, which is to say it was largely occupied by a grass tennis court, several formal rosebeds and three willow trees overlooking the second garden below. Flanking the tennis lawn, descending pathways followed the line of two boundary walls against which grew fig, pear and plum trees. On the second level lay the kitchen garden, its fruit and vegetables arranged in big squares and with a central path arched with apple trees that joined two curving flights of steps to the third level. Here stood three long hothouses crammed with black and white grapes and exotic flowers. At this lowest level there were also chicken houses with some fifty chickens wandering in and out of the potting shed, garage and coal yard with its wonderful mountain of black coal, perfect for climbing.

These gardens at Brocket 'were as good as many of the walled gardens in large country houses', my father wrote. From 'asparagus to onions, from gooseberries to quinces we had it all!' He especially liked the black, red and white cherries that gave their fruit in rotation and 'could have fed a small army of children'. Nevertheless he and his brother would sometimes balance themselves on the top of the potting shed and, using a butterfly net mounted on a long bamboo rod, steal some of the horribly sour cooking apples from the garden next door. 'It is the only intimate thing I ever remember doing with my brother as a small boy unless you can count watching my father start the car on Sundays.'

Compared with Kenneth who was a massive three, almost a monumental four, years older, and Yolande who, being a year older still, was almost an adult, Basil seemed a Richmal Crompton urchin-child. But he was happy. He had his own tomboy friend Joan and he lived in a secure and exciting world until the war – not the Great War, but that 'war of my own' which was fought out at his preparatory school.

Scaitcliffe School had been founded in the early eighteen-eighties by the Reverend Doctor Charles Crosslegh. He chose its rather perilous name after his seventeenth-century family house in Lancashire, taking out a ninety-nine-year lease on Crown land near Windsor Park in which to start a cramming establishment for prospective candidates to the Royal Indian Engineering College. Twenty-five years later it had been bought by Ronald Vickers, a classical scholar who, turning his back on the family armaments and engineering business, converted Scaitcliffe into a boys' preparatory school for Eton, Charterhouse, Wellington and other prominent public schools. His family was wealthy – several of them had been painted by John Singer Sargent – and he ran a private school 'because he liked doing it', my father observed. By the time Basil arrived in 1917 the school had some forty boys and was very much a Vickers family enterprise.

My father's difficulties at Scaitcliffe were largely caused, he felt, by his brother. Kenneth had actually left the term before Basil arrived, but his reputation stayed on. He had been a great success: doing wonderful things on the cricket and football pitches, excelling as an intrepid diver into the school plunge, performing miracles in the gym and, despite only scraping into the lowest form at Eton, gaining the approbation of the headmaster. This was not easy. Ronald Vickers was 'a remote austere figure, despite his underlying care and interest', his son Richard admits in the school history. '. . . Discipline was extremely strict.' Except for his academic record, Kenneth 'was everything I wasn't!' my father exclaimed. 'At first my life was absolute hell. I was scared stiff of the bigger boys and when frightened I talked my head off instead of being quiet. I was the butt of the school bullies. My locker was ransacked, my belongings stolen.'

This glimpse of rampageous school life differs from the picture of an extended family presented in the school history. There is no illustration in this book of the most visible Scaitcliffe master, Edgar Ransome (nicknamed Rampoo), but there is a fine description of him which contrasts rather dramatically with my father's boy's-eye view at the age of ten. Richard Vickers writes:

> Despite his great size – he weighed over 20 stone – he was a slow bowler of considerable skill who regularly attended nets each morning of the summer term. He was also a fine amateur pianist, whose rollicking songs were always an amusing interlude on winter evenings. His class presence was truly formidable, so woe-betide any boy who was slow to learn his tables or whose writing strayed from the line during copy-book exercises.

Certainly he must have had a lasting effect on my father whose writing never strayed from the line until his final illness. Ransome was the junior form master at Scaitcliffe for twenty-six years before retiring to be a tobacconist in Basingstoke. To cover his bald head he always wore a cap, and became 'pre-eminent' among the 'great characters of the school's early years'. But my father greatly feared and disliked him. 'I never quite understood how Ransome got a job at Scaitcliffe,' he wrote.

> He was a particularly coarse old man with a large stomach and a big fleshy hooked nose from the end of which hung a permanent dew drop. He couldn't even speak correctly, so heaven knows why [Ronald] Vickers, a purist, came to engage him.
>
> One of my worst recollections of Scaitcliffe was being made to stand in the corridor for bad behaviour. Should Vickers happen to come along the culprit got six sharp

cuts with the cane. Edgar Ransome, who took the lowest
class of very small boys, loved to inflict this form of
punishment. His classroom was opposite Vickers's Study
door, so the unfortunates were particularly vulnerable.

Basil could not wait for the holidays. During the war, the
family spent more time at Brocket, but because of school he was
seeing less of Joan. By the age of twelve his best friend had
become his dog, a mongrel officially named Pat whom he called
'Woorah' – 'I don't know why.' Looking back at this period he
was to write: 'I loved my dog dearly but did nothing for him. Nan
[Kate Griffin] fed, sometimes bathed and generally looked after
all our animals. My contribution was to reckon up how long he
could live and imagine there would be no world for me when he
died. And now I can't even remember how he died or when.'
Knowing as I do his last solitary years with his dog, this passage
has for me an almost Johnsonian tone of self-recrimination.

My father's last year at Scaitcliffe was more tolerable.
Memories of his glamorous elder brother were receding and he
himself was a bigger boy now – not someone who could easily
be bullied or have his locker ransacked. He was playing cricket
and football not too badly. He had escaped from Ransome's
form and there were fewer beatings. He had even learnt when to
be quiet and not talk his head off. 'I wasn't too unhappy,' he
concluded. 'I kept out of the way.'

I have no photographs of my father at Scaitcliffe, only one of
a school group taken in the grounds shortly before he arrived,
with my Uncle Kenneth standing eyes half-closed in the back
row, and the formidably handsome Ronald Vickers seated at
the centre, the solitary adult, with a cricket ball in his hand: an
intimidating figure.

Between the ages of seven and eleven my father didn't notice the
Great War much. The same seemed to hold true for Fraser. His

brother Pat, having been transferred to a regular battalion of the Royal Welch Fusiliers in 1915, made his Will and went off to fight in France. By 1917 he was back with the reserve battalion and retired after the war while in his forties. It was said in the family that he suffered, this amiable man, from shell-shock and that this was aggravated by domestic warfare. Certainly his career was modest by the standards of the two major-generals, his father and father-in-law, and he seems to have been a disappointment to his wife Coral who, according to my father, taught both their children (in particular their son Ivor) to despise him.

Coral already despised Fraser who took no part in the Great War allegedly on account of his varicose veins. So how, apart from fathering his three children and being 'of independent means', did my grandfather occupy himself in the first twenty-five years of his marriage before the big disaster?

At the beginning he seems to have had a notion of taking up the law. On 22 November 1899, some seven months after his marriage, he entered Gray's Inn (where George Sowley Holroyd had been admitted the previous century), enrolling at the private college run by the Bar Council. The Register of King's College, Cambridge, has a note of his studentship, and the Uppingham School Roll notes that he went on to qualify as a barrister. Actually he took no law examinations but shortly after the death of his first son he left the college to look after Adeline.

Over the next fifteen years he seems to have done very little but look after Adeline. She needed looking after – indeed she insisted on it. All the children could see what was going on. Their mother got more attention at home than any of them did. She was their rival. Whenever she didn't get her own way, she would have violent hysterics – like firework displays they were – and Fraser, who was a naïve and kindly man, was pricked with self-reproach. For he had really married the Corbet family, and the barometer of his happiness shot up whenever he was among them *en masse*. Bang wasn't allowed any of her tantrums when her sisters were around – they teased her too much. 'What's the difference between a man and an umbrella?' her sister Lizzie called out at one of Bang's bridge parties. All the card players stopped and looked up. 'Really, Lizzie, whatever are you talking about?' Bang answered. 'I'm sure I don't know.'

'Well, you damn well ought to – you've been under both of them.'

The implication was that sex was as enjoyable for Bang as a rainy afternoon. She lusted instead after a refined life. When none of her sisters were at Brocket, Adeline would put on operatic performances, crying out that she was not long for this world, that people would miss her when she was gone. She would send up many quivering Hail Marys and pray for the good Lord to take her – she was still playing these scenes fifty years later when I was among the audience. Alarmed by her mysterious illnesses, Fraser sent her to many specialists. They gave her their most expensive attention, but the mystery of her illness remained unsolved.

In 1900, after leaving Gray's Inn, Fraser had been made a director of the Rajmai Tea Company and would regularly see his brother Pat at the board meetings. These meetings were pleasant social affairs, spiced with tales from the East. Pat and Fraser enjoyed spending this time together without their wives.

But everything began to change in 1914. Adeline could not compete with the war. All men had to do something then. So what did Fraser do? According to the Uppingham School Roll, he joined the Stock Exchange. The Stock Exchange itself has no record of his membership. But my father remembered that Fraser had got a job with a shrewd German financier called Lowenfelt two or three years before the war. Lowenfelt started a firm called the Investment Registry in Waterloo Place. It was a lucrative business and Fraser made some money by taking Lowenfelt's advice to invest in rubber shares. Unfortunately, he did not take Lowenfelt's advice as to when he should sell the shares, and lost much of his gains after the development of synthetic rubber. Nevertheless he made some profit.

It was probably a mistake for my grandfather to have left the Investment Registry – it was to carry on in Grafton Street and London Wall into the nineteen-sixties. That he did leave was partly due to the uncomfortable sensation of having a German as his partner during this war against the Germans. It had an unpatriotic air. Besides, Lowenfelt was also a Jew which in those blatant days was additionally unpopular in England, though it hadn't told with Fraser before the war. In any event, listening to others, he seems to have persuaded himself that there was something 'ungentlemanly', if not actually illegal, about Lowenfelt's manipulation of the share market. Lowenfelt was a man ahead of his times, and already Fraser was falling behind the times. My grandfather's modest success at the Investment Registry persuaded him that he was 'a safe pair of hands' in business matters. He debated whether to pick up a more suitable business partner or go it alone, and then steered somewhere between these choices. In 1915 he decided to buy a patent cleaner from a naval captain he had recently met. It was a miraculous machine which, Captain Jennings assured him, would revolutionise the world of house decorating. There was nothing, not even the most dulled paintwork or delicate fabric, that this restorative device, filled with its fizzing formula, could not make new – and so quickly it took one's breath away. My breathless grandfather wanted to call the new company he created round this machine 'Brevis', signifying its amazing speed, but this name had been taken by another company, and so he named it 'Breves' meaning nothing at all, which is what he got. He took premises at the Knightsbridge end of Sloane Street, employed some staff and, as company secretary, chose a charming and penniless old man who had been hammered on the Stock Exchange. He had a long white silky moustache, always dressed immaculately in spats, and was devoted to my grandfather for rescuing him from poverty. Like schoolboys, the two of them would disappear behind a locked door to mix buckets of the secret formula which were then reverently handed to the works manager. It took a year, following the unexplained disappearance of Captain Jennings, for them to conclude from the flaking paintwork and faded fabrics that their magic substance, known as 'the Breves Process', did rather more harm than good.

My grandfather was determined to turn expensive failure into expansive success. He acted boldly, moving from 15 Sloane Street to larger premises, Imperial Court, between Harrods and Harvey Nichols, round the corner in Basil Street. Here he sought to develop the business. In the nineteen-twenties directories, Breves is listed as 'builders, decorators, electrical, heating and sanitary engineers, furnishers, designers and manufacturers of panelling, parquet floors, upholstery, carpets, bedding, curtains, blinds, picture restorers, vacuum cleaners, removals'. In short, Breves did everything and, like a circus performer, did it all at once. It made a small loss each year.

But my grandfather was still a man of wealth. Brocket, his home at Maidenhead, was an imposing, red-brick, Edwardian house with attics and cellars full of servants. The family owned a carriage and pair and, after 1908 when Fraser bought an Enfield Allday, they had a car. The ex-coachman, Thatcher, drove it during the week and my grandfather took over the wheel at weekends. Then there was my grandmother Adeline, 'one of the most accomplished backseat drivers in the country', according to my father. Fraser himself did not drive for long: the new technology did not suit him. The Enfield Allday, for example, having no self-starter, had to be 'wound with a starting handle', my father remembered. 'There was too a petrol tap which had to be turned on to allow the petrol to flow from the tank to the carburettor. This small point my father always overlooked. My brother and I used to hide behind the garage and listen to him trying to start the car. It was rare entertainment.'

My father's time at Scaitcliffe ended abruptly. In his account he wrote: 'When I was twelve Vickers made me sit for the Common Entrance examination. He did so, he said, to accustom me to sitting an exam. He made it abundantly clear that I hadn't the faintest chance of passing, so it was to everyone's dismay that I achieved the bottom form at Eton.' He was still in the lower half of Scaitcliffe and had been there little more than two-and-a-half years. He had obviously longed to get away, but did so just as he was beginning to enjoy the place.

What he had endured at Scaitcliffe, he now endured again at Eton, only it was worse because his brother was not simply a glowing memory but a very obvious presence in the school – 'one hell of a big fellow'. And he was not pleased to see his younger brother turning up so unexpectedly. Kenneth was 'in the library' which meant he was among the elite of their school house. He played for the 'twenty-two' (Eton's second cricket eleven) and also had his Field colours (which meant he was in the top team of that peculiar Eton game which somehow fails to combine the qualities of soccer and rugger). Above all Kenneth was a member of the fabulous Eton society known as 'Pop' which meant he could wear fantastically coloured waistcoats and 'stick-up' white collars that dazzled younger boys. In the school hierarchy it was impossible for such a swell to talk to a lower boy. Not understanding the social oligarchy of the school, Basil was hurt that his brother with whom he sometimes stole apples from the potting shed roof at Brocket had no word for him at Eton. 'My brother actively disliked me and avoided as much as possible having anything to do with me,' he remembered. He obviously embarrassed Kenneth. 'As usual when nervous I gave my half-witted display,' he concluded with a Thurber-like touch, 'and set a seal on my misery.'

In his diaries, the novelist Anthony Powell, writing some seventy years later, remembers being in the same division as my father, whom he described as being 'red-faced, hearty, one would say boring'. But he adds that he 'did not know him at all'. Since there was two years' difference in age between them, this Holroyd seems more likely to have been my uncle who was closer in age to Powell and, by Etonian standards, far more boringly successful.

Basil forgot the trick he picked up at Scaitcliffe of keeping 'out of the way' and reverted to his nervous habit of talking 'my head off'. That was the voice my mother was first to hear on board the *Suecia* when she sailed to England, the voice which was so raucous on bad days and, on good days, could 'talk anybody into anything'. That he did not relearn the discretion of his late Scaitcliffe period may have been due to his removal from Eton after a little over two years. 'I got double pneumonia and was taken in an ambulance to Brocket.' After an examination by the family doctor and a period of convalescence looked after by Nan, he was sent to Leysin in Switzerland. 'I was pronounced in good order within a few weeks,' he wrote. 'Then came the question of whether I returned to Eton or not. My mother, still convinced that I was ailing, opted for a Swiss education. She found the story of my fight for life very tellable at her weekly bridge parties. So I was sent to Chillon College.'

There my father's narrative stops. The difference between Chillon and Eton 'was immense', he wrote. 'I had spent most of my time loathing Eton.' Yet he would have preferred to return there than remain a prisoner of Chillon. Kenneth had now left for Clare College, Cambridge; so Basil had survived the bad years, and happier times lay ahead. I never heard my father speak of Chillon College which must have been near Geneva but which no longer exists (neither the Municipalité de Leysin nor the Fédération Suisse des Ecoles Privées has any knowledge of it). It was evidently one of those private boarding schools that

specialise in educating American, British, French, German and
Italian nationals, some of whose parents work in Switzerland,
others of whom are sent abroad to be 'finished'. For my father it
represented exile, under the shadow of failure at Eton.

He remained in Chillon for the best part of two years. But
now that people could travel abroad again in the early nineteen-
twenties, his family was able to visit him, starting their holidays
in Switzerland and travelling leisurely back through France. It
was at Dinard, the fashionable watering-place in Brittany, my
father remembered, that during one of these journeys Fraser
first saw a display of Lalique glass. Later, in about 1926, he
went to a Lalique exhibition mounted at showrooms in Great
Portland Street. It had been brought over to London by the
Curzon family following a grand exposition of decorative art in
Paris. Though the glass did not attract great attention in the
British newspapers, it impressed my grandfather who went over
to Paris the following year, saw René Lalique and tried to get
himself appointed sole agent for the glass in 'Britain and the
Empire'. He was just too late, the agency having been acquired
by 'a likeable rogue' called Keir. But Fraser managed to pull off
a deal with Mr Keir. He now had the magical ingredient, like the
earlier 'Breves Process', necessary for success.

Between the mid-nineteen-twenties and the mid-nineteen-
thirties my grandfather pursued an extraordinary strategy. He
sold for cash, or lodged with Barclays Bank as a means of raising loans, all his Rajmai Tea shares – indeed he got rid of ninety
more shares than he actually possessed (these ninety shares were
'sold' to his friend 'Nipper' Anderson and must have been part
of a 'gentleman's agreement'). He then acquired another 1,000
shares and used them to get more loans. By these means he
raised the equivalent today of almost one million pounds. What
was so strange about this programme is that it went against
everything in which he believed. He disapproved of selling
shares, most especially Rajmai shares, because it struck him as

an act of disloyalty. It was this rapid buying and selling, this playing of the market, that he had disliked in Lowenfelt. Also, tea was doing rather well in the nineteen-twenties before the government placed a fourpenny tax on it. The Industrial Fatigue Research Board had come up with the finding that 'a cup of tea aids efficiency and curbs industrial discontent'. It was patriotic to drink Indian tea in Britain. You drank it for prosperity as you would later dig vegetables for victory. A survey in 1927 showed that the British were drinking more tea and less beer – and also that birth rate figures were falling.

But Lalique glass dazzled Fraser and, though they did not guess why he had taken this dramatic change of direction, it seems to have been uniformly popular in his family. Adeline liked having it around the house; Yolande thought it beautiful; and the two boys, Kenneth and Basil, saw a future for themselves in this new family business – a far brighter future than on a tea plantation. René Lalique, then in his mid-sixties, had become recognised as a pioneer in this Age of Glass. He was an astonishingly versatile artist who exploited its texture and colour, using motifs from nature (flowers, fish, birds, animals) in the jewellery, sculpture and ornamental tableware he designed in his Paris studio. Fraser gazed at this glass as if it were a magic crystal. He looked about him – there were hunger marches, miners' strikes, lengthening dole queues and street demonstrations protesting against unemployment throughout Britain; there was the Wall Street Crash in the United States, civil disobedience in India, the Japanese invasion of Manchuria, revolution in Argentina, revolt in Peru, the rise of Hitler in Germany and Mussolini in Italy, and throughout the world an economic crisis – Fraser looked and saw, reflected in his glass, that all was well. The omens were good, he decided, for further business expansion.

The Basil Street offices were converted with a Chinese-style background into glittering showrooms by 1928. A gallery, with beige carpets, walnut veneers to the showcases, and brown walls paling into ivory at the ceiling, was prepared during the early nineteen-thirties in New Bond Street. A special lighting division was set up in Newman Street, off the Tottenham Court Road. There was also a smart office in Brown's Arcade near Oxford Circus and an apartment in Carlyle Square in Chelsea, where orders were dispatched and drinking glasses, salad dishes, scent bottles, flower vases, car mascots, glass sparrows, fish, cocks, horses, eagles and other amazing objets d'art sent out on approval. The Breves Lalique catalogues during the late nineteen-twenties and the nineteen-thirties show the wonderful range of goblets, bowls and plates, jugs and decanters, statuettes, paperweights, ashtrays that became available, decorated with leaves, dragonflies, peacocks, beetles, swallows, sunflowers, cupids, water-nymphs – a witty, decadent array.

My grandfather gave a magnificent fancy-dress party in Knightsbridge for everyone associated with 'Breves Lalique Galleries'. It was opening time in the West End. The lights were switched on, and all stood dazzled and ready for the boom which my grandfather sensed would sweep through the business world, bringing prosperity to the nineteen-thirties and a well-earned peace into which he could retire in the nineteen-forties.

This was to be my father's future. Meanwhile, the School Clerk's records at Eton have him going up to University College, Oxford, in the summer of 1925. But if that was his intention he did not carry it out. Instead (and to my surprise since he never referred to it) he turns up as a pensioner (that is, an ordinary student without financial assistance from the college) at Trinity College, Cambridge, in the Michaelmas term of 1926, having passed one paper in mathematics for the ordinary Bachelor of Arts degree in Easter that year. The examination he took was called 'The sun, the stars, and the universe'. But as he studied only one subsidiary course, 'I do not think that your father was intending to take an ordinary B.A.,' writes Jonathan Smith from

Trinity College Library. 'Your father's social life here is a bit of a mystery. Unfortunately he does not show in our personal names index to club and society records, nor does he make an appearance in the *Trinity Review*.'

What a contrast to Kenneth at Clare College! He appears in pictures of all sorts of clubs, teams, societies with a sheen of maturity spread over his rather blasé handsome features, so resplendent in his gleaming blazer, so sophisticated with his casual cigarette. And he had worked a bit too. He is listed in the third class for parts I and II of the Architectural Diploma, and in the second class for part III. It is not a bad record for someone who had entered the lowly Third Form at Eton.

My father stayed only four terms at Trinity and 'left without a degree'. He had left Scaitcliffe early by accident; he had left Eton early through illness; why had he left Cambridge early too? No one has the answer to this until I happen to mention it to one of Kenneth's stepsons. He tells me that my uncle (his stepfather) revealed that Basil had celebrated his return from Switzerland by amassing spectacular gambling debts at Cambridge.

It must have been shortly after my father went down from Cambridge that Fraser, having paid off all his debts, made him and Kenneth directors of Breves Lalique in the late nineteen-twenties. 'In my brother's case it could have been all right,' my father commented, 'but in mine it was madness.' Yet it was a fine madness, and nothing is so becoming in Fraser's career as his championing of Lalique with his two sons in the decade before the Second World War.

6

The Coming of
Agnes May

To all but his children, Fraser had kept his marriage looking reasonably harmonious all these years. But he was deeply unhappy. Why was Adeline so discontented? Was it his fault? He was always buying her costly trinkets – surely she had everything she wanted? And that was probably the trouble: she wanted such unrewarding things and did not know why they failed to satisfy her.

Of all the Corbet sisters, Adeline had probably made the best marriage – or so it seemed. Yet she was the one who always complained. While she was crying out that she was at death's door, it was the others who actually died. And when she prayed to God to relieve her of some disaster, it seemed that these disasters were visited on her sisters. Two of these sisters, the delicate Atty and the mysterious Sloper, had passed away very young and long ago in Ireland. Then the beautiful Alice, having finally married 'Nipper' Anderson, was drowned while sailing away with him for a new life in the United States. Iley now had Parkinson's Disease – they would put her hands on the piano and she would play a few bars, then stop: and soon she stopped altogether. Lizzie's life was also clouded by an awful tragedy, one of her twin sons having been run down and killed in the road outside her house. Her brother-in-law, the jovial Tom White, had grown enormous – over eighteen stone – and on medical advice taken up golf (though it was said he could never see the ball). He and his wife Minnie (a mere sixteen stone) would play together at Maidenhead. One day Tom broke his club and seemed to explode. He was presented with his death certificate on the sofa afterwards at Brocket. Minnie went on playing rather half-heartedly, but did not long survive him. Lannie had by this time received her passage money to Australia – had in fact received it more than once. But she would not go, even though her beloved daughter Joan, now living with her lesbian girlfriend in England, had quarrelled and refused to see her any-more. But after her 'protectors' Tom and Minnie died, she could no longer stay. So finally she went, and was given a pittance by her son and restricted access to her grandchildren over what was to be a lonely exile in Australia.

That was how life had treated those delicious Corbet girls who, in my grandfather's eyes, appeared to possess the very secret of happiness.

Fraser had attempted to shield Adeline from such disasters. Perhaps he had shielded her too much. Was there some extra apprehension that called forth his protection – a fear of the unknown, untreatable by her doctors? So much was unknown to Adeline. She had learnt little at school and little from her married life. No one had really bothered to teach her anything, and her imagination never came alive except when sensing danger. The world was teeming with danger: a shopping trip to London, a matinée in the theatre, lunch at a restaurant – all had their risks. Being uncertain of so much, she pretended and was perceived as being pretentious. She did not really love anyone, was loved neither by her husband nor her children, and never realised what was lacking or how she might attract it. All she knew, as she went on with her bridge parties each week and giving attention to her dogs, was that life had turned out a disappointment.

Adeline and Fraser had been together for over a quarter-of-a-century, and perhaps theirs was no worse than many marriages. People did not get divorced so easily then. But the times were changing. They were to change for Fraser and Adeline after the General Strike of 1926.

After the war my grandfather used to be driven by Thatcher in his Lancia each day from Maidenhead up to Basil Street in Knightsbridge. Passing through Hammersmith in the second week of May 1926, he told his chauffeur to stop the car and give a lift to a woman who was standing on the pavement – many people were giving lifts during the General Strike. As a courteous gentleman Fraser must have thought it his duty to help this voluptuous-looking, well-dressed young woman in distress, with her fine eyes, full lips and welcoming smile. It was the very least he could do – indeed he desired to do more. In the car, they got talking and by the time they reached their destination in the West End they found that they had not exhausted all they had to say to each other. So they arranged to meet that evening and continue their conversation . . .

The lady's name was Agnes May Babb. She was thirty years old – that is twenty years younger than my grandfather – though she admitted to being only in her late twenties. And she was married – in fact had already been twice married, though it seems unlikely that my grandfather knew this. Agnes May's first husband had been a young accountant called William Reynolds Lisle. He was made a Second Lieutenant in a London regiment shortly before she married him in 1916. Both of them gave their address as Rose Cottage, Barrow Green Lane, Oxted, in Surrey. He was the son of a solicitor (who had recently died leaving him a nice inheritance) and, on the marriage certificate, she agreed that her father too had been a solicitor, and was also dead.

Rather curiously she gave her Christian names as 'Maimie Archie' – almost as if she had not been quite sober at the time. But that perhaps was understandable as her husband was off to fight in the war. Against the odds, Second Lieutenant Lisle survived the war. In his petition for a divorce, which came to court towards the end of 1919 and was made absolute on 19 July 1920, his wife's name is correctly given and she is cited as respondent. But there is no co-respondent which suggests that she deserted him almost immediately after the marriage.

Then she went up a couple of ranks. Eleven days after her divorce came through she married Thomas George Symonds Babb, a thirty-three-year-old, previously-unmarried Captain in the Royal Engineers. Both gave their address as 187 Ladbroke Grove, a large late-Victorian terraced house some three hundred yards from where I am writing this book.

Thomas Babb was the son of a hotel proprietor in Minehead, and on the marriage certificate Agnes May agreed that her father too had been a hotel proprietor. As soon as they married they left London, but six years later she is separated from her husband and back in London, standing on the pavement in Hammersmith, waiting for a lift.

How much of this past history my grandfather got to know I cannot tell. Certainly Agnes May's two husbands were not meant to find out that she was the daughter of a humble glass-grinder, Joseph Bickerstaff, from St Helens in Lancashire – her sophisticated voice showed little trace of a north country accent. She was unlike any other woman my grandfather had known, a fast smart modern woman of the nineteen-twenties as thrilling to him as the Corbet sisters had been thirty years ago in Ireland. He quickly became infatuated with her. But what was he to do?

What he did shocked everyone – it was so dramatically out of character. He left home and put himself up at the Royal Automobile Club's palatial Edwardian hotel-and-headquarters in Pall Mall (sometimes called 'the Chauffeurs' Arms' by members of senior clubs). And he bought a twenty-one-year lease on an apartment a few hundred yards away in Piccadilly into which Agnes May moved in the summer of 1927. From the second floor of Berkeley House, 81 Piccadilly, on the opposite side of the road from the Ritz Hotel and not far from Lord Palmerston's old house, her rooms looked pleasantly across Green Park towards Buckingham Palace. The yearly rent of this love nest was £1,250 – equivalent to no more than £40,000 a year in the late nineteen-nineties.

But this was not my grandfather's only fresh expenditure. He had to make separate provisions for his wife and children. This he attempted to do by means of a legal arrangement, the trustees of which were his old friends 'Nipper' Anderson (who had of course been married to Adeline's sister Alice) and his partner in the tea business, Richard Magor, whose father had befriended Fraser's father in India.

It was on his 'Indian fortune' that Fraser was relying to support his new way of life. From 1 July 1927 he covenants to pay his trustees, for the rest of his life, one-half of his income from the Rajmai Tea Company for the benefit of his wife and three children. Rajmai Tea shares are not the sort of happy-go-lucky shares that are bought and sold by anyone and everyone on the open market – the sort of shares from which Lowenfelt made his dubious profits for the Investment Registry. On the contrary, they were shares in a private company, reliable shares owned by one or two families and their loyal friends that had the same nominal value of £10 a share as they had when Major-General Charles Holroyd listed them among his assets in the previous century. Of course, if they somehow did make their way on to the Stock Exchange, there is every reason to feel that by now they would fetch considerably more than £10 apiece. But there is no need for them to be traded in that fashion: they are rock solid, part of Britain's undented tradition. The nominal value of Fraser's shares is a little under £30,000. But their true worth is incalculable. They are, in the Holroyd family's legend, priceless, invaluable, beyond dreams.

Apart from this income Fraser allows Adeline and their children the occupation of Brocket and the use of its contents. In the event of his death there are binding guarantees reaching into the next generation. But he retains the right to sell his Rajmai Tea shares if 'he shall in his absolute discretion think fit', then reinvest his fortune and divide the renewed income in the same proportions.

My grandmother made it clear that she would never consent to a divorce. After all, she was an Irish Catholic and knew her rights and duties, knew what was proper, knew that the shock of it all would kill her and that her husband would forever have it on his conscience. But that Fraser, who for thirty years had given every appearance of being ruled by conscience, could so far have forgotten himself flabbergasted her. She had thought him such a safe pair of hands. She did not keep quiet about the catastrophe. She told everyone. She wrote letters to Ireland and Australia; and she made terrific and terrible scenes in Maidenhead. Everyone at Brocket was familiar with her ascending Hail Marys, her dramatic pleas for wingèd death to carry her off; but their repetition and the increase in their volume chaffed at the children's embarrassment. They wished she would shut up, though reluctantly recognising that this time she had some justification.

Yolande, Kenneth and Basil all preferred their father to their mother. His was the more sympathetic presence, and yet they were not really close to him. 'He is not of a nature to confide in others, & keeps his feelings to himself,' his own father had written to Oscar Browning, and that was how he remained. The

Archbishop of Canterbury was soon to announce his approval
of free sexual discussion. But such a thing was absolutely impossible for my grandfather and his children. The only intimacy
they really shared was one of English awkwardness. Yolande,
Kenneth and Basil were in their early twenties, easily shocked,
quick to judgement. 'We were horrified by the slur cast on the
family name,' my father wrote in the fragment of his account.
'How could we ever hold up our heads again? How could he
have done it?'

It seems that Fraser told them almost nothing, that he could
not bring himself to speak of such things, could not even bear to
see his children. They were left in a vacuum. 'We cannot judge a
man,' one of Yolande's friends wrote to her, 'as their temperaments & everything are so different from ours & they do things
hastily.' Among the family at large there was general incredulity.
'I'm absolutely lost for words to say about Uncle Joshie,' wrote
a cousin from Australia. 'It all sounds to me like a dream as
Uncle Josh was the one man in the world that I believed in . . . I
think that temporally he must be unbalanced and that sooner or
later he will realise the great mistake he is making . . . he was
such a model I simply *can't* convince myself that it is true. If my
own father left, heavens I would be singing a hymn of thanks-
giving . . .' But none of Fraser's children were thankful he had
left. And none of them seemed capable of understanding what
had happened.

Except for the allusive couple of pages my father wrote fifty
years later and a strange legal document, there was nothing to
mark or record the break-up of the marriage. The few photograph albums among my Aunt Yolande's possessions suggest an
uninterrupted passage of smiling summer holidays. There are
groups of the family with dogs and tennis rackets at Brocket;
and snaps taken on trips to Greece, Turkey and Sicily – the
Acropolis at Athens, the Sancta Sophia and Blue Mosque at
Constantinople, the Chapel of the Royal Palace and the

Monreale Monastery at Palermo, all visited in 1927. But mostly there are holiday shots of Yolande in the South of France: at Antibes in 1928; Juan-les-Pins and Cap Ferrat in 1929; Monte Carlo between 1930 and 1932. There she is sunbathing and picnicking on the beach. I am astonished to see her water-skiing behind speedy motor-boats. She still takes almost as good a photograph as she did when she was a precocious child, and she looks happy with her friends Cathie and Cynthia and Freda, though this is the period of her father's decampment. Clearly these holidays, longer and more luxurious than at any other time, are designed as an escape from this distressful family break-up. In the background occasionally, and sometimes in a group posed on deckchairs, Adeline appears; but of course Fraser is never to be seen, nor are Kenneth and Basil often there. They have their own friends elsewhere, and besides they are now directors of the famous Lalique enterprise on which the family fortunes, including the continuation of these holidays abroad, will depend. Apparently it does not occur to them that their father's change of business life may be part of his emotional and sexual change of life. They do not see the disposal of the Rajmai Tea shares as a letting-go of his family past, or the purchase of Lalique glass as his embracing of Agnes May's contemporary glamour. But then they do not know that Agnes May's father had been a glass-grinder.

Kenneth and Basil themselves kept almost nothing from their past, and among Yolande's three or four cardboard boxes there is little except the photograph albums of people and dogs – the people, if not the dogs, usually unidentified. There are a few papers, but they are mainly notes for the milkman, old cheques for tiny sums, reminders from the Eastbourne Mutual Building Society, a newspaper cutting on 'the ABC of Purchase Tax', a receipt for shoe repairs (3s 6d) and an advertisement recommending analgesic tablets. Some of these items are stuffed into a torn and ragged evening bag of soft red morocco. There are several old letters too, among which is the one already quoted, from a cousin in Australia, dated 20 December 1926, expressing amazement at Uncle Joshie's temporary madness. Otherwise the creased and faded bits and pieces belong to later years. But in the lining of this dilapidated red bag I find three or four extra papers that cannot have seen the light for more than half-a-century. One is apparently in code. It is scribbled in pencil and difficult to make out even with a magnifying glass in sharp light. I call in a second opinion, my wife's. As part of her biography of Angus Wilson, she has been doing research on the codebreakers at Bletchley Park, and after a few minutes she solves the puzzle. We are reading a special recipe for de-worming dogs. The other pages come from three short letters written by Fraser and sent to Yolande from the Royal Automobile Club in October and November 1926.

My grandfather's handwriting has not altered greatly since he wrote the only other letter I have seen – to Oscar Browning in 1895 – which is in the library at King's College, Cambridge. He has a clear, handsome, flowing hand with, nevertheless, the odd word regularly crossed out. The first letter is simply a note to be delivered by hand:

> I have been very seriously ill and am not yet in a
> condition to stand further worry.
> With all my love
> ever yr fond & devoted Dad.

This serious illness, whatever its exact nature, recalls his breakdown at Cambridge. The other two notes his daughter kept are also written from the RAC apparently one month later, and both are incomplete. The shorter of them concerns some money for Yolande's wedding. 'I enclose a cheque value £20 to pay for your wedding clothes,' he writes. 'Early next month

£175 [£150 has been crossed out] will be paid into your a/c making £275 since last June.' This amount (equivalent over six months to £8,000 in the late nineteen-nineties, or presumably £16,000 a year) is an allowance the details of which, her father adds, can be better explained by a Peter Rawlins of 45 King William Street, London Bridge. The handsome Peter Rawlins had been an admirer of Yolande's Aunt Lannie in the days before she went to Australia. So Fraser is keeping everything, as it were, in the family. Yolande has evidently been sending letters to her father at the RAC, and eventually he agrees to see her. He also agrees that, as a wedding gift, 'you can certainly have a piece of Lalique'. The note ends at the foot of the page without a signature. 'My love and affection for you have not changed & I am not the character some may wish you to believe.'

Perhaps the separation between husband and wife had been too long postponed. In any event it seems to have been peculiarly bitter, and whereas the unpleasantness of it all paralysed Fraser, it released a hailstorm of recrimination from Adeline. Her husband is now a wolf in sheep's clothing. The children cannot credit this. Certainly they do not want to, but they do not know what to believe. The worst that can be said of him, they think, is that he is weak. For years they have seen how weak he has been with their mother. Is he now being weak with another woman?

Yolande's pressing letters to her father are obviously not unsympathetic but they express her bewilderment. What were the facts? Surely it must be possible to put everything right by a family discussion about it all? Fraser's last note is his reply to this suggestion.

Discussions more especially on subjects where I am
unable to make concessions are distressing, & when I
know that your minds have been poisoned by
misrepresentation & the withholding of important facts.
    I am grieved that you have felt the strain of the

position – your letters were greatly appreciated – but because I am not for the *moment* able to confide in you please trust me & do not believe all you hear. Time will I am sure show that your belief in me is not misplaced & this will I hope repay you for the sorrow you have suffered.

I have been wronged for years and it was only my love for you three children which enabled me to endure so long.

You are & will always be in my thoughts – I have no wish to ostracise . . .

And there the letter stops. There is no mention of the woman in the case. Perhaps, by staying at the Royal Automobile Club, Fraser was concealing her presence in his life for as long as possible. But by the early summer of 1927, after he bought her the flat in Piccadilly and made his legal Settlement with Adeline and his family, the truth must have been known to them all. It was the old story. Adeline was aged fifty and Agnes May thirty. Adeline had given birth to four children; Agnes May apparently had no children. She was a glaringly attractive woman – an expensive tart, my father irritably thought when he eventually met her, whom Fraser insisted on treating as a great lady. But she was also sympathetic and understanding, sexy and loving to Fraser who believed that Adeline's loveless complaints over the years had worn away all good feeling and were the real cause of their failed marriage. At any rate, he could stand no more. He had that special sensitivity to women that some men whose mothers die early retain all their lives. The fact that his mother had killed herself may have acted on him as an inhibition – though I do not know whether he was ever told that she had killed herself. In any event, his need had grown so acute through neglect that he was driven to actions which people who thought they knew him found incredible.

But what had attracted Agnes May to Fraser? He was in his early fifties, six feet tall but rather bent, with ears that stuck out as if straining to understand what was going on, and bald though his face was decorated with what, after the rise of Hitler, was to be known as a Hitler moustache. He was a generous but not a glamorous man, a gentleman in the Edwardian style who, though desperately wanting to be young, could not shimmy or foxtrot or even 'Tip-toe through the Tulips'. He would have liked to belong to the new generation with its jazz and tangoes, its naughty sentimental songs, but he could not really join in. His moment of youth had been too long delayed; and what Agnes May gave him, however vital and necessary, was probably as much part of his imaginative as his physical life. He did not care much for nightclubs and cabarets, _thés dansants_ and musicals. Also he felt guilty at being unable to 'do the right thing' and offer Agnes May marriage, and did not object when she called herself Mrs Holroyd.

The affaire lasted four years altogether, during three of which Agnes May lived in Piccadilly as Fraser's mistress. Then he had grown tired and she had become bored. The arrangements for their separation were spelt out in an extraordinary Deed of Covenant dated 5 May 1930 and drawn up by a solicitor in Clarges Street, round the corner from Berkeley House, representing Agnes May. In consideration of 'past services' and from 'motives of concern for her interest', Fraser states that he is 'desirous of securing to her' the payment of £33 6s 8d each month – or in other words £400 a year (equivalent to £13,000 seventy years later). The first payment has already been made on 1 April, and these monthly payments were to continue for ten years or during the joint lives of them both 'whichever of two such periods shall be the larger'.

But there are conditions attached to these payments. Agnes May must lead a chaste life. If she 'returns to cohabitation with her husband' Thomas Babb, or divorces him and remarries, then

THIS DEED OF COVENANT is made the *fifth* day of May One thousand nine hundred and thirty BETWEEN EDWARD FRASER ROCHEFORT HOLROYD of Berkeley House, 81, Piccadilly, London, W.1., (hereinafter called "the Grantor") of the one part and AGNES MAY BABB c/o Stanley Attenborough & Co., of 4, Clarges Street, London, W.1., (hereinafter called "the Annuitant") of the other part WHEREAS the Grantor in consideration of the past services of the Annuitant and from motives of concern for her interest is desirous of securing to her the payments hereinafter mentioned NOW THIS DEED WITNESSETH as follows:-

1. The Grantor for the consideration aforesaid hereby covenants with the Annuitant that he the Grantor will provided and on condition

Arbitrators or an umpire whose decision shall be absolutely conclusive and binding on all parties and this shall be deemed an agreement for a reference within the Arbitration Act 1889.

IN WITNESS whereof the parties hereto have hereunto set their hands and seals the day and year first above written.

SIGNED SEALED AND DELIVERED by the   )
above named Agnes May Babb in the   )
presence of :-

Agnes May Babb

the monthly allowance will be forfeited. And there are other things she must not do: she must not call herself Mrs Holroyd any longer; she must not 'come to reside within two miles' of Fraser's family house at Maidenhead or 'hold any communication' with his family; she must not lay claim to 'his Lancia car' or become a bankrupt (though there seems more likelihood of him entering bankruptcy than her). If these conditions are met, the allowance will continue to be paid to her on the first of each month, and she agrees to inform Fraser through his solicitor of 'her exact place of residence' every three months – providing that he does not disclose this address to his family as she does not want to be molested by them.

This strange document has lain for many years with a small bundle of my father's out-of-date Wills, divorce and tenancy papers, long ago forgotten. 'She faded out of the picture with a minimum of fuss,' he wrote of Agnes May in his brief account. 'I suppose she was given some money but I've no idea how much. At the end of it all we were very broke.'

The Deed of Covenant is signed by Agnes May Babb in a spiky, slightly backward-leaning hand. I touch it with my finger. It is this signature alone that has given me her name and provided a small crack in the dark, enabling me to find out more about her.

By trawling backwards over the years at the Public Search Room at St Catherine's House I came across Agnes May's previous marriages and her birth certificate. Now I travel forwards to find out whether, after she had separated from my grandfather, she remarried. From my grandfather's point of view the good news (since it put an end to his monthly payments) is that she did marry again on 15 February 1934. Her husband was a thirty-year-old divorcé and 'company director', Reginald Alexander Beaumont-Thomas.

Agnes May Beaumont-Thomas (formerly Babb, previously Lisle and initially Bickerstaff, who for two or three years adopted the name Holroyd) calculates her age on the new marriage certificate as thirty-six (which is only two years short of her actual age) and she describes her father as a hotel proprietor which she remembered having copied down on her certificate of marriage to Thomas Babb. Her father appears to have had a biblical ability to die and come alive again fairly regularly. At the time of her first marriage, she writes that he is 'deceased' as her husband William Lisle's father was; but he was alive four-and-a-half years later when she married Thomas Babb (whose own father was alive), and had died again by 1934 now she was marrying Reginald Alexander Beaumont-Thomas (whose father was also dead). Actually he did not die until 1942. He died intestate, so there is no mention of a daughter. Despite her wealth, his estate, which went to his widow, was valued at only £207 3s 6d.

The Beaumont-Thomases are married at Biggleswade in Bedford and Agnes May gives her address as 'The Red Lion Hotel, Sandy'. But to have remarried, she would have had to get divorced. The decree nisi had been granted on 13 June 1933, and the bad news for my grandfather is that he has been named as co-respondent – though it is more than three years since he has been living with her. Perhaps this is no more than a legal convenience since his name is written with no great accuracy on the divorce proceedings – Edwin (instead of Edward) Fraser Rochford (instead of Rochfort) Holroyd. It seems unlikely that damages would have been sought against him but he may well have had to pay the court costs. What is surprising is that even an inaccurately-named co-respondent has been necessary, since husband and wife were living apart for more than eight years (had she gone back to him, her adultery with my grandfather would have been condoned). The speed with which she marries again is spectacular – even quicker (three days versus eleven days) than her first remarriage. For this was a very good marriage she was making. Her late father-in-law, Richard Beaumont Thomas (the name was not then hyphenated), a steel and tin-plate manufacturer of Brynycaerau Castle, Llanelly, Carmarthen, had left £419,285 18s 9d to his three children on his death in 1917. Such a sum would be worth £14 million at the end of the century.

For two years Agnes May Beaumont-Thomas continued living with her company director husband in Campden Hill Gate. Then they leave London – perhaps to one of the properties he had been given in Gloucestershire, perhaps abroad (his first wife had been French and they had married in Paris). I can find no further trace of them. So Agnes May disappears from my story, like an alarming comet passing over the night sky.

*

But was there nothing more I could discover about the ramifications of this affaire? Suddenly I recalled the mysterious 'Holroyd Settlement' my father had mentioned in the account he wrote for me of his early years, and which still provided him in his old age with a couple of hundred pounds or so a year from the National Westminster Bank. This Settlement had occasionally been spoken of in hushed and hopeless whispers during my early years. I remember my mother telling me how she and my father took me, aged six or so, to the home of a famous lawyer, Sir Andrew Clark, who had been a friend of my Uncle Kenneth's at university. He was reputed to be the cleverest barrister in England and was much disliked for his arrogance (he later gained fame for a brilliant investigation into the Ministry of Agriculture known as the Crichel Down Inquiry, and also for cutting off his daughter with exactly one shilling when she married an unacceptable man). My mother was terrified that I would smash one of the precariously-placed objects in his drawing-room as I wandered happily from table to table and my father appealed to him to release us from the iron grasp of our family Trust. I broke no china that afternoon, nor was the Trust Deed broken. My grandparents, my uncle, my aunt, everyone wanted it broken: and yet it could not be broken. The letter of the law was too strong. Somewhere in its legal depths, like treasure in a long-sunken wreck, lay the money we so desperately needed. It remained as if in a chest whose key is lost, its contents slowly disintegrating.

But what the origins of this complex affair were I never knew. At my request the National Westminster Bank now sent me the documents from its vaults and I could see what I had begun to suspect: that the 'Holroyd Settlement' was the legal arrangement made by my grandfather in 1927 after he left his family, together with a Supplemental Deed dated 27 May 1932 which reveals something of what happened over those five years. It is a ruinous story.

Two properties are identified in this Supplemental Deed. The first is Agnes May's expensive love nest in Piccadilly, the lease of which did not expire until June 1946. The second is an oddly-crenellated, nineteenth-century town cottage with a small garden. It resembles a gate house to some grander building. Auckland Cottage, 91 Drayton Gardens, in unfashionable Fulham, is where my grandfather retired in April 1930. The rent on this house was £200 a year (equivalent to £6,000 in the late nineteen-nineties) and the lease did not expire until March 1944. These two properties Fraser handed over to Magor and Anderson, his trustees, in place of his Maidenhead house. They were to sell or sub-let them once he returned to Maidenhead so that his payments to his wife and children, promised in the principal deed, could be kept up. All his Rajmai Tea shares were now in other hands. A small design shows the details of these loans and overdrafts he had so far secured.

Amount owing	Name of Bank	No. of shares
£24,500	Mercantile Bank of India Ltd.	1,000 Transferred to the name of the Nominees of the Bank. 100 Collateral.
£8,000	National Bank of India Ltd.	227 Transferred to the name of the Nominees of the Bank. Guaranteed by Messrs. Geo. Williamson & Co.
£10,000	Major Holroyd (He owes Lloyd's Bank for this amount.)	300 In Major Holroyd's name.

£5,000	Barclays Bank Ltd.	125 The amount of £5,000 is being repaid at the commencement of June.
Total number of shares		1,752

All the family were required to sign this new Deed, Basil getting
as his witness the British Consul in Venice where he happened to
find himself in the early summer of 1932.

But he was back in England that July and accompanied Fraser
to a nursing home near Blandford in Wiltshire where his Uncle
Pat had gone following an operation. My father hardly knew his
uncle, beyond recognising him as a handsome, mild-mannered
man with a liking for drink. In the account he wrote for me
almost fifty years later, he recalled 'finding my Uncle Pat tiptoeing down the stairs at Brocket when he was staying a few days
with us. It was one o'clock in the morning and he was on his
way to the dining-room for one more whisky.' According to my
father it was whisky that killed him at the age of fifty-eight. He
was suffering from a duodenal ulcer, an infected appendix, a
blockage of the intestinal canal and chronic constipation. That
was how Fraser found him at the nursing home. As with their
father, and with his son who died in infancy, Fraser is again
'present at the death' on 15 July 1932. Even Basil's regular high
spirits temporarily drooped, those high spirits on which he
depended to overcome his sense of being unwanted, 'an evident
mishap'. He never forgot that awful white room in the nursing
home and 'my father's great distress at his brother's death'.

On the death certificate issued three days later, Fraser gave his
address as Brocket, Maidenhead. The signing of the
Supplemental Deed that summer of 1932 had been his act of
negotiation back home. But it cannot have been a happy return.

His two sons lived mostly in London, and Brocket was a household of squabbling women – even their dogs quarrelled. Yolande by now hated her mother, and her mother hated Nan who had stayed on after the children grew up despite Adeline's many high-pitched invitations for her to leave. All Yolande's filial affections seemed to have been transferred to Nan. Between the three of them there were incessant plots and counter-plots, and much yapping at the ankles.

But Fraser was a man of illusions. It was to these illusions we were responding when retrospectively we pictured him as a brilliant mathematician, barrister, athlete and so on. Though his romantic illusions might be shattered, his financial illusions still glimmered in the city of glass he had attempted to create in the West End of London. His optimism shone blindingly forth. Were there moments of panic and doubt? In any event, there was nothing for it but to go on and hope for the best.

When my father had his signature witnessed by the British Consul in Venice on 18 May 1932, he was endeavouring to sell glass to the Venetians. Over the next couple of years he talked Fraser into forming a new department for glass light fittings: table-lights, wall-lights and hanging lights which were sometimes inverted fruit bowls suspended from the ceiling by ropes, decorated with opalescent shells, and fitted with flared flames of frosted or tinted glass. These had several seasons of popularity and were installed by some famous restaurants including Quaglino's and Claridge's. But they were not profitable because of the breakage when drilling the glass to the metalwork. One of his designs appears on the title page of this book.

But Basil was keen to develop this side of the business and made contact with a German glass manufacturer called Stensch which, following the Anglo-German trade agreement of April 1933, appointed Breves Lalique as its British agents. Early in 1934 Basil went over to Berlin to meet the Stensch family, and made friends with their twenty-year-old son Rudi, who had been sent down from Bonn University. Being a Jew, he explained to Basil, he had been 'retired' from Bonn as a result of the national boycott on Jewish professions introduced by the new Chancellor, Adolf Hitler. Possibly the non-completion of a university career did not strike my father as so very grave a matter. In any event it was his easy-going habit to offer anyone he liked a job in Breves Lalique. He had come over with one of his cousins from Australia (the one who had begun so promisingly in the IRA) and together 'these two exuberant, extrovert fellows painted the town of Berlin red', Rudi remembered. '. . . For us Jews, then being very subdued under the first impact of nazidom, it was a wonderful tonic.' Their air of innocence, their very ignorance, was appealing. For they lit up the hope that this anti-Semitic phenomenon would soon blow away almost as if it had never been, like an illness that passes, leaving no marks, and is forgotten.

Rudi took my father and his cousin to Leipzig where they were to make a reconnaissance of Germany's major commercial trade fair. 'I particularly remember when we all went to the local firemen's ball,' Rudi wrote to me, 'and your father and his cousin insisted on driving our car right into the hall and in the centre of the dance floor. They then snatched the helmets of the worthy firemen, donned them on their heads, appropriated the buxom partners of these firemen and began to dance some weird Scottish jig. The impact of these young blades on the oh so German "Spiessbürger" [petit bourgeois] was quite sensational . . . Heinrich Himmler, you should have been there to watch it!' For a moment the world of P.G. Wodehouse rode triumphantly over the Nazis' campaign against decadence.

After a week Rudi returned to Berlin and a few days later he received a telephone call from Basil who sounded in deep trouble. 'In a muffled voice he told me that he was at the Eden Hotel in Berlin and would I please send him immediately a wire saying that I had heard from London that your grandfather [Fraser] had been taken very ill and would Basil please return post haste. I would get an explanation later.'

My father gave his explanation next day at a *thé dansant* on the roof of the Eden Hotel. It appeared that he and his cousin had become involved with two young women they met at a Leipzig bar, and all four of them spent the night at a hotel. The cousin promised to take his companion to Paris the next day. This gave my father no option but to add that he would take his lady to Stockholm. But next morning he woke to find his Australian cousin had gone in the night. He was left with a girl on each arm and two hotel bills. He paid off the bills and saw that one of the girls got home in a taxi, while the other girl – who appeared in the daylight to be a dramatically painted woman with a loud Saxon voice (a veritable Saxhorn) – he took by train to Berlin. The fake telegram arrived and 'the histrionic performance of your father when he explained to the girl that, alas, he could not proceed with her to Sweden and how all his life his greatest pleasures were being spoilt by quirks of fate, was masterful', Rudi wrote. 'We both took her to the station and put her on the train to Leipzig.' Then the two young men went on to another railway station in Berlin's working-class northern district, where my father was to catch the train to Stockholm. Over a few drinks while waiting for his train, Basil repeated his offer for Rudi to come over and work as a trainee for Breves Lalique in London. 'At that time I faced the problem of many young German Jews whose careers had been suddenly aborted – what to do with my life,' Rudi remembered. 'So I accepted with alacrity. I had been in London once before as a schoolboy and had felt at home. If I had to become a refugee there was only one country I would choose.'

It was in the autumn of 1934 that the great Lalique galleries finally opened at 4 New Bond Street. 'The ornamental glass associated with the name of M. René Lalique deserves recognition as the first attempt in Europe to explore the full possibilities of glass as a plastic material, and Messrs Breves, its agents in London, are to be congratulated on the general effect of their new galleries,' wrote *The Times*. 'A plain shopfront faced with travertine, with the name in white metal above, opens to a deeply recessed window which allows a clear view of the whole interior. As far as possible all the working features such as doors, and the decorations of the new galleries are constructed of Lalique glass, in association with stainless steel.' René Lalique himself, a shy seventy-three-year-old with a white moustache, arrived from Paris hidden in an enormous overcoat, almost two hours late, missing the ceremonial speeches by the French Ambassador and the Mayor of Westminster. But he was not too late to avoid a reporter from the *Manchester Guardian* who noticed him among the guests (including everyone from Lady Oxford to Princess Bibesco) and described his 'somewhat brisk military appearance suggestive of Cheltenham rather than the Champs Elysées'.

About this time my mother arrived from Sweden.

7

A Triumph and
Disaster

Ulla was pleased to be getting away from Stockholm. She had an adventurous spirit and she loved travel. Nor did she mind leaving her mother. It was not that she and Kaja didn't love each other, but they needed to be independent. Living together, they were like two dancers each treading on the other's feet. Ulla's feelings for Kaja were a world away from anything Yolande had ever felt for Adeline, yet both daughters had their difficulties. Adeline liked to stop Yolande from going to parties in London. But when Ulla said she was going out to a party in Stockholm, Kaja would dress up and go along too. And what a power dresser she was! The rustle of her dress before she entered a room and the lingering perfume in the air after she made her exit were potent spells that lodged in many imaginations. She had such a sharp eye too and was still so strikingly smart that her presence grew immensely oppressive to Ulla. The trouble was that Kaja, then in her early forties, seemed so terribly old to her daughter, yet she simply refused to behave like an older person. She was delighted when people took the two of them for sisters. Because she preserved such a strict manner at home, it was only gradually that Ulla realised what was going on. Though her mother kept a single gentleman admirer, the distinguished-looking Birger Sandström, famous for his cravats, who escorted her through the high places of society, she also kept company at other times and in lower places with all sorts of amusing bohemian artists. One of them painted her in a fur coat, earrings and lace bodice (I have the painting in London). It was also rumoured that Picasso – or was it Picabia or even one of the Pissarros – had become infatuated with one of her feet while she was travelling abroad. It was usually Picasso in these stories and part of Kaja's foot was said to appear in his *Guernica*. Her own collection of pictures, near masterpieces all, hung like trophies on the walls of her apartment, the names of the painters – 'Fragobard', 'Valminc', a rare 'Edouard Monet' – echoing discordantly their famous reverberations (she left me a small 'Verner' and what looks like an unusual 'Whatho'!). The distraught Birger Sandström found himself obliged to fire off many agitated telegrams.

'What a mother! What a daughter!' exclaimed one of Ulla's schoolfriends. Stockholm seemed too small to hold them both. So Ulla was not unhappy to be escaping. She would be particularly pleased to miss that one day a week when her father was allowed access to her. She didn't mind being taken to the opera by him and felt proud of his musical knowledge (though she was embarrassed when he started humming – and besides, opera was not the sort of music she really liked). But what she hated were the evenings he came to dine with her and Kaja. There was absolutely no conversation at all, simply an icy silence and then dreadful bickering.

Ulla had been to France but never to England before. Her English was not bad and under the pressure of events would quickly get much better. Of course she felt a little apprehensive, but on the whole she was excited. It was the summer of 1934, she was seventeen, and she wanted to have fun.

On board the *Suecia* as it set off from Göteborg, Ulla sat at the Captain's table – Kaja had arranged that. Everyone dressed for dinner, there was a formal toast, and a dignified atmosphere prevailed – at least it would have done had there not been so much noise from one of the other tables, in particular from one persistent raucous English voice. 'I was annoyed and kept turning round,' my mother remembered. On the second evening a man swayed up to her table and with exaggerated correctness requested the Captain's permission to ask Ulla for a dance. The Captain assenting, she found herself waltzing with the ghastly-voiced Englishman. He explained that he had been smoking too many Gauloises, and then went on jovially talking. 'He could talk anybody into anything,' she later wrote. He told her he had recently been in Germany and then gone to Sweden to meet important people in Kosta Glass. He spoke brilliantly of the beauties of Lalique and his own rich future in glass. Before they reached Tilbury, he had talked her into giving him her address and telephone number. And also a promise to see him in London. This man was to be my father.

Ulla's first experience of England was a shock. She was living at Beckenham in Kent with a Mrs Malmburg who received pupils for English language tuition. No. 48 Coper's Cope Road (a name which struck her as incredible – it came from a handsome eighteenth-century house with quoins and a pediment on giant pilasters at the end of the road) was partly a guesthouse, partly a small school. The regime was deliberately English and included kippers for breakfast at 7.30 a.m. which made my mother sick. She was pleased to get an invitation from the man on the boat, asking her to lunch with him at the Grill Room of the Hyde Park Hotel. But Mrs Malmburg felt anxious – until Basil spoke to her on the telephone. By the end of their conversation, she was convinced that Ulla could hardly be in more distinguished company than this Old Etonian director of Lalique.

So Ulla went up to London. She was worried over this first journey by train and bus to the capital. The Hyde Park Hotel, which flew the Swedish flag whenever King Gustav stayed there, was only two minutes' walk from the elegant Breves showrooms in Basil Street with their 'Chinese' wallpaper and permanent display of Lalique. At the Grill Room, Basil ordered Ulla what she took to be a lemonade but was actually Jimmy the barman's speciality, a Gin Fizz. After the first shock, she found it delicious and had to be driven home by car. But she had sobered up by the time she reached Beckenham, and Mrs Malmburg, impressed by her description of the Hyde Park Hotel, was happy to let her go on seeing Basil. Ulla was allowed to spend weekends at Maidenhead which, to Mrs Malmburg, sounded a pretty safe and proper place. Here Ulla met the amiable if rather distant Fraser, the baffling Adeline (a small figure with tall hair), Yolande dashing everywhere in her short tennis skirts, and Kenneth encircled by his aristocratic friends. Thatcher, the family chauffeur, had retired and his place was taken by Frederick who would drive Fraser, and sometimes his sons and their friends, up to London on weekdays. Ulla used to wonder what he did there until it was time to drive back again. She was always wondering things like that.

Ulla's English had improved, though she still found the English Js awkward and would speak of waving a 'Union Yak at the You-billie'. Basil taught her some slang and several naughty words, and he and his friends started calling her Sue or Suzie instead of Ulla which rather stuck in their throats. She was becoming quite anglicised, and picking up extra English culture from her visits to Brocket – the weird offerings of hot-water bottles, the ritual of early-morning tea, the ceremonious walks with the dogs, and the strange procedures when everyone sat down to dinner.

Brocket was then in the last phase of its glory. The lease had come to an end in 1933 but Fraser, still hoping for good things, renewed it year by year. 'It was a lovely brick house,' my mother remembered, 'covered with green ivy, a drive and two gates.' It had been designed by a young architect called Clifton Davy who became well-known for his domestic work along the Thames Valley. The upper part of the building was built of solid oak half-timbering with herring-bone brickwork, and the house itself divided from Boyn Hill Avenue by an ornamental brick wall. Above the heavy oak front door two quotations had been cut into the stone: 'Through This Wide Opening Gate None Come Too Early None Return Too Late'. And, more conventionally: 'Welcome The Coming Speed The Parting Guest'.

My mother was obviously impressed by Brocket. The large hall with its light oak panelling, its beamed and rafted ceiling, was a perfect place for parties. The French doors opened on to a veranda some six feet above the tennis court and, when the evenings were warm and the lamps lit, there was no better place for sitting out between dances. It is not difficult to imagine how exciting these dances and parties were for my mother now that she was not under the watchful eye of Kaja.

Ulla wrote regularly to Kaja who was delighted with her daughter's progress into British society. These Holroyds with whom she was spending so much time appeared to be a wealthy and well-appointed English family, with some Irish and perhaps Scottish ancestry as well as an Anglo-Indian chapter in their history. Basil himself, curiously christened after a herb, recommended himself as an Old Etonian and a Cambridge man whose central names (De Courcy Fraser) had to Kaja's ear a reassuringly rare Anglo-Saxon elevation. Kaja was pleased that her daughter was enjoying herself. It was all most satisfactory.

But events were to move with a speed and unorthodoxy that took Kaja aback. 'You must have been conceived,' my mother hazarded, 'on the canebacked sofa in the drawing-room at

Brocket' – which rather puts paid to her speculations over my conception at the Hyde Park or Basil Street hotels. Perhaps it was that same sofa on which Norah Palmer Holroyd had lain, her pretty hair spread out, before her final journey into France in 1913; and the sofa on which the enormous frame of Tom White expired after breaking his golf club in the early nineteen-twenties. Dr Johnson once boasted that he could write the life of a broomstick, and it would need him, or Virginia Woolf, to tell the common reader the story of a sofa.

My father was twenty-seven on 20 October 1934 and my mother celebrated her eighteenth birthday on 20 November which was probably also the date of my conception (but since I was apparently born almost a month off schedule it is difficult to tell). The two of them were then secretly married at the Registrar's Office at Bromley, not far from Beckenham on 15 December 1934. One of the witnesses was the taxi-driver who drove them there and then took them up to London through the rain (it was pelting down that day according to the Meteorological Office). They spent their honeymoon at the Basil Street Hotel, which had some good Lalique glass in its art deco interior (it was only a few yards from the Breves showrooms). Then they went off to spend Christmas in Stockholm where, rather belatedly, my father asked Kaja for permission to marry her daughter. Kaja answered that she wanted them to have a decent period of engagement, which was awkward – no one thought of consulting Ulla's father Karl whom Basil never met.

To set things off correctly Kaja took Ulla to be fitted for her white wedding-dress, at which stage I can make out the word 'Calamity!' in my mother's handwriting, dramatically under-lined as she underlined other decisive words such as 'pregnant!' and 'married!' There was no hiding the pregnancy from Kaja's sharp eyes. Ulla was too sick for that; after which there was no point in hiding the marriage. Had they intended to stage a second marriage in Sweden? I believe they had. It would have been a good joke: and everything still had the air of a joke. But Basil now admitted to the marriage – and his wife's pregnancy. It was certainly not what Kaja had had in mind: a Registrar's Office in Bromley. For a time, a rather short time, she looked severely about her, then relented. 'I think Kaja was glad to see me "happily settled" as she thought,' my mother wrote, 'since she herself was busy with poor old Birger Sandström.'

The white Swedish wedding was called off and the married couple sailed back to England in January 1935. After Basil had brought his parents up to date, they settled into 91 Drayton Gardens, the cottage in Fulham to which Fraser had retired after leaving Agnes May. My mother's labour pains came on that August in the Fulham Forum, the cinema at the end of the road. She was taken to the London Clinic and Kaja arrived from Sweden just in time for my birth at 4.20 p.m. on 27 August. My father, who had been playing golf, was late – which may account for him assigning me a birthday two days later.

Kaja stayed on in England for the autumn and came to visit us again in 1936. The regime at Drayton Gardens seems to have been pretty comfortable. There was a Danish housekeeper called Vera who looked after my parents; and a nanny who looked after me – 'she fell in love with the milkman & had to have all her teeth out (nothing to do with the milk)', my mother explained. There were also two small town dogs, Snaps and Popples (which sounds like a breakfast cereal or perhaps a circus act), a tabby cat that discovered things and was called Christopher Columbus (he had been bought from the grocer for one penny by my mother who believed that it was 'bad luck not to pay for a cat'). We also owned two goldfish, Dalgleish and Pullen, named after a couple of architects my father knew.

All this was agreeable enough, but what my Swedish grandmother liked most were her visits to Brocket. English society might be incomprehensible, but its incomprehensibility was impressive. What for example could she have made of the family

Arms and Crests and Latin mottos – those Demi-Griffins Wings
Endorsed, those Roses Gules and Pierced Mullets in Saltire that
occupied a more prominent position at Brocket than the lavatory
of my father's flat in Surrey that was to be their hiding place
years later? Whatever she made of them, I feel sure she was glad
they were there. Only they should not have been there. What
Kaja could not have known, since no one else knew, was that
none of these Holroyds, not Fraser nor his father Charles, nor
even their eminent forebear Sir George Sowley Holroyd, nor the
first Earl of Sheffield himself, had established through the correct registers and pedigrees, the right to ancestral Arms by
inheritance. So this parade of exotic Conquerfoils, that Fess
Dancetty Argent, those many Escallopes Gules, diamonds and
lozenges, the very Pierced Mullets themselves were all assumed
without proper authority.

Never mind. Basil took Kaja round the house. Off the hall
was a large drawing-room with two silent grand pianos where
Adeline held her bridge parties. There was also a cosier 'morning-
room' and a rather dark formal dining-room, its refectory table
lined with straight-backed chairs. This led on to an Edwardian
conservatory full of ferns and garden furniture. Down some
stairs by the side of the dining-room were the kitchen quarters –
a pantry and spacious kitchen off which stood the cool larder
and a scullery where vegetables from the garden were prepared.
Basil introduced Kaja to the staff in the Servants' Hall, but did
not take her of course to their rooms which were on the top
floor and reached by the back stairs. Kaja's own room when she
stayed at Brocket had once been Kenneth's, and contained a
magnificent Hepplewhite four-poster bed. It was on the first
floor, as were Fraser's and Adeline's bedroom and their two
dressing-rooms (one of which, with its separate door on to the
passage, had by now become Fraser's bedroom). At the south
west corner of the house, overlooking the garden, was Yolande's
bedroom which no one else entered. There were three other

guest bedrooms and along one side of the corridor two bathrooms, as well as a spare room that had once been the children's nursery.

Basil ended his tour where they had come in downstairs, at the entrance hall with its medley of sticks and umbrellas, and its two lifesize figures of a black man and black woman that had fascinated him as a child but that somewhat perplexed Kaja. Yet it was the quality of her perplexity that was important. Indeed she exaggerated the grandness of life at Brocket and when offered a pot of Russian caviar at lunch, served by the parlourmaid on a silver salver and with a silver spoon, she took the whole pot and had to be corrected by her daughter in Swedish.

Another foreign visitor to Brocket and to Drayton Gardens was Rudi. He had first come over as a trainee at Breves Lalique for a few months in 1934. The following year the Nazis introduced conscription and he had to submit himself for a medical examination. Standing stark naked before a panel of senior officers, he was congratulated on his excellent health and asked in what arm of the services he would prefer to serve. Surprised, he replied that, as a Jew, he was surely ineligible for any service, but was told by the presiding Colonel that the new 'Reichswehr' (German army) needed strong 'Burschen' (members of the student fraternity) like him, and that he should not believe all he read in the newspapers. It was this incident that finally decided him to seek his future abroad, much to the chagrin of his father and his 'Aryan' partner who were both convinced that the Nazi nightmare would soon be over.

By 1935 the United Kingdom immigration laws had been tightened. No one could arrive and simply look for a job. Only prominent people – capitalists who brought money to invest – were welcomed and given a home. Rudi's grandfather had recently died leaving him £750 (equivalent to approximately £25,000 at the end of the century). This he proposed putting into a new company my father was starting called Holroyd

(Glassware and Lighting) Ltd. His money, my father promised, would guarantee Rudi a junior partnership. But there was a difficulty. It was impossible to transfer money out of Germany legally, and illegal currency smuggling was now a capital offence.

It was then my father came up with one of his ideas. In the rather kitsch range of table-lamps made by the Stensch factory in Berlin were some with a stem cast in the shape of a gnarled tree with a variety of animals lurking in its shade. Among this odd zoo was a herd of elephants, the largest of which was so big that the front and back parts had to be cast separately. What my father was proposing sounded like one of his innocently dangerous pranks which were becoming less innocent and more dangerous as the decade advanced. Why shouldn't one of these huge elephants convey Rudi's inheritance abroad? Basil ordered six of the table-lamps for his company, and suggested that the loaded elephant should be marked with a scratch on one of its heels. So this was agreed. When the lamps were ready for dispatch, Rudi's father and his partner sent the nightwatchman out on an errand, concealed the fortune inside two of the raw elephant halves, soldered the parts together and put the whole elephant in a patina bath. Then they scratched the prearranged code and substituted this elephant for one of the six already waiting export.

The consignment arrived at London and, instead of waiting for customs clearance and dispatch to the warehouse in Fulham, Rudi went to the docks at my father's suggestion and took possession of the elephant with the damaged heel. 'I was very nervous and in the taxi riding back tried to break the beast open,' Rudi remembered. 'I made such a racket that the Jewish cabbie asked what the hell I was up to. I revealed the secret to my co-religionist, whereupon he took a big spanner and somewhere on the Commercial Road, smashed the elephant to bits, revealing the hoard. Cheers all round: my future was secure.'

My father had one more suggestion. He had changed his

young wife's name from Ulla Knutsson-Hall to Sue Holroyd. Now he indicated to his new partner that the name Rudi Stensch would sound less well in England than in Germany. Forty years later it was Ronald Stent who, having read one of my biographies, wrote to me from Ealing asking for my father's address.

But my father did not now want to give his address. He was getting old, he was poor and he lived very modestly with his dog in Surrey, having been left by his third wife. He could not invite anyone there, and he did not want to go anywhere else or to see people, or write to people, or read what people wrote to him. He simply did not want people. Or even the absence of people. He did not know what he wanted. Or whether he still had wants. He did and he didn't. In any case he was no longer the jovial personality who could 'talk anybody into anything'. When he compared his meagre circumstances to those heady expectations of the early nineteen-thirties, a sense of humiliation spread through him. That was perhaps one reason why he could not continue with the account of his life he had written for me beyond his uncompleted schooldays. Besides he did not wish to be reminded of those mad escapades when he was a damn fool in his twenties. So I learnt of his adventures with Lalique from Ronald Stent who in the late nineteen-thirties used to push my pram along the Hammersmith Road; and also from Hazel Truman and Merle Rafferty who happened to see in a newspaper a picture of my mantelpiece on which stood my Lalique legacy, three glass sparrows. 'I remember meeting your grandfather and your grandmother,' wrote Hazel Truman, 'both of them aristocrats in my opinion. Your mother we (that is the staff) thought was so beautiful and so very young.' 'Basil often appeared with friends to "borrow" a dinner service which came back with breakages,' Merle Rafferty wrote, 'but his father was always long suffering where his younger son was concerned.'

In my library I have a copy of the general circulation edition of T.E. Lawrence's *Seven Pillars of Wisdom* with its curious subtitle: *a triumph*. It has been inscribed: 'To Mr E.F.R. Holroyd with every good wish from the Staff. Christmas 1935.' There is a photograph of them all in their best evening clothes taken the following year. Fraser wears his white collar and tails, Adeline one of her long black dresses with a silver fur stole; Yolande sits next to her in a patterned dress – she is already beginning to look like her mother; then comes Ulla, a blonde beauty, still very Swedish, still in her 'teens; and standing behind them is Basil, smiling in his dinner jacket; and also Kenneth nearer the centre looking very smart. There are over a hundred people altogether, including Hazel Truman and Merle Rafferty. It is like the last picture of a royal dynasty before the republic comes in.

Everything moved quickly after this. My parents left Drayton Gardens (the lease of which was sold to help pay off debts) and moved to Latymer Court, a block of flats in the Hammersmith Road. Brocket was given up in the summer of 1937, Fraser discharged most of the servants and took Adeline, Yolande and Nan off to a much smaller house a few hundred yards away called Norhurst. Lalique had begun to go out of fashion and the family business was running into the ground. By the time war came Fraser had to tell what staff remained that it was all over – there was no money for anyone.

Ronald Stent, alias Rudi Stensch, was rounded up during the panic of June 1940 and, along with thousands of other German Jews and people of alien origin, interned on the Isle of Man. He had plenty of time to reflect on his half-dozen years with the Holroyds. They had introduced him to a segment of British society to which few refugees had such easy access. 'Its upper-class lightheartedness and devil-may-care attitude was in such contrast to my own background,' he wrote, 'and the fraught surroundings from which I had escaped.

My education into a would-be Englishman was really an amalgam of what the Holroyds showed me, and what I learned from Speakers' Corner; my spelling of English had always been better than that of the Old Etonian Basil; my vocabulary over the years was enriched by the Daily Telegraph crossword puzzles; but my accent I could never shed.

Ulla, alias Sue, had also become anglicised and was more adept at shedding her accent, though she still made mistakes such as ordering 'two whitebait' for supper at the 'fishmongler'. She no longer had a housekeeper, though I had a new Scandinavian nurse, Nanny Tidy, who was so ferociously tidy and had such emphatic views on hygiene that my parents were seldom allowed to touch me. 'She was much too strict,' my mother admitted, 'but I was only nineteen and had to take her advice.'

The war threatened my mother with what seemed to her a more terrible internment than any imposed on 'enemy aliens' on the Isle of Man. Against the rising note of the first air-raid warnings, Basil announced that it would be too dangerous for them to go on living in London. He had given up the lease of their flat in Latymer Court and they were moving down to the safety of Norhurst, his parents' new house in Maidenhead. My mother realised that he was thinking of my safety, and perhaps also of hers, but she objected to being informed of decisions in which she had no part. My father insisted on treating her like a child. 'He never really told me anything,' she wrote.

So the three of us moved down to Norhurst 'lock, stick and barrel', as my mother wrote. 'Disaster!' she added dramatically. '<u>End</u> really of life.'

INTERVAL

8

Literary Lapses

At the beginning I was no different from anyone who wants to write poetry, novels and plays. Being a solitary child, books soon became my friends and the means by which, from the privacy of my bedroom, I travelled all over the world and off to other worlds in my imagination. I much preferred these voyages to actual journeys, full of anxiety and incomprehension, I was obliged to make with my parents.

I also liked having stories read aloud to me. My Aunt Yolande would take on this duty, reading to me beside the Aga cooker in the kitchen. She read from a thick, tattered, black-boarded volume with drawings which she had loved in her own child-hood. It was full of the adventures of a racy girl called Mathilda. I could not get enough of her exploits and, when we had gone through them all, I craved to hear them just once more, every one of them, and then all over again from the beginning to the end – if only they would never end.

During the war my aunt drove a library van round prisoner-of-war camps in the Home Counties. She was then approaching forty and it was her first job. She often used to take me, aged six or seven, on these exciting expeditions to our enemies. I remember wondering whether they ever escaped. They never did, apparently, and I picked up the notion that my aunt's choice of thrillers, romances and detective fiction, held them captivated behind the friendly barbed wire.

I owe much of my early interest in books to my aunt. Though I never actually caught her reading – she read in bed at night, she let it be known, and seldom slept – she was one of those people who are said never to be without a book. Her bedroom was her library – even her bed rested on books. Books were part of our furniture at Norhurst. We used them for propping open doors, supporting windows, balancing tables, reaching things, and also lining the air-raid shelter.

Some years later I joined the new public library at Maidenhead. I lived like a lord there – like little Lord Fauntleroy – with a trained staff and a parade of authors lined up alphabetically before me on the shelves. It was a handsome building in a town not noticeable for its architectural events, and in due course it became my university.

My Aunt Yolande soon grew curious about this place. She herself patronised the private lending library at Boots the Chemist in the High Street where she could pick up a bestseller with her toothpaste and soap. Eventually, her curiosity growing, she followed me to the public library at the end of the town. What she saw amazed her. It was like a palace. Abandoning Boots she became a new member, though she never lost the habit of lightly roasting the books she borrowed in a medium oven for the sake of the germs. Many cautious booklovers did this, and you could tell the most popular volumes by passing the palm of your hand along the spines and bindings and sensing the residual heat from middle-class Aga and Rayburn cookers.

That library became my club, my home from home, my place of recreation and learning. It was a democratic place – we were of all sorts, ages and conditions. And it was here, sometime later, I came across my first biographies: *The Life of Oscar Wilde* by Hesketh Pearson, and Hugh Kingsmill's *Frank Harris*. From Hesketh Pearson I eventually learnt something about the craft of non-fiction storytelling. I read Pearson's biographies in my 'teens to find out what was going to happen next in the past. He didn't take you into the recesses of history, but brought his characters – Walter Scott, William Hazlitt, Henry Labouchère, Tom Paine – into the present so that they seemed to fill the bedroom where I was reading. He didn't bother with dreary documentation, but relied on good anecdotes, skilful use of quotation, pen portraits done in primary colours and with solid underlying draughtsmanship. It was exhilarating stuff.

From Hugh Kingsmill I learnt about the business of serious comedy. His *Frank Harris* was a small masterpiece, it seemed to me, of poetic irony. What F.R. Leavis was for many of my generation, Hugh Kingsmill became to me. He was my guide. He belonged to no school of writers, no literary group or movement. He was an isolated figure as I felt myself to be. And I had found him for myself. Kingsmill divided the world not into men versus women, not by colour or class, not geographically or by politics: in short not by any of the usual categories. He saw the world as being occupied by two species of human beings: men and women of will who sought unity by force if necessary (and so often it was necessary): men and women of imagination who could detect a harmony underlying the discord of our lives and used it as their compass. He identified the real struggle in modern times as being fought out between these two species of human being over the battleground of public opinion. But all of us were composed of will and imagination, and were tempted to externalise the enemy within. The charting of these impulses was the main theme in his biographies of Samuel Johnson,

Charles Dickens, D.H. Lawrence and Matthew Arnold.

The early influences of Pearson and Kingsmill propelled me towards becoming a biographer. But there were other causes too. The books at Norhurst – volumes of Andrew Lang and Winston Churchill; also dusty romances by Rhoda Broughton and Marie Corelli (which Adeline had devoured long ago) – did not appeal to me. I loved the adventures of Rider Haggard and Conan Doyle, and was astonished when my grandmother told me that Conan Doyle's historical novel *Micah Clarke* was the finest work of fiction ever written. This was especially strange because Doyle's re-creation of seventeenth-century puritanism had originally been rejected by publishers because 'it has next to no attraction for female readers'. The book first came out when Adeline was fourteen, and perhaps she remembered her father reading it in Ireland.

It was my grandfather's opinion that literature had flourished in the age of Shakespeare and pretty well come to an end in the twentieth century, though he granted special status to a few remarkable men who happened to write such as Winston Churchill, Lawrence of Arabia and an American homosexual nutritionist called Gayelord Hauser who, at an advanced age and on a diet of cider vinegar and black molasses, hazelnuts and soy bean oil, was said to have enjoyed an affaire with Greta Garbo. On account of his deep knowledge of Hauser, Fraser was, we all maintained, 'better than any doctor'. We seldom bothered to call in the family practitioner Dr Flew (whose full name, I believed as a child, was Dr Influenza) unless one of the dogs was off colour. But though he had this reputation for learning, Fraser seldom read anything except, with trembling indignation, the newspapers. It was not the author but literature itself that had died in our house. It had been ingeniously recycled into a batch of doorstops, makeweights and steps up to the tops of cupboards.

'What shall we do with the boy?' my grandparents would

ask, and everyone would turn and stare at me. There seemed no answer to the question. Other people, the people I read about, had narrative, it appeared to me, while I hovered in a vacuum. Inevitably I began absorbing the pace and condition of my grandparents, which is to say the regime of seventy-year-olds when I was still seven or eight. It was an odd form of precocity, a jump from early childhood straight into second childhood. Having compensated with book-adventures for the compulsory inactivity in Maidenhead during the war (like living at the dead centre of a storm), I later went one stage further by stepping from my own life into other people's where there seemed to be so much more going on.

But before I thought of taking up biography I tried composing verse, the influence of which veered drastically between Wordsworth and T.S. Eliot. The effect of this upon my father was extraordinary and, by the beginning of the nineteen-fifties, we found ourselves collaborating on a history of the world in verse. I was very much the junior partner in this herculean enterprise which, in its heroic hexameters, extended over a hundred closely-typed foolscap pages. We put a light blue cover on it, sent it off to the publishers Faber & Faber, and waited. And waited. After a long dazed silence, and in response to our eager telephone calls, we eventually received a report which, though congratulating us on our quixotic stamina, concluded that the satire was not sufficiently satirical for publication – a statement that, as we pored over it, struck us as worthy of the Delphic Oracle. Later on I showed our *oeuvre* to the writer and artist Colin Spencer who thought our best chance of success lay in running it as a hilarious serial, illustrated with cartoons, in *Punch*. But by that stage my father and I were moving along very different avenues of literature.

I was hardly out of my 'teens when I began writing a novel largely in the historic present which I had picked up from reading Joyce Cary, though the mood was intended to be Chekhovian, and my patterns of writing were partly derived from the novels of Patrick Hamilton who had brought fame to Maidenhead with his thriller *Hangover Square*. I worked on my novel for a long time but could find no way of ending it. A first draft in a thick exercise book marked 'Ideal Series' peters out after 110,000 handwritten words. A second version, this one typed, appears to reach some sort of exhausted conclusion on page 626.

My father, seeing what I was up to, soon joined me in fiction-writing, polishing off four or five full-length unpublished novels and several unpublished short stories. This was all the more remarkable since over this period he had a full-time job as a salesman which involved a good deal of motoring round the country, leaving him only a few evenings and some weekends for novel-writing. But he was growing to dislike his work and, feeling apprehensive over the future, hoped that this book-writing business might rescue him. He acquired a literary agent who liked what he wrote, but sadly never a publisher.

Only one of his novels, an 80,000-word typescript called *The Directors*, survives. It is competently done rather in the manner of C.P. Snow. But since it describes the business world he was anxious to escape, and is rather full of bank managers and solicitors discussing delivery schedules and production returns over dinner, it did not make for glamorous reading. However, it is rather well-plotted and with some editorial pruning, some helpful advice, might have been published. Its weakness is that the men are somewhat undifferentiated and speak with the same voice – which is my father's voice. The women are of two sorts: those who, in their roles of wife or secretary, protect and mother their immature charges; and those who wreak havoc either by their addiction to sex or by provoking unquenchable sexual appetites in the men. Sexual excess rather than business chicanery is the villain of *The Directors*.

My own novel, the incompetencies of which struck one good-natured publisher as marks of originality, was largely autobiographical. It described my grandparents' life at Norhurst, my parents' marital exploits, and my own limping attempts to become a writer. But since I seemed unable to harness these first two subjects to the advancement of the third, I eventually put the manuscript away and turned to what in due course would emerge as a biography of Hugh Kingsmill. Then, coming across the manuscript in the mid-nineteen-sixties, I suddenly saw how I might carve out the first quarter of this spacious family saga and make it a self-contained novella covering twenty-four hours of family life, which I called *A Dog's Life*. Once I had accomplished this I sent the typescript to William Heinemann Ltd, the publishers that were about to bring out my *Lytton Strachey*. My typescript went to the editorial manager, Roland Gant, who was himself a novelist and a translator from the French. 'This is a difficult novel to describe,' he wrote in his report.

> Age and particularly old age dominate it . . . these are not the tragic or coy old people created by novelists. They are comic but not laughable because they are so true to life. Like many old people they have lowered their sights and narrowed their field and live in grumbling contentment within their prescribed limits . . .
> As I am usually over-sparing in praise, I could add that reading *A Dog's Life* gave me the same kind of sensation of being in the presence of real talent as did the first production I ever saw of *Three Sisters*, listening to *Under Milk Wood*, and reading *Mrs Dalloway* for the first time.

Heinemann were to offer me an advance on royalties of £500 which was ten times what they had given me for *Lytton Strachey*. Roland Gant did not wish to publish *A Dog's Life* until the two Strachey volumes were out of the way. But since Penguin Books wanted the novel as a paperback and my publisher in the United States also sent me a contract, I was happy.

But my father was not happy. He had given up writing novels by then and assumed that I had done so too. He had read an early draft of my novel guardedly, reassuring himself perhaps that it would never be published. When I posted him the later shortened typescript, his reaction was more sparing in its praise than Roland Gant's. 'The typescript of your book arrived,' he wrote, 'and I read two or three chapters before I was so nauseated that I had to put it down.' Since the first two chapters covered five pages and the third chapter reached the top of page eight, this was not encouraging. Of course he had read more, though he could not bear to finish the book. But he wanted to impress on me as dramatically as possible how dreadful my novel was. When I urged him to complete it (it was not long), arguing that the death of Smith, the family dog, brought out the underlying sympathy of the characters (a sympathy sunk so deep, one reader was to write, that you needed a diver's suit to reach it), he simply refused. He hated everything about it.

> Your formula is evident. Take the weakest side of each
> character – the skeleton in every cupboard – and magnify
> them out of proportion so that they appear to become the
> whole and not part of the picture . . . Surely you could
> have written a study of old age and loneliness without
> photographing your own family for the background?
> Why should they be pilloried? You go out of your way to
> avoid any redeeming features in anyone's character. One
> would have thought that you could have waited a few
> years until we were dead before appraising the world of
> our misery.

If I went ahead and tried to publish the novel, my father promised to bring legal proceedings against me and the publishers. Publication would, he believed, expose to savage ridicule the whole family, especially himself and Yolande.

As you know I work in a firm with a staff of several hundreds. Were you to publish the book I should have to give up my job. I am too old [aged sixty] to stand the sort of humiliation you wish to heap on our heads. I am also a little too old to get a new job and start again.

In the circumstances – for my sister's sake and my own – I must do everything to prevent this book being published *anywhere* till we are dead, and I am prepared to take whatever steps that are necessary legal or otherwise.

I was appalled by this hostility – as appalled as he was by what he felt to be my hostility. The next four months, during which I tried to negotiate some compromise, were deeply unhappy for us both. When I asked my father what pages he would like changed, he answered rather wittily: 'Why not introduce a few fictional characters? It would of course entail rewriting but you would discover whether you are a novelist or whether – as I believe – you are not.' Here lay one of our difficulties in reaching an agreement. For where I would refer to *A Dog's Life* as a novel, my father insisted on calling it a 'distorted biography'; and where I pointed to inventions, he saw lies. But it was of course true that the first drafts of my characters were closely sketched from life. 'Had you written down the name and address of the family you could hardly have done more to ensure that they were identified,' my father stated. He did not allow that this problem might be solved by my using a pseudonym since he believed, probably correctly, that my identity would soon be uncovered. When I sent him Roland Gant's report and an approving letter from another editor, he merely replied that they were 'not on the receiving end', and repeated that 'the whole family are together in their dislike of this distorted picture you have drawn of them'.

But this was not really true. Adeline, my grandmother, knew

nothing of this book and never would; while my mother, who was now living again in London, described it as 'a hoot' (though it was very far from the kind of novels she really liked, which were big American bestsellers featuring very rich people misbehaving in Cadillacs and swimming pools). Her acquiescence however did not impress my father. 'Your mother may not object to anything you say about her under the misapprehension that – her surname being different – she will not be so easily identified . . . She is as usual generous at others' expense.'

My mother was changing her surname so frequently that I doubted whether any pack of investigative critics could catch her. But I was shocked by the ferocity and unfairness of my father's anger, not realising how many bruises I was pressing on. For example, I called the character based on myself after my Uncle Kenneth. I did not know my father's earlier years had been lived under the shadow of his elder brother. 'Could it be that he is the worldly & financial success you so admire & is therefore not to be offended?' Such a question nonplussed me. For years my father had been accusing me of a lazy disregard for the financial ways of the world. The truth was that he envied Kenneth's success and resented his inability to give me some of it.

Being obliged to reread *A Dog's Life* for the first time in almost thirty years, I do not find it hard to understand my father's dismay. As Henry Farquhar he appears 'inclined to fatness, jovial in manner and vociferous in his denunciations'. He bulges out of his green suit, the colour of which clashes with his complexion (a patchwork of mauve and crimson), and by various means he spreads consternation and panic through the house. At one time he is innocently using up all the hot water for his bath (drowning the clamour of complaints at the bathroom door with his lusty singing); at another he is filling the dining-room with smoke, sparks and a snowstorm of tobacco as he attempts, between terrible volleys of coughing and a blind staggering from wall to wall, to light his pipe.

My father had a rather bullying manner of speech. What left him as no more than an intended hearty pat on the back would land as a telling slap on the other person's face. It was a trick that opened him up to caricature. He would prefix his honest advice with phrases such as: 'Don't be an utter fool . . .', and invite other people's opinions by asking: 'What pearl of wisdom are you about to let fall?' His general conversation was peppered with recommendations to 'Be your age!' or 'Take it from one who knows.' He could not understand the reactions some of this well-meant banter produced. In my novel I tried to catch this tactless style of talk and set it in a more sympathetic context. 'Even at his kindest, Henry somehow contrived to sound offensive. He was shy of his generosity, awkward in exposing his good nature,' I wrote. '. . . For all his apparent robustness, Henry hated the sight of pain or illness, and was far more sensitive than he dared admit.'

Such passages had no effect on my father, if he ever read them. 'I must admit a feeling of great distress when I read your true opinion of me,' he wrote. '. . . I quite agree with your statement that I am a failure. I am well aware of it.' In vain did I tell him that this character in my novel was not a failure in the way he meant – he actually brings off an important business merger on which he had set his sights. The 'failure' lies elsewhere: in the inability shown by each one of the family (including 'Kenneth') to break out of his or her separateness and (except at the moment of tragedy) touch the others. 'After the long-awaited triumph of the merger that he [Henry] could share with no one, after the thrills of the drive that no one wanted to hear, a great weariness overcame him. He couldn't continue this kind of life forever.' Yet we continued. That, it seemed to me, was our predicament.

Heinemann gave me moral support over this difficult period, which is to say that they distanced themselves from the battle, frightened of a Pyrrhic victory. They could not afford, they warned me, to win a court case over a novel. The cost of injunctions, delays, extra storage etc. would be too great. It was therefore up to me to settle matters amicably. Since this proved impossible, production on the book was stopped and *A Dog's Life* never appeared in Britain.

When I asked my father about publication abroad, he replied: 'Of course I agree that were the book to be published in Hindustani or Erse there would be little likelihood of it affecting anyone, but this does NOT apply to the *English Language*.' He relented a little, however, over the United States. 'If you alter the story as far as Yolande is concerned this is all I ask of you,' he conceded. 'She, not I, must be the judge of this.'

I had given the character of my Aunt Yolande the name Mathilda after the dashing young heroine whose adventures she had read to me in the kitchen when I was a child. In the novel I raised her to over six feet tall, made her Henry's aunt instead of his sister (and gave him a special moustache and a naval background). My American publisher then took the advice of a New York lawyer who declared the novel to be potentially libellous if the Holroyd family were indeed in the corned beef business in Canada (my equivalent of tea in India), if my father lived with his family and was 'in celluloid', if my mother was married to an industrial agriculturalist, and so on. In any case, the lawyer concluded, there would be no substantial risk of libel because 'the Holroyd family simply isn't that well-known in this country'.

I decided to go ahead and publish in the United States. I felt I had done what was reasonable to protect everyone, including myself, and no one should be hurt. I did not tell my father or my aunt. I alone was to be the judge.

A Dog's Life was published in the United States in 1969, reviewed surprisingly well considering how English it was and, less surprisingly, sold not so well. I was in New York at the time of publication, beginning research for my *Augustus John*. When I returned, bringing with me my advance on royalties due on publication of the novel, I found that my father was in great financial difficulties. Everything he had feared about the future of his business and had once hoped to escape through a new career writing novels, was coming true. So I handed him my advance – the best part of £2,000 – without him knowing that it came from the American publication of *A Dog's Life*.

What then happened remains obscure to me. Some months afterwards I received a letter from the Official Receiver in Bankruptcy. It appeared that my father's new company, Seamless Floors Ltd, was already in liquidation. 'I note that you are named as a party in the debenture created by the company on 6 January 1970,' the Receiver wrote to me. Evidently my father had been interviewed with his solicitor at the Board of Trade offices. Beyond the fact that this was bad news, I understood nothing. There were references in the letter to 'the provisional liquidator', a 'floating charge' and 'Section 322 of the Companies Act 1948'. The letter ended: 'Will you please consider the matter and let me know your views?'

It seemed to me that my views would be without value and were therefore useless. But I must have replied (I have a second letter stating that the contents of my reply 'are noted'). The correspondence has long ago been destroyed by what is now called the Insolvency Service (which is part of the Department of Trade and Industry) and in any case I heard no more. My 'investment' had not been enough to save my father.

It must have been about five years later, when I gave him the American edition of *Augustus John*, that my father suddenly realised my novel had actually been published and also that I had handed him my royalties. There were many ironies in the situation. He appreciated, I think, my fine act of revenge. None of the family had been troubled by its publication, and it all seemed history now. But my father wanted to 'balance the books'. He wanted to 'pay me back'. He did so most ingeniously by means of some far-flung tea shares from a colony of the Rajmai empire that had somehow escaped the liquidation of Rajmai itself in the late nineteen-sixties. I still have these shares. Indeed I cannot get rid of them. Each year I am sent details of the severe local weather, the fresh damage to crops, the lower prices and higher production costs. Some years the directors (who until recently included a member of the Magor family, a new Richard Magor) are unable to recommend a dividend; other years when they do, they are nevertheless unable to pay shareholders abroad because of Foreign Exchange Regulations. I have become the apotheosis of Holroyd business enterprise. The rupee stops with me.

Looking back, it seems to me that my father probably had the better of our long rally (those tea shares were really his aces). But I am left with an unexpected feeling of gratitude to him. He saved me later embarrassment. Also the troubles I had over my novel-writing, though intensely depressing to me at the time, reinforced my desire to tell non-fiction stories by adapting some legitimate fiction devices. Besides, I have my father's novel *The Directors*, and the letters he wrote to me about *A Dog's Life*, which together with the remaining draft of my own unpublished fiction-writing, lay down various stepping stones after his own account ends, and help me to pursue my story.

PART II

9

Some Wartime Diversions

At Drayton Gardens I was a placid infant sleeping in my pram in the garden whatever the weather and waking punctually for my 'meals'. My mother had been unable to breastfeed me because I 'bit too hard', so she gave me 'Cow and Gate' milk from a bottle. It was mixed with water and if the mixture was too rich I came out in vivid spots. One day my mother added a mashed banana. I consumed it, stared frantically at her, and turned blue. She quickly gripped me by the feet, held me upside down and shook me until I started breathing again. But I had made no noise.

At Latymer Court I was a backward baby, literally crawling backwards into the furniture whatever temptations were waved or frisked in front of me. This habit of going backwards across the floor into crevices and corners grew so pronounced that my parents eventually consulted a child specialist. As they explained my curious problem to him I entered the room crawling forwards.

I have no memories of my mother living with what she called 'the old people' at Maidenhead. They seem to inhabit different worlds. But she had two memories of me there. In the first, she is laying me wrapped up and fast asleep on her bed while she goes off to prepare my 'lunch'. When she gets back with the tray I am gone. The window is open and in a panic she wonders for a moment if there has been a kidnapping. Anyway, there is no kid napping. Not on the bed. Where was I? What should she tell the family? Will she ever get me back? She does get me back after a search reveals that I had turned over and slipped off the bed on the side next to the wall and am now sleeping quietly under the bed. The story is satisfying since it explains, or so I like to think, my preference as an adult for low beds to the insecurity of sleeping in high ones.

Her second memory gives a dramatic glimpse of the family as I got to know them and later tried to recreate them in *A Dog's Life*. At the beginning of the war Fraser arranged for a large shelter to be built under the vegetable garden at Norhurst. I can remember the strange hump of the vegetable bed like a stilled wave, or the channel made by a monster worm as it furrowed its way from one side to the other. The interior smelt of wet earth and concrete, and possessed a curious other-worldly aroma that infected all our spirits. I used to play innocently on top of it during the day, but underground it did not seem quite so innocent. My father and our gardener were the architects. At night they had stolen out and returned with wheelbarrows of materials from a road that was being built near by – pioneers of privatisation. Inside, there were concrete slabs to sit or lie on, and hanging oil-lamps, and an enormous stack of tinned foods; but the German Luftwaffe never put us to the test of discovering whether we also had a tin-opener.

Before this hideaway was completed we used a lighted store-cupboard in which to conceal ourselves during emergencies. It was here we would place the large chest full of fragrant Rajmai tea sent to my grandfather from India each Christmas – a comforting companion in a crisis. This small cupboard under the stairs seemed to me a holy place that would surely afford protection from any war as it had previously protected my grandmother from thunderstorms. But we had dug for victory and had our new shelter ready for the Battle of Britain.

Being only thirty miles from London we sometimes heard the buzz and drone of the bombers and saw the night skies crossed by the moving lines of the searchlights. We had been issued with 'siren suits' as the proper clothes in which to greet enemy aircraft, and we were to be given rubber gasmasks which made us look ridiculously frightening and suggested death from suffocation. Among my aunt's possessions is the first draft of a letter and a form which reveals that she had applied for gasmasks for the dogs – my grandmother's bad-tempered sealyham, the few miscellaneous terriers attributed to my grandfather, my mother's faithful scottie Popples, and the various labradors or sheepdogs owned by my aunt herself.

When the first air-raid alarm sounded at night we were more than prepared. My grandmother, who gave the impression of spending most of her nights poised at the door of her bedroom waiting for burglars, rushed straight into my mother's room and snatched me (I was then aged four) from her bed. She was followed by Fraser running from his room without his dentures and quite naked save for the truss he was obliged to wear for his hernia. The two of them began wrestling over me while through a window, mingling with the sustained wail of the siren, could be heard my aunt screaming for the dogs. There was turmoil as everyone fumbled over the zips of their siren suits, hunted for torches, gasmasks and other impedimenta. Then we all struggled downstairs. We unlocked the back door (no easy matter) and made our way over some flowerbeds down the garden, cursing the irregularities of the route, the bad behaviour of the others' dogs, the Germans, and one another. As we tumbled at last over the marrows and cabbages into the shelter, the 'All Clear' sounded, and we began tottering back. 'I was spellbound, but had to follow the "circus",' my mother later wrote in her account for me. 'Back to bed and you really did not know anything about it as you were half-asleep all the time – so was I.' But I do recall the illuminations in the night sky, the cold air, and a general mêlée.

My father was to join the Royal Air Force, and my Uncle Kenneth, who had been in the Territorial Army (he was a member of the Artists' Rifles in Chancery Lane) was immediately made a Captain in the Rifle Brigade. On 20 October 1940, 'being about to leave the United Kingdom of Great Britain and Ireland and to serve for a time in foreign parts', he gave Basil power of attorney over his affairs. My father is still described as being a company director and his address is given as Norhurst, the family home.

While training in the Rifle Brigade earlier that year Kenneth had come across his cousin Ivor (son of 'Uncle Pat') who was a regular soldier. He had been impressed initially by Ivor's devotion to discipline, but soon, seeing how far it went, wondered whether he was 'off his head'. At Maidenhead we always enjoyed these stories of 'mad Ivor' and used to speculate on whether he suffered from early sunstroke or something more devious.

But why, I wondered, hadn't my father joined up at the same time as Kenneth? His service record, which refers to 'rheumatoid polyarthritis noted in 1932', suggests that his entry was delayed by poor health. He did not become a member of the Royal Air Force Volunteer Reserve until the spring of 1941, his civilian occupation during 1940 being given as a sales manager in Birmingham. I never heard him refer to this job (he was probably selling off his glass company there), nor did my mother mention it in the last pages of her account, simply covering this period with a note: 'Couldn't stand the strain.'

It is clear that by the end of 1940 their marriage was pretty well over. At Maidenhead they slept in separate rooms, though this was partly because there were no proper double beds in Norhurst, and my mother always insisted on nine hours' sleep at night – otherwise she had 'no eyes' in the morning and would have to place teabags on her eyelids during the siesta hour. In a Will my father made on 20 March 1941, shortly before joining the Royal Air Force, he appointed his brother and sister as his joint executors and trustees and as my guardians. There is no mention of his wife in the Will, and in his service record he gave his father as his next-of-kin (though in a moment of absent-mindedness describing him as his wife).

Later that year Flying Officer Basil Holroyd was posted to Wilmslow in Cheshire – and my mother went too. It was their last chance together. Once they had settled into a boarding house (the first of four), she came and fetched me from Maidenhead. I had been attending a small nursery school which I was taken to along a lane known as Folly Way. The school was called Highfield and all I can remember now is learning to crochet and 'colour in' surrounded by an indiscriminate noise as the boys rushed around the top of Castle Hill. At Wilmslow I went to a new school of which I recall nothing except a big green field. But my mother wrote about a prize-giving day in the summer of 1942 with crowds of parents in the garden. It was evidently one of those amiable occasions when the sun shines and 'all shall have prizes'. But when my name was called out I was too shy to go up to the headmaster's table, and my father had to collect the prize himself. It was too literal a version of what he wanted from me.

My mother worked at the refreshment bar of the Church Army Canteen inside the RAF station at Wilmslow. Pumping the milkshake machine and cutting the fruitcake passed for glamour in those days – it was certainly livelier than Norhurst. She made several friends, in particular the vivacious Shirley Morton whose husband Ivor became a semi-celebrity playing the piano with Corporal Dave Kaye at the entertainments which included Gracie Fields among the visiting stars. We sometimes heard them on the 'Light Programme' of the BBC too playing chirpy dance tunes, and patriotic songs, 'Roll out the Barrel' or 'Hang out the Washing on the Siegfried Line'. I remember the great hangar where they played against a clatter of plates and cups and glasses in the background. In the evenings, as one of the 'Wilmslow Wheelers', my mother (they still called her 'Sue' in those days) would join the convoy of bicycles off to the pubs. Bicycling back in the black-out on her upright but uncontrollable Raleigh was always a tricky business and there were many spills. Though this was the time when I heard loud arguments at night between my parents, the wartime spirit of forced gaiety and compulsory conviviality in public never seemed to flag. 'Basil was always one over the 8 in those days,' my mother wrote in her idiomatic English.

But my father did not like my mother's new friends or approve of her going out with them at night, leaving me in the boarding house. He was often away himself at RAF stations in the north of England arranging the supply of provisions overseas and would have preferred my mother to go back to Maidenhead, taking me with her. But she would not go. They argued violently. 'We really could not stand each other by then,' my mother wrote. Though she makes no mention of another man in her account, she told me never to mention the name of a certain RAF officer there, and not having mentioned it, I have forgotten the name.

It was at Wilmslow that my mother began having affaires. In his novel *The Directors*, my father wrote: 'Thelma's first affairs hurt him bitterly . . . She was constitutionally unable to exist without the admiration of men . . . She didn't even feel very deeply about any man she went to bed with and usually forgot all about him as soon as the brief intrigue was over. Then the excitement of a new affair would prove irresistible.' I have no doubt that this passage comes from these times at Wilmslow.

During one of the school holidays in 1943 ('it must have been summer', my mother wrote, 'although you were wearing your pale blue overcoat'), my father announced that he was taking me down to Maidenhead. 'But he never brought you back to me,' my mother continued. '. . . After a few months, when the Mortons left Wilmslow, I went with them.' She stayed with her friend Shirley Morton for several weeks in London and then moved to a boarding house in Cresswell Gardens, off Drayton Gardens where she had begun her marriage. I have no memories of this upheaval, only of the repercussions that would follow.

My father, soon to be promoted to Squadron Leader and unexpectedly benefiting from his exile at Chillon College, was being trained as an RAF interpreter. In 1944 he was posted to Paris. Before leaving, he drove me over from Norhurst to begin my first term at Scaitcliffe, the boarding school he had described as 'absolute hell'.

10

Notes from Norhurst

'What shall we do with the boy?' That cry comes back to me whenever I think of my early years at Maidenhead. As if to answer the question, my father, in the intervals from his career in France, would turn up at Norhurst with some devastating present – an air rifle, chemistry set, conjuring tricks or even golf club – and after a few flourishes and gestures, a few words of encouragement and a laugh, leave the fine tuning of my tuition as rifleman, chemist, magician or golfer to my aunt while he returned to fight the Germans or encourage the French. My aunt did her best, but I remember thinking one rainy day as we quarried out some lumps of ice to put on her forehead while waiting for the ambulance to arrive, that we shouldn't have chosen the dining-room to play cricket.

Most of these events passed my grandfather by. He got little sleep at night and would catch up during the day with a series of 'forty winks'. Besides he had his own disasters to occupy him.

The post would arrive, he would shake his head and on the backs of the envelopes begin a sequence of calculations that never seemed to come out well. Distracted, he would suddenly stand up and crash his poor head against some unexpected corner of furniture and then, blaming the government and all its works, stick on another piece of Elastoplast.

This Elastoplast, like the impasto of an expressionist painter, covered the dome of my grandfather's head which, because he was bald and somewhat bent, he appeared to be accusingly presenting to us all. His face too, with its changing surface of bumps and bruises, was something of a battlefield largely because of his shaving habits. He was not a skilful shaver. His chin and cheeks, as well as his nose and neck, were sometimes dotted with tufts of cotton wool and crossed with thin red lines like alleged Martian canals. Late in life my father gave him an electric razor. After some experimentation in the privacy of the garage, he found this gadget easiest to use while standing on the seat of the upstairs lavatory from where he plugged its dangling cord into the overhead light. In the darkness the whole operation lasted nearly half-an-hour, for he sometimes submerged part of his kit in the cistern. It was impossible for the rest of us to use the lavatory over these periods. My aunt, my grandmother, Old Nan and myself would line up outside, rattling the door handle and crying out in exasperation. But he felt protected by the comfortable whining of his machine. Occasionally he would shave the same side of his face twice since there was no soap to guide him. But over a week things would even out.

From time to time, amid panic and pandemonium, my grandfather was required to travel up to London for a meeting of the Rajmai Tea Company, and once or twice I went up with him on the train. When he arrived at Paddington he would hand up his neatly-folded copy of *The Times* through the smoke of the hissing engine to the train driver who touched his cap and nodded his head as he took it. My grandfather always came back looking worried from these days in London, and the dogs themselves would sneak into the corners of the rooms.

Part of his difficulties arose from increasing deafness, though this also afforded him protection from the perpetual squabbling that filled the rooms at Norhurst. As a child I had the double experience of my parents' marriage that had unhappily broken up, and my grandparents' marriage that had been unhappily kept going. At one point I was to make an attempt to run away from Maidenhead to join my mother in London; at another point, I attempted to run back from London to Maidenhead. The family was baffled: but I do not feel so baffled.

Norhurst was to be my intermittent home for twenty years. Everyone was very kind to me, but the atmosphere had become saturated with unhappiness. It was a ritualised unhappiness, repeated in the same formula of words through the awful succession of meals, housework, and more meals that was our routine, every day, all year. I can hear their voices still:

> *I declare unto goodness I don't know what's wrong with*
> *you . . . Are you perfectly potty? Are you insane?*
> *Sometimes I think you should be certified . . . Shut up!*
> *You bitch! . . . You are disgusting! How dare you speak to*
> *me like that? I do have ears you know . . . One can't open*
> *one's lips in this bally house . . . Sorry! Sorry! Sorry!*
> *Sorry! Will that do? Or would you like me to go down on*
> *bended knees? Why don't you arrange for me to be shot*
> *at dawn? . . . I'm sick to death of you all. I wish I were*
> *dead! I wish we were all dead, dead and gone.*

Sometimes they shouted all this and more, much more, from separate rooms. At other times I would come across one of them practising these same words under her breath. During meals, above the immaculate reports of wars, natural disasters, weather and sport issuing from the huge wooden wireless in one corner of the dining-room, they confronted one another with the same shouted phrases yet again. From another corner of the room my grandmother's parrot 'Mr Potty' (though we realised after she produced an egg that we had got her gender wrong) croaked back to us our shrill invective from her vast cage.

Into this echoing pit of abuse had tumbled 'Josh and Bang' from their heady days in Ireland; also their daughter Yolande who had looked so engagingly bold and lively in her early photographs, so happy with her friends in the South of France; and even the kindly Kate Griffin, the 'Nan' who had nursed my father so carefully through his illnesses and was now called 'Old Nan' by me. It was their collective unhappiness I had tried to recreate in *A Dog's Life* that so distressed my father – and that probably accounts for my avoidance of arguments today. 'They sat around in dismay, bowed, overcome,' I wrote. 'The words came from them mechanically, as though they existed under a spell . . . They had passed and repassed on the same staircase, twisted the same door handles, sat in the same old chairs around the same old table, and heard the same monotonous voices . . . and as time wore on they had somehow grown into strangers – strangers to themselves and one another.'

We lived at Norhurst as if in a capsule. No one visited us – we would never let anyone in. If by some mischance a person came to the door and rang the bell, we suddenly stopped our insults and froze into silence until he went away. When the telephone rang (Maidenhead 336) we panicked, rushing with frightful cries from room to room until it ceased ringing and we could relax again into our hostilities. We were certain the telephone was not 'safe', that the world could hear every syllable we said, though we had nothing to say and could hardly hear what others were saying to us. We did not want to hear. The truth was that we were frightened of the world outside. We had locked ourselves in an awful embrace and forgotten how to communicate with strangers.

And yet, because of its familiarity and my insecurity, I was attached to Norhurst as my father had been to Brocket, which was only round a corner but a generation away. That house lay in sunshine, this one in darkness. On the ground floor the 'morning-room' was without light and occupied by the telephone, like a monster in its cave; in the large hall, like the remnants of a beleaguered army, had been assembled the last cracked pieces of Lalique glass: the jardinière with gazelles and the eglantine powder box; the archer ashtray and the water grasshopper in opal, green and blue; the goblet with dogs and the vase with egrets; the amber carp, the dahlia bowl, the mulberry and mistletoe lights, the cockerel mascot. One or two of these, with a cry and a curse, we smashed each year until there was almost none; at the back of the house a gloomy dining-room gave on to the garden where the sparrows, chaffinches, thrushes and blackbirds waited noisily for their three meals a day; also at the back was the kitchen, the only warm room in the house, and a dilapidated scullery where frightful battles over washing-up raged. Off the landing upstairs stood five small bedrooms and two bathrooms – one for my grandmother, the other for the rest of us. But baths were discouraged. A bath a day was unthinkable. As my grandmother remarked (referring to my mother): 'Some people must be bally dirty if they need *that* amount of washing.' The boiler, which was encased in a shed outside the kitchen and which we fed night and day with coal and coke and much else besides, seemed to have fallen asleep. Whatever mixture we gave it, whatever knobs we twisted or levers pulled, it continued dozing and we got barely enough tepid water for our washing-up contests. The trouble was that we all had contradictory notions of how the boiler should be operated. 'Now look here,' my grandfather would begin, taking out a pencil and the back of an envelope to demonstrate his theories to Old Nan, the only person who was obliged to listen to him (though he would raise his voice so that his message reached everyone). On Fridays a gardener called Western came in to help with the leaves and twigs, enabling the rest of us on Saturdays and for the rest of the week to blame him for getting everything wrong. 'Western must have been putting grass in the boiler again,' my grandfather would grumble, shaking his head mournfully. He was very fond of Western whom he often called 'a damn fool, and no mistake', beaming as he said it.

It was the garden I loved at Norhurst, with its hovering dragonflies and bumblebees, its ladybirds, butterflies, chaffinches, robins. It was a long and narrow garden, divided into three sections. Nearest the house was a lawn which belonged to the crowds of birds except in wartime when we turned it into a vegetable patch. In peacetime, it reverted to green grass with rosebeds, a place in which to savour Rajmai tea on a summer afternoon, and get my aunt to send down her lethal-sounding leg-breaks to me with a tennis ball. The middle section was wilder, incorporating a small rock garden and a dangerous pond with its mighty toad, and a large tree in which I could hide. Further down, where the shelter had been dug, was a sandpit for me to jump in. It lay beside some enormous marrows and elongated hanging beans. At the end stood a garden shed and, over the fence, the peaceful insecurity of All Saints' cemetery.

Though once or twice a cousin was invited to play with me (the boy who was whispered to be Rex Harrison's son and who then suffered from an ophthalmic illness that made his eyes bright red), on the whole I played alone. I hid and found myself in the tree; captured and released myself from the shed; raced myself up and down the length of the garden past the sundial and the dogs' graves; threw a tennis ball high on to the roof and, as it spun down out of the blue sky, caught it; and contrived a complicated game with a ball against the garage doors, simultaneously winning and losing.

The garage, guarded on one side by a peach tree and on the other by a walnut tree, was a sombre fascinating place, an

Aladdin's Cave, piled high with treasures from the past – a broken rocking-horse, a strangely-painted screen, a still-working radiogram, pictures of girls and horses by Lewis Baumer and Anna Zinkheisen, suitcases, ladders, illustrated catalogues and mildewing books, one or two imposing pieces of furniture and large threadbare carpets with faded colours, a bowler hat belonging to my aunt, a walking stick that turned out to be a gun, and bottles of cider that I was sometimes allowed to drink in the evening with my grandfather. It was obvious treasure. There was even room for a car, a little eight-horse-power Ford that my aunt no longer used.

I sometimes sat in my aunt's old car and listened to records on the radiogram. My grandparents had no interest in music and my father seemed actively to dislike it (he could be propelled to his feet if told that a piece from Gilbert and Sullivan was the National Anthem). But my aunt had a collection of 'seventy-eight' records – 'Miss Otis Regrets' or 'Dinner for One Please, James', 'Bye-bye Blackbird', 'It Had to be You', 'Who's Sorry Now', 'Always', and Charles Trenet singing 'La Mer'. They were scratchy but curiously poignant and appealing. My aunt never took them into the house to play – she never played anything. I did not know why. But I played them, and then I played my own records. How I first heard classical music, how I got hold of my records, I cannot remember. I daresay I listened to the wireless and then demanded these records as birthday and Christmas presents. I would take Schubert's *Unfinished Symphony*, Verdi's *Requiem*, Wagner's 'Ride of the Valkyries' out to the garage, and sit there absorbing them in the dark. My favourite composers were Tchaikovsky and Beethoven whose symphonies I got to know by heart. I suppose these garage concerts began when I was aged about nine, and continued for eight or nine years. I would turn up the volume, open the car door, and sit enthralled. Sometimes I could not sit still but had to stride up and down through the dusty bric-à-brac waving my arms, lifting up my voice, joining in. This music, and the imaginary adventures I was led on upstairs by Conan Doyle, Rider Haggard, H.G. Wells and others, were no artistic luxury for me but the essence of my life. I would come in from these hours in the garage, or down from my bedroom, glowing with happiness and fortified against the family warfare that was more real to me than any combat against Germans, Italians or Japanese. I was at the centre of this domestic warfare and regarded the world war as mere orchestration for it.

Though I was an excessively timid child, the boredom that timidity induced would sometimes get the better of me, and I became for a few moments vicariously bold. One day I found some nice fat cartridges inside a desk in the morning-room. Remembering the walking stick that was a gun I took these cartridges to the garage and found that they fitted. I then went off to find my grandmother who happened to be in her bathroom, not having a bath. I showed her the walking stick, put it in her hands, pointed to the trigger and asked her to pull it. She was reluctant to do so, but I begged her and begged her until eventually she did pull it. There was an enormous bang and a hole appeared in the floor through which our feet dangled, emerging, I daresay, like strange stalactites in the garage below.

I got into grave trouble for this exploit and my father arrived back from France to punish me. But really everyone blamed my grandmother. She had become a figure of blame round whom all the irritation in the house seethed and beat itself. The sight of her struggling downstairs, or patting the cushions, or rearranging the chairs, or humming as she sauntered indecisively between rooms, or simply eating, provoked surges of uncontrollable indignation from us all.

In his novel *The Directors*, my father has a breakfast scene in which John Maitland, a distinguished character with 'a Victorian conscience about anyone who is dependent on him', sits reading *The Times* while his wife chatters uninterruptedly without ever gaining his attention. She is an empty person, without occupation or interests, a child in a woman's body, who has become completely dependent on her husband and so made him her prisoner. This is a picture of Fraser and Adeline at Brocket while my father was young. 'John had bought the old Georgian house shortly after their marriage and she had fallen in love with it at first sight. She still loved it when she wasn't feeling bored – which was all too often. Time hung heavy on her hands . . .'

After almost half a century of time, Adeline (whom Fraser now called 'Di', rapping it out like a terminal injunction) makes her appearance in my novel as I saw her when I was young at Norhurst. She is now a 'bent and fragile old woman, bravely pessimistic', with a parchment face, and lips coloured crimson so inaccurately as to make her mouth leer across her cheek like a Hogarthian trull. I pursued her in *A Dog's Life* as she advances to her breakfast.

Her sparse metallic grey hair lay chaotic and unkempt, crushed by a dilapidated hairnet. From her left ear hung an earring; on her right foot a sober black gumshoe. Around her neck was suspended a fantastic chain of imitation pearls that stretched, as though elastic, far below her waist, and, when she got down from her stool, almost to the floor itself . . . Before her on the table was piled an assortment of articles, reminiscent of a junk shop. There was a ballpoint pen and a bottle of ink, one ball of string, a bottle of aspirin, some soap, a book, two flashlights and a small tin of boot polish. She was prepared for almost anything.

My father did not object to this passage, or to my other descriptions of his mother. 'Strangely enough, you seem to have dealt more gently with your grandmother,' he wrote to me. 'This

I suppose is only to be expected considering she caused most of the misery. It was greatly due to her spendthrift habits that father got into trouble with the banks. Anyone who was dependent to any degree on her paid pretty dearly for the pleasure.'

At various times in the course of her life we had all been dependent on her. Adeline had spent the family money, my father believed, and given the family no love in exchange for that money. Fraser and Basil were consequently 'embarrassed', both in the financial sense and in their vulnerability to attractive women like Agnes May and Sue who, they calculated, did give love for money. My father, who lacked self-esteem, talked women into marriage with glowing descriptions of financial happiness to come. He could not credit that anyone would accept him 'for poorer'.

I cannot believe that readers would find the hunchbacked, haphazard figure of my grandmother, as she appears in *A Dog's Life*, with her meaningless patter and mad apprehension, more sympathetic than the other characters. Her days, I wrote,

> succeeded one another in a dull, identical pattern, each one finding her a little older than the last, a little more tormented by monotony, a little more fearful of the approaching end to her monotony . . . she waited for several seconds listening, but not knowing what it was she expected or even wished to hear. For Anne seemed convinced that there existed some secret in life which she had never discovered, but which was always being discussed behind her back. She hurried from place to place, from one shut door to another, in the hope of a sudden revelation . . .

My father was convinced that his mother never loved him because, being her son, he genuinely was unlovable. And he could do nothing about it except make a million. Then he would be worth something. Money would transform him. Though it was worse for him because she had not even wanted him born, he knew that Adeline had not really loved his brother either, or even his sister, or her own husband, or anyone else so far as he could see. Until now. For she loved me. If Basil 'put a foot out of line just once he heard about it till kingdom come', I wrote in *A Dog's Life*. But I 'could get away with sheer bloody murder', as I almost had done with the gun in the bathroom.

Now that her bridge partners were 'dead and gone' and her wicked pack of playing cards put away, Adeline had nothing to distract her until I came to live at Norhurst. She at once offered me everything she had – everything she had somehow been unable to give her own children. I became another version of herself. 'There's nothing much to occupy a child in this rotten place,' she would say. 'It's all gone to rack and ruin.' She continually gave me things, often really absurd things like extra carrots for the night. She saved up her rations for me, saw I got second helpings of spinach and dried eggs, stood over me as I tried to eat them urging me on, plucking at my sleeve, trying to pull out of me some loving words. 'See anyone you liked better than yourself while you were out this morning?' she would ask. But this was not a promising gambit for a heart-to-heart talk because she never wanted me to go out of the house at all. 'You'll catch your death,' she would say, before warning me to keep clear of strangers. She was terrified when my father arrived with a bicycle, and would endanger her own life leaning far out of her bedroom window looking up and down the road until I wobbled safely back. If I was taken to the Plaza or Rialto cinemas – expeditions that would send me almost ill with excitement – my grandmother would raise up her arms to heaven at the sheer folly of it and then force quantities of formamint tablets on to me in case I 'caught something'. She, who had apparently been so carefree over my father's illness, fretted all the time over mine. 'Your eyes look like two burnt holes in a blanket,' she would greet me in the mornings. She waited vainly for gratitude. 'Now do buck up and be a comfort,' she pleaded. But what could I do? Too often I felt irritation, impatience and the need to escape as she hovered near me, watching, worrying, plucking at my sleeve. 'I declare unto goodness the boy never tells me anything,' she would complain. But I had nothing to tell her. The important things for me were my book and music adventures and they could not be told to anyone. 'Don't waste your time speaking to your poor old grandmother. All right! All right! I'm not going to hurt you. But you'll miss me when I'm dead and gone. "I wonder where she went," you'll say. "She was good to me when she was alive, poor old soul."' And so she was good to me. But it was too late and there was too much distance between us to make something of that goodness.

11

Yolande's Story

Whatever was to be done with 'the boy', it was usually left to my aunt to do it. Apart from reading to me in the kitchen and playing cricket on the lawn, she would take me to films in Maidenhead. She herself loved musicals and romances which I didn't like; and I loved comedies and thrillers which she didn't like. But in those days there were two films in a programme so we usually came out reasonably pleased. She also took me occasionally to matinées at the Theatre Royal in Windsor. We would get on the bus and rattle through the fields and villages to the theatre that stood under the shadow of the castle, round a corner from the river. These were journeys of painful excitement for me. But I was dreadfully disillusioned by the Windsor pantomime, sitting through the first part with unutterable expectation, and then with awful impatience through the long interval during which trays of tea and cake were passed along the rows of seats in the stalls. I watched the final act with dismay, hating

the silly jokes and longing for the entrance of the pandas – for I
had got it into my head that I was at a *pandamime*. I have never
since enjoyed pantomimes.

My aunt was aged forty in 1943, the year I returned from
Wilmslow to Maidenhead. To assist with what was called 'the
war effort' she had taken a night job at the telephone exchange.
She never told us what she did there, but I liked to imagine her
in the dark decoding secret messages. Most of her days were
passed 'walking the dogs'. No extremity of weather kept her
indoors – she could not abide frowsting with the rest of us. She
would start out at a terrific pace, almost running, as if to catch
up for lost time, over the Bath Road, up All Saints Avenue,
along the playground and across the fields. Then she would
strike for home through Maidenhead Thicket. The dogs were
exhausted when they arrived back. But my aunt seemed driven
by a frantic energy. She never had meals with the rest of the
family. She could not bear the sight and sound of us eating, the
uproar, the spectacle: my grandfather's loose dentures, my
grandmother's regular farting, my own obstinate mess, even
Old Nan's insistent chomping. However late we were, she
would burst into the house halfway through lunch and was
always welcomed by Adeline with: 'We were beginning to
wonder where you'd got to.' By way of reply, she would cry
out: 'This place is like an oven!' Then she banged open all the
windows and, as we cowered at the table clutching our white
napkins like flags of surrender, she would turn on us and snatch
away our half-full plates of food for the first round of washing-
up. Adeline sometimes tried to hold on to her plate, not because
she wanted to eat what was on it but because she wanted the
privilege of washing it up. 'Now do be sensible, Yolande,' she
would cry. 'Do leave everything! You're in no fit state. I'll see to
it all later.'

'I'd save yourself the trouble if I were you,' Yolande would
spit back. 'I'd only have to do it again afterwards.'

'Leave the whole bally thing alone!' Adeline would scream, as they struggled for the plate.

Old Nan, who sat in her usual curiously tilted position, the top portion of her body bent acutely forward so that it seemed, despite being anchored to the chair by her substantial lower self, that she simply must crash forward, would aim her disapproving cough at Adeline and reach for her sewing or knitting like Madame Defarge beside the guillotine.

Every move in the choreography of this family quarrel was achingly familiar to us. There were of course minor variations. Sometimes my grandmother, taking advantage of my aunt's absence as she ran out to feed the birds, would put some knife or fork under the tap, and my aunt would snatch it from her as she raced back in and put it under the tap again. It was all done with extraordinary anguish and venom.

The only meal my aunt liked was tea which she ate alone at about six o'clock as the bells from All Saints Church began sounding through the garden. She loved sweet things, drinking her cups of Rajmai with plenty of sugar, and eating biscuits and cake. Then she would disappear off to the telephone exchange or into her bedroom with its columns of magazines which, besides the few films we saw together, were the only spot of glamour she allowed herself.

Writing *A Dog's Life* in the mid- to late nineteen-fifties I gave a picture of my Aunt Yolande as she appeared to me in her fifties.

The last ten years had brought her to her knees and made her irretrievably old before her time. Like the fine strands of a spider's web, a thousand tiny lines had spread across her face, making her appear, even in her sleep, incredibly harassed. She did not flinch from this truth; she did not even regret the past – but . . . whatever happened she must not make an exhibition of herself. Life went on regardless of misfortunes . . . in an angry voice she began to lecture herself

'Mathilda Farquhar!'
'Yes?'
'This will never do!'
'No.'
'Pull yourself together!'
'Yes.'
'Stop all this nonsense, this instant!'
'I will!'

I can remember my aunt fiercely lecturing herself under her breath in this manner at Norhurst. In my novel the event that brings on this self-tutorial is the death of her dog Smith. But behind this loss rises the memory of another loss years back, that of an Italian boyfriend or lover whom she thinks of in her bedroom that night.

> It was difficult to believe that she was the same person as she was now, difficult to believe that any of it had ever happened at all . . . he had been a terrible rogue of course, everyone knew that. Still . . . whatever anyone cared to say about him . . . she often wondered whether she had really had such a lucky break as the family liked to make out. Anyway, he had given her what real happiness she had ever experienced, for however short a time, and no one had been able to take his place afterwards – no, not with all his faults!

It was this page that particularly alarmed my father, I now see, and made him insist that I 'alter the story as far as Yolande is concerned'. I must have picked up some rumour of my aunt's early life, otherwise I would not have chosen an Italian for 'Mathilda'. But only now can I begin to assemble some of the pieces in my aunt's story.

At the end of 1926, when Yolande was aged twenty-four, her

father had sent her some money from the Royal Automobile Club 'for your wedding clothes'. But there was no wedding and the following year he is writing of 'the sorrow you have suffered'. If something went wrong it may have been due to 'the slur cast on the family name' by Fraser's notorious escapade with Agnes May. This episode made all his children ask the question, as Basil put it: 'could we ever hold up our heads again?' But in his novel *The Directors*, he put forward another reason why his sister did not marry.

> Thelma grew into an unbelievably lovely girl and her
> Mother was determined to salvage the family fortunes by
> getting her daughter a rich husband. Thelma was paraded
> round all the smart places but she was never allowed out
> with anyone on her own. Wherever she went her Mother
> went too . . . A great many men wanted her, but those
> whom her Mother considered ineligible were turned away
> whilst the few who were permitted to pay their addresses
> soon decided the old lady to be too great an obstacle.

I have no doubt that this is my father's summary of the relationship between Adeline and Yolande. It was far easier for the sons to escape into their other lives. The little hammers of duty boarded Yolande up first at Brocket and finally in Norhurst. 'You – as much as any of us – must know what hell has been made of your aunt's life,' my father wrote to me after reading *A Dog's Life*. 'Your grandmother ruined what chance she had of marrying when she was a young girl.' Certainly it would have been all the more difficult for Yolande to leave her mother after Fraser himself had left. And when he returned early in the nineteen-thirties her wedding clothes had not been bought. 'I have been wronged for years,' Fraser declared from the Royal Automobile Club. But as the years unrolled it was Yolande who seemed most grievously wronged.

The pictures of her in the South of France between 1928 and 1932 show a sunlit smiling face. She looks happy. She is usually with other women also in their late twenties. There are few men.

But there was a man.

When my mother began visiting Brocket in 1934, she saw Adeline playing bridge indoors and Yolande playing tennis in the garden. They would meet on the veranda for some light bickering before the tea ceremony. Yolande had her little Ford, the very one that, later stabled in the garage at Norhurst, I was to use for my private concerts of Tchaikovsky and Beethoven. But at Brocket in the nineteen-thirties Yolande was chiefly buzzing about, my mother noticed, taking Adeline to and from her bridge parties. Yolande was disappointed that Ulla (she pronounced it 'Oh-la') did not play tennis. She was running out of partners. But unlike Norhurst, Brocket did open its doors to visitors, and people 'popped in'. Mostly they were Yolande's friends – Cathie, Cynthia, Freda, Nina and a few others who lived near by. And my mother also met Captain Hazlehurst whom everyone called 'Hazel'. There is a snap of a yacht among my mother's miscellaneous photographs which apparently belonged to Hazlehurst on which my parents and my aunt spent a weekend in the mid-nineteen-thirties. Among Yolande's albums there is no photograph of Hazel himself. But this man, my mother wrote, was the love of Yolande's life.

My father assumed I knew about Hazlehurst, but I never met him and can recall no more than the hushed whisper of his name. Among the cheque stubs, vets' receipts, bank statements, odds and ends my aunt preserved at the end, lay a few small bundles of correspondence. They are mostly letters of condolence on her parents' deaths, letters from building societies and banks, and one or two letters with foreign stamps including a couple from myself posted in the United States. There are also about a dozen letters dating from the nineteen-thirties. These are signed 'H'.

*

And now arises the question of whether I am entitled to read these letters written sixty or more years ago, and use them in this book. For as I write, though in her advanced nineties she can hardly speak or hear, has no memories and does not really know where she is, Yolande is alive.

It is a question with which biographers are naturally familiar, but never in my own writing life has it arisen so acutely. For if I read them am I not trespassing? And if I quote them do I not commit the sin of which my father so angrily accused me? Or is this my chance of atonement?

To other people I know that I appear reticent. This surprises me, since I do not always *feel* reticent or keep my opinions to myself. Have I not been in tears while writing parts of this book – tears of laughter sometimes? Doubtless I have a self-protective manner, the reasons for which are scattered through this narrative. Nevertheless, despite my appearance of reticence, I have gained something of a reputation as the biographer of Lytton Strachey and Augustus John for beating back the frontiers of reticence in other people's lives. So what can I do in this near-autobiographical story? To some extent I am obliged to reflect the silence and repression within my family – a code of privacy shared by most ordinary people of those times – because they do not hand me the codebreaking clues of any correspondence. So what I can reveal emerges more between the lines of my writing.

My father and mother kept no letters from me or anyone else, and my aunt has not kept these few letters for publication. It is merely bad luck that her nephew turns out to be what James Joyce called a 'biografiend'. In a sense she has not deliberately kept this correspondence at all – its incompleteness and the haphazard way in which it is scattered through miscellaneous bits and pieces of paper indicate that these letters are merely 'undestroyed'. For the act of destruction is like a sentence of death, a second death, which we cannot easily bring ourselves to commit on those we have loved. But can others do it for us? Is that an act of mercy or an act of vandalism? And does the passing of time alter the purgatorial state of these papers, raise or lower them from a heartbeat to a text? Then, if I keep them and they are never used what of that? Does their interest gradually leak away? Have I been cowardly? Why should my aunt be any different from the band of semi-public characters who have been dragged in to play parts in my biographies? If there is a principle that entitles me to do this to them, what principle permits me to act differently with her? Remember that, though the contents of these letters may not shock a reader at the end of the twentieth century, their publication would have been considered highly indiscreet only fifty years ago, quite unacceptable to my family, and absolutely unthinkable to my aunt herself. For here, in its muted form, lie moments, private moments, from what is perhaps the most vital part of her life. And if I feel a need for self-protection, so may she.

'No serious biographer working in the twentieth century will have failed to lay down some ethical foundations to his craft,' I wrote in a lecture on biography.

Far from adding a new terror to death, the good
biographer gives an opportunity to the dead to contribute
to the living world. It is understandable and right that
people should seek to protect themselves and others close
to them during their lives. We all need our prevarications,
evasions, our sentimentalities and silences. We have a
need, too, for the privacy out of which our work comes.
But I make a distinction between the living and our
friends the dead. I believe we pay a compliment to the
dead by keeping them in employment to assist the living.
For if we have all these necessary prevarications,
evasions, sentimentalities and silences as our guide to
conduct . . . we will make ourselves unnaturally miserable
by imposing impossible standards on ourselves.

The general pattern of my aunt's story is not uncommon. But whenever the chorus of conventional family sentiment bursts forth, she should be able to step forward with others, including perhaps her own aunt Norah Palmer Holroyd and her grandmother Anna Eliza Holroyd, to remind us of what families may inflict on themselves. What happened to Norah and Anna is largely irrecoverable, but an outline of my aunt's predicament may be traced. Now that she can no longer be hurt by me, by her family, by those who knew her, by any of us, surely I may open her letters and use them to help tell her story? But I hear my father's warning: 'Please remember that one day someone may have to write your biography.' I devoutly hope not. Like many others, I do not want a biography of myself written. I have all the familiar objections. Whoever tried would get it wrong. I would prefer to do it myself – and perhaps this is what I am indirectly doing. But then of course I am merely alive, and when dead may think differently. Or I may think and feel nothing. Besides, as the examples of T.S. Eliot, Somerset Maugham, Jean Rhys and many others testify, the dead have never been able to control the living, nor the living the dead. What matters is the spirit in which they communicate, the imaginative link made between us and those who 'though dead, yet speaketh'. At any rate, I feel I must go on and do the best I can.

Hazlehurst's letters are mostly undated but a number of the envelopes exist which have postmarks, so it is possible to arrange the others chronologically by matching writing paper and addresses. The correspondence opens with a dramatic argument. From a letter sent to Brocket on 1 June 1933 from Yacht Frothblower in Cubitts Yacht Basin at Chiswick, it appears that Yolande had recently accused Hazel of 'making use' of her while 'looking for someone else'. It emerges that he has had two previous love affairs about which she knows, and that both women have 'moved on'. But he is convinced that Yolande now has grown tired of him and is herself about to 'move on'. For she too has had romantic attachments. What about her near-marriage in 1926? And that was not all.

In one of her photograph albums there is a picture of an upright gentleman in hunting regalia seated on a white horse, its ears pointed. He looks about thirty and the caption unusually identifies him and not the horse. He is 'Major Ogilvie'. The date is in the late nineteen-twenties, probably 1929. Also in my aunt's box of papers are three letters she has kept from 'Og' written from the Whittington Barracks in Lichfield. It appears that they had known each other only a few weeks, but that he has fallen in love with her and wants to marry her. However, she is already engaged or committed to someone else. He apologises for worrying her with his declarations and attentions: they were, he tells her,

> the result of day dreaming, of sitting in the sun &
> thinking of the impossible & making it seem possible,
> and impossible though it was I hadn't really, in my heart
> of hearts, given up hope . . . I have had enough
> experience of the world to know how intensely
> unwelcome unwanted love letters are, so when I write it
> will be just as a pal. This time, though, I am going to
> transgress & tell you I miss you & want you & love you.

Perhaps because he is to have an operation, Yolande writes affectionately back, sends him at his urgent request three photographs of herself and altogether, as he gratefully acknowledges, 'makes a fuss of me' by going up to London to see him at the King Edward VII Hospital for Officers. 'It's funny dear,' he writes, 'that though I didn't know your name six weeks ago, it will be your hand I shall be holding when, in a few minutes, they wheel me out to a great adventure, & it will be your photographs I shall find by the side of my bed when I wake up again . . . I am so happy that I love you.' After the operation he writes once more: 'I often look at your photographs & wish you belonged to me.'

But it was to Hazlehurst, apparently, that she belonged. By 1933, however, they both have doubts about the other's commitment. Hazel has the idealistic notion that women are naturally of finer clay than men. In any event he felt 'damned inferior', he admits, to his previous loves, and Yolande is 'very much more superior' to both of them – which means of course that he is 'worse off'. Is he trying to 'move on' himself and giving her the most flattering grounds for doing so? He blows a lot of froth as he sails round his predicament.

> Suffering as I do from stupid shyness, I must imagine a
> lot of things that are not meant and yet, although I
> know this, I haven't the sense to coordinate this
> feeling. In the almost impossible hope that you won't
> discover too quickly my gross inferiority, you had
> better keep this as evidence against me, and in the
> likely event of my backsliding produce it to stimulate
> me up again.

This convoluted Victorian sentiment leads on to a simple nineteen-twenties conclusion. 'I suppose the only way to look at things is to live for the present. The past gone, tomorrow unborn – to-day is sweet.'

But can Yolande be part of this sweetness? 'I was quite the proudest man in London to be even seen with you,' Hazel writes. 'You must know how awfully attractive you are, & how any person would give anything for the privilege of your presence . . . You are too adorable. I cannot think of even one tiny flaw in the whole of you. I cannot say more . . . Do believe me. You are too sweet to me.'

The two of them spent much of that summer together. It was

easier for Yolande to get away now that her father had returned to Brocket, and Hazel could come and stay there too. Their affaire was full of 'naughty things', but Yolande was generally careful to 'restrain' herself, and seems to have made no final commitment to her lover. Though he would frequently profess his love for her, she could never quite bring herself to say 'I love you' however passionately he invited her ('I live for the day'). Did she find such exchanges silly? Was she, like her father, having difficulties in showing her feelings? Or did she shrink from what must inevitably follow such a declaration? For he had spoken of marriage, or at least it was implied in much he said. Of course there would be obstacles. He was not rich ('I must make haste and make enough money for you'), and Adeline would certainly oppose the match, wouldn't she? So they must be careful, very careful, and meanwhile he would cultivate the rest of her family. All this lies in the second surviving letter of the series which he writes from his home in Teddington in the second week of September 1933.

Yolande has gone the previous month to Monte Carlo. She is probably staying with her girlfriend Cathie who has an apartment in the boulevard d'Italie. Hazel, anxiously waiting for news, imagines 'all sorts of things such as you finding someone else'. When a letter from her does come he is elated. 'To me you are just too wonderful, & it is still incomprehensible that you should deign to look at me even much less like me. Darling one . . . I never missed anyone so much and never felt so completely dependent upon one person . . . I never hope to be fonder of anyone for it really hurts, & I'm afraid so very afraid.'

Hazel has been staying again at Brocket and has invited Yolande's family to visit him that weekend at Teddington, some twenty miles east of Maidenhead. It is 'sweet' of him, Yolande writes. But there is more to it than this, he explains. He likes her father and brothers and 'some day it might stand me in good stead if your mother ever commenced to go off the deep end'.

Kenneth and Basil arrive while he is writing this letter – it is twelve pages long and occupies him intermittently all weekend. Adeline does not turn up. Instead she telephones regularly and when she learns that Kenneth has a temperature and is in bed, she creates tremendous scenes, 'crying copiously all day' and telling her friends of the calamity. It is essential that Adeline's nervestorms do not break over Yolande and Hazlehurst themselves, at least not yet. Because of his work, 'I shall not be able to come to France,' he tells her. But he suggests 'sneaking a night' by meeting her at Dover on her way home. 'What do you think?' he asks. 'Even if I met you in London and we went away somewhere. As I am back on the boat I can go anywhere . . . But, darling Yolande, if there is the very tiniest chance of upsetting things then like you [I think] such a move would not be worth considering . . . I am waiting for the marvellous time you promise me when you return . . .'

What happened when she returned, what developed between them secretly, cannot be traced through any subsequent correspondence. They went on seeing each other, but the next letter among my aunt's papers was written from Yacht Llanthony on 16 May 1939 and sent to Norhurst. Yolande is still 'Darling' and he is still 'H'. But inevitably the tone has changed in the intervening six years. The passion has disappeared, though they are emotionally at ease with each other. They are almost like a married couple – only for some reason they aren't married. Since Yolande is in her thirty-eighth year, the possibility of them having children has probably been eliminated. She writes to him about her 'canine troubles' and of Nan's health; he is full of sailing adventures and tells her of an enthralling trip up the Rhine ('we only just made it . . . I wouldn't have missed it for anything. The whole river is full of wrecks & broken ships so you can guess the thrill . . . will go into detail and places visited when I see you').

The remaining nine letters are all written during the war. In

August and September 1939 he writes from Yacht Goddess which is moored at Tilbury Landing Stage as part of the River Emergency Services, and describes the 'complete chaos' of the first air-raid warning during which he is trying to buy milk ('really the war is most inconsiderate'). He tells her he has been ordered to report to Liverpool. 'Here am I the head man perfectly comfortable in possibly the safest place in the land & have to go and leave my comfy bed & home and go to some perishing outlandish heathen hole to do God knows what.' He signs his letter 'As ever, H'. But this is a world away from the man who half a dozen years ago had felt so emotionally dependent on Yolande, and cried out when she was away in France: 'I miss you hellishly & long like the devil to have you back again, Darling, darling, so much.' Yet there is the habit of an attachment, the assumption of an understanding, between them still. He telephones her, is careful to let her know where he is going, hopes 'I can come to you or you to me depending on petrol', and exhorts her to 'Cheer up, be good, & happy.'

The next letter in the series comes in mid-October from the General Hospital at Ormskirk, some fifteen miles north of Liverpool. Hazlehurst is not adjusting well to the war. 'In the black out after an Air Raid Practice I fell into a concrete shelter 10 feet deep on my head,' he explains. Some 'damned fool' had left the door open 'against all orders' and there would have to be a Court of Inquiry. Meanwhile he lies bandaged in bed like a hero, with concussion, cuts to his face, an amazing black-and-red eye, sprained shoulder and thumb and broken tooth. 'I am as beautiful as ever,' and of course he is 'as ever Hazel,' he assures Yolande. He hopes to be coming down to London in a week – to see his dentist.

Over the following eight months Hazlehurst's letters from 'C Camp' and elsewhere near Liverpool show how greatly people's lives have changed since the nineteen-thirties. London itself seems far away and long ago. 'What a long letter!' he exclaims somewhat in dismay at reading Yolande's news from Maidenhead. He does his best to take an interest, but really his own news is much more interesting. The simple, active, open-air life of the army is beginning to suit him. 'I have over 500 men in my company,' he informs her. His only complaint is the cold. 'If you ever knit anything other than jumpers, you might try your hand at a pair of gloves,' he suggests. It is the only opening he allows her, and Yolande immediately responds by sending him 'a lovely dressing-gown & gloves. They are grand, but how naughty you are to spend so much money.' Then he returns to his war-talk about Baldwin, Chamberlain, Churchill and that 'damned clever man Hitler'.

'I have always impressed on everyone I know that we have been taking the [war] too lightly,' he writes. '. . . We are now fighting literally for our lives and everyone must do something.' It is probably this call to duty that persuades Yolande to drive library books to prisoner-of-war camps and then join the telephone exchange in Maidenhead.

For reasons of security, Hazlehurst is not allowed to 'say of course what we are doing'. But he cannot help revealing some of the 'eventful things happening', the hectic hours of work in twelve-hour shifts, and the fact that 'we are all in tents'. He has had a sense of seriousness forced upon him. It is a difficult grafting process and, in moments of reflection, he feels that he has 'rarely if ever been so depressed about things'. The happy world of yachts and picnics and long summer holidays that he and Yolande inhabited has vanished. 'There will be very few parties & fun in London in less than a month,' he writes on 20 May 1940, ten days before the British forces are to evacuate Dunkirk. All the same he is curiously well, and he repeatedly urges Yolande to 'keep fit, & happy and above all don't worry about anything'.

Though he signs off with 'all my love', there is no actual expression of love in these letters. Yet it seems unlikely that he is writing so openly to anyone else. Yolande is a real friend, a confidante, a pal. Realising that he is revealing to her more than he should of his military life, which is now all his life, he asks her to burn what he has sent her. But of course she cannot. This correspondence is all she has of him, and she continues sending him long domestic letters from Norhurst.

By the autumn of 1940 Hazlehurst has been posted with the 14th battalion of the King's Regiment to the Isle of Man (where Ronald Stent had recently been dispatched). He feels cut off from everything. 'No bombs even,' he complains. His duties include escorting the Governor's wife to cocktail parties, raising funds from charity events, and starting an officers' club. 'I want to get abroad & do something in this war,' he writes impatiently, 'and not sit back in England all the time . . . Better to see some real action than listen to a lot of bloody huns going overhead dropping their loads . . . If only I were a bit younger,' he adds, 'I should be in the RAF.' This is the time of the Battle of Britain, the German blitz on London and the intensification of U-boat warfare in the Atlantic. There are rumours that Hitler is planning to invade England. Hazlehurst by then must have been in his late forties. 'Even now the age limit may cease to function & if the worst comes the old brigade can have a go,' he tells Yolande. But apart from the news that he is being made Brigade Major, 'I don't appear to have anything else to say.'

By the summer of 1941 Yolande has some war news of her own. Kenneth has been captured in North Africa by the Italians and taken to a prisoner-of-war camp in northern Italy. From here he escapes, is hidden in the mountains by Italian peasants, but then recaptured and taken to a prisoner-of-war camp in Romania. Basil, in the RAF at Wilmslow, seems to be at war with Ulla; and German planes have again been flying over Maidenhead, dropping a few bombs on their home runs and driving Adeline into hysterics. Hazel is the only person to whom Yolande can confide such things, for he is as it were part of the family, part of herself, and so she is not betraying anyone by

telling him. 'You have had a perfectly bloody time,' he acknowledges. Kenneth, as a prisoner of war, is 'fairly sure of decent
treatment', because 'we hold such a lot of their people, &
reprisals would be easier for us'. As for Basil and Ulla, they
'appear to be behaving up to their usual form. I'm afraid I did
not expect anything else. If Basil can put up with what seems to
be a fairly promiscuous wife, well he is a poor boob. I'm damned
if I would. I would have too much pride to accept her second-
hand from that fat slob Thurnell.'

Thurnell, I now recall, was the name my mother told me never
to mention within the hearing of my father. Hazlehurst's reaction
to her affaire with him must have been the conventional one.
This was the climate of opinion in which my father made his
decision to take me back to Maidenhead and, since she would
not go there herself, leave his twenty-six-year-old adulterous
wife to fend for herself in wartime England.

What Hazlehurst wrote was intended to comfort Yolande.
His own opinion surely supported hers. How well she had
behaved, and how badly Ulla was behaving, in this war crisis.
But the hypothetical reference to his own wife, so impersonally
thrown into the argument, may not have brought Yolande much
comfort after all. Who is to say what was in her mind when
introducing this scandalous family business into their correspondence. But Hazlehurst is preoccupied with Hitler and no
longer feels so intimately involved with Holroyd affairs. 'It is
none of my business,' he writes, 'so we will forget it.' The rest of
his letter is full of news which Yolande could hear any day on
the radio or read in the papers or, if she ever went to such places,
pick up in the pubs. It is the stuff to give the troops (Hitler 'has
got his hands full with Russia . . . the terrific pounding the RAF
are giving the hun cities in the Ruhr must be having its effect',
etc.).

There is one more letter in the series. It is difficult to date,

being without an envelope, incomplete (ten from what appear to
have been fourteen pages) and scribbled in pencil on the writing
paper of the Cheshire Regiment. Hazlehurst has been ill with
shingles and 'crops of boils in the most awkward places'. This is
due to his not having 'relaxed literally for years' and to 'never
[having] had any leave'. When he does get leave, 'I propose to go
& have a fish or something to give me a complete change.'
Without the 'Yolande darling' on the missing first page and the
regular 'All my love' on the last, the letter reads as if it were written to another man.

Hazlehurst did eventually get one of his wishes. After
Mussolini fell from power in the summer of 1943, he was sent
out to Italy. Less than three years after declaring war on Britain,
Italy then declared war on Germany, and Hazlehurst found himself in a friendly country. He must have written a letter to
Yolande, but she did not keep it. 'She learnt one morning that
her fiancé had married an Italian woman of 20 (he was nearly
fifty),' my father indignantly explained.

The consequences of this – Yolande's endless running with the
dogs across the fields, her inability to tolerate us as we sat about
gulping down our meals, the barricading of the house against
visitors, the fiery outbursts at her mother, the putting away of
her records in the garage, her retirement into her bedroom – I
could see every day at Norhurst. But I could not interpret it and
did not try until I came to write *A Dog's Life*. 'Poor Yolande!'
my mother exclaimed in her account. My father's reaction was
one of outrage. 'She was reduced to unpaid nurse to three old
people,' he wrote to me after reading part of my manuscript in
1968. 'Not much need to ask you to remember what sort of life
she leads now – you see it often enough.'

What had gone wrong? And why had her brothers done so
little apparently to help her? Perhaps that is the question of a
single child, and brothers cannot be used in this way. Besides, it
is impossible to tell from this packet of letters whether Yolande

really loved Hazel or whether he was the only man she really knew and somehow not quite the right man. Whatever the reason for this sad end to their affaire, her mistake, whether from excessive loyalty or a failure of nerve, was to have gone on living with her family. She may well have protected her father from his wife, but he could not protect her from the consequences of living with them both. And the consequences were awful.

12

Scaitcliffe Revisited

Scaitcliffe had not changed very much since my father's time there. The school had grown from forty to fifty-five boys between the two world wars, and one of the classrooms had been enlarged. A squash court and rugby fives court which had been built were 'in constant use', the prospectus assured parents. An extra playing field had been bought from a farmer, extending the grounds to some twenty acres. Otherwise the red-brick, late-Victorian pile stood with its chapel in Crown land as before. My father would also have been able to recognise some of the names – Riley-Smith, Cornwall-Jones – of boys whose families, like himself, were continuing to send their sons to Scaitcliffe. So he was doing the customary thing. Yet after reading the account he wrote towards the end of his life of the hell he endured there, I cannot help being surprised. Why did he do it? One answer is that Scaitcliffe was the only preparatory school he knew, and there was little opportunity during those war years of getting to know other schools. But I don't think that he would have wanted to act differently whatever the circumstances. Though he spoke to me kindly about homesickness, I had no idea he had been miserable himself at Scaitcliffe. Quite the contrary. The only clue lay in a book he gave me, F. Anstey's *Vice Versa* (which I later saw filmed by Peter Ustinov as *A Lesson to Fathers*). In this story the father, Mr Bultitude, who is much given to praising his time at school as the happiest days of his life, is magically obliged to change places with his son and re-experience the tortures of his boarding school. I enjoyed this novel, but I did not pick up the signal my father was sending me.

He was an optimist, my father. He wanted to believe that things were getting better and all was for the best. He had suffered because of his brother, but I had no big brother overshadowing me. Besides, it was only when he was approaching the fragility of his second childhood that the miseries of these early years came back to him. In his late thirties, during these war years, the ups and downs of school life did not seem such a big business.

Yet my father was eager for me to do well at school. He had never really come to terms with missing so much through illness when a boy. Success had been blazing away somewhere else while he languished in Switzerland. When had he ever been applauded or thumped admiringly on the back? He won no silver cups, wore no coloured badges. He breasted no tapes ahead of others, saved no penalties, never scored a century. Everything he had missed now seemed to return and take hold of his imagination. I was to be his second chance, play another innings for him, take the field as his substitute. I ran, I jumped, batted, bowled and kicked for him – and looking through the school records I find I represented him not badly. At the age of twelve I made the winning long and high jumps (13ft 2in and 4ft 4in); I won the Senior Challenge Cup and a cup for fielding; I became vice-captain of the football and the cricket teams.

By far the oddest of my accomplishments was as opening batsman for the cricket eleven. The family money had dwindled so drastically by then that my father and grandfather could no longer afford to buy all the equipment I needed. So they were delighted when I came in from the garage at Norhurst one day carrying my Uncle Kenneth's bat and pads. He had put them to good use at Cambridge in the nineteen-twenties, but would not be needing them now, we all agreed, in his Romanian prisoner-of-war camp. So I could have them. We would write and tell him they were in use again, and he would be pleased. Many years later I wrote an essay called 'Not Cricket' in praise of this bat and pads.

The pads were deeply yellow and reached almost to my
shoulders. I peeped out from them unafraid. The bat was
a mature instrument, well-bound and fully-seasoned,
giving out a deep note when struck, like a groan. I
admired that bat – but I could not lift it. I was ten or
twelve; the bat was more than a quarter-of-a-century
old . . . I would drag it to the crease and then, as it were,
leave it there. As I took guard there occurred a total
eclipse of the stumps. The bowler had not even a bail to
aim at . . . We stood there, my uncle's bat and I, keeping
our end up, while runs flowed and wickets fell at the
other end. I had a good eye and would watch the balls
swinging my way with great keenness, making lightning
decisions as to what shots I could play. But I never played
them except in my imagination.

The Scaitcliffe School Notes record that, like my grandfather at Uppingham, 'Holroyd was the soundest and most correct [batsman], but a slow scorer.' That was a polite understatement. Occasionally, over the seasons, a ball would glance off the edge of my uncle's bat and flutter through the slips bringing me a run.

But it had to go almost to the boundary to gain me time to reach the other end in those pads. What the score sheets do not reveal is that, despite my meagre totals, and though going in first, I was often out last doing something desperate with the bat, handling it as if it were a Scottish caber. I was the nightwatchman who watched the day, and my perfect total was nought not out. If I was not popular with the other side, I was scarcely a hero with my own. My batting partners were obliged to score most of their runs in boundaries, and those lower in the batting order seldom got much of an innings. Once, when stranded between wickets with my vast anchor of a bat, I was run out, I could not tell which team uttered the loudest cheer.

Nought not out summed up my achievements at this age. There seemed to hang about me an undefined air of promise that prevented me from doing anything at all. I seldom spoke first and never took an initiative. To attract attention, it seemed to me, was to ask for trouble. I strove for invisibility. What I liked most, because I had never experienced it before, was 'joining in' whatever was going on. I liked the Sunday walks in our blue suits through beechnuts, conkers and sweet chestnuts (which we were allowed to take back and toast for tea) to the 'Copper Horse', the equestrian statue of George III that looked towards Windsor Castle down an avenue of trees three miles in length called 'the Long Walk'. Sometimes we walked to the Duke of Cumberland's Obelisk at Smith's Lawn, heads bent, on the alert for pieces of shrapnel. I loved also the epic games of 'Convoy' in the wilder reaches of Windsor Great Park, hiding in the heather or behind trees, then veering off between 'destroyers', or 'submarines', 'minesweepers' and 'battleships' as we risked finding out who was what and then tried to remember as we raced for headquarters. On our way back, walking in crocodile past the flaking white façade of Fort Belvedere, we would glance around for items of the Crown Jewels which Edward VIII had thrown over the wall and into the park, we believed, when told he had to abdicate. I remember too the excitement of climbing into one of the massive hearse-like Daimlers that took our teams to play matches against other schools: Sunningdale and St Pirens; Heatherdown and Earlywood, each with their tribal rallying from the edge of the playing fields. I even enjoyed lining up with all the others for Nurse Minima to spoon us our 'Virol' or 'Radio Malt' each morning; also lifting up my voice in the chapel and losing part of myself in the collective singing: Decani versus Cantoris.

My moments of happiness often came from these conspiracies of self-forgetfulness. I also made at Scaitcliffe my first two friendships. One was with a boy called John Mein with whom I often paired off during our Sunday walks. One Sunday afternoon he came back with me to Norhurst and I showed him the walking-stick gun with which I had almost shot my grandmother. As a precaution, it had been hidden on the top of a tall dresser in the dining-room, but unfortunately my grandfather had not unloaded it, and we unintentionally shot a cartridge past the parrot and into the ceiling. No one found out, and after the shock we had to hurry into the garden and burst into laughter. What we laughed about at other times I no longer know, but we were always laughing and the joy of that laughter I remember vividly. Sometimes we laughed ourselves into sheer helplessness. '*I'll give you such a smite, Holroyd!*' one of the masters cried out in despair after John Mein and I had spread our staggering laughter through the complete cast of the school play, a historical drama with us attired as General Wolfe and the Marquis de Montcalm at Quebec. It was a passion, this laughter, that released me from innumerable apprehensions. At another time when I went to stay at his mother's house in Sussex, we almost drowned ourselves in a boat so uncontrollable was our condition. John Mein remembers taking me ferreting that week and 'you didn't like me wringing the rabbits' necks – but you always were a tender soul!' I have no memory of this, though I recognise my squeamishness. For me John Mein was a poet of the ludicrous and an imaginative storyteller, who lost his shyness in comedy and stories, and taught me how to do the same.

Another wonderful storyteller was my friend Christopher Capron. He would fill Wellington dormitory after lights-out with glowing tales of adventure and mystery. I could never have enough of these stories. 'What happened next?' I would demand, and he would give another spin to the plot. One by one the other boys, Bowman (the clever one who was bullied), Drummond (who played the piano), Molins (who was always being beaten), Palumbo (who was our sports star) and Stirling (who had a secret society with a language no one understood) fell asleep. But I was always awake at the end, clamouring for more.

I knew John Mein and Christopher Capron only four years of my life, but I count them both as lifelong friends, one the Muse of Comedy, the other a Keeper of Stories, because their liberating influences have lasted all my life.

Scaitcliffe was probably no worse than other preparatory schools of the time, and in one respect it was certainly better. In the grounds, between the playing fields, lay an excellent kitchen garden from which, for much of the year, we had fresh fruit and vegetables to add to our war diet of dried eggs and baked beans, our porridge and chocolate tart. Other schools loved coming to play us at cricket and football because they could wolf down such scrumptious teas. This was largely due to Mildred Vickers, a believer in milk and, fortunately, in cream. She studied our diet sheets, and prescribed Haliborange to supplement our rations.

Ronald Vickers, the formidable headmaster of my father's time, had died eighteen months before I arrived. In the attic at the top of a pitch-pine staircase lay the first Mrs Vickers. Or so we believed. Mr Vickers was now up there too, of course, encased in lead, awaiting arrival of his second beloved wife. After lights-out we dared one another to climb the stairs to this attic and look through the keyhole. Chetwynd minor said that when he did so the handle of the door had turned and a voice whispered 'Come in!'

Ronald Vickers's twin sons, whom my father had seen when a boy being wheeled across the lawn in their double-pram, were abroad fighting in the war, and the acting headmaster was Denis Owen.

Denis Owen was a remarkable man. As a teenager, he had won an exhibition to Oxford but was unable to go there because his family had no money. In 1927 he had been recruited by Ronald Vickers to take the place of Edgar Ransome, that twenty-stone 'coarse old man' my father had so hated. All the distinction of the school during my time there derived from Denis Owen. His career was spent teaching the sons of well-off families who did go on to university. He was a small, wiry, tough character with a hooked nose, dark hair, a grim expression and demonic energy. He coached us brilliantly at cricket and football; he ran a debating society, played the organ in chapel and gave the sermons, took shooting lessons, taught Latin, French and English, worked himself and us, indoors and outdoors, round the clock. Though boys from other schools envied us our delicious teas, they were glad not to have our strict and strenuous regime. We were woken at seven o'clock by the clashing of a bell handled by one of the gardeners, and after washing at the bowls of decanted water in the dormitories and hurriedly pulling on our grey shirts and shorts, our ties and sweaters, we proceeded in line to our first service in the chapel where the biblical figure of Denis Owen was already at work on the organ. Then, following a ten-minute scripture lesson, we went in to breakfast. The rest of the day was crowded with Latin gender rhymes, fielding practice, multiplication tables, gym, English grammar and spelling, cross-country runs, the recital of dates in history, and appalling plunges into the open-air swimming pool (an uninviting arrangement of concrete and corrugated iron in which we nakedly splashed, watched by the keen eye of Mr Bailey who also took us for drill). Most of the teaching was unmemorable, but Miss Stanton's hesitant French lessons, and the spitting and shaking of Mr Perry's mathematics reinforced by something known as 'the Perry Punch' (a clenched fist, one finger angled, delivered to a painful spot on the upper arm) stay in my mind as being peculiarly terrible. Mr Perry was an irritable old man, stinking of tobacco, whose large yellowing moustache concealed a bullet hole from the First World War which was, in our opinion, his one distinction. Worst of all were the piano lessons in a tiny room called 'the sardine tin'. When I struck a wrong note I was immediately stopped, my finger taken and placed on the correct note, and then forced up and down on it, again and again, jarring the sound through my body. I gave up piano lessons, saving my father three guineas a term, but have regretted it for the rest of my life. Perhaps the war was responsible for such bad teaching. Perhaps it was the same everywhere.

But Denis Owen commanded our respect if not our affection. I think we all recognised that he was somehow special, though we also thought he was extremely frightening. 'He certainly petrified me,' John Mein remembered. The beat of his footsteps through the corridors of the school, especially at night, started a wave of pounding fear ahead of him, and we would hold our breath until the sound receded. Maybe I feared him more than most, for I was ridiculously sensitive. I can still blush when I remember the eruption of laughter in class when I pronounced surgery as sugary, called a Quaker a Quacker, came out even more disastrously with an 'earthquack', and gave the Thames two phonetic syllables. Mr Owen appeared unaware of my sensitivity, however, until awareness was forced on him by a sensational episode.

One morning when the bell clanged outside and we all got out of our beds, I noticed across the lower sheet a large cherry-coloured stain. Nurse Minima noticed it too and I was closely questioned. I answered that I did not know what it was and felt quite as baffled as she did. That evening I was summoned to Denis Owen's study and after waiting nervously in the passage, that same passage in which my father had sometimes waited thirty years earlier, was severely questioned again about the red area on my sheet. At first I had thought it must be blood, but I had no wound or nose-bleed. It was inexplicable. My ignorance must have been transparent, and perhaps Denis Owen suspected that I had been the victim of a practical joke by the other boys in the dormitory. In any event I was not beaten that night. Instead I was told that, whatever the stain had been, it must never re-appear. I thoroughly agreed and returned upstairs. But a week or two later it did reappear, bright cherry-red across the sheet – and this time I knew what it was. In the early hours of the morning I had half-woken, found that I had wet my bed and, still half-asleep, put my red dressing-gown underneath me before going back to sleep.

Nurse Minima sent me back that evening to the headmaster's study and Denis Owen, who was busy, told me that I must come to him next day with a convincing explanation. This was more difficult than it sounded, not only because I felt the explanation to be unspeakably humiliating, but also because Denis Owen was so awfully unapproachable. Between the formal lessons, the organ-playing and sermons, he appeared to inhabit Olympus. I saw him once that day striding across a distant field with that grim expression on his face, and I ran some way after him but did not get near. The thought of interrupting his progress with my dreadful story was simply impossible.

That evening I was again summoned down to wait in the pas-sage outside his study. Then he called me in, told me it was too late now for explanations, bent me over a chair in my pyjamas and began beating me. However, I was by this time in an extreme state of nerves and, at the first stroke, releasing all my pent-up emotion, let out a vast cry. It was as much a shout as a cry, mingling protest and pain in a great emotional eruption. The sound, I was later told, travelled upstairs and into rooms throughout the school. No one knew what it was, but everything came to a stop. Nothing so loud and unexpected had happened since the famous night when a public house nearby called The Bells of Ousley had been blown up by German bombers. Even Denis Owen appeared shaken. He told me to go back up to the dormitory, and at the end of term wrote a devastating report to my father, questioning him as to whether I was really fit for the rough-and-tumble of a boarding school. It was, I now think, an opportunity for my father to tell me about his own 'absolute hell' at Scaitcliffe, but I do not recall that he did so. He was worried by the practical difficulties of having to remove me, as he had been removed for different reasons. So I went back all the more determined to develop my skills of avoiding attention.

My last year at Scaitcliffe was the best. I did not actually like going there after the holidays, but then I did not like going back to Norhurst at the end of term. I did not know what I liked or where I was going: whether to Maidenhead with my aunt and grandparents; or to various places in France with my father; or to London with my mother, and then across the North Sea to meet my other grandmother in Stockholm and roomfuls of my incomprehensible Swedish cousins in Borås and Göteborg.

I needed everything to be simple. But by the end of the war my parents' lives were growing more complicated, and these complexities began infiltrating my own life.

13

Three Weddings
and a Funeral

My mother wrote that she was 'without a penny' at her boarding house in Cresswell Gardens, and that there were 'days when
I only had a glass of milk'. She lived largely on what Kaja was
able to send her from Stockholm via the Swedish Consulate.
Occasionally she would come down by train to Scaitcliffe, and
sometimes also to Maidenhead 'where you were left for me to
see for a few hours. We always had tearful partings – you
wanted to come back with me. I was desperate & believe that
you were too.'

Everything began to change after my father left the Royal Air
Force. In the first week of April 1946 he attended a medical
board which found that he was still suffering from rheumatoid
polyarthritis. His disability was rated at forty percent and, 'with
regret', he was declared unfit for further service. He had been
billeted in Paris for eighteen months 'chez Madame Dimier' in
the rue Sergent Hoff, a small street near the Arc de Triomphe,

and after his discharge he continued living there. It was a solid, spacious apartment block built in 1912 and decorated on its balconies by sandstone flambeaux containing quivers and arrows, also pineapples and lions and swags of dependant fruit and flowers. Above the large portal with its art nouveau decorations was fixed the head of Silenus framed with grapes and vine-leaves. Inside were marble floors, and a slow and stately lift up the five floors. I remember visiting my father there during my holidays and being astonished by Madame Dimier's ability to pour forth rapid continuous loud incomprehensible French without ever taking breath. It was an artillery of sound that killed off all other speech and covered everything we did, or thought, or saw, or imagined. I wondered how my father, no mean speaker under ordinary circumstances himself, could endure such a perpetual battering of noise. And then I suddenly realised that he had fallen in love with Maman's voluptuous daughter, Marie-Louise, or Marlou as everyone called her.

Marlou was the most glamorous woman I had met. She was always elegantly dressed, had gorgeous raven hair that was swept back but kept falling forwards, rather pouting lips, and large expressive eyes with hooded lids that fascinated me. Her sultry looks made the climate around her seem warm and relaxing. I thought her the height of sophistication. I liked her too, but felt shy after my father took me to one side and asked me to give her a kiss each night because she was unable to have children of her own. This revelation led to a brief man-to-man talk about the 'facts of life' which left me rather unconvinced by the unlikeliness of it all, and wondering whether I had misunderstood. I doubt if, in my nervousness, I was as affectionate to Marlou when she came to say goodnight as I should have been. She took me to various fashion shows and praised my taste; and she gave me a camera with which I took a spectacular shot of the Eiffel Tower, making it appear like the leaning tower of Pisa.

Marlou's full name was Marie-Louise Deschamps-Eymé. She

was in publishing, her business partner being Marcel Brandin, 'a cool, slim, bitterly disillusioned ex-Resistance fighter', as the novelist Winston Graham described him, 'who saw France returning to its old corrupt ways.' It was in their publishing company, Editions Begh, that my father bought a directorship, using the invalidity money he had been granted by the RAF. He also brought with him an idea, which was to corner the market in translations of books that were being, or stood a good chance of being, made into films. Winston Graham, whose Poldark novels were later to be such a success on television, was one of his early authors; another was the well-respected, now-forgotten novelist Claude Houghton (whose 'novelisation' of Jerome K. Jerome's play *The Passing of the Third Floor Back* was also filmed). Love and money were to be the ingredients of their success, but it was love and money that undid them.

Marlou was known to be the mistress of a millionaire newspaper owner on whose financial support Editions Begh largely depended. Nevertheless, my father proposed to marry her – once he had divorced my mother. In the summer of 1946 he hired a London detective who soon came up with the evidence he needed. The decree nisi cites Rowland Hill as co-respondent. It is not a name that appears in either of my parents' accounts or that I ever heard them mention. In the London telephone directory of 1946 there is one Rowland Hill. He is living in the Marylebone Road, but disappears at the time of the divorce.

This divorce legally freed both my parents for fresh chapters in their lives. Or so they believed. In fact, probably because my father was in Paris, they forgot to take the formal step required to make their decree absolute. The result was that, though they never knew this, they actually remained married to each other, and all their later marriages were invalid. Fortunately perhaps they did not have children by these four subsequent marriages, though from time to time I was presented with a new stepbrother or stepsister for the holidays.

Late in 1946 my mother, still aged only thirty, moved into a nice small flat on the eighth floor of Sloane Avenue Mansions, near the King's Road in Chelsea. I often stayed with her there before and after our journeys to Sweden. How I hated those awful bucketing voyages across the North Sea! We would start out from Tilbury in one of the regular Swedish boats, the *Suecia*, *Saga* or *Patricia*, creaking and groaning, swaying and heaving – and I was soon down in the cabin groaning and heaving with sympathetic sea-sickness. But my mother was not ill. She was popular on board, never missing the *smörgåsbord*, or the music playing and the sun shining, and the company of strangers. Occasionally I would crawl up on deck and see her talking to some admirer and exchanging addresses. I remember only one of these gentlemen, a Mr Smith, who wore his watch with its face on the inside of his wrist. I was so struck with the novelty of this that I turned my own watch round, and have worn it so ever since. Later, 'Mr Smith on the boat' became a generic term, and I would tease my mother about this ever-recurring gallant on her travels round the world.

It was unusual during those years immediately following the Second World War for people to go abroad, and for a time I became a person of exotic interest to other boys. I would return to school like a mariner disembarking from some exciting piratical expedition, with strange glowing booty: a Lapland knife in its multicoloured leather-and-fur sheath; a brilliantly exciting board game of ice-hockey; a vast marzipan pig with chocolate features; a magically tilting wooden maze over which, like a minefield, you could steer a silver ball. Such treasures made me appear like a magician in those drab years and granted me an illusory popularity. 'Can we borrow your ice-hockey, Holroyd?' I can hear their voices still. I always said yes and was proud when my best friend 'Cuffy' Capron made an astonishing score on the tilting maze in the school sanatorium.

This was the best feature of my travels overseas: the popular return. For though I loved my mother and could imagine no worse calamity than her death, I never found a way of life that fitted her style and rhythm of living. The fact is *she was always lying down* when I wanted to be bounding around. Dawn, it seemed to me, was the right time for leaping up. But left to herself my mother would not get out of bed till nine or ten o'clock. It was an agony lying in bed and waiting for her to wake. And when she did get up she almost immediately *lay down again* to sunbathe. The least glimmer of the sun and she would *lie down*. Is there anything more tedious than sunbathing? In my view there was not. But my mother loved nothing better unless it was, after the sun had gone down, to dance.

My mother's dancing was not boring: it was excruciatingly embarrassing. She knew no shame. She would sing the tunes, kick up her heels, smile stupidly, drink all sorts of coloured drinks, make jokes in five or six languages. And she would dance. She could not be stopped. It was not beyond her to grab a waiter and propel him laughing round a restaurant. I saw her dance on tables too. I would close my eyes and long to disappear. It was then that I first determined to master the secret art of disappearing. But the penalty you pay for this vanishing trick is that your past vanishes with you. Now, as I bring those scenes back, I curse the terrible self-consciousness I felt that hardened into an inhibition preventing me from speaking the languages my mother spoke, and a paralysis that all my life has stopped me dancing, though I love to watch other people dance – indeed it is one of my vicarious passions. I rejoice now in the memory of my mother whirling about those floors and tables, but I could not possibly join in. All is in retrospect for me.

When she was surrounded by her family in Sweden, my mother was obliged to behave more formally. I was reminded of our large family gatherings at Easter or Christmas or on St Lucia's Day when I saw Ingmar Bergman's film *Fanny and Alexander* in the mid-nineteen-eighties. We preserved something of the same strict protocol of hospitality, the correct toasts and then the growing merriment and finally a soaring into surreal entertainment. It was all fantastical to me, for though everyone addressed me in English, they spoke fast incomprehensible Swedish among themselves. And then, though they were all introduced to me, my mind had somehow wandered and I did not know who most of them were anymore.

It was a relief to get back to London, even back to school sometimes. Coming up from Scaitcliffe to my mother's flat at Sloane Avenue Mansions, I would crowd my uncle's bat and pads into the hall, and eat up huge plates of bangers, beans and mash, followed by trifle and tinned cream – my mother knew what schoolboys liked. I did not realise that her 'cabin in the sky', as we called it, was rented for her by a man named Edouard Fainstain, nor that my mother was his mistress. She took me to meet 'Edy' and, what was most important, she borrowed his car, a sparkling blue Packard with an open 'dicky' or jump seat at the back in which I travelled dramatically in the sun and the wind. With this wonderful machine she would whizz down to Scaitcliffe, a blonde bombshell in a blue racing car, astonishing the other boys whose own mothers appeared so much older and dowdier. 'You were notorious, pitied and envied, because your parents were divorced,' my friend Christopher Capron remembered. I was the only boy at Scaitcliffe with divorced parents and after my mother began driving down on Sundays, I gained a certain status – Christopher Capron spoke of the 'rather daring wickedness' surrounding me. Once or twice I invited Christopher Capron or John Mein out to lunch with my mother at a rather grand hotel on Englefield Green. But she found it difficult to say anything that interested us, and we wandered around the gardens rather bored. Her notoriety was more potent from a distance. My great fear was that she might bring down Kaja on one of her visits to England. Occasionally she did this, causing me anguish over lunch when my grandmother examined the menu through an exquisite pair of eye-glasses held prominently by a single handle – 'my *lorgnette*' she called them. Another time, which was almost worse, she glared through an imposing monocle, looking like an aristocratic pirate. The embarrassment in case another boy, Bowman or Drummond, Palumbo or Stirling, should see this exhibition of adult eccentricity was agonising.

In 1948 Edy Fainstain was divorced from his wife Ida and on 25 February 1949, at the Kensington Register Office, he married my mother. 'Then things were O.K.,' she briefly noted in her account. She moved into a splendid maisonette on the top two floors of 24 Wetherby Gardens, a house once occupied by Viscount Allenby and round the corner from Drayton Gardens where I had spent my first couple of years. I was given a bedroom of my own and introduced to the first of my stepsisters.

Edy Fainstain was a Hungarian Jew whose father had been a farmer. For their honeymoon he took Ulla to Stockholm and, with his strong sense of family, was shocked to discover that she scarcely knew her father. He insisted that Kaja invite Karl to her apartment, and she absolutely refused. But nevertheless he still insisted, and so it went on over the honeymoon, this rally of obstinate insistence and absolute refusal until, to her own surprise, Kaja found herself conceding. She knew that, at some level of respectability, Edy was behaving correctly. And it would look so bad if, in however dignified a fashion, she went on refusing. Her own family liked Karl, or Kalle as they still called him. They thought him 'charming and colourful', a man of 'humour and humanity'. Did they blame her for his lack of promotion in the army? Everyone had expected him to be made a general, but his inability to impose harsh discipline was said to have been held against him. He had behaved better to his men, Kaja sometimes thought, than to her. He had not grown aggressively drunk with them. She knew that some of her family still believed that the marriage had been broken up by her own persistent flirting with men of higher rank. Of course it was absurd – was he not a flirt also? – but that is what they thought. It must have been difficult for her to telephone this man who, she had told Ulla, had made her life so awful during the late nineteen-twenties and early thirties with his demands for money, his venereal disease, his threats of violence. But perhaps she exaggerated his vices. Neither she nor my mother had seen him for over fifteen years, though he was living not far away with his second wife Marianne. But Kaja spoke to him, and he accepted an invitation to a cup of coffee at her apartment in Artillerigatan. Edy then went back to his hotel so that Karl could spend some time alone with his daughter. 'Pappa Kalle arrived – pale – drawn – nervous – with a bunch of red carnations,' my mother wrote. 'A very awkward hour – Kaja made it so. I felt sorry, but also quite a stranger after so many years. Kaja never sat still & kept looking at the clock & bringing up awkward moments in the past. I did my best & I knew he knew that. That was the last time I saw my father.' He was to die less than three years later aged sixty-five, at Växjö, on 14 December 1952. 'This chilly December day when Karl Hall's life ended seems very far from the idyllic warrior's life in the happy 1920s,' wrote the obituary writer in one of the Swedish newspapers.

> Now when we are all middle-aged, the officers and men and the young ladies of the ball, we treasure the memory of this chivalrous heartbreaker, Captain Hall . . . Yet in this moment of farewell one doesn't chiefly remember the carefree Kalle Hall from the balls and evenings of song, but the silhouette of Major Karl Knutsson Hall in the saddle after the company's hard day-long marches or night manoeuvres . . . The tall horseman has passed the last post on his journey.

His brothers and sisters and his widow went to the funeral at Växjö, and so did Ulla. But Kaja did not go. There was no mention of her among the mourners, or in the obituaries. From this time onwards she reinstated her own family name, calling herself Kaja Jagenburg Hall. Her husband had already been as good as dead for many years, and such was the annihilating force of her feeling that my mother sometimes echoed it. That was probably why, in her account, she had written that her father had died in 1945. It surprises me now that he was alive while I went on my trips to Sweden, and that I never met him. But I was not interested then in the past.

My new stepfather must have been a relief to my mother after her sequence of inadequate Englishmen. Edy was forty-five at the time of their marriage, some thirteen years older than his wife. He was the sort of person men instinctively distrust and women like. But I liked him, as all young people did. He gave the impression of having lived a generous life, not all of it respectable. On the marriage certificate, as his 'rank or profession' he put 'Company Director', the profession that had by then supplanted the rank of 'Gentleman' on such documents. He was a director, I understood, of several property companies; the owner, or one of the owners, of 'The Brief Encounter', a smart café-restaurant opposite Harrods, and an expensive furniture shop round the corner in Beauchamp Place. It was here my mother met 'a charming man' to whom she sold a *chaise-longue*. He was a Mr Haigh, soon to become notorious for a series of acid-bath murders. But that, as Kipling would say, is another story. Or might have been.

Edy had entertaining cosmopolitan friends: a white Russian; a much-photographed model; a radio scriptwriter; an actor. Jon Pertwee, a future Dr Who, came and sang to a small guitar, greatly irritating me. Was this the sort of performance you had to put on to get adults' attention? Was this what my mother admired? I despised his pattering jokes, his insistent strumming, and refused to smile or even listen, knowing I could never do such tricks myself. Edy belonged to a far more glittering world than any she had known in Beckenham, Maidenhead or Wilmslow. It was a world she thought she had been entering when she married my father – and very near his Basil Street showrooms and the hotel where they had spent their honeymoon. Among Edy's scattered properties was a villa called 'L'Oiseau Bleu' near the village of La Turbie, just above the Grande Corniche overlooking Monte Carlo. The world was opening up for my mother.

But it was beginning to close in for my father. He had married Marlou in 1948, having talked her and everyone else into believing that his ideas would liven up their publishing house in Paris. The ideas were good enough, but they needed money to implement them. 'Editions Begh went down the drain when the millionaire withdrew his financial help,' Winston Graham later wrote. 'If Marlou deserted him for your father, perhaps this is the reason.' Probably it was. By the beginning of the nineteen-fifties my father returned to England; Marlou eventually got a job with another publishers, Les Editions Mondiales, in the rue des Italiens; and their partner, the cool slim Marcel Brandin, accepted an offer from André Malraux to become his *chef de cabinet*.

There was one more family marriage in these years. My Uncle Kenneth, having escaped from his prisoner-of-war camp in Romania, had been captured once more and ended the war in a German prisoner-of-war camp. We saw him at Maidenhead again in 1945, terribly thin and ghostlike. But he had plenty of stories for us – stories of hiding in the Dolomites with Italian peasants; stories of living on a diet of turnips in appalling conditions; stories of death and friendship; stories of humane or inhumane commandants and guards – and the awful retribution afterwards; stories also of the ingenious methods he had picked up for passing time (he had even learnt, my grandmother was delighted to hear, how to play bridge). We listened to these stories with fascination at first and then, despite our valiant intentions, with overwhelming boredom. He was so nice, so quiet, so achingly dull. We were all experts in tedium and recognised a master. He took an infinitude of time to tell his stories and he told them in an unwavering monotone. Perhaps it didn't matter. We were all pleased to see him. But we felt that, after all he had endured, we really should keep our eyes intent, our heads set at intelligent angles, our smiles and frowns coming and going. Doing all this I almost fell off my chair, so overcome was I with drowsiness. The others were no better. My grandfather could hear so little, my grandmother never listened, my aunt could not keep still, Old Nan gave no sign of anything as these ghastly tales of war slowly unfolded before her, and my father, seething with impatience on his visits to us, tried unsuccessfully to insert some RAF anecdotes. As for myself I was mainly anxious to hold on to my uncle's bat and pads for my last cricket season at Scaitcliffe. Poor Kenneth!

My father's marriage to Marlou caused no surprise at Norhurst. He was known to be hopeless over women. First a Swede, now a French woman – my grandparents almost laughed out loud, and my aunt nearly joined in. But when Kenneth married, the same year as Basil, they fell back into tortuous explanations involving his long imprisonment (wedlock being in their experience another form of imprisonment). After all, as my grandmother reminded us, Kenneth was only in his mid-forties, 'no age at all for a man'. The infinite perambulations of his speech had not prepared us for such precipitate action. We were all thoroughly shocked, and went about the house tilting our heads, clucking our tongues and raising our eyebrows to the ceiling. In the family saga, Kenneth had seemed cast for a similar destiny to Yolande. Like her, he was on the verge of matrimony in the nineteen-thirties: and then it all went wrong. He was one of the admirers of 'Brownie' Hollway, the beautiful daughter of a distinguished Rajmai Tea director – indeed he appeared to be engaged to her. But when he introduced her to one of his younger aristocratic friends, she suddenly ran off with him and, at the end of 1939, became the Marchioness of Tavistock. That may have been one reason Kenneth was so keen to get abroad quickly in the war.

After he returned, having survived so much illness and danger, he found that Brownie Tavistock had recently died. And it seemed to us watching him, so frail and spectral, that his adventures must now be at an end.

He shared a London apartment at Nell Gwynn House with two ex-prisoner-of-war friends, one of whom got him a job in the Anglo-Iranian Oil Company. There was a strong bond between these ex-prisoners, quite a few of whom were to die within a year of one another from the same cause (cancer of the pancreas) brought on by their prison diet. Their reunions became a way of recovering the years they had missed. At their parties it was almost possible to believe that there had been no war and everything was continuing without interruption from the nineteen-thirties. Time itself was cheated and all wounds healed.

During one weekend tennis party at a house on West Heath in Hampstead, Kenneth met a woman in her early thirties called Sheilah Sayers. She was the widow of devil-may-care 'Mike' Sayers, a spectacularly good-looking and popular Irish sportsman and army officer who had been killed in an air crash at the end of 1943. When she met Kenneth three years later, Sheilah was living in St John's Wood with her two young sons. Mike Sayers had not been a rich man, but Sheilah was an heiress – one of the three daughters of William Lawrence Stephenson, founder and first chairman of Woolworth.

She lived pretty grandly in those post-war years with a resident cook, a maid and governess, a gardener, daily cleaning woman and half a boilerman whom she shared with the musician Sir Thomas Beecham. But what some of her suitors did not know was that her millionaire father disapproved of inherited wealth and had taken no steps to avoid the full rigour of death duties (then set at eighty percent).

Though she was beginning to put on weight, Sheilah was still a good-looking woman and it soon became obvious that Kenneth adored her. He seemed quite unlike the regular pack of admirers who escorted her to theatres and cocktail parties. He was not keen to spend her money – indeed he appeared embarrassed by their financial incompatibility. His gentleness too impressed her as romantic, and her two boys almost hero-worshipped him. But what really touched her was his need of her. Without her love, it appeared, he had no future.

We all went up for the wedding in September 1947 and there is a picture of us standing in a group before the Marylebone Registry Office. I am at one end of the front row wearing my light suit and dark shoes, gawky, smiling faintly but not knowing what to do with my arms. Also in the front row are my new step-cousins, Christopher (who has forgotten that he is being photographed) aged nine, and Michael (who is giggling) aged seven. Old Nan, whom they call 'Big Nan', looms hugely between us in her coat. In the back row my father, temporarily wifeless, is wearing his Old Etonian tie. Further along are Adeline, in a tall improbable hat, and Fraser, the very image of a storybook grandfather. The rest of the group is made up of Sheilah's family whom we don't know. At the centre are Kenneth, whom Sheilah's family all call 'Larry', looking handsome and serious; and Sheilah herself, a little wary in her brilliant silk dress.

But there is one figure missing. Yolande is not there. She was of course invited and I feel sure she went. But she has missed the critical moment, as she often did, as if it were another meal to be avoided, as if there were a dog to be exercised, as if the implications of it all were too painful.

At the far right of the wedding group stands Bill Stephenson, an active-looking man who is glancing across at the rest of us. He has just given his new son-in-law a cheque for £100,000 (roughly equivalent to two million pounds at the end of the century) to ensure that he will be financially independent of his wife.

Kenneth was to use this money in two different ways. After the birth of his daughter Vicky in 1950, he left Anglo-Iranian Oil and bought a 300-acre farm in Sussex, hoping to combine a healthy life for the children with a modest profit-making enterprise. But this romantic notion never really worked. The children loved the farm, but after the boys left it became more of a 'gentleman's estate', like a comfortable prison camp, where Sheilah grew fat and idle and shut herself off from visitors.

Kenneth used some of his capital to rescue Fraser who had been obliged to raise a double mortgage on Norhurst to pay my school fees. Kenneth paid off these mortgages, bought the freehold of the house for £2,750 and then handed Norhurst back to his father. He also bought back all Fraser's shareholding in the Rajmai Tea Company, invested in it himself and became a director.

So for a brief period it seemed possible to believe that the family fortunes were restored. At any rate my father felt optimistic enough to send me on to Eton.

14

Eton

I left Scaitcliffe at the end of the summer term in 1948 – in fact I left two weeks early. My father wanted us to travel together to the South of France for a holiday with Marlou. I resented this premature leaving bitterly, being unable to say a proper goodbye to my friends Christopher Capron and John Mein. My father, perhaps sensing this, presented John Mein with a wonderful French banknote. 'I miss Holroyd very much,' Mein wrote to his mother the next Sunday. I was almost in tears as I handed over a book on the Arab Legion as my farewell gift in the headmaster's study – that same study from where I had briefly brought the whole school to a halt with my howl of unhappiness.

About a year or eighteen months after I went to Eton, my father found he could no longer afford my school fees. He had almost bankrupted his own father who was gradually being raised to the surface and floated again by Kenneth. But this was a vessel without treasure and there was precious little more help to be salvaged from Norhurst.

In his novel *The Directors*, the character based on my grandfather, head of a business company (i.e. family), is accidentally killed through the inept financial machinations of a junior director. There is no doubt that my father felt uneasy over borrowing money from Fraser. But the very last thing he wanted was to remove me from Eton, as he himself had been removed. I must complete what he had begun. So he turned to my mother and her husband, Edy Fainstain. It cannot have been easy for him. 'Edy paid half your Eton fees,' my mother wrote. 'Edy loved kids so he gladly stepped in so that you could finish your education.' There is no mention of Edy's assistance in my father's account.

I soon noticed around this time that Edy was beginning to question me about the nuances of cricket. Were leg-breaks as painful as they sounded? Could you get far with long-hops? Were yorkers invented in Yorkshire? His middle-European accent combined with much gurgling laughter did not unsettle me as Kaja's *lorgnette* had done, and I did my best to respond to these overtures of friendship. But my answers were often lacklustre. I think we liked each other, but we belonged to different cultures and talking together was rather like walking uphill. We were soon out of breath, having run out of things to say.

To prepare me for my first summer at Eton my father had asked the greengrocer in Maidenhead High Street to give me a few nets while he himself made one of his last forays to sort things out in Paris. In the corner of a large field one evening, this greengrocer sent down a vicious outswinger that clipped the edge of my uncle's bat. Sparks seemed to fly in the dusk. He bowled again and I saw the bat, like an old ship in a tempest, begin to break up. There was nothing I could do – there never had been. By the end of my net practice my wicket was intact, but my uncle's bat lay splintered and demolished. The pads too were sprouting strange yellow and grey matter. On the way back to Norhurst, I heaved the wreckage on to a rubbish dump. It was the end.

My reputation as a chap who might force a draw from an impossible position had travelled to Eton before me, and I was immediately placed in the top game. What happened I have described in 'Not Cricket'.

> Approaching the crease in my gleaming new gear I seemed to be walking on air. Where was my ballast, my anchor? . . . My new bat wouldn't keep still. It sent the first ball I received for an astonishing four through the covers. I felt like apologising. After all I had done no more than contemplate a cover drive: the bat had done the rest. To the second ball it offered a leg-glance, and I walked off the field while the wicket-keeper righted my leg stump.

This was disappointing for my father. He had done his bit in the war and, when acting wing-commander, had worn a series of gleaming blue stripes up the arms and across the shoulders of his uniform and around his hat. Now he was a civilian again, he looked forward to reflected glory from my Etonian accomplishments. In his generous imagination, he saw me scoring for the Oppidans at the Wall Game, captaining the Field Game, distinguishing myself against Harrow at Lord's. I performed none of these noble deeds and there was very dim glory for him to bask in. I doubt whether my stepfather understood the enormity of my failure. Boys went to Eton in the hope of being capped with amazing colours, quartered or striped, and walking the streets under a halo of athletic glamour, shimmering with their cream blazers trimmed with blue, their high collars with butterfly ties, their exotic flowered waistcoats. They didn't go, for heaven's sake, to learn algebra, but to shine in this fancy-dress parade. However, I pretty well gave up cricket, never rowed, played almost no tennis (largely because I couldn't find the tennis courts), and never saw, let alone took part in, the famous Eton Wall Game. And I was no good at algebra either. Was I there at all? I sometimes wonder.

One of the troubles was my housemaster, R.J.N. Parr. There was really rather a lot of him, some sixteen stones approximately, all of it signifying very little. He was a portly, well-waistcoated and bespectacled man, and had a very red face. Everyone called him Purple Parr. He was rumoured to be some relative of Catherine Parr, Henry VIII's last wife, and was himself married to a very thin widowed lady from Ireland, Mrs Murphy, whose meagre glamour we occasionally glimpsed, but who took no interest in the house or its boys. Purple Parr, so far as we could discern, took only a remote interest in us. For a man of his bulk, he spoke in a curiously soft voice muffled by continuous catarrh. In the evenings, like some amphibious monster, he would glide quietly along the perspiring corridors, occasionally stopping, entering a room at random and lugubriously passing the time of day. These sudden appearances, their pointlessness, and the nasal snuffling that would sometimes erupt into hooting volleys of sneezes, were mildly disconcerting. By trade he was a mathematician, but he also took us for Latin in pupil room – a sort of homework. As a teacher he was uninspiring, as a housemaster damp and undynamic. His main interest appeared to be 'real tennis' as opposed to what he called 'lawners' – the sort of stuff they played at Wimbledon. He would sometimes introduce this or that arcane aspect of real tennis – the origin of the 'Dedans' or the significance of the 'Tambour' – as a means of initiating an informal conversation. He was, it now occurs to me, a shy man and probably insecure. He appeared more at ease with furniture than boys – indeed he loved good furniture. His long letters to our parents showed that he noticed far more than we realised, distanced as we were from him by his unsympathetic qualities of pedantry and snobbishness.

We felt more comfortable with 'm'dame', the house matron Miss Grieve, a cheerful woman with dumpy legs, who spent her summer holidays on the Isle of Wight. I only once saw her seriously rattled. At lunch one day I heard myself uttering the words: 'the caper sauce is capering, m'am'. The meaning of this remark, beyond its experimental play on word-sounds, I cannot now decipher, nor I suspect could anyone else at the time. But, caught unawares, and feeling that they must contain some impenetrable impoliteness, possibly even a profound obscenity (the food was certainly not good), Miss Grieve reported me for insolence.

Purple Parr was a comparatively new housemaster and had inherited his house in its vintage years. When I arrived in the autumn of 1948 it still possessed a tremendous reputation. The dining-room glittered with the trophies it had won on the river. At the centre of this display stood the magnificent Aquatic Cup itself, a proud mass of silver. But over my first year, as we were bumped or bravely beaten in one race, then another, these cups, shields, medals, honours were removed until we were left with nothing at all. We entered the nineteen-fifties, by popular consent, as the worst house in the school. This is no empty boast. I write with authority. For two years, despite playing no games, I was the Captain of Games; and in my last half, despite an indifferent academic record, I was also Captain of the House.

Carlton, Holroyd, MacLeod, Philipps, Valentine: those were the new boys in September 1948. Our parents came with us the first afternoon, and were given tea and cake by Purple Parr in the drawing-room which, on the other side of a green-baize door, was to be a world away from our ordinary life at Eton. They shook hands, these adults, joked and laughed, then slipped guiltily away. It was as we were standing around indecisively afterwards that someone said something to me. I jumped back, not being used to such attention (indeed having gone a long way in the last year or so to avoid it), then saw it was Philipps who had spoken to me. He still had some cake in his hand and was asking me about my uncle's bat. I recognised him. He was a large crouching sort of boy, with a round face, hawk-like nose, hanging arms and intent brown eyes. Through his feet most of my sparse totals had trickled on the occasions when Scaitcliffe played Sunningdale. I had seen him with cake in his hand before, at our tea intervals, and I remembered his alert yet curiously blank expression. He appeared to miss nothing, while taking no part in anything. I told him about my uncle's bat and he immediately understood. During a walkabout round the school on which Purple Parr led us early that evening, we got talking and I learnt that his parents, like mine, were divorced. Over the next five years Griffy Philipps became my special friend.

He called me 'Hagga', an odd name that caught on in the house to the extent of Purple Parr sometimes using it when he had drunk too much in the evenings. 'Dear Hagga,' Griffy writes to me, attempting after an interval of forty-five years to explain the derivation of this name. 'At the time you always looked, and indeed probably still do, though for other reasons, quite haggard. Also at that time I was reading the works of H. Rider Haggard (*She* etc.). Hence the name Hagga.'

Griffy came to believe that the catastrophic fall in our house 'from majesty to disrepair', combined with the unsupportive, discouraging nature of Parr himself, affected us all. Can there really, I asked myself, have been long-term consequences? Were we in any way exceptional, Carlton, Holroyd, MacLeod, Philipps, Valentine? One of us became an alcoholic, killed two people in a car crash, and died himself; one of us went to prison; one of us, perhaps the most fortunate, was removed prematurely from the house; one of us was informed in his last school report that he would never achieve anything worthwhile; one of us was striving to become invisible. I reckoned we were an average intake.

Having come from 'broken homes' and finding ourselves now

in a broken-down house probably did have some effect on Griffy and myself. 'I opted for a quiet life and studied *Wisden*,' Griffy wrote to me. He hardly does himself justice. He was the very spirit of *Wisden*, that bible of cricket, and the greatest scholar of the game I have met or could imagine. His command of bowling analyses, stretching over continents and back years, was breathtaking. Batting, too, in this respect, was no difficulty to him. I would have backed him in any quiz, and he was never dull. When he quoted statistics, they danced and sang for him. He spoke with a quiet passion and authority that touched even oarsmen and tennis players.

But no one bothered to encourage him as, over a short period, they tried to help me. Though Griffy knew everything about cricket, no cricketers knew about Griffy. Our Captain of Games in 1949 was Peregrine Pollen, a tall chap who looked like the Knight of the Sorrowful Countenance, and who later became a top man at Sotheby's. He wanted me to recover my cricketing status by turning into an experimental spin bowler. Under his tuition at the nets I invented a new recipe for the googly which seemed less risky for the umpire. My bowling was acknowledged to be unusual, but no legend adhered to it as it had to my uncle's bat. While I sweated at those nets with this mournful, kindly Don Quixote, Griffy, it now shames me to remember, volunteered to come along and field the balls that were clouted over my head. Fielding was all he ever did.

I made Griffy the hero of my essay 'Not Cricket'. The top game at Eton was played with frightful earnestness, but all the other games were circuses of misrule. I felt happy neither with the solemnity of the one nor the lawlessness of the others. Having no river-ambitions (I could barely float), I descended into what was contemptuously called a 'slack-bob'. But Griffy never gave up. He would be dispatched to obscure pitches on the edge of the school territory, yet his keenness and devotion to the game were never extinguished by the drudgery of his

experiences. In the evenings I would come across him oiling his
bat and turning over his arm against the day when he would be
invited to bat or bowl. That day never really came. One of the
consequences of his parents being divorced, I understood, was
that he didn't own a pair of cricket boots. But this didn't
matter in the games he played. Nothing mattered. 'They were
less cricket matches than exhibitions of anarchy,' I wrote in
'Not Cricket'.

> No one bothered if you turned up or didn't. Philipps
> always turned up early. Sometimes he had to wait almost
> an hour before enough people ambled along to make up a
> couple of scratch teams . . .
>   Philipps took his role as spectator to the centre of the
> field. He knew more than anyone there and he remained
> there, year after year, waiting to use his knowledge. I
> would see him in the summer afternoons setting off to the
> fields like clockwork . . . Possibly because of his divorced
> parents, he never got a new bat or pads or anything else
> during his five years at Eton. In a sense they weren't
> needed. Everything looked new: but smaller. By his last
> year all this miniature paraphernalia with which he stood
> waiting to try his luck looked Lilliputian.

While Griffy Philipps lay at anchor in the mainstream of
Etonian sport, I was carried off into an odd tributary. Avoiding
the conventionalities of team games, I would make my solitary
way down a long avenue of fives courts with their stone 'pepper-
pots' to a cluster of huts grouped in a shallow valley, like a
primitive African village. These were our squash courts. Squash,
unlike rackets and fives, was not a fashionable game in the late
nineteen-forties. It gets no mention in a well-known book on the
school called *Eton Medley* that was published in 1948, not even
in 'Sport', the longest chapter in the volume. But this obscurity

appealed to me. After a winter storm no one could feel quite confident that these hutches would still be standing. Usually they were for the most part, and I devised ingenious games of water-squash among the copious puddles.

Dominating this village were two superior courts. When their lights were turned on (a complicated business involving numerous keys and switches) they glowed like magic places. To see the illustrious senior players, you climbed up a wooden staircase and stood on a platform in the freezing weather viewing them through a wire mesh from above – like opera-goers standing in the gods. I venerated the Keeper of Squash, Ian de Sales la Terrière, whose exotic name seemed to add lustre to his elegant play.

Ian de Sales la Terrière, who later played for England, was influenced by the great Egyptian player, Open champion of the world, M.A. Karim. In fact, we all were. Karim wore long, cream-white flannels and he gave this sweaty, thundering, claustrophobic game a quiet and classic beauty. While others laboured, gasped, pounded around the court, Karim stretched and stroked the ball this way and that. He had what all legendary figures must have: he had mystery. His style masked his intentions so cunningly that, however hard you studied him, you could never tell whether it was a lob or a drive, a deft reverse-angle or a tender drop-shot that was coming. We were like children watching a magnificent conjuror.

I modelled my style of play on Karim, though not being very strong, I was obliged to hold the racket very high up its handle, and was much criticised for this eccentricity by the master in charge of squash, Dr Lefevre. Nevertheless, despite my handicap, I thrived. Players with the smartest of Etonian names, Colin Ingleby-Mackenzie, Richard Williams-Ellis, eventually fell before my blade. Though I made a speciality of losing very brilliantly, I went on to win the public schools under-fifteen cup, and then in 1951 the British Open Junior Championship for under-sixteen-year-olds.

This was not of course a triumph on the playing fields of Eton where the Duke of Wellington was reputed to have said the Battle of Waterloo had been won (and where, according to George Orwell, the opening battles of all subsequent wars were lost), but it was something my father could enjoy. He liked telling me of a famous Egyptian player of his day called the Amr Bey, Open champion in the nineteen-thirties. His deadly lob, so altitudinous, so accurate, was unreturnable, my father boasted. He was of course speaking up for his generation, but it sounded as if he were playing the shot himself, and I was sceptical. Karim, I told him, was in a different sphere. He made even the finals of the world championship, I explained, look like exhibition matches. I used to go and watch him play at the celebrated Bruce Court at the Lansdowne Club off Berkeley Square, where all the major championships were held in those days. His victories rose above national pride. I felt delighted that squash possessed such a miraculous player and would come away from his matches exhilarated as from a ballet at Covent Garden or a concert in the new Festival Hall.

In 1951 a rumour began buzzing round the squash world of a remarkable new player from Pakistan named Hashim Khan. I was in the gallery of the Bruce Court when Hashim met Karim in the final of the Open that year. In his dazzling flannels, Karim glided and stroked the ball everywhere, and Hashim ran hectically after it. Often he ran in the wrong direction. But it didn't matter since he seemed able to change direction in mid-air. It was obvious to me that no one could go on running like that and not collapse. I felt sorry for Hashim. What happened however was that Karim collapsed – not physically, but morally. What was the purpose of out-thinking, out-manoeuvring your opponent if he still won the point? The game was reduced to a simple test of speed and stamina. Hashim won the match 9–5, 9–0, 9–0.

The impossible had happened. I could hardly credit it. But perhaps it was a freak of history. Next year the two of them met again in the final to decide the future of squash rackets. I saw the first game proceed very much as in the previous year. But in the second game Karim made the supreme effort and they reached seven all. I had never known anyone run as Hashim ran. He dived and swerved and hurled himself around this way and that, always smiling cheerfully, and sometimes when he was completely outplayed breaking into laughter. Karim played with agonising beauty. The wonder of his stroke-play was beyond anything I could conceive. There was such wit and grace, eloquence, ingenuity in those strokes. I cannot explain the happiness they gave me. They made squash an aesthetic pleasure where thought and movement were one. There were gasps from the gallery at the mesmeric combination of these rallies, first the delicate potency of Karim's play, then the impossible retrievals of Hashim. I can see again Karim's dazzling figure moving so easily about the court, embodying something vital to me. But he lost 9–5, 9–7, 9–0, gave a small bow as he left the Bruce Court, and never returned.

It was the end of squash for me. The game was changing and so was I. As I became less competitive and more of a joker, I switched to the unserious (though rather dangerous) game of doubles and actually helped to win the Public School Doubles and then, partnered by a future amateur champion, Nigel Broomfield, the Palmer Cup, a doubles competition for under-twenty-one-year-olds. This may not wholly have satisfied my father, but for eighteen months, as Keeper of Squash at Eton, I was able to join the margin of that Vanity Fair up and down the High Street wearing a dark blue cap with crossed rackets stitched in gold at the front, which mystified the 'lower boys'. Yet the glamour of this position, which appeared so bright when Ian de Sales la Terrière occupied it while I was still a junior boy myself, seemed curiously to dissolve like a mirage once I reached it. I had however scored a satisfying technical victory over Dr Lefevre. The new Open champion, Hashim Khan, held his racket as far up the handle as I did. I had wandered briefly into fashion.

No sooner had I achieved this particle of glory than, it seemed to me, my father turned his mind to graver matters. I think it must have been shortly after he appealed to my Hungarian-born stepfather for half my school fees that his character appeared to change. 'We need to have a serious talk, Michael,' he said to me gravely one day at Norhurst. I braced myself, as we entered the gloomy morning-room with its lurking telephone, for what I assumed would be another attempt to explain the facts of life to me. But on this occasion it was the economic facts of life my father wanted to explain. The family fortune, such as it was, had gone down the drain, he told me, and I could expect an inheritance of serious debts. It was essential therefore that I wasn't a damn fool. I mustn't fritter away my chances. I must use my education to prepare myself for a modern business life. Being out of work himself, he had been thumbing through advertisements for jobs in the newspapers and seen how huge the demand was for plasma-physicists, chemical engineers, radiologists and other scientific people. He wished to God his own father had spoken to him as he was now speaking to me. I would thank him later – not that he wanted thanks, not that he had ever received thanks for anything. No. Never mind that: it was probably too late for him. But it was not too late for me to become a plasma-physicist or whatever. I must specialise in the sciences if I knew what was good for me.

This was a bleak prospect. My instinct recoiled from all my father was saying, but I had no arguments to marshal against what appeared to be his formidable common sense. To my mind school was something you got through as agreeably as possible. My father, in his concern for me, made adult life sound so appallingly grim that I averted my mind from it. I had little sense of school being a factory which trained you for some profession, or of exams being used for money-making – and nor, I believe, had many of the masters. Of course I knew that I would have to begin a career sometime, but that belonged to another chapter in my life, and who could tell how that would eventually be drafted? My father despaired at the impracticality of my attitude, and I lamented over the impracticality of his anxious planning. But though I trusted to my instinct to direct me in due course, I agreed to my father's schemes because I could offer no plausible alternatives. Besides, I knew that once I had agreed I would hear fewer cautionary tales from the business world.

So I returned to Eton and, from the age of fifteen or sixteen, specialised in arithmetic, biology, botany, chemistry, geometry and physics – with a little astronomy thrown in at night. Over the next two years, my days became filled with a maze of logarithmic tables, geometric angles, and a blackboard covered with algebraic signs and letters that needed to be solved. I can remember vividly the dead frog, saturated in evil-smelling formaldehyde and crucified on a wooden block, at which I picked with my scalpel each week, identifying bits and pieces of its body. From among the bunsen burners with their firm blue and orange flames, and between the array of retorts, flasks and pipettes with their coloured powders, liquids, gases, I can see the exasperated face of our Czechoslovak teacher appear, like a pantomime demon, as he tried to beat back our happy ignorance with eruptions of barely intelligible English. Occasionally, too, a few of us would climb to the top of a remote school building after dark to gaze blankly at some blob of light in the sky and solemnly utter its Latinate name. I believed that I had some interest in astronomy, but it lay in the lure of the unknown, the mysteries of time, the question of our origins and the problem of our destination, rather than this recital of named stars. In short, I was a poor science pupil. But then my teachers were poor.

The Head Master when I arrived was Claude Elliott. 'Elliott did not neglect education matters,' writes the most recent historian of Eton, Tim Card. This was fortunate in a schoolmaster.

He was later knighted for 'services to education', though 'few headmasters have been more determinedly not educationalists'. He was perceived by us to be a kindly and cautious man, rather deaf, somewhat dull, and known by some of the masters as 'Muttonhead'. His influence on the school was far less marked than that of the most outstanding housemaster Oliver Van Oss, an energetic man with some interest in the arts, who bustled about the streets catching our attention, but who failed to catch the attention of the Fellows in his bid to become Head Master himself.

At the beginning of my second year, Claude Elliott was appointed Provost of Eton and a new Head Master arrived. This was the historian and social scientist Robert Birley who was reputed to be a blazing socialist and nicknamed 'Red Robert'. Some of the masters felt apprehensive over this new Head Master. When ripples of their fear reached us, we began whispering among ourselves how he would make early school half-an-hour earlier. The fact that he was coming from Germany (the Labour government having appointed him educational adviser to the military governor in the British Zone) seemed to make him a hostile figure. In fact, he turned out to be a liberal-minded Conservative voter whose red politics were later attributed to a portrait of Johannes Brahms in his office having been mistaken for Karl Marx.

With his white hair and stooping gait, I thought of Robert Birley as an elderly man and am shocked now to discover that he was only forty-six when he came to Eton. I occasionally heard him lecture and realised he was an inspired teacher. But the general quality of teaching at the school, in so far as I experienced it, was fairly lamentable. Worst of all was 'Bloody Bill' (H.K. Marsden), a tall, bent, grim-visaged, churlish, prying mathematics master with a relish for power and a devotion to the theory and practice of corporal punishment. He terrorised generations of boys and was disliked by everyone except a few favourites. But some Old Etonians, having survived the tyranny, later found themselves congratulating him on that fact.

More amiable, though hopeless as a teacher, was 'Hojo' (William Hope-Jones), another mathematics master who had spent almost all his life at Eton. In 1902 he had appeared with Maynard Keynes in a school performance of *Much Ado About Nothing*. After three or four years at university, he then came back to Eton as a master. By the time I arrived in his class he had been teaching there for over forty years and grown into one of those gnarled 'characters' around whom cluster stories that vastly amuse people without much sense of humour. In Tim Card's chapter 'Eton between the Wars', he appears as a celebrated oddity who won boys' hearts by his eccentricity and goodness. 'Was there a more imaginative teacher of Mathematics in his day?' the author asks, '. . . many boys who were not natural mathematicians were glad to be up to Hojo.' But I am not one of them. He was in his mid-sixties by the time he taught me and seemed almost out of control – of his subject and of us. Perhaps, poor man, he was ill. In any event, Eton was no longer between the wars and, though he hung on, Hojo's day was past.

Among the other masters was Tom Brocklebank whose 'difficulties' we attributed to his once having become stuck near the summit of Everest; 'Leggy' Lambert, the Lower Master (later Vice Provost), who used his desk as a kennel during thunderstorms; and Babington Smith who marked our papers out of ten thousand instead of ten.

But there was one teacher I admired. Sydney Watson, our precentor and musical director, was afflicted with such an insistent stutter that some people who heard him utter his full name in public believed he had a knighthood. But his passion and zest, his sheer skill as a choral conductor, turned this terrible hesitation into eloquence. He was known to us as 'Daddy Watson' and, as he led us through the complexities of Haydn's *Creation*, Bach's *St John Passion* and Handel's *Messiah*, through songs by

Brahms and Vaughan Williams, Stanford and Parry, making the rough places plain, it seemed indeed as if he were our father and we, of the Eton College Musical Society, his family. The ECMS was the only society I joined, the one 'team' I played for. We sang in the evenings at a schoolroom in the Eton Wick Road. It had steeply-banked rows of desks up which Daddy Watson would leap and round which he strode, encouraging us, correcting us, explaining, expounding, exemplifying, sometimes tapping his baton to prevent us going off the rails, then urging us on again. I did not read music but, holding the sheets in front of me, I could see roughly where the notes went, could pick up a tune, follow a narrative; and so for some four years as treble, alto, tenor, bass, I belted it out, giving my best, feeling my best.

On Sunday afternoons, I used to sneak off to the Music Schools with Michael MacLeod. We weren't really allowed into this building, not being proper music students, but no one minded us occupying a room with a piano if no one else needed it. Over some weeks, we 'composed' a piano duet that, beginning with a pastiche of chopsticks, went on for almost eight minutes. We were proud of this marathon, but having nothing more in our musical vocabulary to add, wisely forgot about it when we returned from our holidays. But my recollection of it now, when so much else is forgotten, marks it as an emergence from my musical beginnings in the garage at Norhurst. Certainly Daddy Watson gave me a wider liking for music, and after fifty years or so I can still summon up a few of the songs we sang, and startle friends with an odd line or two.

I had been at Eton for two or three years when one night, sometime after midnight, Purple Parr opened the door of my room as I lay sleeping and told me to come to his drawing-room. As I put on my slippers and dressing-gown I remember wondering whether one of my parents had died. But when, a few minutes later, I stood before him, Parr began asking me in a solemn voice a series of innocuous, almost meaningless questions. Who were my friends? Did I have friends in other houses? When did they come and see me? Or did I go to their houses? And so on. After half-an-hour of this surreal interrogation, he told me I might return to my room. When I woke next morning, I thought perhaps it had been a dream. But I soon found that a number of other boys had been taken from their beds and similarly questioned. What was happening, we concluded, was a homosexual inquisition or purge.

Was there homosexuality at Eton? Well, of course there was. Romantic passion and amorous speculation hung in the valley atmosphere of the place, and seeped into our imaginations. With almost 1,400 teenage boys closeted together in some twenty-five houses, how could there not have been infatuations and intrigues, spiced with exciting rumours over who was 'gone on' whom? Boys exchanged signed photographs of one another as marks of favour, and would send each other complex paper knots containing confidential messages which were delivered from house to house by fags scampering through the streets. These running figures seemed to match the palpitating hearts, the breathless tension and suspense, of the correspondents. Our hours were steeped in vague delicious daydreams and pleasurable scuffles on the floor in the evenings that might turn at night into masturbatory fantasies. To all our emotions there was a rhythm that seemed to change with the changing seasons. In the schoolrooms we read poetry that, though filtered through sanctioned translations from dead languages, told of exquisite friendships and carried erotic signals from the past. But we were very much alive and curious as to how we might translate these sentimental stories into present-day adventures. Surely this, in addition to the taking down of Latin Unseen and the recital of gender rhymes, was part of our education? We wanted to live our literature for, as Cyril Connolly wrote in *Enemies of Promise*, 'a schoolboy is a novelist too busy to write'.

In the scandalous twentieth-century novels of public school

life, from Alec Waugh's *The Loom of Youth* (1917) to Simon
Raven's *Fielding Gray* (1967), there is a potent homosexual
ingredient, sometimes disguised, often unenacted, that is nevertheless sensationalised by athletic brilliance, or exploited by the
system of fagging and the habit of boys legitimately beating
younger boys (the very rare beatings by housemasters were inter-
estingly called 'screwings' at Eton). There were, of course, tides
of fashion in homosexuality (we never used the words gay and
lesbian then), and to the general reader one period may seem saturated with it, another quite arid. But we rely on accounts which
have been written either by some of nature's celibates or by
those who were very sexually aware. In earlier days, when some
unmarried housemasters would bestow long kisses on tolerant
boys in their rooms after lock-up, a general unawareness of sex
may have made emotional life simpler. 'Women did not play a
large part on the Eton scene,' concedes Tim Card in his survey of
Eton from 1860 to 1990.

> . . . It would seem that sex may have caused increased
> problems between the Wars . . . Most Housemasters were
> constantly on guard against any physical sexual
> activity . . . Boys were left in little doubt that they would
> be sacked . . . The adult world was still officially very
> hostile to homosexuality, but among the boys it was
> recognised that romantic friendships were natural.

Purple Parr sent my father a letter warning him that I should
be careful of the company I kept. He must have written to a
number of parents about this lurking peril of 'keeping company'.
Evidently something dramatic had happened and a hunt was
on – I think one boy may have been sacked. This was something
that must have taken place every few years. But my father was
astonished. He braced himself to do his duty and informed me
that homosexuality was 'worse than . . .' Here he paused, trying

to be fair, yet still dramatic. '. . . Worse than burglary.' I would like to think that he coined the phrase 'buggery is worse than burglary', but I cannot honestly say he did. It was all made more difficult for him by having to voice his dismay down the telephone while I was staying with my mother in London. I remember him whispering that during his time there had been 'only one queer at Eton' and he was pretty odd – no one had liked him. My father was whispering because he did not want my stepfather to hear of this scandal, and his whisper made everything sound additionally dark and dreadful. In Norhurst style, he continued lowering his voice on the telephone until it grew hard to pick up his plunging syllables. What he had to say, as it became more buried, also became more infernal. He had instructed my mother not to breathe a word of this affair to her husband, but in order to bring home to me the gravity of it all, he also instructed her not to take me to the cinema while I was in London. My mother, however, was unable to take Parr's letter quite so seriously. For about thirty seconds or so she attempted to show concern, then we went off to see a film together (with me swearing never to breathe a word of this to my father).

We were all in a muddle because no one had decided how much sex-life should be allowed between boys of fourteen to eighteen (many of whom without sisters knew no girls at all). In fact nothing had really changed at Eton in the thirty years since Cyril Connolly was there. In 1920 he had found himself among those boys who were floundering through on 'surreptitious experiments' that were suspected by the masters and would have led to his expulsion if they had been actually discovered. Eton, he came to believe, encouraged 'continence officially and homosexuality by implication'. This tantalising suspension of the emotions, with all its intensity and irresolution, fixed many public schoolboys in perpetual adolescence.

Nothing had changed: but much was about to change. Things simply could not go on like this. Those of us who left Eton in or around 1953 were impatient for the better life that was to begin ten years later 'between the end of the Chatterley ban/And the Beatles' first L.P.'. Though this change came a bit late for us, our impatience was, I like to think, a necessary preparation for this change, a hammering at the door.

Though midnight interrogations and solemn letters were high points of anxiety, my main anxiety over the first three years at Eton was figuring out how the place worked. The streets were busy with boys hurrying from one place to another as if they instinctively understood the choreography of the system. Perhaps I too looked like this as I walked along. But I had great difficulty finding out, keeping up, arriving at; and for years afterwards I was afflicted with exhausting nightmares of following people and losing them, of failing to reach some destination and never discovering what it had been. When Purple Parr, making his amphibious progress through the damp corridors, glided into my room one evening to describe his shame at having a Captain of Games who apparently played no games, I was sympathetic but could not bring myself to explain that I did not quite know how these games were arranged, or even sometimes where they were played. No wonder, as Griffy Philipps observed, I looked haggard.

But in my last year I found there were some blissful advantages to this ignorance. For if I was not quite all there, as it were, perhaps I would not be noticed; and if no one noticed me, then I was free to do as I liked; and if I did what I liked surely my anxieties would evaporate. And they did. There were penalties to be paid for this style. If you affected a forgetful air, you soon found yourself forgetting things you would have preferred to remember. But as a way of avoiding trouble it seemed to suit me well enough, though it meant I avoided other things too.

At the beginning of one half in my last year a boy I had known at Scaitcliffe, Nicky Winter, came to see me. He told me that he had suggested my name for 'Pop', the élite Eton society to which my Uncle Kenneth had belonged. No one, he was able to report, had a word to say against me. In fact, no one had anything to say at all. Between legendary appearances on the squash court, I seemed to disappear and was unknown. However, if I would put myself about a bit, Nicky Winter said, and make some effort, he might perhaps get me in at the next election. It was a kind gesture and I was tempted to do something about it. But I found that I was unable to do anything. It was as if I were already programmed for invisibility and could not reverse the process.

There were to be other symptoms of this process, such as the vanishing of blatant facts and events. I have no idea where I was when President Kennedy was assassinated or Queen Elizabeth crowned; I do not remember my army number; I do not know what examinations I passed or failed at school. Of course I could find out about the exams, but perhaps the truth is better conveyed by not doing so. For I have never been questioned about my qualifications and nothing in my career has depended on them. I do remember that I had the choice of going up to either Oxford or Cambridge (though I cannot recall to which colleges), and that this was partly based on interviews.

My one anxiety during this last year at Eton was how to escape my father's generous plans for me. I simply did not want to be a plasma-physicist. During the holidays, I had continued my intermittent and alternative education at Maidenhead Public Library and become convinced that I was more at home in the arts. One evening at Norhurst I tackled my father, blurting out that I could not go up to university and read science – I really had no talent for it. He gave a long sigh and entered the battle. We argued quite violently into the early morning, and my father, by brute force of speech, appeared to demolish my carefully-prepared position – though I continued to defend it with desperate obstinacy.

Much of what my father said was true. Many people had

made sacrifices to send me to Eton, he reminded me, and now I was proposing to throw it all away. Very well. He could not stop me. But perhaps I would be kind enough to inform him what I was going to do – other than live off other people all my life. There was, of course, one practical alternative open to me, and it was an index of my thoughtlessness that I had not mentioned it. He was referring to the Rajmai Tea Company. This was a fine business, he would not deny that. But if I wanted to go in that direction it would mean my travelling out to Assam and starting at the foot of the ladder. Did I have the guts for this? Did I have any guts at all? If I had he would do everything in his power to help me. He would have a word with my grandfather in the morning and set the wheels in motion. I was lucky. Not every boy had a second chance like this. I had only to say the word. When I mentioned that I had been tentatively thinking of taking up writing, my father sat back and laughed. It was not a happy sound. No one, he assured me, would prevent me writing. How could they? My evenings and weekends on the tea plantations of Assam would be my own, just as my school holidays had been. Perhaps I already had some masterpiece in my pocket. He would very much like to read it. He really would. Meanwhile we had better come down from 'Cloud Cuckoo Land'.

I hardly slept that night and felt wretched in the morning. But my father, who had been so triumphant in the night, also looked drained. His tone was now altogether different. He told me that he had hit on a solution to the problem. If I could argue so persistently why shouldn't I take up a profession that paid me to argue? He meant the law. Many of the Holroyds had been lawyers, so perhaps their genes were shaping my destiny. I had probably left it too late to read law at university, but I could become articled to a firm of solicitors. He knew some solicitors in Windsor and would make inquiries if that was what I wanted. The relief between us was palpable, and I welcomed his suggestion gratefully. It would mean postponement of my National

Service, but that was no disincentive. I had little desire to go to university because I had little notion of what life there might be like. In any event, it seemed beyond my range. What would I do there? I was not attracted to the idea of reading Classics; I had never heard of the humanities; and besides my father would certainly not have paid anything to see me waste my time on such subjects. Later, it seemed to me, I had been shut out of Eden and that everyone at university was clever and in love, and the sun always shone there. Later still, I reacted from this sentiment and congratulated myself on the advantages of having so little to unlearn. Now, I see the advantages and disadvantages as more evenly spread.

There was a strange postscript to our night of argument and morning of reconciliation. For, although my father had dominated the agenda, one of its eventual consequences was to be our collaboration on a history of the world in verse – which really was entering 'Cloud Cuckoo Land'.

For the last few months of my time at Eton I left my dead frog in its formaldehyde haze and the bunsen burners with their orange and blue flames, left my logarithmic tables and blackboard algebra. But what was to replace them? I asked Purple Parr whether I could study English Literature. There were not many boys who did this at Eton and Parr, not liking to take the risk, shook his head. It would hardly be appropriate, he thought. I had heard there was a subject called Psychology and I asked him about my chances there, which gave him the opportunity of explaining that I didn't have the brain for it. Eventually it was decided that I should start Spanish (and resume French) in my last half. From this new language I retain just one phrase, 'Que lástima!', which sums it up.

But it was during this last half that I came across a genuine intuitive teacher among the masters. This was Peter Spanoghe, a name that does not appear in the volumes I have read about Eton. He was not one of those caricatures, like 'Bloody Bill' and

'Hojo', garnished with stale school jokes. There is no obituary of him in the *Eton Chronicle*, and none of the Head Master's files of that time survive. Nothing exists about him beyond a note that he arrived in 1934 and taught German and French. Yet he was a remarkable man. He lived in Willowbrook, was married to a beautiful woman in a wheelchair, was himself partly disabled and walked with a pronounced limp. He was nevertheless one of the most active people in the school. He taught me French – and suddenly I was top of the form. Spanoghe knew no boundaries and we moved easily between French and English literature, from the past into the present and back again. Before this, French had been taught to me as a dead language; English was presented as a set of grammatical rules and obstacles; history a procession of dates and battles, kings and treatises. Spanoghe changed all that. He was quick-witted and made it all fun, made it easy. Somehow he engaged me in the subject so that my feelings were involved, I came alive and no longer felt slow. This was the magic of teaching, and no sooner had I glimpsed it than it was time for me to leave.

I left Eton at the end of 1953, and Peter Spanoghe himself was to leave a year later. I heard a rumour that he was involved in an affair with some girl and I was told that Pamela Spanoghe was divorcing him. Eton was still ludicrously sensitive about such matters (only ten years before, the Provost had informed a housemaster who married the innocent party in a divorce case, and whom he had met only after the divorce, that he was a habitual adulterer). I caught sight of Spanoghe one more time, at a delicatessen in Chelsea during the mid-fifties, but was stupidly too shy to go up and thank him. He must be long dead now. Looking through the telephone book, however, I see there is a P. Spanoghe listed as living in Chelsea still, and suddenly it becomes a matter of urgency to contact him. I telephone: but there is no answer. Then I write. But I am too late. He died a few months earlier, his widow tells me, and so I have missed him again.

What I would have thanked him for, besides his teaching, was a letter he wrote to Purple Parr which was forwarded to my father. Though he lost it, he was impressed by the notion that I was rather a promising tortoise. It also had some influence on Parr himself, 'I agree very much with Spanoghe's letter,' he wrote to my father.

Michael has indeed a critical mind and its full value will probably not be appreciated for a long time. Indeed, it is in some ways a handicap at the moment. He is still very much an observer of life, even though he cannot detach himself completely. He sees more sides to a question than most schoolboys and is slow in decision because he genuinely wants to be right rather than merely expedient . . . He is neither a disciplinarian nor a rebel, and much of his work as Captain of the House must have seemed to him not right or wrong, but merely petty . . . He is not nearly (thank goodness!) at his peak yet: his honesty, determination, shrewdness and sensibility will come into their own when he has become, as inevitably he must, a little coarser-grained.

Parr's previous reports had emphasised rather less appealing aspects of what he called my 'doubtful temperament': my nervousness, indecision and egocentricity. He thought, though I cannot recognise this in myself, that I was swayed by superstition ('he lacks robustness against omens!'), and told my father that I had a disbelief in ultimate success that I communicated to others – though this, I think, reflected Parr's own disbelief in my success. But after reading Spanoghe's letter, he gave a far more amiable interpretation of these qualities. 'He has been exceptionally mild, but not thereby ineffective,' Parr wrote. 'He has been respected and liked by all classes . . . I could have wished that he had, in his Eton life, ventured further outside the house.

But he kept to his own ploy and was in consequence little known. From those who have known him he has always earned golden opinions . . .'

My mildness, and the ripples of popularity it briefly spread, can be accounted for by a decision I made to discontinue house beatings. I did not announce this as a new policy (not being a rebel), but simply beat no one. This was unusual in the early nineteen-fifties, but I got away with it because it became the practice almost before anyone noticed.

In his last letter to my father about me, Purple Parr described himself as 'a friend who has now known and liked him a long time'. But over five long years he had been unable to communicate this friendliness. His shyness, detachment and egocentricity (qualities I saw in him curiously similar to those he saw in me) put him beyond my reach, and beyond the reach of other boys.

A year after I left Eton, in the autumn of 1954, I wrote to Purple Parr asking him for information that the Law Society needed relating to my registration as an articled clerk. In the course of my letter I mentioned that I was writing a book. 'I imagine [it's] a novel,' he sighed. '. . . I should think at least one leaver every half writes (or at least begins) a novel in his first year away. You wd certainly be surprised at the number who have from my house.'

This characteristic, slightly discouraging comment was to gain unexpected irony a few years later when David Benedictus published his *succès de scandal*, *The Fourth of June*. Benedictus, who had also been at Purple Parr's, was three years younger than myself. Like me, he became Captain of the House and abolished beating. But by then Parr's was once more becoming a brilliant athletic house. The dining-room glittered again with silver cups and shields, and the dull brown and mauve quarters of his house colours excited admiration on the playing fields. One consequence of this new climate was that David Benedictus had a more awkward time than I did, and was not permitted the same 'mildness'. His novel, written partly in reaction to these difficulties, is a satire that shows up Eton as a totalitarian city state of snobbery and sadism. 'It is inevitable in a book of this kind that some lonely person somewhere will imagine himself portrayed,' he wrote in a careful preparatory note. '. . . care has been taken to avoid such portrayals.' In the novel itself the word 'lonely' is applied to the calculating pusillanimous housemaster, Manningham, and, despite the care taken to convert him into an imaginary character, no one who reads the book and knew Parr can fail to recognise some borrowings. Parr himself read the book in 1962 and was obviously affected. It was adapted for the theatre and, around the time we all saw it in London's West End, he suddenly died, leaving us with very ambiguous feelings of regret.

15

Legal and Military

My first half-dozen years after leaving Eton were strikingly indecisive. They began with two minor operations. The first – to correct some complications in my right knee caused by squash-playing – was counted a success (though it actually masked an injury that led to more serious damage years later). I was given a general anaesthetic and stayed several days in hospital. It was the first time I had been in hospital since having my tonsils and adenoids out as a child, and I was taken aback by how much the experience disturbed me. In the ward men lay groaning, men lay dying. Between the rows of beds marched a starched army of nurses with glinting thermometers and watches, and among them moved a clattering rabble of cleaners and kitchen staff wheeling their trolleys. They looked exceedingly happy, often stopping and laughing among themselves, overcome with hilarity, as if unaware of the sounds of pain and fear all round them, as if they were somehow inhabiting a parallel world where these ranks of sick people were invisible. I could not believe what I was witnessing. I felt I was in hell. After my operation I told the ward sister that I wanted to discharge myself and complete my convalescence at home. But during those early years of the National Health Service, patients were not moved along like a fast-moving queue of 'customers' or treated as expensive 'consumers' to be 'targeted' with medicine; and the practice was to keep them in hospital until the doctors were confident they had fully recovered. The ward sister told me not to be so stupid and, as a precaution, hid my clothes. But I found them, dressed myself, hopped out into the night and took a taxi back to my bedroom at Wetherby Gardens where I felt much better.

It was in this bedroom that I went through my other operation – a succession of primitive and painful clearings of the nasal sinuses by an ear, nose and throat specialist called Miss Wadge. She would stick a thin metal instrument right up my nose, above my eye, and pump sterilised water through it for an hour. After half-a-dozen visits, I was cured of sinusitis. Not long afterwards I suffered the first of a long, though not frequent, series of migraines in the very place where Miss Wadge had been needling me. Perhaps unfairly, I have always associated my migraine attacks with her operations.

Around this time, and in the same bedroom one night, I had a frightening experience that enables me now to tell a miniature non-fiction ghost story.

It is a wild night, reader, and a storm has blown up slashing the sky with rents of lightning, with tremendous bangs and rumbles of thunder. I am at the top of the house and my attic window suddenly opens. The wind frantically agitates the glass panes, the curtains streaming in, and the commotion of the storm outside wakes me. I hear the window shivering, see the curtains flapping, the rain driving in, and feel a strange coldness in the room. Perhaps I have woken from a nightmare. Certainly I feel odd and cannot tell for a few moments whether I am really awake or asleep. I take my arm out of the bed and stretch over to turn on the bedside light so that I can get up and close the window. The thunder roars and crashes. Then, as my hand reaches the light switch I feel another hand fixed upon it, a damp, cold, unattached, inexplicable, horrifying hand. My heart gives a thump, I force the terrible thing away and switch on the light, dreading what I will see. What I see is my other hand which has completely 'gone to sleep' and through which I can feel nothing. I am my own ghost.

In later years I have had three or four similar experiences. An animal, perhaps a snake, maybe a rat, lands dramatically on my chest in the middle of the night a second after I have woken. I start up and fling the brute away, but it immediately lands back on me and I cannot get rid of the monster, whatever it is. What it is, of course, is my own absolutely senseless arm I am wrestling with in the dark. For some moments, without the circulation of life, it is a terrifying experience.

Eton had gradually become the most secure of all my living places, and I missed the friends I had made there, Griffy Philipps, Michael MacLeod and a few others. I continued shuttling between Maidenhead and London, Sweden and France. I was travelling to France not with my father now, but my mother. We used to speak of L'Oiseau Bleu as our villa in the South of France, though it was little more than a stone shack with a glorious view of Monte Carlo from above the Grande Corniche. I hated it. I could do nothing with the view or anything else. In my opinion there *was* nothing else – nothing that interested me. I was scared of the frogs, lizards and scorpions that leapt and scuttled about my bedroom, and I disliked the wearisome business of carrying water each day from the village of La Turbie, a mile away. While my mother lay in the sun, I wandered around doing silly things like falling down a mountain, climbing a tree and making myself ill on unripe figs, or simply getting severe sunburn. I was an awful nuisance.

Eventually my mother suggested that I invite my friend Griffy Philipps to join us. We met him at Ventimiglia railway station just over the Italian border, and he stayed three weeks. 'Apart from some alarm about scorpions,' he writes to me, 'nothing very controversial happened.' But it was much better doing nothing together than alone.

On another occasion Kaja came with Birger Sandström who smoked a wonderfully long cigar and wore dazzling co-respondent's shoes. Edy brought his daughter Gay, and we all stayed in a hotel at Antibes. Gay was a couple of years older than I was, and something of a tomboy. Together, in great excitement, almost hysterics, we put on an excruciating 'entertainment' of music and recitations, through which everyone was politely obliged to sit.

On 16 April 1954 I began a five-year term as an articled clerk. The solicitors to whom I was articled, T.W. Stuchbery & Son, had their offices at the corner of Park Street in Windsor. So I was still very close to Eton, though my new life was a world away.

Messrs T.W. Stuchbery & Son had never entertained an articled clerk before and appeared to have little notion of what to do with me. I was technically articled to one of the senior partners, Ian Hezlett, a Falstaffian character of uncertain temper who had been a drinking companion of my father's (signs of his beer-drinking could be detected after midday on his extravagantly frothing moustache). But I saw little of him in his grand office on the first floor after our initial encounter together with my father. 'We'll start him on tort,' Hezlett announced. 'Donoghue and Stevenson.' My father laughed heartily, and I looked blank. Then I was sent up to a modest office under the attic where a thin, bent, sun-starved, middle-aged solicitor called Mr Owen worked, encircled by papers. An extra desk was moved into his office and I sat at it. I was also equipped with blotting-paper, pen, pencil and rubber. And that was it. All I did in the first weeks was to practise making tea and coffee. But gradually, over the months, my duties were extended. I released Mr Owen from some of his imprisoning papers, filing them in the shadowy attics crammed with documents tied in faded pink string, and covered with dust. Occasionally Mr Owen, who was a well-intentioned if unexciting man, would take me to the County Court in Windsor to sniff the legal atmosphere, and I would sit out the long days there. On one of my first visits, trying to keep awake during the afternoon, I unintentionally released from a large metal radiator a fountain of tepid water over some witnesses. I could not tell afterwards whether Mr Owen was amused or appalled, but I noticed that he began giving me increasingly odd jobs out of the office and would question me quite keenly when I got back as if hungry for some specks of entertainment. I was able to tell him how I had been shot at while attempting to serve a writ (the marksman taking aim through a caravan window as I approached, waving a white handkerchief, across a field), how I had accidentally been locked into a huge fridge among various carcasses which belonged to a litigious butcher who was, I felt, exaggerating the oven-like qualities of his cold storage. Apparently encouraged by my misadventures, Mr Owen saw to it that Stuchbery's craziest clients, those in search of therapy rather than legal opinion, were sent up to me for consultation. I daresay that many country solicitors, before the widespread use of psychiatry, provided such services for those who could afford them. I remember one elderly woman who used to come in fairly regularly complaining of nudity among her neighbours. At twilight, she confided, and at even more revealing times, they would dance in the garden and were, she concluded from the noises she heard at night, tunnelling under her house. I made notes on my pink blotting pad, gave her some of my tea, and eventually prepared an invoice in mock-legal jargon which I think she appreciated.

My worst offence occurred in London during a complicated divorce case. I had made a summary of the husband's and wife's letters to each other – something of an education for me – and was allowed by Mr Owen to attend the court hearing in London. But the case took an unexpected turn while Mr Owen was in the lavatory, and our Counsel, murmuring to the judge that he needed to take fresh instructions, turned to me. By the time Mr Owen returned, the case had been adjourned and the disgruntled parties found themselves still married.

I did not know what I was doing. What I was meant to be doing was reading law under Ian Hezlett's supervision for some of the time, and working in his legal practice for the rest of the time. In those Dickensian days, articled clerks were not paid salaries, but actually paid the solicitors to whom they were articled. This was not an obvious solution to our financial problems, though my father persuaded himself that it was an astute investment. At the beginning of my second year, acknowledging that I was receiving no training or tuition, but simply doing errands for Mr Owen, Ian Hezlett decided to pay me a modest wage. My father, ever the optimist, interpreted this as a promotion rather than surrender, and for a brief period allowed himself to feel almost happy at the way things were shaping.

The only point of law that was explained to me at Stuchbery's was one that involved a snail in a bottle of ginger beer. 'Do you know Donoghue and Stevenson yet?' Ian Hezlett called out to me one day on his way to the pub. Then it was Mr Owen's turn. 'May I recommend that you peruse the case of Donoghue versus Stevenson?' he said seeing me gazing out morosely at the buses which went one way to Dedworth, the other to Gravesend. 'How are you getting on, young chap?' a visiting solicitor quizzed me. 'Mastered Donoghue and Stevenson have you?' I mastered nothing else, having received the impression that if I got the hang of this famous snail which had gone in its bottle all the way to the House of Lords to establish the manufacturer's duty of care, then I would have cracked the legal code and all would be well.

The most cheerful aspect of my legal career was that it deferred my two years' National Service. But eventually I could endure the pointlessness and boredom no longer. I simply could not credit that people spent their lives shut up in such gloomy buildings, counting themselves lucky as they shuffled through old papers from Monday morning to Saturday lunchtime day after week after year, with only an annual fortnight's holiday, until the long holiday of retirement and the permanent vacation of death. It seemed awful, but then I was intensely lonely, having lost touch with my companions from school and being unable as yet to replace them.

There was at the office a girl who lived on a caravan site which I used to pass in the bus that took me each day from Maidenhead to Windsor and back. She was in her early twenties, slim, dark-haired and with glittering eyes that shone and flashed in my imagination at nights. Was it only in my imagination that she seemed to be making some signal that we might see each other outside the office, in the evenings or at weekends? I will never know. In those days it was difficult for a girl to take the initiative in a relationship, and I was handicapped by poverty and paralysed by shyness.

From these legal experiences I was later able to add to my family's foreboding of bankruptcy my own writer's apprehension of libel. But the only law that genuinely interested me was criminal law, and that is less an interest in law than in human nature. After eighteen months at Windsor, I braced myself for another confrontation with my father. 'I am not angry because you don't like the law,' he wrote to me.

> I am angry because you are apparently prepared to chuck it up without an effort. The world is not an easy place & I don't want you to miss the boat.
>
> I have met hundreds of men of my own age who are down & out in life and the story is always the same with

slight variations. They are men of good education who
because of indulgent parents never settled down to any
job . . . Heaven knows, I don't want you to hate your
work, but I don't want to see you a drifter – for I have
seen only too often the mess they make of their lives.

My father promised me that I would hate the army even more
than the law. A legal qualification, he argued, would be my best
insurance policy. 'Your life must be more competitive than mine.
If you pass your examinations you still have a big pull over the
others because you were at a Public School, but not unless you
can back it up with the necessary qualifications.' He stressed the
awkwardness of reneging on my articles, but if I was determined
to chuck the law then it would be better, he told me, to join the
army as a regular soldier rather than a national serviceman. 'At
46 years of age you retire with a lump sum or pension.' Then I
could afford to write books. 'You don't know how hellish life
can be if you get on the rocks,' he warned me. My father was
then, I calculated, forty-six. 'Had I had a firm hand to guide me
when I was young I would have been in a damn sight better position in life to-day.' But, he concluded, if I would not continue
with the law, not join the regular army, I must simply go my own
way.

Things might have been a little easier if I'd known that my
grandfather had left Gray's Inn in 1900 without taking any
examinations. But though I was still living at Maidenhead, he
said nothing to me. In any case my father would have seen this
precedent as being out of date. Nevertheless I would not have
felt unique in my record of failure as I terminated my articles
and, going my own way, prepared for two years' National
Service.

Conscription had been introduced after the Second World War
partly as a reaction against Britain's military unpreparedness

during the nineteen-thirties. Both the Conservative and Labour parties supported it, and it was popular among the majority of older civilians and ex-servicemen. By the end of 1955, when I joined up, two years' military service (followed by three-and-a-half years in the reserves) seemed a natural part of growing up though, since women were exempt, it prolonged the unnatural segregation of the sexes.

'Some of you,' Captain Carlton-Smith announced to our group of raw recruits, 'will be lucky enough to see active service!' There was a titter of disbelief and general air of incredulity. Few young men objected to military service on conscientious grounds because few of them thought they would actually be called on to fight. Ten years after the end of the war, we were still in a state of stunned reaction. Over the eighteen years of its existence, though 395 national servicemen were to be killed in action, parents did not regard National Service as dangerous until the Suez Campaign of 1956. It was generally spoken of, rather vaguely but quite sincerely, as a training for life – something that developed the character, allowed many young chaps to see a bit of the world, made them physically fit, and gave them an opportunity of finding out where their talents lay. It conferred none of these benefits on me.

I joined the Greenjackets because my Uncle Kenneth had been in the Greenjackets. That was how the army worked in those days, at least among its officers. The Greenjackets were barely tolerated by the battalions of Guards, but looked down their noses at the line regiments which in turn were contemptuous of the Royal Pioneers and the Education Corps, which hated the whole lot of us. And the regular soldiers despised the national servicemen who thought the regulars slightly mad. Such was our comradeship. It was, I now see, very much like Britain's education system and operated as a means of keeping separate the various classes and categories in the country. I applied for a Russian course in Cornwall as an alternative to serving in the army, but after the mid-nineteen-fifties this was discontinued. So when I was summoned to Winchester for my basic training, I went like a lamb.

But the Greenjackets at Winchester were not expecting me. There had been a mistake and I was that mistake. The adjutant studied my papers critically and asked me why I had not arrived with the regular intake. I did not know. He was not best pleased, and being uncertain what to do with me, eventually ordered me to 'clear off back home' for a fortnight.

Something similar was to happen at the end of my ten weeks' basic training. The Ministry of Defence suddenly noticed that my mother was Swedish, and decided that this called for an investigation. So while everyone else went on to their next posting I was held in limbo at Winchester with one other national serviceman (who was suspected of having tuberculosis). The barracks were suddenly empty and for two or three weeks there was positively nothing for us to do. We went once or twice to films, stared pennilessly at girls in the street, lay in the sun on St Catherine's Hill overlooking the town. We even managed to commandeer a Land Rover and, with my new friend at the wheel, patrolled the summer countryside. These days, being timeless, have remained with me. But suddenly one day I was ordered to proceed *soonest* to Chester. I never discovered whether my friend had TB.

I was to spend sixteen weeks under the improbable shadow of the Officer Cadet School near Chester. Eaton Hall was a 'Wagnerian palace', as Nikolaus Pevsner described it, with intricate Gothic pinnacles and grandiose battlements, that had once belonged to the Dukes of Westminster. The lodges, chapels and stables, the lakes and neglected rose gardens descending to the River Dee, had been dramatically transformed to cater for the peacetime goings-on of our amateur infantry with its bustling captains and bristling sergeants. Jeremy Isaacs, who was there at the same time as myself, recalls that one of our sergeant-majors was called Blood and another Leach; and that the Regimental Sergeant-Major was Lynch. 'Much gallows humour resulted.'

Eaton Hall was the sort of fantastical place where my late Great-Uncle Pat, the innocent Major of the Militia, might have enjoyed performing manoeuvres and parades. But I did not enjoy the platoon marches and marathons, the kit inspections and fatigues. 'Training consisted of drill with spit and polish,' Jeremy Isaacs writes, 'firmly, but not ferociously insisted on; giving lecturettes; planning and leading field exercises.' Jeremy himself made a brilliant night attack on a group of boulders that he believed were the enemy. I landed in a swamp, sinking with my bren gun up to my shoulders. On Sundays we headed for the comforts of Blossom's Hotel in Chester to forget our humiliations of the week.

Because of my deferment as an articled clerk I was older than most of my fellow officer cadets. Griffy Philipps and even Christopher Capron and John Mein from my Scaitcliffe days whom I might have seen again, had all finished their National Service. I found some boys who had been junior to me at Eton were now my seniors at Eaton Hall. My smiles of recognition often went unanswered. I had become an anachronism. But I did not fall seriously out-of-step until I finished my officer training, was given the rank of Second Lieutenant, and had the good luck to miss active service.

It must seem odd that I became an officer. At the War Office Selection Board near Andover I had not performed well. I used the wrong method of getting a log over a stream and, using arguments of unassailable ingenuity, reached an incorrect con-clusion in the written examination. But I had achieved all this error and misjudgement with the aid of proper grammar and the right accent. So, between ends and means, I was an awkward case. Everything depended on my lecture. I spoke on 'Sense of Humour' without a single joke. It was an intimidating perform-ance (extensively cribbed from George Meredith's lecture 'On the Idea of Comedy and the Uses of the Comic Spirit', and also from Harold Nicolson's little book *The English Sense of Humour*): and it worked. For what I was really being tested on was not, fortunately, my military skills, but my acting abilities. Could I convince other ranks that there was no danger in the trenches, that we personally hated the enemy, that our cause was glorious and everyone else's vile? On the strength of my 'Sense of Humour', the War Office Selection Board decided that I could. But I had not passed with distinction and was to be transferred from the Greenjackets to the Royal Fusiliers, at the request of the Greenjackets.

Before I joined my new regiment I was granted three weeks' leave. It was the autumn of 1956. I remember going to John Osborne's *Look Back in Anger* at the Royal Court Theatre and watching many of the red-faced audience leave in the interval. I also went to Ingmar Bergman's sombre film *The Seventh Seal*, and during the Pathé News was surprised to see several of my colleagues from Eaton Hall gesticulating blindly from the screen. Their trapped expressions, like zoo-animals', stared vacantly down at me, while the commentator described the embarkation of the Royal Fusiliers to Egypt. National servicemen, as well as the regular army, were being 'given the privilege of serving their sovereign' by recapturing the Suez Canal from Colonel Nasser.

There spread through me a sense that something was wrong. Surely I should have been up there on the screen instead of in the stalls? That evening I telephoned Griffy Philipps and tried to make a joke of it. 'Will they shoot me?' I laughed. He considered the question far too long. 'I should think, Hagga, that they would grant you a court martial,' he replied, 'first.' Fifteen years later I wrote an account of what happened for B.S. Johnson's National Service anthology *All Bull*.

Next day I telephoned my adjutant ostensibly on a small matter connected with dress . . . Cutting across a detailed

query on buttons, he demanded to know 'where the hell' I
was. Did I realise I had missed the war? I was to put
myself under close arrest and escort myself to the Tower
of London . . .

I arrived at the Tower of London later that morning
and, standing to attention, was cross-examined by two
senior officers. Why, they asked, had I not responded to
the urgent telegram summoning me to active service?

I spent the night in 'Napoleon's Room' at the Tower.
The following day, unexpectedly, came a reprieve . . . It
appeared that the adjutant, in the heat of war, had
addressed the telegram to himself. In the circumstances
there was little they could do, except have me up on the
minor charge of being improperly dressed.

'You are wearing the wrong buttons, Mr Holroyd.
Kindly take a week's Orderly Officer.'

However I was not yet out of trouble. The *News Chronicle*
that week reported that the Union Jack on the Tower of London
was flying upside down. This was certainly news to me since I
did not know that the Union Jack possessed an upside down. Yet
as Orderly Officer, I was responsible. I think they were happy at
the Tower to see me leave at the end of that week. I can still hear
the voice of one major who had the job of deciding what to do
with me. 'Take a walk, Mr Holroyd,' was his solution. The tone
of the sergeant who presented himself in my bedroom one night
after I had failed to turn out the guard was more alarming.
Snapping on the light, he took three paces forward, came to a
crashing halt and after sharply saluting me as I lay in bed,
shouted out: 'Permission to speak, sir?'

I had been posted to Connaught Barracks on the heights of
Dover cliffs which the Royal Fusiliers had left when setting off
for the Suez Canal, and which was now filled with refugees from
the abortive Hungarian uprising against Soviet occupation. After

my recent misadventures, I was morbidly anxious to get things right. But it was not easy. For example, I had been told on the Saturday night to report on Monday morning in Dover wearing 'mufti'. This featured a bowler hat. I did not have a bowler hat. In desperation I called at Norhurst on the Sunday and retrieved from the garage a very old bowler which my Aunt Yolande had once sported. 'Crowned with this, like a small black pimple at the top of my head, I descended properly dressed upon Dover,' I wrote in my essay for B.S. Johnson.

> My instruction had been to make the refugees 'feel at home' on the cliffs. This was not only vague, I discovered, but a euphemism. For my job actually consisted of juggling with inadequate supplies of light bulbs and contraceptives so as to ensure that those Hungarians occupying unlit barrack rooms were protected with French letters, while those left unprotected were bathed, like battery hens, in a permanent glare. The supplies were to be alternated each night. After a few weeks the Hungarians went forth and multiplied.

So ended my first year in the army.

During my second year I perfected the art of being over-looked. Previously I had unwittingly drawn attention to myself by being in various ways out-of-step. Now I used my wits to camouflage myself. At first I had been nonplussed by military terminology – the practice, for example, of indicating a tree by calling it a 'bushy-topped object at four o'clock', which seemed to me a complicated method of attaining soldierly simplicity. I was bemused, too, by the exaggerated way of walking called marching, by the barking out of curious sounds called orders, by the loss of privacy in the general hubbub and frenzy. I decided not to try and analyse all this commotion but to copy, even car-icature it. I watched what the others did and then did it myself, starting a fraction late perhaps but doing it slightly quicker. I positioned myself in the middle rank, towards the middle, and was gratified to see that people were finding it increasingly difficult to pick me out. I always answered with a shout to a number, not a name. I was losing my identity, fading from notice, and feeling all the better for it. When alone, I equipped myself with a board to which I attached some sheets of paper. Carrying this, and a short swagger stick, I hurried round Connaught Barracks after the regiment had returned from Suez, looking urgently at my watch and studying the blank sheets of paper with an expression of severity. It was obvious I was up to something pretty important. I would strut, ostensibly from one significant place to another, though actually from my bedroom back to my bedroom, occasionally calling out the words 'Carry on!' to groups of soldiers slightly beyond earshot. One day, while I was standing alone in the Officers' Mess, someone opened the door, looked round the room where I was standing, and shouted out to some people behind him 'No one here!' And I knew I had achieved my ambition of becoming invisible.

In the army I trained hard as a non-volunteer, shooting up my hand barely too late for everything except the job of Orderly Officer during Christmas and other regimental holidays when the barracks would empty and there was again positively nothing to do. The guard had to be inspected of course, but these were the years of IRA quietude, and there wasn't anything to guard against. All was quiet. The adjutant at Connaught Barracks was a man in his thirties called Dick Jones. He was something of an intellectual but, in the manner of T.E. Lawrence, wanted to change himself into a man of action – and was to die tragically young, climbing a mountain in Wales. He lent me his collection of gramophone records and, while the regiment went on leave and I was alone, the Officers' Mess on top of Dover cliffs was filled with the sound of Sibelius and Nielsen symphonies – to which I later added the Swedish composer Franz Berwald to make up my Scandinavian trio. These musical intervals are what I remember most at Dover.

The problem I gave the army was not so different from the one I had presented my grandparents. What were they to do with me? I found myself appointed Motor Transport Officer despite being unable to drive and could, I believe, have awarded myself a driving licence instead of waiting till my mid-thirties. I also became 'Mess Officer', a phrase that quite accurately describes my catering skills (the Royal Fusilier curries were indistinguishable from the innocent fruit salads that usually followed them). Also, for a season on Salisbury Plain, I was appointed ADC to our Brigade Commander, the formidable-looking Brigadier Bernard Fergusson (who had himself been ADC to the legendary General Wavell and written a biography of him).

Despite his ferocious appearance – a flashing monocle and rampant yellow moustache – Bernard Fergusson was a civilised, literate man. Discovering that I was a reader of books and dreamed one day of being some sort of writer, he engaged me in conversation about James Elroy Flecker and Siegfried Sassoon, and then invited some writers he knew – Peter Fleming the travel writer, and the novelist L.P. Hartley – to dinner so that I could meet them. I was very nervous on these occasions and once poured the Brigadier a sherry and soda instead of his whisky. But L.P. Hartley gallantly rushed to my rescue, claiming that he had distinctly heard Fergusson demand sherry and soda. I read his novels with additional admiration over the following weeks.

When Peter Fleming came to dinner, Fergusson invited me to bring along my friend Anthony Howard who became spectacularly drunk by the end of the evening. On leaving the house, he accidentally put on the Brigadier's hat instead of his own. Spotting his sudden promotion when we got back to camp, we then spent the rest of the night employing all the military tactics we had been taught (short of bayonet drill) smuggling the Brigadier's hat back and retrieving his own. Anthony Howard was the only other national serviceman in the battalion addicted to the reading of books, and his company and conversation were a great support to me. There was between us an unintentional rivalry as to who was more ill-adapted to this peculiar way of life – a contest, I believe, usually settled in my favour.

It was my job to get Bernard Fergusson to the place of military action each day on Salisbury Plain. But such were my map-reading skills that we never witnessed a single hostility. Fergusson was marvellously patient, but sometimes his exasperation broke through and once, approaching midnight, miles from where we should have been and still no warfare in sight, he insisted that I come to a halt and give him some salutes.

The last months of my army career were unorthodox. While the Royal Fusiliers retreated to Sutton Coldfield, I was dispatched to a department of the War Office in Colindale, on the northern perimeter of London. Here, with one other national serviceman called Smout, I tackled the vital task of redundancy. These were early days in the amalgamation of regiments and the rundown of the army – 'streamlining' it was bravely called. National Service itself was soon to end. Smout and I divided the country in half and went through the applications from all field officers. Some had applied to continue their military careers, others wanted to accept the money that was on offer for early retirement and enter the priesthood, run a toy shop in Slough, start an egg farm in the Hebrides. We would read through these applications and, knowing what percentage of these officers would have to go, make our recommendations. One of the names that came before me was that of the Colonel-in-Chief of the Royal Fusiliers. He was not a popular man, partly because he owned a brightly-coloured cat called Cooper which, many officers thought, made the regiment look ridiculous on parade. At night the Colonel would emerge from the Officers' Mess and call: 'Coopah! Coopah!' And various subalterns concealed in the bushes would miaow back. Our Colonel was one of the officers who left the army and I later heard he had got a job as television critic on a new fascist weekly.

My knockabout career through the army was crowned with the honorary rank while in charge of redundancy of temporary, acting, unpaid Captain. It all seems more entertaining to me now than it did at the time, and has left me with a weakness for Gothic fiction and barrack-room farce. Then suddenly, after what had felt like a life sentence, it was over. But during the next couple of years, one of my Royal Fusilier colleagues with a genius for practical jokes (he once removed my entire bedroom and reassembled it with the bedside lights shining prominently on Dover cliffs) would telephone me in the early morning and, in stentorian tones, announce that, because of the crisis in Algeria, Cuba, the Middle East, or even Notting Hill, all National Service reserves were being called up: and for a few blurred moments the horror would return.

In *All Bull* B.S. Johnson was to conclude that 'the Army itself did very well out of National Service'. When the book was published in 1973 I sent a copy to Bernard Fergusson who, as Lord Ballantrae, had recently retired as Governor-General of New Zealand and been appointed Chairman of the British Council. He replied: 'National Service may or may not have been a good thing for the nation; it was a bloody awful thing for the army . . . [it] dried up regular recruiting almost entirely: men didn't want to join something voluntarily when it was compulsory for others.' He also deplored the amalgamations of the English line regiments and the formation of 'Big Regiments' without territorial identity, in the initial stages of which Smout and I had been employed. Then he apologised for this 'out-pouring' and thanked me for his 'honourable mention in dispatches', adding: 'You could have had much fun from making me look a real Charlie, instead of just a benevolent old blimp.'

In 1980 I saw him at one of the Literary Society's dinners at the Garrick Club. He was then in his seventieth year and his wife had recently died. He looked pale and fragile, a ghost of the terrific brigadier I had known. We laughed over our exploits as a British Don Quixote and Sancho Panza twenty years before on Salisbury Plain. Then he went out into the night, and I read his obituary not long afterwards. I remember him with gratitude as the first person after Peter Spanoghe at Eton to give me genuine encouragement.

16

The Third Mrs Nares

Although the nineteen-fifties was an indecisive decade for me, my mother was making plenty of decisions. One morning while I was still working as an articled clerk in Windsor, she telephoned me to say that she had discovered her husband Edy had been having an affaire with Mrs Hanbury, a tenant on the first floor of Wetherby Gardens. I was surprised by this news and felt curiously disappointed. Frances Hanbury's husband Ronnie was a writer of radio scripts for a famous comedy team, Ben and Bebe Lyon. I enjoyed these programmes but could never believe that Ronnie Hanbury, a peculiarly unfunny man, had written them. 'His wife was a voluptuous blonde by daylight,' Griffy Philipps reminds me. 'With the benefit of hindsight and having read one or two books by Iris Murdoch, I suspect that Mrs Hanbury was much taken by you . . . As an Etonian of that era you were alarmed, and took great pains to enter the front door so quietly that Mrs Hanbury would not delay you.'

It was suddenly clear to me that Griffy's assiduous reading of contemporary novels, though alerting us to a real drama, had seriously misdirected us as to its plot. It was not for me that Frances Hanbury was waiting, her ears alert for the telltale click and muffled crash of the front door, but for my stepfather Edy Fainstain. I had been tiptoeing round the house quite pointlessly. And though I had felt a tremor of alarm at what Griffy insisted were Frances Hanbury's advances, I now felt deprived by the knowledge that she had no romantic interest in me at all. I could have done with some of her delay.

'What shall I do?' my mother suddenly asked. She seldom took any action during the nineteen-fifties, however ruinous, without first asking my advice. But it was awkward giving advice over Mr Owen's telephone in Windsor, with Mr Owen himself standing humbly by me, though his office was packed to the ceiling with valuable precedents. The quality of my advice, its timbre and sheer slowness of delivery, had gained me an odd reputation for maturity. I would pause a good deal and produce a series of noises in my throat that conveyed gravity and experience. My silences, hedged around with an air of pondering wisdom, sounded powerfully deep. When I did speak I used 'whereas' and 'nevertheless' and 'on the other hand' pretty freely. While I was putting on this performance, the other person would usually make it clear what he or she wanted to do – and I would then triumphantly chime in with that conclusion.

What my mother wanted to do, rather to my surprise, was to divorce Edy and start another chapter in her life. Perhaps it was the presence in Wetherby Gardens of Mrs Lupu Fainstain, clothed in black, that had unsettled her, since Edy felt it right to give his mother priority over his wife in most things. But I suspect that Ulla already had her next chapter sketched in and was eager to get on with it. The decree nisi was granted on 25 January 1955 and made absolute in the second week of March.

They had been married almost exactly six years. My mother was now aged thirty-eight.

While these legal matters were proceeding she took off for Stockholm, arriving back with enough kronor in her handbag to pay for several weeks at the Royal Garden Hotel in Kensington. This became her habit: vanishing into Sweden during emergencies and then reappearing with these handbags of kronor – until eventually Kaja was to die a poor woman.

A dozen years after the war people in Britain were just beginning to recover themselves financially in preparation for the good days to come in the nineteen-sixties. But we had gone down too far to recover. Even the richest of us, my Uncle Kenneth who had 'married money', left only £45,000 at the end of the nineteensixties. The rest of us had become a species of distressed, not-so-gentle folk, downwardly mobile, indeed charging downhill, led nobly by my grandfather. He was to leave £6,000 in the early nineteen-sixties, having been given more than this amount by Kenneth. My mother, it is true, left £40,000 in the mid-nineteeneighties, but this included Kaja's estate and the flat in Chelsea I had recently completed buying for her. When I sold the contents of my father's rented flat in 1988, they fetched less than £50 altogether.

My mother made two more telephone calls to me at Stuchbery's that year. One was to tell me that Edy had suddenly died of a heart attack (Griffy wanted to know whether Mrs Hanbury had been with him). I could tell she was genuinely distressed, feeling perhaps a little guilty, at least regretful. Edy died in France. There is no mention of my mother in his Will, and I am surprised to see that he left only £28,000. Some years later, when passing through the South of France, I went to see his gleaming white grave in the cemetery at La Turbie. High in the Alpes Maritimes, overlooking the Mediterranean, such a glorious site I thought was appropriate for a good property owner. And if I could have said this to him, I think I might have heard his gurgling laughter again.

My mother's other telephone call was to tell me she was marrying once more. Her third marriage was celebrated at the Chelsea Registry Office on 12 May 1955. She wore 'a Dior dress of pink and black silk organza and black velvet' according to the evening newspapers. The marriage was widely covered by the national press and there were also reports of it in Sweden. This was partly because my mother had recently begun modelling clothes for the dress designer Charles Creed, having shown the spring fashions that year for the Incorporated Society of London Fashion Designers to Queen Soraya of Persia. The marriage was additionally newsworthy because she was marrying the son of a famous actor-manager.

My new stepfather, David Nares, was a forty-one-year-old advertising executive who managed 'the Martini contract' for the Crawford Agency. He was the son of Owen Nares, a celebrated 'matinée idol' between the wars, and star of several silent films – melodramas and romances such as *The Sorrows of Satan*, *Young Lochinvar* and *The Private Life of Don Juan*. In his *Who's Who* entry, he listed only one son, but there was another, David's younger brother Geoffrey. He had been homosexual, and died in Cairo from a tumour on the brain during the war. Looking back, it seems clear that David was anxious to suppress a somewhat feminine strain in himself. He liked firing off reverberating letters to the *Daily Mail* and *Sunday Times*, calling for a stronger British 'fighting force' against the red menace of Soviet Russia, or cursing young people in modern society for expecting something for nothing. 'Let us roll up our sleeves,' one of his letters exhorts readers, 'and get down to hard work.' He himself was a hard drinker and would sometimes roll up his sleeves at dinner when explaining how alcohol was a necessary solvent in his line of business. This was his third marriage, as well as my mother's. He had a very pretty daughter, Caroline, who had been distantly educated round Europe and was to be one of the last débutantes presented to the Queen. A picture of

my new stepsister at the front of the *Tatler* at the age of seventeen shows her already beginning to dress like the Queen
Mother, as many young girls with their matching accessories
dressed before the nineteen-sixties. Nevertheless, the few times I
saw her she appeared so dazzling that I was simply unable to
speak, and when she invited me to her coming-out dance, I did
not turn up.

For the first year of their marriage my mother and stepfather
lived in Ennismore Gardens, near the Brompton Oratory in
Knightsbridge (it was the same street in which Edy Fainstain had
kept a secret apartment for his meetings with Frances Hanbury).
They then moved to Turners Reach House on the Chelsea
Embankment. Their ground-floor flat, with its wonderfully theatrical split-level drawing-room looking out on the Thames, was
directly below the apartment where George Weidenfeld gave his
famous publishing parties, and was itself bought, my mother
later told me, by the filmstar Sean Connery. She was entering,
she believed, a world of glamour.

'MODEL TO MARRY. SHE WILL BE THE THIRD MRS NARES' ran a head-
line the day before my mother's marriage.

Ulla Hall is a statuesque blonde from Stockholm in her
early thirties who was visiting England just before the
war and stayed here. During the war she drove an
ambulance. She took up modelling a few years ago and
appears regularly in the collections of the Top Twelve.

According to this Stockholm beauty, who divides her
life between the two countries, it is easy for a Swedish girl
to model English clothes 'because we Swedes wear suits
and tweedy things like the English women'.

This girl with her cool Nordic look would be at home
practically anywhere. She speaks French, German, Italian
and Swedish, and is now learning Spanish.

Ulla plans to continue modelling after her marriage.

This article, about a woman who has never been quite 'at home' even in her homes, is a good reminder for biographers not to accept newspaper information naïvely, or to rely on sources where the code of ethics forbids the revealing of sources. My mother, who was actually in her thirty-ninth year when she married David Nares, enjoyed a career of three or four years modelling for Charles Creed who had a fashion house behind Harrods, at the opposite end of Basil Street to my grandfather's Lalique showrooms. There are pictures of her showing clothes to the Royal Family in the nineteen-fifties, and as one of the 'Twelve Smart Women' selected to display British *haute couture* at Lancaster House. 'The blonde Mrs Nares has a flair for enhancing elegant, classic clothes,' declared a reporter on the *Daily Telegraph*, 'which is why Creed chose her.' Charles Creed himself claimed that his wife, the fashion editor of *Vogue*, knew more about the 'mysterious business' of women's clothes than he did. He knew nothing. Though his family had been in tailoring for four generations, you could get more sense on the subject, he would boast, from Crinnie, his small corgi dog. He was buoyantly shallow; never read a book (not even his ghosted autobiography); had no interest in politics or the arts; and listed watching golf and snooker on television as his hobbies. He was very popular.

After leaving the army, I would occasionally call at Creed's couture house to collect my mother for lunch at La Vache à la Cave, a few houses along Basil Street, past the beauticians and hairdressers. Creed's settled belief that fashion 'always comes round to meet the couturier who refuses to follow it' was leading him into an unfashionable hinterland from which he never escaped. The waistless, short-skirted line of the nineteen-twenties, which came round again in the nineteen-fifties with its beads and fringes, had little in common with his tailored suits; while the more abandoned styles of the nineteen-sixties were deeply unappealing to him. To my young and partial eye, one reason why my mother modelled so well for him was that she made women in their forties and fifties believe they could look flatteringly young.

Despite the novelty of this modelling, my mother was not happy in the late nineteen-fifties, and nor was my stepfather. Seeing them together, I could not understand how they had ever wanted to marry one another. Each, I imagine, appeared to offer the other some social advantage. As she glided, glassy-eyed, around the cocktail parties, my mother presented from a distance an image of serene drawing-room credibility. My stepfather, who was anxious to burden himself with the equipage of an English gentleman, gave the impression of being considerably richer than he actually was. Both of them were quickly undeceived.

I occasionally stayed a few days at Turners Reach House. 'I don't want you treating the place like a hotel,' my stepfather welcomed me. But it was difficult not to do so if, simply by going in and out of the front door, you were judged to be downgrading the house in this way. On the other hand, my stepfather added, it would be a pleasant relief to 'enjoy some good conversation for a change'. Women, he suspected, were incapable of conversation – certainly my mother was. The sort of newspaper talk that passed for conversation at Chelsea Embankment struck her as intolerably dull. My stepfather liked to ask me, man to man, what I thought of 'the Cyprus situation', or the CND march to Aldermaston protesting against the hydrogen bomb; and I was clearing my throat, tilting my head, when suddenly my mother would spring up, switch on the radio, and start whirling round the room clicking her fingers. My stepfather, abandoning Cyprus and the CND, unavailingly called her to heel. Both of them were already fairly drunk, my stepfather having tanked up at various clubs and bars on his way back from the office, and my mother having fortified herself against his homecoming with several secret whiskies. At this stage, my stepfather usually said something offensive about Swedish neutrality in the war, and then announced that he was going to 'change for dinner'. He would make his way to the bathroom and we heard the splashing of bathwater. Twenty minutes later he would reappear in exactly the same clothes, except for a new white collar above his old striped shirt. Dinner was served by Giacomo, a young Sicilian who later enjoyed an erratic career in the black market. In the belief, apparently, that he was displaying aristocratic manners, my stepfather called my mother 'Mrs Nares' over dinner, though at no other time. This struck her as unfriendly and led to an increase in her drinking. When she was drunk, she became extraordinarily silly and fell down a lot before passing out altogether; when he was drunk, my stepfather became aggressive; when I was drunk, I was sick.

That was how matters usually stood when, at the end of the evening, my stepfather would bang the table with his fist and shout out the word 'Bed!' He would do this even when there were guests; or go off to his bedroom and then come back in his pyjamas and dressing-gown to show those who still had their wits about them that it was time to leave. My mother did soon leave.

It was, I think, sometime in 1957 that she telephoned to ask again for my advice. She had recently been on holiday with Kaja to Baden – or was it Baden-Baden? Anyway, they had been abroad for the sake of the air or water, and my mother had encountered a very polite Viennese gentleman who apparently manufactured everything from ballpoint pens to motorbicycles somewhere in South America. She had often dreamed of travelling to South America and she wanted my advice as to whether she should set off there now. She had a handbag full of Swedish kronor after leaving Kaja which would take care of the fare (her husband, she reminded me, never gave her anything). Egon, her new admirer, had promised to meet her off the plane. He was wealthy, she added, and passed all his summers in Europe, so she would be able to see me each year. Perhaps, when all else failed, I could come over and manufacture motorbicycles myself . . .

I replied with one of my profound pauses, made a few gravelly noises in my throat and uttered a perfectly-balanced sentence with a 'nevertheless' at its centre. Then we got down to planning her journey. Before she went off to the airport, my mother asked me to draft an explanatory note for 'your stepfather'. This she copied down, leaving it for him on his return from the office.

That evening my stepfather telephoned me to say that 'your mother' had gone abroad. His voice sounded wobbly, and I went over to see him. This was a different conversation from the ones we usually struck up, and all gentlemanly airs and pretences were shed. My stepfather was somewhat bald but had a good growth of hair at the sides of his head which he kept tugging until these tufts stood out fantastically over his ears. We drank several tumblers of whisky, man to man, but for once he did not grow aggressive and I was not sick. Eventually he asked me to help him draft a letter to my mother who had left a forwarding address. 'You're a writer,' he said. 'You can put it on paper.' This was the first time he had acknowledged my wish to be a writer. Much gratified, I took out my pen, the very pen with which I had recently drafted my mother's farewell note, and hoping the whisky would inspire me, began writing.

Some three weeks later I heard from my mother in Acapulco. She had received, she wrote, a very curious letter from 'your stepfather' and was wondering how she should reply. Would I help her? I did try to help her. I drafted an answer. So began what, for eighteen months or so, was to be an elaborate international correspondence with myself. I was not really aware of what I was doing, of the irony of what I was doing, as I bent over these letters, acting barrister for, almost being the biographer of both husband and wife. But I did notice that I was beginning to pay myself extravagant compliments – 'your excellent letter' and so on.

While this correspondence was slowly trundling back and forwards (my stepfather did not like wasting money on airmail), and I was still trundling between London and Maidenhead, writing a paragraph or two in one place, crossing them out in the other, I spent two long summer holidays with my mother's new entourage, moving through Denmark, France, Austria, Germany and Italy. These were extraordinary summers of affluence. A shimmer of sun and beach, the glitter of casino and nightclub, buoyed me up, blinded me, as I floated agreeably off the known map. I hardly knew where I was sometimes. I remember arriving in Vienna and being astonished by how amazingly wet the streets were – before realising I was in Venice. Egon Hessel and his ebullient brother Walter would spend their days in luxuriously carpeted hotels and gorgeous restaurants, their nights at gambling tables and bars – and I went along too.

While we were in Austria, Griffy arrived for a couple of weeks and he was able to explain to me that we were at a lakeside resort called Velden which had once been frequented by socialites from the Austro-Hungarian Empire, and was now haunted by émigrés returning from the New World. At the further end of the Wörthersee, in which we were presently bathing, was Klagenfurt, once a prisoner-of-war camp. Griffy told me that he had been shocked to see one lady who had a death camp number tattooed on her arm. Velden, he thought, was one of those places where a large Jewish community lived before the war, many of whom, like the Hessel brothers, now returned each year. Despite this Germanic piece of scholarship, I noticed that whenever Griffy and I went out to lunch beside the lake, the two of us would land up with three portions of food due to Griffy's habit of confusing *zwei* with *drei*.

Egon Hessel was a leathery sort of man, of medium height, with a crumpled figure and creased features – a smiling, paper bag of a face he had. He could easily have disappeared in a crowd. But the crowd around us was very aware of him because of his wealth. He was a generous, level-headed man, a rock in this fermenting sea of social life and a contrasting figure to his brother Walter with his wicked air of scandal and fountain of gossip. My mother, I think, saw Egon as representing an appealing form of security; and he was attracted to her because she brought a transparently innocent sparkle to his life. They seemed to trust each other. That, at any rate, was what Griffy and I decided as we ate our way through our curiously large lunches.

Griffy had taken to calling my mother 'Madam'. At various stages of our holiday, often quite late at night and from the edge of the dance floor, he would cry out in an anguished voice: 'Steady, Madam! Steady!' But my mother had little grasp of steadiness, and perhaps it was we who needed more unsteadiness. It was as if she were younger than we were, as if she were providing us with an education that we lacked. 'This is where Madam excelled,' Griffy writes to me.

> She was always on the lookout for some fun. She was game to try anything and if it involved a party she would do her best to see that things went with a swing. This ability to enjoy herself was infectious and a wonderful tonic for others. I think she had an uncomplicated and almost childlike approach to life and was not much given to great thoughts about herself or her future. Although she had left Sweden long ago, it never left her. I have learnt never to be surprised at anything which a Swede may suddenly do.

Griffy surprised himself later by marrying a Swedish girl (a friend of one of my cousins) and becoming something of an expert, he believes, in Swedish ways. But at the various stopping-places used by the Hessels as they moved like a travelling circus through Europe, Sweden was represented in its purest form by my grandmother Kaja. She had always dressed up and gone out to my mother's parties, and continued doing so. Though she was not quite at ease in these exotic caravanserai, she wanted to see Ulla safely settled at last. She often looked, I thought, like redoubling Griffy's cries for caution, and made something of a confidant of the remarkable head waiter at the hotel restaurant at Velden. He was a man of terrible dignity and momentous tact with the appearance of an archduke and the spirit of Bernard Shaw's wise waiter in *You Never Can Tell*. I think he impressed my grandmother as the one obvious aristocrat among this miscellaneous throng of middle Europeans.

The following summer, when Egon and Ulla reached Munich, my mother summoned me urgently. She had gone into hospital for an operation to remove one of her ovaries and her womb. Though the operation, for which Egon was paying, was successful, it had a lowering effect on her. It was as if she were at last heeding Griffy's appeals to steady herself. She told me that she did not want to go on with this life of perpetual travelling. She wanted to return home. Home was now London rather than Stockholm. Home was Chelsea. She missed the King's Road. Over the last eighteen months or more, she reminded me, she had been receiving a number of nice letters from David Nares. He had promised to be more friendly to her in future and not call her 'Mrs Nares' when summoning the salt and pepper. He also promised to be more generous and let Kaja come to stay. He had written repeatedly that he wanted her back at Chelsea Embankment, and she had decided that she wanted to go back. But how could she tell Egon? He had been so kind to her. Lying in her hospital bed, rather tearful, she told me that she was not up to telling him. Would I do it for her before I left Munich? Why didn't I explain everything to him that evening over dinner? It would be an immense relief to her.

I was then twenty-two, but an inexperienced twenty-two. This was one of the penalties I was paying for all my mannerisms of maturity and that patina of sophistication I had acquired as a protective carapace. I dreaded the prospect of speaking to Egon, but I did so that evening in a half-empty restaurant, explaining away my mother's decision as a post-operative condition, but one that would persist. I could see he was surprised and I believe he was hurt. As a rich man, he could never be certain that people really liked him and not his money. Though my mother enjoyed much of the brightness that money switched on, she was never commercially-minded, and Egon liked that. He hardly said anything that evening.

Before the end of the year, and after a short spell in Stockholm, my mother was back in London with David Nares. Then, early in 1959, she left him again and, employing me as her travel agent, returned to Egon Hessel in Mexico. Both return flights were disastrous. At Turners Reach House, everything soon reverted to pomposity and drink. Despite what I had drafted in my letters trying to negotiate some common ground, they remained completely incompatible. I had achieved, in a more devastating form, what I had accidentally done while Mr Owen was absent from the divorce court: prolonged an irretrievably unhappy marriage.

What did I feel about this? The answer is that I did not fully recognise at the time the part I had played in it all. Being then in my twenties and quite familiar with the rapid changes in my parents' lives, I was not so worried on my mother's behalf as I later became. I had no moral objections to anything she did. Life, it seemed to me, was a matter of trial and error, and error had legitimacy. I thought of facts and the factual lure of fantasy more than of faults. My own anxieties arose from inaction and experience delayed. Like my grandfather. If I did not really understand my mother's life, it never occurred to me to condemn it.

But what went wrong the second time round with Egon

Hessel? For some time I wondered whether he had deliberately lured my mother back so as to seize the initiative and end the relationship on his own terms. I do not believe he wanted revenge, though his shock and disappointment in Munich could have damaged his feelings. I asked my mother afterwards what happened and she said Egon found out that she had altered the date of her birth in her passport. Looking through so many birth, marriage and death certificates for this book, I am amazed how regularly men raise their status and women lower their age. I have my mother's passport from that time in front of me and can see that she has changed the year of her birth from 1916 to 1918. It seems a harmless vanity, though maybe some customs official noticed it and caused them embarrassment as they crossed from one country to another. But if Egon saw my mother as luminously innocent, perhaps this deception was significant to him, symbolically changing who she was. In any event, his feeling for her altered 'when it alteration found'.

After another short spell in Stockholm with Kaja, my mother returned to London and by the end of 1961 was living in Ebury Street, not far from Sloane Square and the King's Road where she felt at home. In February 1962, David Nares presented a petition for divorce on the grounds of desertion. It was uncontested, and David found himself free to marry for a fourth time on his fiftieth birthday. Two or three years later, when working on my biography of Lytton Strachey, I came across a letter from his father Owen Nares to Strachey and sent him a photocopy of it. 'I'm in good heart,' he replied, 'and now that I've risen to dizzy heights at Crawfords am reasonably affluent, though heaven knows what will happen to us all when Wilson's recent measures begin to bite. Why not come and have a drink before they do?' We met at Turners Reach House and discussed, man to man, Harold Wilson's six months' freeze on wages and dividends. David had already fired off a couple of explosive letters to newspapers and had another, he told me, in the barrel – mercifully they were not the sort of letters he needed any help in writing. This was the last time I saw him. We did not mention my mother and there was no sign of his wife.

Though still only forty-five at the time of her divorce, my mother never remarried. Apparently she had no need to do so – no financial need. Egon had promised to pay her a quarterly allowance. I cannot remember how much this was – something between four and five thousand pounds a year. But unlike my grandfather's arrangement with Agnes May Babb, this was an unwritten agreement and no one knew how long it would last.

17

Flight into Surrey

My father (unlike my mother) was very commercially-minded, but unfortunately he had no money. He found the post-war world difficult to understand. Everything appeared topsy-turvy, and he could not manoeuvre round it. After the failure of Editions Begh, he retrenched at Norhurst, still married to Marlou. Then he went west to work as sales manager for a company called Concrete Construction (Wales) Ltd, with its headquarters in Pontlliw. Though it had been my uncle who read architecture at university, it was really my father's interest and, guided by this enthusiasm, he now attempted to make a career in the building trade. Pending success, he lived modestly at a boarding house in Swansea, working at our history of the world at nights so as to save money he might otherwise have spent in pubs or at the cinema. How we actually began this grand enterprise I cannot now remember – perhaps it was after one of the occasions when my father was teaching me the correct way to drink wine. I visited him two or three times and remember reading Joyce's *Ulysses* in the back bedroom there (I was reading Proust in my bedroom at Maidenhead). Then I would go further west to stay with Griffy Philipps at his father's house near Carmarthen. Sir Grismond Philipps, Lord Lieutenant of Carmarthenshire, looked like a Grenadier Guards' version of the Italian film actor Vittorio de Sica whom we had all seen in *Bread, Love and Dreams*. Griffy sometimes referred to his father as 'the Commanding Officer' and, on returning to Swansea, I tried out this formula on my own father as a means of circumventing the difficulties of 'Daddy' or 'Basil'. He took it pretty well and was soon signing his letters to me 'C.O.', while my mother became 'Madam'.

Grismond Philipps followed his son's habit of calling me Hagga. He was an amusing man, with a sophisticated style of humour, who enjoyed teasing me. Initially I found this rather disconcerting until, noticing my discomfort one day, he remarked: 'I only tease you, Hagga, because you're so good-natured' – after which he could tease me as much as he liked. He continued doing so to the end, and even a little beyond by bequeathing me a brace of stuffed parrots (alleged Flaubertian parrots that later turned out to be commonplace pheasants).

My father came once to collect me from Carmarthen and drive me back to Swansea. 'The first impression on seeing him was that he had very blue eyes and was extremely talkative,' Griffy writes to me. 'He was a most unlikely Old Etonian and very hard to categorize. He appeared to possess an optimism and an ability to cope with unpromising circumstances. To me he always seemed a generous person, blessed with enormous energy and probably putting too much trust in the wrong people.'

Before the war the C.O. had been famously able to 'talk anybody into anything'. Now he was obliged to talk himself into anything. It was his way of coping with what Griffy calls 'unpromising circumstances'. I remember him telling me one

evening, in his dingy room in Swansea, of the genius of his partner in the construction company, the jewel-like virtues of
concrete, and the dawning success awaiting them just over the
Welsh horizon. The room itself seemed to glow with early rays
of this throbbing success as he strode excitedly up and down,
filling it with his splendid vision of the future. A couple of years
later the concrete construction had collapsed and the brilliant
partner was revealed as a dark villain.

This fall of concrete broke up his marriage to Marlou. She
was striving to find a secure place as a publisher in Paris while
the C.O. had been driving desperately round Wales, covering
100,000 miles in two years, selling concrete constructions to
people who didn't want them. Fighting all the way, he was enormously successful as a salesman – and that had really been the
trouble. Concrete Construction (Wales) Ltd simply buckled
under the volume of reluctant orders that poured in. The bad
debts rose, the company sank, and the geniuses became fools.

At the end of his life the C.O. kept on his mantelpiece a
photograph of only one of his wives, fiancées and girlfriends of
a lifetime, a picture of Marlou. She is glancing down, her sultry
looks partly concealed, her raven hair falling a little forward, her
hooded eyelids appearing to guard some secret. That is how I
remember her.

The parting between them was wholly amicable. They simply
could not find a way of living in the same country. Marlou asked
the C.O. for a peculiar acquisition at their divorce: the right to
use one-and-a-half of his Christian names as her future surname.
She became, at Editions Mondiales and elsewhere, Madame de
Courcy, that 'de' adding lustre to her career.

Ten years later I wrote to Marlou asking her for information
about various *penseurs* whom Lytton Strachey had met at
l'abbaye de Pontigny in 1923. She gave me the facts I needed and
offered to introduce me to André Maurois. But Maurois was ill
and died before I could meet him. Then, in 1968, after publishing

Lytton Strachey, I sent her a copy and she asked me whether she might act as my agent in France. I happily agreed. But when my British publisher raised contractual objections, I was obliged to rescind this agreement. I did not realise how swiftly the wheel of fortune spins. Then in her early sixties, Marlou needed my help, and I could not give it to her. Whatever we did, it did not quite work, and there trailed behind us vague shadows of regret.

Back again at Norhurst for a spell, the C.O. was reduced to selling carbon paper. Even then his optimism did not dim. It seemed obvious to him that, with the advances in typewriter technology and the increasing use of the written word, carbon paper was set to proliferate into the twenty-first century. He was on to a winner. He could even see a way, our verse history having run into the buffers, of writing a bestseller on carbon paper, he jubilantly told me – a prose work that would dramatise an imagined board-room battle between the 'Stable Standby' and the 'Finer Flimsy' as a metaphor for contemporary culture. In short, he was labouring at a novel during the Maidenhead evenings.

By 1957, though still pursuing fiction, he was back in the building trade. Timber, he explained, not concrete, was the stuff of the future. He'd been a fool not to have spotted this earlier. He was now blessed with a business partner who had a genius for all things wooden – a Pinocchio figure he appeared in my imagination. In any event, the future was bright.

Though I still needed my father's help during the nineteen-fifties, I noticed that he was beginning to want my approval. While lying angrily becalmed at Maidenhead, he would some-times take me off in his car to some public house, and later in my bedroom I would make notes of our conversations. These notes then reappeared as chunks of narrative below the printed surface of *A Dog's Life*, in that vast unseen mass of my novel that was never published. The character emerging from this narrative is someone who regularly goes through a transformation scene that, despite its familiarity, always takes me off guard. Alone with me, he is a serious and sensitive person, but as soon as we enter the pub he suddenly changes into a figure of burlesque. 'Now I think I'll have a sherry today,' I record him as calling out to the panic-stricken barman.

> Have you a good amontillado? On holiday in Spain we used to drink the Tio Pepe. But while I was in France I rather lost the habit, I must confess, and now I prefer the medium dry. The French, of course, never were great sherry drinkers. Still, there's no place quite like Paris . . . Oh yes, we'll sample a couple of your amontillados – looks as if you've talked us into it. Ha! Ha! [To me] Here you are, an amontillado sherry. See what you think. Wash it round the roof of your mouth with your tongue – that's the correct way, so the experts tell us. Don't gargle!
> [To the barman] This is my son and heir. The one that inherits the overdraft. Ha! Ha! Says he wants to be one of those writer-johnnies. I ask you! Still, stranger things have happened I don't deny – though I tell him we all have to ditch some of our fancy ideas in life. He's not got much taste in wine yet, I'm afraid. Said he liked a Sauterne the other day. I told him it's just a woman's wine, though you can taste the grape in it, I grant you. You'd never think he'd had a French stepmother. Of course we're divorced now . . .

This is hardly an exaggeration of our pantomime performances in pubs played out against the struggles of a barman desperate to get free, the rising clamour of the drinkers rhythmically thumping their glasses, and myself, the straight man of the act, staring fixedly into the distance. I daresay that the copying of it down was an act of revenge for my embarrassment.

When I left the army at the beginning of 1958, the C.O. was

temporarily 'cooling his heels' at Norhurst. He took me several times to different pubs to have a serial conversation. It was impossible, he explained, to talk at Norhurst in case someone heard him. Not that anyone ever listened to anything he said, but they were uncannily quick at picking up the wrong end of the stick. Then he came out with the reason for his nervousness. He wished me to meet someone. In fact he rather thought I'd like her. But we would have to be discreet for reasons he would later make clear. Anyway she wanted to invite us both to her flat 'not a stone's throw as the crow flies' from Maidenhead railway station. She was a damn good cook, so it was not an occasion to be missed. She might not be a literary genius, but she'd read a few things in life, and was a good sort. We fixed a date.

Sonia was a well-built woman of thirty-eight who pretended to be petite and rather girlish, it seemed to me, while at other times affecting ladylike airs. She had been obliged to work in a shop at Maidenhead since the dissolution of her marriage, and had a son, to my irritation also called Michael, who had recently gone to what the C.O. described as 'a really rather good minor public school'. It was an impossible evening. The C.O. was dreadfully anxious that we should be immediate friends. He was like an intrusive theatre director, full of gusto and hilarity, putting us right, urging us on, speaking our lines for us until neither of us could behave naturally. The more the C.O. enthused, the more silent I grew, the more wrong notes Sonia seemed to strike. We simply could not hit it off and more than once got into a terrible mix-up over which Michael was being singled out for praise.

In my unpublished novel, I gave an unflattering portrait of Sonia which, because of the guilt I felt for being so disobliging, rises to moments of Dickensian excess. I quote from it, not as an accurate description, but as evidence of my hostility.

She is a large woman. Her head is large and so obviously are her arms and legs. Her hips are very large indeed. The

texture of her face is mottled and spotted like a Spanish
Omelette. But its principal feature is a nose of great
prominence bent upwards at a sharp angle like a bottle
opener. Above it are a pair of wandering eyes of an
indiscriminate pastel, round and wobbly as two lightly-
boiled eggs. Her pallid complexion is offset by deep black
hair which has sprouted into a fuzzy mass.

Why was I so aggressive? Was it because the C.O., then in his
fiftieth year, could apparently attract all sorts of women, and I
could not? Or did I resent the feigned admiration he kept pumping out of me? Or was it simply that Sonia and I did not very
much like each other? As he drove me back from this disastrous
first evening, the C.O. was bubbling with enthusiasm. And I was
so laconic that he had to supply the answers to his own questions.

Good-looking woman, isn't she? Yes, I always believe in
choosing attractive women in life. Pretty good cook, too,
don't you think? That soufflé! You must come over again
when you're not too busy with your masterpiece. She
obviously took a shine to you. Told me so. Can't imagine
why. She's had a pretty rough time of it and coped bloody
well. I'll tell you all about it.

That 'rough time' was an allusion to Sonia's marriage and
divorce. Rather to the C.O.'s chagrin, Sonia often spoke in dramatic style of her ex-husband: how violent he was, what a bully,
how deranged – 'a thoroughly nasty customer', my father concluded. All this seemed to be borne out when he turned up one
evening at Sonia's flat and made a scene. The police were called
and the C.O. described the rumpus to me in his special low
voice. But the police were apparently powerless to do anything
'unless he's committed a few murders recently'. Something
would have to be done.

For several weeks the C.O. had been confiding to me how the family was 'driving him crackers', how he could not spend much more time at Norhurst 'getting ticked off like some infant in swaddling clothes'. But things were looking up since he met this prodigy in timber and been made sales director of Seamless Floors. Now he had a spot of cash in his hands, he was going to change his life. Not that he would jump the gun. But he had decided to take the plunge. In short, get hitched up again. To Sonia. He didn't like to think of her alone at night while this madman roamed the streets. Of course it would be impossible to marry in Maidenhead. They must do it somewhere he wouldn't find them. The C.O. had already alerted estate agents.

They were married on 2 September 1958. It was a strange day. 'We'll lead him a merry dance if he tries to follow us,' the C.O. grimly announced, referring to Sonia's ex-husband. He dreaded telling the family at Norhurst and left it to the last minute on the grounds of not breaching security. 'I only hope she's a bit better than the last lot,' Adeline said by way of congratulations. We set off early from Maidenhead, driving at a furious pace but by a circuitous route out of Berkshire and up to Hendon in Middlesex where the ceremony was to take place. The C.O. and Sonia were in the front of the car, I and my new stepbrother (the other Michael) sat in the back with orders to look out for pursuing vehicles. On the marriage certificate at Hendon Registry Office, the C.O. described himself as 'Sales Manager (Timber Buildings)' and gave as his home his new partner's address in north west London which enabled him to claim residence in Hendon. Sonia put a line through the box marked 'rank or profession', and we two Michaels signed up as witnesses. After a furtive celebratory lunch, we struck southwards, zigzagging into Surrey where the C.O. had rented what looked at first sight like sheltered accommodation next to a cemetery. The day ended with the exhausted couple planning redecorations to their new home.

Over the next few years I used to go down intermittently for Sunday lunch. Sonia, I thought, was soon showing signs of boredom with life in Surrey. In any event the redecorations were never finished. She would attempt to prise exciting news of London from me. But though I did take myself to cheap seats at plays, concerts, films, I had little that was interesting to tell. I felt grateful when she changed her line of questioning from myself to my mother. The C.O. would listen sardonically, giving an occasional chuckle, as I described a few of my mother's goings and comings. Sonia wanted to know whether I had really drafted my mother's farewell note to her husband and, if so, what I had written. I reproduced it to the best of my ability. Soon afterwards she wrote a very similar note herself when taking her leave of the C.O. Though I never knew the details of their separation, I got an impression that after half-a-dozen years both of them were happy to be shot of one another. The divorce petition came to court in 1966, and I see that the C.O. did the gentlemanly thing by allowing his wife to be the petitioner and appearing himself as respondent. But the document makes curious reading. For the co-respondent is Sonia's previous husband, the 'madman' from whom we had made such a dramatic flight, and back to whom, after this interval of marriage, she now escaped from the C.O.'s insolvency in Surrey.

18

Scenes from
Provincial and
Metropolitan Life

'Is everyone still alive?'

I had forgotten this cry and the collective groan that, mounting in volume as it went from room to room, rose to meet it three mornings a week as our cook opened the front door at Norhurst. It was thanks to my Uncle Kenneth that we still employed a cook. By buying the house he had saved my grandfather £150 a year in rent, besides the heavy repayments on our double mortgage raised to pilot me through school.

Our cook was a morbidly cheerful character who refused to take offence at the family's barrage of insults. 'Go on then, knock me down! String me up!', she would cry in ecstasy. And then, to my grandmother: 'I know you don't really mean it, madam.' She went on joking in the kitchen until she eventually forced a smile from my grandmother. This did not recommend her to Fraser, Basil, Yolande or Old Nan, all of whom were on shouting but not speaking terms with Adeline. If only she would spend less time gossiping with the cook, they sighed, they might get a few meals.

Our gardener still came too, his pale face and wavering smile lighting up as we shouted at him that he was a 'damn fool' and a 'bally idiot' after seeing how he had planted, in a straight line, all the weeds we had dug up the previous week. We were also visited by a daily woman who came weekly. She was a remarkable diplomat. With her understanding smile, the appropriate exclamation, a supporting shake of her head, she managed the all-but-impossible feat of getting along with everyone. We called her a 'treasure' until, after many years of loyal service, we found she had been steadily stealing our cutlery, china and still-unbroken pieces of Lalique (the Narcissus mirror with frosted glass, the lotus cups, the bowl with sirens, the Avalon vase). By the time I got back from the army to live at Norhurst again, almost the only Lalique left were the eagles, fish and sparrows with which Yolande had decorated the dogs' graves in the garden.

Everything was agonisingly familiar to me. The passing of the hours from All Saints Church; the squabbling birds congregating on the lawn for their meals; the leaping red and grey squirrels, the hovering multicoloured dragonflies, all darting here and there; the garage with its music and cider and lurking treasures; the magical tea chests arriving from India with their silver foil under wooden casing, and when they were excavated, like an Egyptian tomb from under the stairs, the bitter-sweet smell of Rajmai tea.

Each morning the family would plunge down Castle Hill into the mêlée of Maidenhead, then lumber slowly up carrying heavy bags of shopping – only to find when all was unloaded in the kitchen that they had bought the same things again and again. The air trembled with recrimination and dismay.

There were changes. Our parrot, the female Mr Potty, had flown out into the trees one day while her cage was being cleaned and though we stood below calling, making bird noises, whistling, swearing, she merely swore back, then flew away.

We were reduced now to one dog, a labrador called Don, whom my Aunt Yolande dragged gasping over the fields and round the Thicket each long day. If she got back in time, we might play tennis together in the late afternoons, rallies rather than games as each of us was frightened of the other one losing. We began playing at the children's playground, occasionally bicycled over to some courts at Cookham (where I once caught sight of Stanley Spencer *en plein air*), and then we played at a private court belonging to Yolande's friend Cathie. This was the Cathie who appeared in family photographs in the South of France during the early nineteen-thirties. But we were nervous of going to the court in her garden too often, not liking to 'trouble' her, though the court was never used. Yolande would telephone, and we pedalled across, darting down the garden from tree to tree, and later darting back again along the line of the bushes so as not to be seen. It was not, I think, Yolande's shame at our poverty that drove her to avoid her friend so assiduously, but dread of Cathie's sympathy.

My grandmother welcomed me back from National Service as if I had been in hand-to-hand combat, thanking God and the Mother of God for the miracle of my survival. She wanted to hear my news, my special news. 'That child tells us nothing of what's going on,' she would complain to the cook and the gardener. 'Just like a bally clam. I don't know where he comes from. He's a proper mystery.'

'Oh do leave the boy alone, Di,' Fraser would interrupt before tumbling out to the garage to find another celebratory bottle of cider.

They all seemed to me significantly older, especially my grandmother. As she meandered from room to room, rattling the door handles, rearranging the cushions, her head full of empty plotting, she looked so small and bent. Yolande, I noticed, could hardly bear to glance at her – the thin grey curls under a dilapidated hairnet, the old powdered and lined face, the bloodshot eyes, her feet in their slippers misshapen with bunions. 'It's high time you went aloft,' she would shout to herself. All her Maidenhead friends were dead, but she lived on. 'Are you decent?' she always cried through my bedroom door. 'Are you visible?' I would hold my breath, knowing I could be invisible but not indecent enough yet. Then, with a sigh, she would wander away, heavy with her uncommunicable love.

An important new feature at Norhurst was our massive television device. It was unlike any other television in the world. My Uncle Kenneth had bought this portmanteau of a set which we stood, a substantial piece of furniture, in the middle of the hall. From a porthole in this object, when the right buttons and knobs were pushed and twisted, a picture could be projected on to a large screen. This screen had to be unpacked and raised up each evening, then folded down at night and put away under the stairs with the tea chests. It was a magnificent contraption – I have never seen anything like it. Our hall, which was the largest space in the house, was converted into a cinema in time for the six o'clock news each evening. It took an hour to prepare the screen which was responsible for new bumps, bruises and cuts ranged across my grandfather's head. But television became his passion, and after a few weeks none of us could remember what we had done before it arrived. He would sit himself behind the machine studying the controls, endeavouring to focus the images, while the rest of us chimed eagerly in with our advice. Old Nan, whose eyesight was failing, sat in a garden chair at the foot of the staircase, crouching forward so as to be almost touching the screen, the outline of her imposing form appearing as a shadow on the corner of all pictures. She watched everything, commented on nothing. Yolande never watched and was audibly contemptuous of the rest of us for sitting hunched up in the dark. It was impossible for any of us to go to any room without passing in front of the screen. My grandmother would actually stand in front of it, achieving an almost total eclipse as she complained to us of the dust created by the contrivance, or simply asked what we would like for lunch next day, switching on the light so as to make sure we heard her. She had found a new way of driving Fraser frantic.

I did not stay long at Norhurst after leaving the army. Smout, my colleague in redundancy, had discovered that we were entitled to special allowances at Colindale, and while we waited for this bonus to come through, I remained there. In my bedroom, still reading Proust, I could hear the whistle of the trains passing along the valley beyond All Saints Church on their way to London and wished I were on one of them. We lived at the respectable end of Maidenhead where nothing happened. But at the other end lay the 'Maidenhead Riviera' with its nightclubs and hotels, expensively lined along the Thames, in particular the notorious Skindles where couples were said to spend illicit weekends, and the smart Guards' Club in whose grounds 260 false wedding rings were later unearthed. The Maidenhead Public Library, near the centre of town, was midway between our respectability and that bohemianism. After a day there, as from a launching pad, I would sometimes take off on my bicycle and look across the Thames with its twin bridges, the red-brick Brunel railway viaduct with its two shallow semi-elliptical arches, and the white-stone eighteenth-century bridge, with its seven small water-arches, that carried traffic to London.

Before I made my way over these bridges, I tried to reconnoitre a literary career from Norhurst, offering my services in the role of book editor or reviewer to our local paper, *The Maidenhead Advertiser*. In fact the paper carried no book reviews, but this did not deter me. Surely, I appealed, they needed for this enterprise, the creation of a book section, someone like myself – young, unencumbered by university degrees, with a bit of legal and military experience to hand, and already deep in Proust.

I am still waiting for an answer.

This reversal spurred me towards London. Maidenhead, it was clear, was a bit off the intellectual map. There was no virtue in the place. But getting a foothold in London was not easy. At first, I could find only intermittent quarters in the Chelsea consulting room of my mother's doctor. On his dark leather couch, the only other occupant a dimly suspended medical skeleton, I passed my nights, rising at dawn to avoid the eager invalids who came beating at the door. Then I stayed with Griffy Philipps at a mews house in Mayfair belonging to his mother. I slept in the attic beside a water-tank, wrapped up on cold nights in brown paper – something between a tramp and an undelivered parcel. In the morning I would descend a ladder to the comfort of the drawing-room where I was transformed into a man of letters in his study.

Griffy at this time was working in the City. I must have murmured something one evening about Rajmai Tea, asked him perhaps whether he could find out anything about it. This obviously took time, but he was at last able to pinpoint it on the map at Boorbarrie and Behora, and, possibly under the impression I was passing on a hot tip, though probably from a feeling of friendliness, or even, I like to think, acting under the spell Rajmai cast on the imagination of all who heard its name, he bought some shares. 'It was better than a seat at the opera,' he writes to me. 'The company staggered from one disaster to the next, but like a lifeboat it always recovered and came back for more. In no particular order I remember floods, strikes by boatmen and porters, rock-bottom tea prices and lastly the Chinese invasion.' At the risk of insider trading, Griffy was receiving unusual dividends.

It was my mother's doctor, Larry Heyman, who at last found

me a more permanent place to live. He was an Irishman with a weakness for the arts who lived with his wife and daughter in Jubilee Place off the King's Road. He was immensely proud of his daughter who was training to be a ballet dancer. She would go in and out of the drawing-room on pointe, showing off her amazing *entrechats* and *fouettés*, performing complicated capers back and forth while her father looked on benevolently. His wife Irene appeared to me a fabulous creature in the high Spanish style. She had been painted by Matthew Smith in Chelsea Cloisters. This portrait, executed in vivid reds and making her appear to be bleeding luxuriantly to death against some flowers above the fireplace, lit up their otherwise gloomy house. When my mother told me at the hospital in Munich that she missed the King's Road, I could tell she had her friend Irene Heyman in mind. They spent much of their time in secret laughter, probably about men. Once they asked me whether I would mind their using my new address for something they wanted to insert in a newspaper. A week later I received a stiff note from *The Times* saying they did not accept personal advertisements of this kind. Irene seemed to have little involvement with humdrum domestic life. On one famous occasion, having bought her daughter a cat, she heard it purring and shouted out in alarm: 'Look out! It's growling.'

Larry Heyman was considerably older than his wife. His hand trembled as he reached for the whisky glass. He enjoyed pontificating in a stage-Irish voice on matters of dance, literature and painting, and passing on titbits about various artistic patients. But he was a kindly man and, having a surgery at Nell Gwynn House, he persuaded the management to let me have a small flat at the back of the building where coincidentally both my mother and my Uncle Kenneth had put up during intervals in their careers.

In my late 'teens I had begun trying to write in collaboration with my father; then in my early twenties I attempted to base my novel partly on my family; finally, when I reached my mid-twenties, I found a subject that had no connection with my parents. It was at Nell Gwynn House that I wrote my biography of Hugh Kingsmill. I had first made contact with the Kingsmill family through his publishers and was invited to meet them for dinner at the flat of one of his daughters, a strapping ex-chorus girl who, after the appearance of my book, became a nun. In my nervousness I arrived too early. Pacing the street I could not fail to notice that the building was in flames, with flashing fire engines outside. However, I was too polite to volunteer help, suspecting that there may have been some culinary disaster about which it would be tactless for an aspiring biographer to inquire. When things had cooled down, I went in. The evening threw up some photographs of Kingsmill's death mask, his smouldering tobacco pouch and other impedimenta, though little of direct literary use. But I refused to be daunted.

Kingsmill's widow Dorothy, once a revue dancer then a dressmaker, nursed literary ambitions which, after Kingsmill mislaid her unpublished novel on the platform of an underground station, found indirect expression in her work as a lay analyst. She was reputed to have freed the novelist Antonia White from a writer's block by liberating her from her husband, the editor of *Picture Post* Tom Hopkinson, and then marrying him herself. When I met her, she had persuaded Tom to take up the editorship of *Drum*, the picture magazine for young Africans, and they were about to sail for Johannesburg. Dorothy acted very flirtatiously that evening and kept calling me an 'angry young man'. Our relationship eventually made me one.

Once I had been given permission to write the book, I went to see Hugh Kingsmill's elder brother, the ski-pioneer and Christian controversialist Sir Arnold Lunn (they were sons of the Methodist travel agent Sir Henry Lunn, Kingsmill writing under his mother's maiden name in order to distance himself from his father and distinguish himself from his brother). 'My wife,' Sir

Arnold warned me, 'doesn't function too well in the evenings.' She was, he added, 'beyond organising sandwiches'. So the two of us went out to dinner, leaving Lady Mabel in bed. She was, I understood, an insomniac. But left to herself for hours on end in the dark, she would sometimes drop off out of sheer boredom. The Lunns were to be away next morning for some eventing in Switzerland, so it was essential that Lady Mabel rest. After dinner we went quietly back to the flat so that Sir Arnold could present me with one of his books essential, he confided, for my biography. Lady Mabel had nodded off. We moved among the half-packed trunks and suitcases like ghosts, Sir Arnold leading with a candle in his hand. He quarried out the book, signed it, and handed it to me with a whisper. I breathed my thanks, then fumbled my way out. On the staircase outside, plunged into total darkness, I felt for the light button and, pressing it, released a fearful peal of bells into the Lunn sleeping quarters. I saw the light flash angrily on under the door and, coward that I was, I fled. Looking through the book when I got back to Nell Gwynn House, I saw it was full of Swiss mountains but without a mention of Kingsmill. My view that he was an unjustly neglected author had been confirmed.

My flat cost £3 a week. The extra money from the army paid for my first few months. My grandparents had also given me some money, attempting to do so secretly but, colliding on the landing at Norhurst, the notes flapping on to the floor followed by their cries of distress and exasperated accusations, the transaction had been well advertised.

It was easy to live cheaply in the early nineteen-sixties; but it was difficult to earn money. From the *Twentieth Century* magazine I eventually received a commission to review an anthology of Oxford and Cambridge writing called *Light Blue, Dark Blue*. I worked on this piece for weeks, revising it intensely – a comma here, a semi-colon there – and at last sent in a review that some months later was published. This was my first writing to be printed. The following year a cheque arrived for a little under £1. Here was success. But could I afford success?

I had notions of supplementing this income with some profitable plagiarism. Taking the hint from an episode in one of Anthony Powell's novels, I went off to the British Museum's newspaper library at Colindale and looked through a number of stories in women's magazines which, I had heard, paid their contributors well. I copied down one that seemed to me very characteristic, then brought it up to date by changing the names of the characters, the speed and make of the cars, the brand of the breakfast cereals and so on before sending it to the magazine that had originally published it twenty-five years ago. I hoped they would be grateful for this made-to-measure contribution. But their letter of rejection, which allowed me genuine promise, decided that the story (which involved a flirtation between a husband and his sister-in-law) was a little too risqué for them.

Though I took one or two odd jobs, it was really the C.O. who made the writing of *Hugh Kingsmill* possible. Early in the nineteen-sixties, he decided to pay me an allowance of £8 a month, and persuaded both my mother and Kaja to do the same: £288 a year (equivalent to some £3,000 in the late nineteen-nineties). This allowance dwindled as the fortunes of its contributors went downhill, the C.O. silently withdrawing after a year, my mother giving up after almost two years, and my grandmother in Sweden carrying on for some three years. But it was enough.

The reason my father offered for this generous arrangement was that I appeared to be 'wasting my time with the right people'. By this he meant two of Kingsmill's friends, Hesketh Pearson and William Gerhardie.

I had written to Pearson in 1958, and over the next half-dozen years received continual encouragement from him. He would invite me over to supper with his wife Joyce or take me out to the theatre (it was with him that I saw my first Bernard

Shaw productions). He also wrote to editors on my behalf so that I could get some reviewing and lent me whatever Kingsmill manuscripts and books he possessed. After his death in 1964, Joyce Pearson told me she thought I had replaced to some extent the son of his first marriage who had been killed in the Spanish Civil War. They had quarrelled over politics on their last meeting, and Hesketh was close to suicide for months afterwards. Perhaps, twenty years later, his goodness to me was a means of reconciliation with his son. Certainly he helped me in ways my father was in no position to do and, without alienating my father, became something of a father figure to me. By an act of imaginative generosity, his assistance was to go on after his and Joyce's death, when his library and copyrights came to me.

Literature was a very tangible affair to Pearson, belonging more to the open air than the study, and reflecting what he saw around him, the people and the landscape he loved. He had once been an actor and knew some of Shakespeare's plays by heart. He was also a man of dramatic opinions. One day, when someone suggested to him that Shakespeare was rather overrated, he stopped the taxi they were travelling in and obliged the man to continue his journey on foot. He was some fifty years older than I was, but we spoke easily, without any sense of a difference in age. Books were not something behind which he sheltered: they were part of his life and he helped to make them part of mine. After cheerless days of doubt, I would come away from an evening with him full of the enthusiasm and vitality he communicated.

Hesketh Pearson described himself as 'a hero-worshipper who likes to take his heroes off their pedestals and get to know them as fellow men'. What I picked up from his biographies was not so much his technique, which derived from his career on stage, as what Graham Greene called his 'sense of life going on all the time'. I admired his ability to tell a story; I shared the endless fascination with human nature from which all his Lives sprang; and I benefited from his gusto and geniality. He was a man without qualifications, an amateur in the sense that he wrote his biographies for love rather than a *curriculum vitae*, who showed me what possibilities might lie ahead and gave me the confidence to follow his example by going my own way.

Kingsmill, like many lonely people, compartmentalised his life, so it was not surprising that his two closest friends over twenty-five years should have met each other only once. William Gerhardie was utterly unlike Pearson, and the most eccentric person I have ever met. Both shared a love of literature and landscape, but whereas Pearson in his direct and upright manner would set off on long vigorous walks in the footsteps of Johnson and Boswell and other favourite characters, his head teeming with lines from Shakespeare and his own explosive phrases bursting with alliterations and assertions, Gerhardie would stay immovably indoors dreaming of what might lie beyond the curtained windows. 'It's a lovely day,' a friend remarked one morning. 'Is it?' he replied eagerly, remaining seated with his back to the window.

In the nineteen-twenties his novels *Futility* and *The Polyglots* had made him, in the words of Arnold Bennett, 'the pet of the intelligentsia and the darling of Mayfair'. He was taken up by Katherine Mansfield and Edith Wharton, H.G. Wells and Evelyn Waugh. 'To those of my generation Gerhardie was the most important new novelist to appear in our young life,' wrote Graham Greene. And Olivia Manning concluded: 'He is our Gogol's *Overcoat*. We all come out of him.'

One of the many articles on Gerhardie in the nineteen-thirties was prophetically subtitled: 'Success: and How to Avoid It'. At this avoidance he became adept. By the nineteen-sixties he could boast of being the most celebrated unknown writer in Britain. He wrote every day but had published almost nothing since 1940 beyond a list of teasing titles in *Who's Who* (an ironical tragedy called *English Measles* for example, and a lyrical comedy entitled *The Private Life of a Public Nuisance*). His background was unorthodox. The son of a British cotton manufacturer settled in Russia, he had been brought up in St Petersburg and being identified as the dunce in the family, sent to England in his 'teens to be trained for a commercial career. During the First World War, equipped with a monocle and a huge sword bought second-hand in the Charing Cross Road, he was posted back to Russia on the staff of the British Military Attaché. When the war was over, he turned up at Worcester College, Oxford, where he wrote a brilliant little book on Chekhov. But by the mid-nineteen-thirties, at the age of forty, he had left the world of travel and adventure, the society of Mayfair and, beginning a career of philosophical speculation, set himself up as a hermit in central London.

William was a good portly man whose figure tapered down to a pair of delicate feet. An amused expression and rosebud mouth, together with his bald head and pink skin, gave him the appearance of a decadent cherub. His eyes protruded in the manner of some tropical fish. He sometimes wore, over his pyjamas, a shiny grey suit and colourful bow tie. I would visit him occasionally at his block of flats in Hallam Street. Whatever time of day you arrived, you were required to ring the night bell, then take the lift to the fourth floor and hammer at his door until you heard him begin to fiddle languidly with the bolts and chains. After a loud exchange of passwords, the door opened and you stepped into the dark guided by William's silhouette. 'This is the gold room,' he would announce with a spectacular gesture, flinging wide an inner door to what appeared like the opening of a coal mine. The floor was crammed with shoe boxes, paper bags and the odd mattress, all bulging with his writings. William moved, despite his arthritis, athletically among the debris. Books were everywhere, but there were no bookshelves except by his bed. A pile of brocade cushions supported him at his typewriter which was itself supported by a tower of empty egg cartons.

Hospitality was a risky business. The flat was freezing and the armchairs, resting on empty coffee jars, slumped to the floor as you sat in them. William shopped by telephone from Selfridges and seemed to live mostly on Coca-Cola and meringues, with the odd sausage thrown in at weekends. But for guests he would go out of his way to prepare something special: a drink of tepid water and raspberry jam called 'All's Well' because, he assured you, 'it ends well'. Few of us got that far. Gerhardie connoisseurs took picnics in order to avoid his prize speciality 'Sherryvappa', a subtle combination of sherry and evaporated milk. After drinking this, you had to be a true friend to come again. The fact was, he did not really want callers. He would insist reluctantly on shaking your hand as you arrived, and then ostentatiously and elaborately washing his own hands. He did not want you going to his lavatory, sitting on his furniture, touching things, breathing his air, seeing what he had written and finding yourself unable to resist making off with his ideas. He could not wait for you to go and, when you did go, would hold you at the door squeezing promises from you to come again.

Gerhardie's early novels, written under Chekhov's influence, explored the comedy of time deferred; his later books, written under Proust's influence, investigated the phenomenon of time regained. He had reached a point of looking into the future with a sense of nostalgia, as if impatient to convert it into the past. Time present remained a fleeting problem. As the solution to its banality, its physical awkwardness, he had hit on the telephone. The telephone avoided problems of actual contact, time could be extended almost indefinitely into the future and then to some extent recaptured with another call. Once we spoke for seven hours on the telephone, and I had two meals during our conversation. Another time I played him a Wagnerian opera down the line. Though he was a very funny man, there was often pathos in his stories. He would be telling an amusing story, suddenly interrupt himself with a cry of 'Oh God!', and then continue with the story. You could telephone him if you were in trouble at any time – three or four in the morning – all time was the same to him. But he was not understanding if you happened to be in a hurry. Once, in desperation, I exclaimed: 'William! I must go! The building is in flames!' But he went on speaking about *The Polyglots*. I noticed, too, how much better I felt if I telephoned him when I was ill – and how exhausted I was at the end of our calls some other times.

I suppose I was flattered that someone who had been taken up by Katherine Mansfield and H.G. Wells should now be taking me up. Unlike Hesketh Pearson, Gerhardie also wanted something from me. He wanted me to take my admiration for his novels like a torch into the future, and light up understanding among a new generation of readers. This I tried and failed to do by writing ten prefaces to a collected edition of his work in the early nineteen-seventies and then, a little more successfully perhaps, by editing with my friend Robert Skidelsky his posthumous book, the ingenious *God's Fifth Column*, in the early nineteen-eighties. Finally I wrote my valediction in *The Dictionary of National Biography*, in the 'Missing Persons' volume of which I also wrote tributes to Hesketh Pearson and Hugh Kingsmill.

The world that William Gerhardie opened up for me was a very unEnglish one without straight lines of cause and effect, where moral certainties are ironically undermined, where comedy thrives as part of tragedy, where progress comes unpredictably and secret lines of communication lie between opposing forces.

According to his biographer Dido Davies, Gerhardie dreamed of possessing all the comely women in the world in a 'cumulative consummate kiss'. His preoccupation with hygiene modified, but did not curb, his obsessive seduction of women. He had picked them up working in shops, strolling in the park, walking home in the streets from their offices, anywhere. Dido Davies herself was one of the girls, then in her 'teens and sometimes with her mother, I met at William's flat. He behaved to her as he did to every girl who visited him. 'Isn't it extraordinary how she resembles Goethe's Mignon?' he would ask. 'Do you find her attractive?' Then, turning to her: 'Come out here into the centre of the room. Why not stand on that table so that this young genius can see you better? And now turn round. What calves!' With obvious pleasure, he would run the palms of his hands lightly up her legs. 'And what fine breasts too, don't you think?' he would add with rich appreciation.

Though these performances were outrageous and embarrassing, I noticed that the girls themselves took a benevolent attitude to William. They giggled a lot but did not feel threatened and were never frightened. For all their shyness, they were not displeased. Everything that was objectionable seemed to have been harmlessly dissolved.

If Hesketh Pearson was a father figure to me, William Gerhardie played the part of a wicked uncle. How was my love life? he immediately wanted to know. My stammering replies did not satisfy him, so he introduced me to his great-niece Jackie, a beautiful dancer who led me into the world of ballet at the time of Nureyev's arrival in Britain and introduced me to the music of Prokofiev.

I could afford to take Jackie out to supper once a fortnight. I would count up to a hundred before telephoning her and try to sound casual. But when we met I had almost nothing to say. I always prepared a few amusing things to tell her, hoping to hide behind these anecdotes, but to my dismay they tumbled out in the first few minutes and then I came to a halt. Twenty-six silent suppers a year were more than Jackie could face, so she made arrangements with one or two of the other dancers at her digs in Earls Court to go out with me in rotation. To waiters at the

bistros and coffee houses we ate in, I must have appeared a regular ladies' man. Eventually one of these ballet girls, Jennifer it
was, listening to some music in Nell Gwynn House after supper,
grew impatient with my lack of initiative. So she got into bed,
my bed, while I was in the bathroom, and so I followed her in.
After ten minutes or so in the dark, she asked: 'Is that all?' 'I
don't know,' I answered truthfully.

   We began to laugh.

While getting a foothold in London, I kept being pulled back to
Norhurst for short spells to see my grandfather. Things had
looked up for him briefly after the war. Towards the end of
1947, at the age of seventy-two, he had gone out to visit the
Rajmai Estate in India and came back with a report recommending new houses, schools and a hospital for the company
employees and their families. The following April he was elected
Chairman of Rajmai. It was a peak in his career. But the board
meetings were nervous affairs. Though he armed himself with all
the regular protective equipment, including a military-looking
umbrella, correct gloves, polished shoes and a venerable double-
breasted suit, he still could not ward off the terrible outbursts
from his cousin 'Mad Ivor', and would sometimes arrive back in
Maidenhead looking very miserable. It was a mystery how his
brother Pat, the mildest and most innocuous of men, could have
produced such an intemperate son. At Norhurst, a rumour soon
sprang up that Ivor was having 'an operation to his head'. The
minutes of Rajmai Tea Company show that he resigned from the
board in 1950 and that there were 'circumstances under which
this resignation has become necessary'. Attached to this minute
is a note: 'In case there may be repercussions legal or otherwise
arising from letters which have passed between Ivor Holroyd's
solicitors and the Chairman, the Board desire to protect and
indemnify the Secretaries against any such eventuality.' The
source of Ivor's anger had probably been Fraser's borrowing of

money from Pat shortly before his death. As an act of reconciliation, Ivor's wife was appointed to the board on his resignation;
and it was from her that Kenneth bought extra Rajmai shares
for himself and his father. When Fraser retired from the chair-
manship in 1952, Kenneth became a director.

Life would have been easier now if my grandfather's health
had not begun to fail. It was his wish to make one more journey
to India and, after various false starts and amid waves of chaos
and commotion at Norhurst – everyone running around in perplexity and the dog wringing its hands – this he achieved in
1955, touring the company's gardens at Assam in his eightieth
year. There is a picture of him there, smiling benignly while various estate workers are doubled up in laughter. Seven years later,
as Chinese troops invaded Assam, we were privileged at
Maidenhead to get our first glimpse of the Rajmai plantations,
edged with Old Nan's silhouette, on our television. But by then
my grandfather was dead.

He had not been well for almost a decade. Indeed for much of
that time he had been stubbornly dying, on bad days in desperation and terror in front of us. He died a little upstairs in his
front bedroom and then a little more downstairs in the morning-
room where the family had made up a bed for him. He died on
a stretcher going down the stairs and in the ambulance going off
to the hospital; and then he went on dying as he was moved in
and out of hospital, back and forth between the wards, again,
again. It took a fearful time his dying, and we all felt we had
died a little with him.

Until I witnessed this, I had thought of death simply as a disappearance, someone walking into another room and shutting
the door; or a trick performed by a conjuror, painless and inexplicable, leaving the sensation that behind the descending curtain
everything was actually all right. I saw the process as we all saw
it in films; a lying down and closing of the eyes on camera.
Nothing more. I had known death only as part of fiction. My

grandfather showed me the fact. I was wholly unprepared for the awfulness of his final years and could not credit what was happening to him. Ours had been the sort of life at Norhurst, blasted with quarrels, saturated with an engulfing misery, that naturally drove us to entreat death – until my grandfather began to die. It was then we realised, all of us, how preferable a living death is to a dead one.

My grandfather died what is called a natural death ('congestive cardiac failure'). He was in his eighty-sixth year by the time the last painful breath had been crushed out of him. So he had had 'a good innings' despite not quite being 'a safe pair of hands'. Surely there could be nothing of which to complain? Yet I was horrified. My father, seeing my distress and suffering distress himself, remarked that through the long horrors of history many people had gone through worse experiences. He began to recite them as if finding comfort from this frightful litany.

In rooms close to where my grandfather was dying, we would gather to discuss his condition, discuss his life. I know more of his life now than I did then. I know that he did not enjoy a successful business career, or a happy marriage, or achieve anything of special distinction. His one romantic adventure had ended in disaster and he had done very little with the fortune he inherited from his father except lose it – indeed he would have ended up a bankrupt had he not been rescued by Kenneth after the war. Yet we spoke of him with reverence, as if he were a truly great man. Not that he ever said anything of greatness. His political opinions, which were expressed as a series of slogans ('Jack's as good as his master') were a hundred years or more out of date and, I believe, copied from his father, the Major-General, who perhaps had more right to them. We thought of him as a Christian Gentleman, though he never went to church and the disgruntled clichés he aimed at socialists were profoundly unChristian. Once he had been a believer, or believed he had been, and he still wanted to believe. But he simply could not. During this last phase of his life, his bible was Gayelord Hauser's *Look Younger, Live Longer*. All his life he had longed to look and feel younger, and now he was striving fearfully to live longer. It was the pathos of his predicament that touched us all so unbearably. Here was a gentle man whose home had resounded with vituperation, nothing if not well-meaning and now coming to nothing, whose long life had been largely unlived and whose fear of hurting others had now turned to a fear of being hurt himself, of being extinguished, buried, burnt.

He had watched his own father die, his infant son Desmond, his brother Pat. And his mother had killed herself. These deaths, I believe, had destroyed his Christian faith. Now it was his turn, and there was to be no miracle. As the realisation spread through him that there was no place for him to go but into oblivion, the change in him became dreadful. His life, for so long incomprehensible and bleak, now appeared wonderfully desirable. He yearned for more of it, for another chance to do better. The remorselessness of his dying made him unrecognisable. All the resilience, good humour, niceness were gradually prised out of him. He did not know how to behave. He was afraid: afraid of more pain, afraid of the nurses, afraid of the medical instruments to which he was attached, afraid of everything. Of what use now were his gentlemanly standards? He had left his card, but the Great Gentleman above was not at home. He was nowhere.

As a source of hope and strength, his vanished faith was replaced by drugs, and these also changed him. They allowed him to sleep, but seemed to give him no rest. His sleep was pitted with nightmares. He shouted out incomprehensible cries, struggled in his bed as if against invisible bonds, and then woke exhausted from hours of wrestling with his unseen opponent. His face sank in, the colour of his skin went to green and purple. The hospital ward was crowded with patients bandaged and strapped like grotesque babies lying in their cots, all alike, all waiting. One day, after a couple of taut hours at the bedside, I was relieved by my aunt who wearily pointed out that I had been sitting next to the wrong bed.

I hated these sessions beside the bed. I seemed to become infected with all my grandfather's fear and sadness. And I could do nothing to help. The wards were like parade grounds where the Last Post was constantly sounding, and marks were awarded for deportment and smartness. By such standards, his own until recently, my grandfather was not making a good death. He was drawing attention to himself, creating trouble, not going quietly, letting himself down, letting us down. This must have been in his mind when he looked across at me and gasped out: 'I'm sorry.'

Those were the last words I heard him speak. On 24 February 1961, the hospital telephoned to say that he had died 'fairly comfortably' early that morning. None of us had wanted him to die and all of us were relieved now he was dead. My grandmother sang out her grief in a frightful dirge that scraped our nerves but gave us a target for our hostility. My Uncle Kenneth began talking, and went on talking, about farming matters to take his mind off it all. 'My God, this is an awful place,' my father unconsciously quoted as we stood together in the undertaker's office. Then my aunt rushed in, looking tired and furious. It was almost as if she were preparing for another washing-up battle over the spoons and saucepans. But then she steadied herself. Her father had been her god. No one could match her sense of loss. We fell back as she advanced upon his corpse, plastered with frozen pink cosmetics. She leant over and lingeringly kissed the gaping face – something I had never seen her do to the living man, or any living man; something I could not do myself.

I do not remember the funeral service, only the burying, so far down in the earth it was, at Braywick cemetery.

A month later a terrific storm broke out at Norhurst as to whether my grandmother was older than Old Nan. Yolande claimed that Old Nan was now the senior member of the household, and Nan herself forcefully nodded her agreement. But my grandmother, bitterly disputing this, appealed to me to get her birth certificate from Cork. This was not easy. The Corbet family, which had once teemed so prolifically over Ireland in the late nineteenth century, dazzling my grandfather, had left no sign of their existence in the Register Office in Dublin, or the National Library, or National Archives. They had vanished. But eventually I did get the birth certificate and was able to show that for the last quarter of a century my grandmother had been lying over her age, and that she was indeed older than Old Nan. The rage this provoked in Yolande took me aback. She shouted that it was a forgery, that you could never trust Irish records, that I had somehow invented it. She put it under a light and stared at it disbelievingly. She was tempted, I could see, to destroy it and swear it never existed. This was my grandmother's one triumph over her family.

She needed a triumph to compensate a little for the shock of not having been left Norhurst outright by her husband. He had given the house jointly to Yolande and herself, and made Yolande his sole trustee 'of my family's financial interests'. It was this deprivation, this sense of being under her daughter's control, of feeling almost a lodger in her own home, that prompted her to assert her seniority and also, perhaps, to commit some strange acts of demolition. She tore up and threw away a number of innocent objects from her past, mainly photographs of better days. I saw the pieces littered across her bedroom and can see now the rents she made with a knife through some of the family albums, obliterating figures she had known.

My aunt believed, or affected to believe, that she had finally gone mad. She pointed to the scoldings my grandmother would give invisible servants, the way she broke inexplicably into French. But she had done such things for years. I could remember as a child hearing her cry out the word 'Jamais!' and thinking it was some kind of confectionery. Besides, the mad have perfectly sane reasons for their madness. Her destruction of these photographs struck me as an act of revenge for the loveless disappointment of living.

She had so often called upon God to take her that her quiet death in hospital, on 21 January 1969 at the age of ninety-two, seemed an anti-climax, like the opening of a play we had long been watching in rehearsal. I remember the funeral service in All Saints Church at the end of our garden: the sudden piercing beauty of a hymn, then nothing.

We kept the news of her death from Kenneth who was himself dying (I visited him in a Sussex hospital and he braced himself on his deathbed to be a perfect host). My grandmother had made a Will at the beginning of 1968 in which she left Yolande and Basil £100 each. But her estate was valued at only £217 and there was nothing left after the payment of debts and funeral expenses. She had signed her name, Adeline Holroyd, on the Will, but added 'also known as Adeline Genevive Holroyd'. None of us knew the name Genevive and it does not appear on her birth certificate. Perhaps it was a special name Fraser had called her in Ireland before their marriage, or a name her father used when she was a child, or possibly an invented name signifying her wish to become someone else.

19

Missing Persons

It took longer to publish my Life of Hugh Kingsmill than to write it. I finished the writing when I was twenty-four, but did not see it in print until I was in my thirtieth year. The book was a labour of love but much of the labour was wasted and the love did not shine through. The words seemed strung across the page like dumb notes on a piano, and my judgements relied too much on other people's opinions. It was also rather incompetently put together, an apprentice work, fumbling, defensive, gauche – otherwise fine. Dorothy Hopkinson never sent the unpublished material I expected, writing from South Africa to say that she was composing a book on Kingsmill herself.

But what chiefly deterred publishers was the towering commercial impracticality of a biography about a forgotten author by an unknown writer. I sent the typescript eventually to sixteen publishers who insisted on returning it to me as if it were a tennis ball sent over to them for that purpose. The rally lasted four years, and I noticed with surprise, as the battered package

My grandparents
with their children
at Windsor:
Kenneth (left),
Basil (middle)
and Yolande

My Swedish grand-
mother, Kaja,
Stockholm, *c.*1913

The schoolboy at Eton

The novelist in London

Brocket in the 1920s

My father with his
schnauzer puppy

Ulla, my mother, when she
arrived in England *c.* 1934

My mother during her
cancer treatment

Haselhurst *c.*1940

My aunt Yolande in the 1920s

The author of *Mosaic* (photograph © by John Foley)

Philippa: while writing *Frank Harris*

Agnes May: the hand-painted
photograph commissioned
by my grandfather *c.*1928

BLUE TINTED MIRROR PENDANT   18½" OVER/ALL DIA.
CHAMPAGNE TINTED COLLAR & LENS BOWL
Nº 1204/12   SCALE ½ FULL SIZE

Illustrations of two light fittings
by the author's father

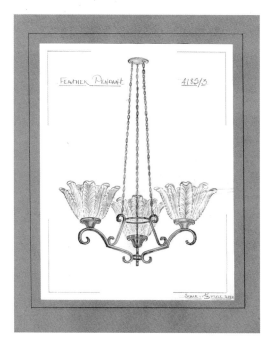

FEATHER PENDANT   4185/3

SCALE ½ FULL SIZE

came back and I posted it off again, an obstinacy mounting in me to a point of exhilaration. Perhaps, as Purple Parr predicted, I had some determination in me after all.

William Gerhardie and Hesketh Pearson did whatever they could to help. Gerhardie wrote a long characteristic article in the *Spectator* entitled 'The Uses of Obscurity'. With my two grand-mothers, he told readers, I had already achieved the status of Grand Old Man of Letters. My *Hugh Kingsmill*, he continued, had received such glowing rejection notices from so many pub-lishers that 'it may fairly rank as the best book never published'. On the strength of this piece I wondered whether to produce extra copies of my typescript to meet the demand. Unfortunately the author of 'Success: and How to Avoid It' had slipped in a sentence indicating that I had once been a promising squash player. 'His father,' Gerhardie revealed, 'though encouraging a literary career, regrets that in pursuit of the quite hopelessly neg-lected Kingsmill, Michael should be seriously neglecting his squash.' Others appeared to agree. From publishers, even from poets and historians – James Michie, Robert Skidelsky – I received letters exclusively on squash rackets. Kingsmill again had been neglected.

Hesketh Pearson wrote to several publishers and gave me a generous quote that could be used on the jacket. It was partly through him that Martin Secker at last offered to bring out the book from his Unicorn Press in the Royal Opera Arcade, allow-ing me an advance of £25. Though this, to use a phrase of Kingsmill's, may have 'looked more like a retreat than an advance', it was a generous gesture since the money came from his own pocket. Equally generous was the long Introduction Malcolm Muggeridge contributed free of charge. Early in 1964 Malcolm Muggeridge, Hesketh Pearson, Martin Secker and myself lunched at the Café Royal, and Martin Secker was able to report that, following a favourable review in the *Observer*, sales had topped thirty-nine copies.

I had, as Dickens might have said, 'commenced biographer'.

To the C.O. it was immediately clear that something extra was needed to transform the book into a popular success. His dog knew the dog belonging to a man he believed to be a band leader. From two leads' distance he suggested interviewing this man and, if his answers proved satisfactory, engaging him professionally for a special launch party. We would have to see our bank managers of course, but it should not be impossible to put on something modestly spectacular. In any business, he explained, some form of advertising, some promotion of good will, was essential. I would be a fool to ignore this. In a spasm of fantastical magniloquence he appeared to be peopling Maidenhead Thicket with literary celebrities such as J.B. Priestley and Daphne du Maurier. He saw them sipping their drinks, moving gracefully around as in some ballet, and putting my book on the map. This plan, or some version of it, was frustrated barely in time by the intervention of a libel action from Dorothy Hopkinson.

Unknown before I came to write about him, Kingsmill has stubbornly remained unknown since the publication of my book in 1964 and the selection from his writings entitled *The Best of Kingsmill* that I brought out six years later. But he had started me on my way. In so far as he wrote biographies himself, Kingsmill had been described as a follower of Lytton Strachey, a categorisation I attempted to refute. So began the pattern of my future work where a significant minor character in one biography develops into the subject of the next.

During the nineteen-sixties and nineteen-seventies I became increasingly absorbed in my subjects' lives. 'Writing is a form of disappearance,' the poet Simon Armitage writes. From my parents I certainly began to disappear. I was like a science fiction character, travelling across time, stretching out and trying to make contact with people I had never met. I travelled on a current of energy ignited by their work, concentrated in their loves and spread around widening circles from their deaths. I was attempting, or so I sometimes felt, to retrieve something from death itself, having been so shocked by my grandfather's dying. Kingsmill and Strachey, Augustus John and Bernard Shaw became the maverick teachers I never had at a university. I learnt emotionally as well as intellectually: and then there was the archaeological digging up of facts. With these I plotted patterns and contours showing different aspects of cultural and political history between the mid-nineteenth and mid-twentieth centuries, and endeavoured to give my answer to a contemporary question: how did we get here?

I led a gregarious and solitary life. My research journeys took me eventually all over the world. Then, back in London, I would shut my door against the world and write for days and weeks in bed. There was no one 'at his desk' earlier than I was, I explained to my father, who seemed determined to catch me napping. All this distanced me from my parents, the C.O. and Madam as they now were.

Ignoring the libel action over *Hugh Kingsmill* (which obliged me to utter an apology, pay costs and rewrite some pages on Dorothy Hopkinson), my mother was happy to see me become self-supporting, as a man should be. The sort of career I had chosen was incredible, but then she had never taken any interest in men's business affairs. *The Sunday Times*'s serialisation of *Lytton Strachey* and *Augustus John* in the late nineteen-sixties and early nineteen-seventies was evidence enough for her that I was properly employed. But her relief could not altogether conceal her wonder that such books could find a single reader.

My father's attitude was more complicated. When I handed him my *Hugh Kingsmill*, he placed it carefully on a table and asked in a tone of urgency how *Lytton Strachey* was coming along. When I eventually gave him *Lytton Strachey*, he inquired gravely after my progress on *Augustus John*. The public was notoriously fickle, he reminded me, and if I didn't bring out a book each year, every year, readers would quickly forget about me. 'Your name has not been mentioned,' he volunteered after reading an article on contemporary writing in the *Daily Express*. I never saw him open one of my books and he was disparaging about my subjects (Strachey was a queer fish; John completely out of fashion; Shaw a cynic whose bluff had been called). His concern on my behalf was somewhat lowering to the spirits. So I was later surprised to find that, after I returned to London, he would go round the village boasting of my achievements to bewildered neighbours.

During the late nineteen-sixties my parents marked time. My mother, who was still receiving a quarterly allowance from Egon Hessel, lived in a series of rather smart apartments taken on short leases. Over seven or eight years she moved from a flat near Sloane Square to another above Elizabeth David's shop in Ebury Street overlooking Orange Square, and then to a mansion apartment near Earls Court. The future frightened her and, unlike William Gerhardie, she lived wholly in the present. It was an attractive quality, especially for young people on whom she spent her money – actually Egon Hessel's money and Kaja's. 'I was young, inexperienced, rather gauche,' my ballet student girl-friend Jennifer writes to me. She had come down to London from Lancashire at the age of twenty and 'to be plunged into your world of expensive restaurants and clubs, taxis everywhere, apparently wealthy people, fashionably dressed was pretty heady stuff'.

> When I think of Ulla I think of champagne. Even her hair, her colouring and a lot of her clothes were the colour of champagne. There seemed a champagne-tinted aura around her . . . I remember Ulla for her enthusiasms and exuberance – the way she greeted the French onion man in Orange Square like a long lost friend; her childlike delight at purchasing in the Portobello Road two green

Chinese vases which were to be converted into table
lamps; and an evening at a restaurant called Chez Victor
where, having said farewell to Kaja that day she was
inclined to sob on the proprietor's shoulder and had to be
restored with champagne cocktails.

In Jennifer's eyes I was a young man with parents, but no
cohesive family. She could discover nothing in common between
my father and my mother. Certainly my father had an innate
sense of fair play, but he believed that the rules of the game had
been unfairly changed at half-time. A vast store of good will
seemed locked in some secret chamber within him and no one
could find the key. But he was still on the lookout for some
woman or business partner who might know where it lay. I
would sometimes go for a drink on Sundays and he would whisper over a sherry that he wanted me to meet someone he thought
I'd like. There was a high-flyer from Epsom to whom he had
given 'one of your tomes'; there was a lady temporarily down on
her luck who worked at Bobby's of Bournemouth ('the sort of
place your publishers should try to get rid of your stuff'); and
there was a woman he had met at the village pub who could type
('might be rather valuable to you, Michael'). But it was difficult
for him to sustain a relationship without money. After the collapse of timber and insolvency of Seamless Floors, he became
'not exactly dour, perhaps sombre or withdrawn are better
words to describe him', Jennifer writes to me. The three of us
would occasionally have lunch in the empty kitchen at his mock-
Tudor refuge where he frantically pressed extra helpings on us.
As his fortunes went downhill he would give me increasingly elevated advice on how to manage my literary career and issue
darker warnings against fecklessness.

The worst of times was beginning for my father, and the best
of times for me. The revolution of the nineteen-sixties reached
me late, but not too late. The sudden freedom between the sexes,

the greater equality too, and the easy atmosphere that allowed us all to resolve many differences into games, came as a wonderful liberation for men as well as women – at least it did for me. A more natural life, with wider emotional horizons, opened up. I moved into it gratefully. To those dead men, my biographical subjects, who had laboured in their fashion for change, and to the living women who transformed my experience of the world, I owe all that I value most. For two or three of the latter I was more than a request stop along their emotional routes. Ideally I had always been 'one for whom the visible world exists'. In these women's eyes I recovered my visibility though some habits could not be changed and I remain invisible to myself. Observation and participation grew so involved that I cannot now separate them. Looking out of the window at the multitude of birds, squirrels and cats in the garden I easily forget myself (I am a cat person unlike my family who were all dog people). If I look out of another window I see the men, women and children walking past in the street, all part of a narrative, each with a story, and I follow them in my imagination. I never tire of watching. I watch, therefore I am; I am what I watch; and what I watch entrances me. This has been my exit from myself.

All these new interests carried me further from my family but when matters began to go seriously wrong I was quickly drawn back. I began my biography of Bernard Shaw where he had begun his life, in Dublin, and was abroad in Ireland and the United States for some two years. The change in my parents after I returned in 1977 was striking.

At the start of the decade Egon Hessel's allowance had suddenly dried up. My mother retreated to a one-room flat in Chelsea Manor Street off the King's Road where I had written most of my *Lytton Strachey* after leaving Nell Gwynn House. Like my father in Surrey, my aunt at Maidenhead, she looked out on a cemetery. 'Moved to Daver Court,' she noted in the account she later wrote for me, 'where I still am – goodness knows for how long – getting too expensive. Bank owns my flat.' She made several visits to Stockholm, but Kaja was not well and needed to borrow money herself. 'Trying to sell my Swedish Pewter this year,' my mother wrote to me. She also sold pictures and furniture that had belonged to Kaja.

She still had a regular 'boyfriend'. Jimmy was not sophisticated or wealthy or romantic. But he was kind and had a whacky sense of humour that agreeably bewildered my mother. He protected her from loneliness. But when she met a rather dashing gentleman with a title (who by a coincidence lived on the edge of Maidenhead Thicket) she could not resist one more escapade. It would be fun to escape again and forget her age, her financial worries. It was a short affaire and the only one, I believe, she truly regretted. 'Wish I had not met him,' she wrote, 'as I lost Jimmy then.'

In her late fifties she was obliged to start work. She took a job as a 'floating supervisor' at Bourne and Hollingsworth, but left it after one week. Then she started working as an occasional interpreter at business conferences and exhibitions. Her letters to me mention events at the Goldsmiths Hall, Earls Court, Olympia, Grosvenor House, the Hilton Hotel in London and the Metropole Hotel in Brighton. For short spells she was working 'like billy-ho'. There are photos of her at gift fairs, electrical exhibitions, brewery conferences ('no free samples') holding a microphone and wearing the glazed expression I know so well (and struggle myself to conceal at committee meetings) as she translates what is unintelligible in one language into what is accurately unintelligible in another.

Now that she was responsible for herself, my mother's life grew bureaucratically more complex. I would receive letters from building societies, banks, insurance companies asking me how long Mrs Ulla Nares had been in my service, whether she was on my permanent staff, what the nature of her duties were and the amount of her monthly salary. 'God help me with the dole!!!' she exclaimed in one letter. She spent many indecipherable hours at the Inland Revenue headquarters being encumbered with the correct assistance. 'Am shaking at the knees,' she wrote to me, 'but say to myself they are trying to help me. Waterford House seems like my second home by now!'

In the autumn of 1976 she was sixty. I was then abroad and did not particularly notice her birthday. Not that she ever forgot mine. She would write apologising for having no expensive presents or exciting news. 'I am thinking of you all the time & wish you all the best in the world in every respect. Love Madam.'

Her moods varied. 'Sometimes I'm glad to be alone & not having to cope with difficult men and their tantrums & whims.' These men, businessmen from conferences, would still telephone on the off-chance, but she could not pretend to enjoy their company anymore and now avoided them. Nevertheless it was not impossible that an incredible someone might ride up and rescue her. 'No social life at all,' she noted. 'Too old & getting very tired of everything. Waiting for the next exciting thing to happen, but I think time is running out and age has taken its toll – but who knows?'

While I was out of the country I asked my parents to telephone each other. 'I spoke to your mother a few evenings ago,' my father reported. 'She seemed very depressed. It's understandable as everything is going from bad to worse. She is complaining bitterly that with your departure she has no one to advise her & I have a nasty suspicion that I've been selected for the post.' In fact he had been selected for another post: that of storing her clothes in the spare room of his flat. 'She arrived down here to collect her winter clothes,' he notified me later. These exchanges of winter and summer clothes marked their first meetings for almost thirty years.

My father's letters over this period are as despondent as my mother's, but written in an aggrieved tone. Shortly before I went abroad he had started a new company called Indus that specialised in brick buildings. Nothing, he remarked, would ever replace bricks and mortar. He wanted to get this business off to a brisk start, but one morning careered his car into a bollard and landed up in the cottage hospital with his leg in plaster. His dog Jonathan was really at fault. My father had bought what appeared to be a miniature schnauzer to keep him company after his wife left him, and this puppy got into the habit of sitting on his lap as he drove around the country looking for work. Unfortunately it soon grew to an enormous size and insisted on its right to occupy the driving seat of the car, squeezing my father to the side, his head and much of his body hanging out of the window in summer and, in the winter months, being displaced largely on to the passenger seat, from which position he did his best to continue driving. He had to chauffeur Jonathan each week between Ewell, the Surrey village where he lived, and Maidenhead because he shared the dog with Yolande (who took sole command while my father was in hospital).

It was a worrying time for my father. He worried, at the age of seventy, that he might be pressed into 'the Great Army of the Unemployed', and become bankrupt as his father had almost done. 'I'll probably end up in quod,' he wrote to me. 'Not a bad way to save money.' He worried too about his dog Jonathan because the Maidenhead vet never agreed with the Ewell vet and both were wickedly expensive. He worried, of course, about me: 'I imagine you may have to do something as well as write about Shaw if you're going to make two ends meet. By the time Shaw comes on the market there'll be no one to buy the book.' But 'I am most worried about Yolande,' he confided.

By the mid-nineteen-seventies Yolande had lived and worked in the house for forty years, looking after her parents, looking after Old Nan. At last, in her early seventies, she owned the house. She felt that she had earned it. She knew she had. She enjoyed having half a dog to exercise, but she dreaded her brother's visits to Norhurst.

What he was writing to me, he was saying to her. To live in a five-bedroom house by herself was utter madness. She had almost no money and 'was trying to live on less and less'. She hardly dared switch on an electric light in case it cost too much, and she never used the heating. She would kill herself and drown the rest of us in guilt. The rooms were so cluttered with rubbish that 'it's hard to find room to put down a plate'. Nevertheless she 'is so set in her ways (like the rest of us) that it's impossible to alter things at all'. He longed to alter things for the better. But how could he when she refused his offers of help? 'I go down weekly and do what I can,' he wrote morosely. He would buy and cook some food for her – a brace of partridges, say, at which she nibbled with distaste. Otherwise she never ate anything cooked at all: only biscuits, bread, cake and fruit washed down with lavish cups of tea. The situation was so bad that 'it really needs me to be there for a month or more', my father concluded. But this was impossible because he was starting up a new company, Framed Building Installations, that made special use of steel.

My father could never understand why anyone should quail before his offers of help. Unfortunately, to help people, he had to make sure that they were worse off than he was. This was increasingly difficult. He was so impoverished now that being the target of his help became a peculiarly depressing experience for the beneficiary. He tormented Yolande with his generosity and advice. Everything he said was factual. But he did not see her fundamental need to keep Norhurst, a need that, though she could not explain it, was stronger than his battalion of facts. 'Yolande won't of course think of leaving as long as Nan is alive,' he reasoned.

Old Nan had stayed on at Norhurst until 1975 and was then moved to the St Mark's Hospice in Maidenhead where Yolande would take the dog to visit her each day. She was to die on 17 May 1976, four months short of her hundredth birthday. My father naturally concluded that 'Yolande is more inclined to think of selling up & getting out, but the trouble is where to get out to.'

But he was wrong. He need not have worried where Yolande was going because she was absolutely determined to go nowhere. Why should she? Why didn't other people mind their own business? The thought that some of the contents of the house belonged to her brother and that their sale would come as a great relief to him, did not occur to her. I argued that since Norhurst was gaining in value it should be sold later. But my father thought differently. He saw the future as so bleak that Norhurst might soon be unsaleable. Its condition was deteriorating rapidly. Besides, everyone knew that property prices would soon take a dive. 'It's on the cards,' he wrote to me, 'that a five bedroom house occupied by one person could be taken over by the State to solve the housing problem. One might get paid some small compensation in a worthless currency.'

We had reached this point in the debate when, one day in 1980, everything changed. Even when my aunt was not looking after her brother's dog Jonathan, she would still charge up to the fields and into Maidenhead Thicket as if leading a phantom pack of all those dogs she had aired and exercised for half a century. She moved amazingly fast for someone now in her late seventies, urging herself on, looking utterly absorbed, fighting old battles. Then, coming into All Saints Avenue from the children's playground, she suddenly staggered, fell, picked herself up, lurched sideways, and began calling incoherently for help. A few people in the street stared and hurried past, probably thinking she was drunk. She tried to stop a car, but it swerved onwards. Eventually she was assisted on to a milk-float and driven slowly back with the rattling bottles to Norhurst. The milkman helped her in, but she refused all other help.

My father, telephoning that evening to make arrangements for Jonathan's next visit, got no reply. After a couple of hours, he spoke to the police. They went round, saw my aunt through the window lying on the floor, and broke in. She was then rushed to hospital.

After her stroke she was severely paralysed. There was no question now of her returning to Norhurst. How could she? But this was what she wanted. She would have preferred to die there, I think, than live anywhere else. The house was full of painful memories. There was no room that had not absorbed years of reverberating anger and the awful atmosphere of our unhappiness. But these echoes from the past now seemed to bring her a ghastly satisfaction. The place was in a terrible state, barely inhabitable, yet she took a grim pleasure living there, a bitter comfort. After all, she had come through. Norhurst was her home. She belonged there: and it belonged to her. There was justice in that, and she did not want to be deprived of justice. To abandon the house, whatever the circumstances, would be a betrayal of her father who had left it to her. She would not abandon it. No one could make her.

Yet she could not go back. She was in a wheelchair, able to move one arm and one leg, but unable to dress or undress, unable to wash, eat or do anything else without help. Years ago the question had been: 'What shall we do with the boy?' Now it was: 'What shall we do with my aunt?'

Until her stroke, I had used whatever male arguments I could summon to support my aunt's need to continue living at Norhurst. But once her course of physiotherapy showed that she was unlikely to regain much movement in her body, I changed my mind. If we sold the house, I told her, we could buy her a flat on the ground floor of the building at Ewell where my father lived. We would have enough money to adapt it for a disabled person, to make it comfortable, and to employ someone to look after her. My soft words sounded so pleasant – almost as if it were worth becoming paralysed to qualify for such luxury. But my aunt would have none of it. From her hospital bed, unable properly to form her words, she fought us all the way. But she could not win because she had granted power of attorney to my father. We were taking away the shell of her life, she believed, wherein her powers of speech and movement might marvellously be restored. She attacked the estate agents even when they brought flowers; she told the auctioneers who sold the contents of the house that they were crooks; and she accused my father and myself of acting as her enemies as we struggled with landlords, bank managers, doctors, the social services and local authorities on her behalf. One day, when she had been particularly dreadful, it seemed to me, about my father/her brother, I stood over her hospital bed as she lay there, still and fearful, shouting at her that she should have had the nerve to leave the house years ago, shouting that her brother had at least tried, and tried again, to make something of his life and been given nothing for his pains, shouting that he was trying now to salvage something of her life as best he could. It was a wretched confrontation.

Norhurst was finally sold for £65,000 and with that money we moved Yolande into a flat close to my father. We had brought over some bits and pieces from Maidenhead to make her feel at home – a couple of Lalique animals, a drawing by Lewis Baumer and one by Anna Zinkheisen, her hairbrushes, a mirror, handbags, familiar china plates and cups – and she moved into her new world.

The contrast with her previous life was extreme. She, who had been so independent, now depended for almost everything on a team of nurses and helpers who came and went from morning until evening. Instead of disappearing across the fields, she sat all day in her wheelchair; instead of eating alone she was fed meals-on-wheels. I did not think she could endure this imprisoned life; I did not think she would consent to continue living. But she adapted to the restrictions miraculously. A peculiar sweetness grew up in her. She was anxious not to cause anyone trouble and, once reassured about this, she became extraordinarily cheerful. Jean and Rita, her two special helpers, wheeled her round the village and up to the library for tea. They wrapped her up and took her into the garden so that she could watch the birds. They brought her clothes, washed her, dressed her, arranged her hair, told her about their families, restored her self-esteem. I was touched by how fond they were of her, and she of them. As an embodiment of her class and time, my aunt would have been regarded as something of a snob in the nineteen-eighties. Snobbishness was her form of self-protection, her superior reason for not doing things that frightened her. She had overcome it in the war; she overcame it again now in her adversity with the help of Jean and Rita and others who looked after her. When she said in her indistinct yet still decisive voice that socialists, foreigners and anyone who criticised the Queen Mother should be shot, Jean and Rita would dance round in laughter – and my aunt happily joined in. All this merriment delighted her. In their game these foreigners and socialists were cartoon characters who could be shot again and again with no harm done. She came to feel quite protective of them.

One advantage of this new chapter in her life was that my father could keep an eye on her. Framed Building Installations had buckled almost before it was set up, leaving him at a loss. But Yolande's illness gave him something to do, and the sale of Norhurst and its contents gave him the money with which to do it. Her affairs occupied him a full year, but when she was finally settled into the same building as himself, things started to go wrong.

It began with his teeth. 'Had to have them all out with a general anaesthetic and a plate made,' he informed me. 'I reckon to finish paying for it around the year 2000.' Then it was his eyes. I took him for a couple of cataract operations: one worked well; the other didn't. Suddenly his handwriting, which had marched so straight and clear through all the ups and downs of his adult life, wobbled and veered crazily off the page. His hearing had also begun to fail. I attempted to get him a new hearing aid in London, but he became irritated with it, being unable to see the tiny batteries or adjust the volume.

My aunt's slithering speech and my father's foggy deafness made communication between them an unhappy business. He would find his way to her flat, his dog Jonathan waddling before him, but within minutes the two of them had grown furious with each other, as if their impairments were being purposely exploited. 'She does it deliberately,' my father complained to me after my aunt had failed again to 'speak up'.

He had forgotten her stroke. Soon he was forgetting more: where he was, what he had gone out for, whether it was morning or afternoon. Though I did not realise it, he was more seriously ill than his sister. I would go down to Ewell, take him out to lunch, then have tea with her. I would telephone beforehand to confirm the arrangements, but when I arrived my father had disappeared. When I did find him in the street, he was surprised to see me: 'Oh hello, Michael. What brings you here?' Once I let my impatience show. Then, in a passionate riposte, he came back at me: 'Wait till you're my age and you'll find out what it's like!' I hear his voice more clearly every year.

His lonely figure had become a well-known sight moving through the village streets, standing at a kerb. He did not drive any longer, but would sometimes stop at the traffic lights as if he were a car, his dog Jonathan looking up at him. Occasionally he went to the pub and also for a time to church, hoping to meet someone. But his deafness, poor sight and other ailments isolated him. People occasionally spoke to his dog Jonathan which pleased him, and there is a picture of them together in the local paper under the caption: 'One Man And His Dog'. My father is not quite in focus, but Jonathan spreads himself amply across the page and appears to be drinking my father's half-pint of beer.

One day my father was unable to find his way back to his flat. Someone got hold of his doctor, and his doctor got hold of me. He sounded indignant. 'I cannot have one of my patients wandering round the village like this,' he protested. On his advice, I took my father to be examined by a specialist who told me his heart was beating very slowly and that he needed a pacemaker to restore his circulation. Later I drove him to the hospital for the operation, after which he seemed more his old self, though still far from his young self. My anxieties receded. But by then my mother was ill.

She had telephoned me one morning after her bath to say there was a lump on her breast. What did I think? I heard my voice, confident, clear, categorical, telling her I thought this the most normal thing in the world, and certainly nothing to lose sleep over. These lumps and bumps were, on the whole, quite harmless and perfectly natural. Indeed, it would be curious, almost worrying in itself, if she'd *not* had one or two lumps by her early sixties – though of course, as a precaution, it must be examined. But the tests showed it to be malignant. Again I spoke with authority. Thank God, I exclaimed, she had not suffered such a thing earlier when they could do little about it. Now, I assured her, everything had advanced, everything was different. It was a well-known fact that most women with this trouble came out of hospital in a few days and went on to live the rest of their lives in excellent health. Modern medicine, I reminded her, was amazing. Of course she would have to endure regular check-ups and that was a bore. But it was no worse than that.

Before her operation, my mother made one more quick journey to Stockholm. Kaja had become almost blind and my mother was trying to persuade her to live in a Swedish convalescent home in London where, because it was technically on Swedish territory, her pension would still be paid to her. But like Yolande at Norhurst, Kaja wanted to spend her last years at her apartment in Artillerigatan, even if this meant never seeing her daughter again. She could barely see anything as it was and would be lost in unfamiliar surroundings. These few days were to be their last together.

My mother went into the Royal Marsden Hospital as soon as she returned from Sweden. This was only a few hundred yards from her flat at Daver Court. Seeing her in the ward, I told her what a good nurse she would have been. She made friends with all the patients, and seemed naturally popular with everyone. Her operation to remove one of her breasts was a success and when she went for a check-up a few months later there was no cancer in her body. But she had great difficulty with an infected sinus in the pit of her arm. She could never again get comfortable whether standing, sitting or lying down. The arm was fastened with bandages and they treated it in various ways. But it got worse and she was soon having to take pain killers.

Nevertheless, for some months, there was an interval in the descent of both my parents' health, as if they had landed on a ledge. I was at that time giving a platform performance at the Lyttleton Theatre before a production of Shaw's play, *The Philanderer*, and I decided to invite them both. This took considerable planning, but I got them there and, as I walked on to the stage, I saw them sitting together in the audience. My mother had her arm fixed at an acute angle like a child in a classroom asking to be excused. My father battled furiously with his hearing aid from which high-pitched bleats were being signalled. After my talk, we saw the play; and after the play I took them to the National Theatre Restaurant. My father frowned a little at the architecture, but not excessively; my mother looked round the tables and inquired if they played music there. It was difficult sustaining a conversation. Over the coffee my father braced himself, clearing his throat, moving uncomfortably in his chair, looking miserable. I knew the signs. He was searching for something pleasant to say about my lecture. I had reassured them both that I could not speak for long as I would be engulfed by the play itself, like a Stoppardian or Pirandello character. 'Yes,' my father said eventually taking his cue from this remark, 'coming to an end must have been tricky. I thought your ending very timely.'

This was the last time the three of us were together – indeed the only time I can remember us together since my childhood.

Not long afterwards my mother's cancer reappeared. So began a long sequence of treatments and operations that are a blur in my memory now, as if everything happened together and went on happening all the time. This dark period began with the suicide of her closest friend, Irene Heyman, and, a year or so later, the death of her ballet-dancing daughter who, with a final *entrechat*, threw herself in front of an underground train at Sloane Square. Poor Larry Heyman, his hand trembling violently round his whisky glass, moved to the top of a tower block in Fulham, and my mother never saw him again.

But other friends came back. Shirley Morton, from the 'Wilmslow Wheelers', reappeared and insisted on getting a second opinion from her own doctor. And Gay, Edy Fainstain's daughter and my one-time stepsister, returned, bringing flowers, bringing comfort, hugging my mother in a way I had never learnt to do. There were women, too, with whom my mother had worked as an interpreter at business fairs and conferences; and, from further back, women with whom she had modelled in Basil Street; as well as a good drinking friend in Daver Court. Arriving at her bedside in the hospital, or at her flat, I would sometimes find a gang of these friends who had gathered to raise her morale. Griffy, too, suddenly turned up from Wales with his Swedish wife Ingrid, filling the place with children and talking of the old days beside the lake at Velden and above the sea near La Turbie. Outside in the street, as he was leaving, he asked: 'Why are we so gloomy when our mothers are so jolly?' Then, after a moment, he raised his voice in answer: 'Stand up, Purple Parr, and be recognised!'

My father would sometimes telephone with obscure messages. 'Your mother is being very brave,' he said gruffly. Then, in a voice from the past: 'Poor Sue.' Kaja also called regularly from Sweden. She was blind now and many of these talks with her daughter ended tearfully.

My mother was a naturally good patient, but as her condition worsened she found it more difficult to cope with visitors, feeling anxious over entertaining them and guilty at the possibility of letting them go away empty-handed. She would make ashtrays from shells, napkin rings from odd pieces of fabric, cards and trinkets from all sorts of scraps and oddments to give them. Sometimes I would feel irritated by all this trivial and unnecessary work she gave herself. But perhaps it was not trivial or unnecessary. I was exasperated too by some of the things she asked me to do, such as negotiating the renewal of her insurance cover on a fur coat we both knew she would never wear again, and arranging for her to be excused the wearing of a seat belt in a car, though she did not own a car and was unlikely to be travelling in one. I was learning how little we can do to help the terminally ill: and how important that little sometimes is.

There were a few practical things I could do, such as buying her flat at Daver Court from the bank to save her financial on top of medical anxieties. Some days I would telephone the hospital on her behalf because 'they take more notice of a man'. And I would occasionally accompany her to the Royal Marsden Hospital, always anxious over my own loss of working time. She might have an appointment at ten in the morning and actually see the doctor at four in the afternoon. She became exhausted by these hours of waiting and dispirited at times by the impersonal quality of the treatment. 'So what seems to be the matter?' asked one doctor resting his elbow on a huge file of my mother's medical records. Each time, it seemed, there was a new doctor in charge of her; each time we started from the beginning; and every time, in case of legal repercussions, a matron or ward sister stood sentinel over us. 'Whichever way I turn,' my mother complained in her idiomatic English, 'my bottom is still behind me.' Occasionally the ambulance failed to arrive; most days it came at unexpected hours; one day, despite her protests, it took her to the Royal Marsden Hospital in Surrey and had to race back, its siren clanging and lights flashing, to the Fulham Road.

One evening when I was visiting her, I went by mistake into an adjacent ward and saw a surreal sight. I was apparently not in a hospital at all, but in a restaurant. A line of smart waiters stood at one end, and the first guests in their dinner jackets and long dresses stood drinking and chatting round a long table set for dinner, its wine glasses gleaming in the candle-light. I stared in disbelief and then, back in the corridor of the hospital, asked a nurse whether I had been dreaming. She laughed at my surprise. For this was one of the Royal Marsden Hospital's fund-raising events, the success of which was marked by a giant financial barometer on the front of the building. As I sat next to my mother's bed that evening, seeing her suffering, conscious of people close to death in other beds, I could not blot out the picture of that formal scene on the other side of the wall, the grotesque juxtaposition of those diners-out and these in-patients – or 'clients', 'customers' and 'consumers of health' as they were soon to be called in the new political circumlocution. I fantasised over wheeling this army of the old and ill next door and overwhelming that table of money-changers from the so-called 'real world' with actual reality and misrule. But of course I could do nothing, and whatever I can do I do now.

One day a nurse brought my mother the news that Kaja was dead, and she cried. Not long afterwards she had another operation during the course of which she regained consciousness. It was this shock, after enduring so much for so long, that broke her spirit. I saw the skull beneath the skin. I saw the skeleton of death. What upset me was that so soft a person had to be so mutilated. Still uncertain of the facts, I went to speak to the doctor in charge. It was again another doctor, with the matron in attendance. He told me that my mother had only three or four days to live – he would not have told me had I not asked directly. It was necessary, apparently, that she endure these extra days of torment. Was it possible, I inquired, for my mother to be given the strongest sleeping pills by night and the strongest pain killers by day? The matron seemed surprised by my request, but agreed.

So often over the years these doctors and nurses had given us bad news, and more often they had given us no news at all. My role was to be Dr Pangloss and give out a continual stream of glowing news. This was what my mother wanted to hear. I returned to her bed and looked her straight in the eyes, those sunken eyes. The worst, I told her, was mercifully over. She had come through. The pain would recede and she would sleep better. Then after a few bad days she would begin getting better. I can only hope she believed me.

Gay was often at her bed when I was not there and for longer periods than I was. She could do what I still could not do. She could kiss her, touch her, bring her moments of close physical comfort. I could not touch her in this way. I must write this again. I could not touch her.

Even with the drugs, even in her greatly weakened state, she was appallingly restless. This was her deathbed and she wanted to get off it. She twisted and gasped. Her hands, like spiders, crept around the blankets and explored the edge of the sheets. The nurses fixed iron railings to the sides of the bed as I sat there so that she would not fall out. I was so tense and my head throbbed so painfully that I asked the ward sister for an aspirin. She refused to give me an aspirin. I went out to a chemist down the street. When I came back my mother was draped across the iron bars of the bed. No one had yet noticed she was dead. A place of death awaits us all.

My father was too ill to come to the funeral. In 1982 he had made his Will appointing me his executor with the duty of looking after Yolande should he die first. But it was his dog Jonathan that died. He immediately bought a new dog, dog William, almost identical, and then added a codicil to his Will with details of dog William's breeding and instructions as to his 'upkeep if I pass out'.

His health was precariously stable. 'I am finding life very tricky,' he scribbled to me. 'It's like trying to walk on a tightrope & I have no doubt I'll come crashing down one day.' I was to take over power of attorney on behalf of my aunt and have a third-party mandate for my father, with both of which I tried to spread a safety net under their lives. After complaints from the landlord I arranged for my father's flat to be decorated and, approaching eighty, he seized the opportunity to go into business with the decorator, leasing him his spare room as an office and, in the role of 'consultant', putting him in touch with people in the building trade with whom he had not quarrelled. I remember some architectural drawings lying on his desk. They looked intricate and palatial and he had obviously derived deep pleasure from preparing them, though he confessed they were merely changing rooms and lavatories for a golf club.

There were days when he recovered his embattled self. Though admitting 'things are very very bad', he drew comfort from the thought that they 'can't be worse than having to live day & night with that arrogant old gentleman Bernard Shaw'. He also enjoyed crossing swords with a writer I knew well who lived in Ewell, John Stewart Collis ('You told me he's a good writer. He must indeed be good at something'). But on the whole he appeared to be growing more vulnerable, shedding a skin, and the sensitivity he had concealed with such flourishes of antagonism and joviality all his life, began to declare itself. I took pains to spare him good news, at least to dilute it. I now drove and owned a car, but pretended I was merely borrowing it and pointed out that it was an inferior automatic rather than a properly-geared machine. With unaccustomed mildness my father remarked that some automatic cars were really quite good these days he had heard – though he himself would not like his gears to be changed in Tokyo or Detroit while travelling round Surrey.

I have written that he found it impossible to give praise or receive money, but that is not quite correct and I stand rebuked by two incidents from this late period of his life. In one of his last notes to me, after I had placed some money in his bank account, he wrote to thank me: 'I never expected the sort of help you have given me and I can't remember ever having received anything so welcome before.' One afternoon I sat in the car with him, having to shout because of his deafness, telling him to spend his money on himself and go off at weekends to hotels with dog William (who was in the car at the time making communication more arduous). I tried to explain that it would be easier for me to help him financially if his capital fell still further, for then the State would assist me in helping him. I shouted that I had ensured in my Will that he would inherit enough money if I suddenly dropped dead. This was not charity, I yelled, but the natural dividend from a fatherly investment through childhood and adolescence, and in the allowance he had arranged for me in the nineteen-fifties. He sat staring out of the window and I could not tell whether he had taken it in. The dog leapt backwards and forwards between us. Then he said: 'Your mother said we could not have had a better son' – and he was fumbling desperately at the car door to get out. It was vicarious praise, of course, and very far from the truth, but it signalled a truce over all our animosities. Later I had a dream in which my father asked me if I'd like a smoke. He passed me a piece of iron piping with concrete knobs attached, bent like the starting handle of a car. It wasn't easy to get going, but we managed eventually and I took a puff or two, remarking that it was surprisingly pleasant: after which he took it from me and began puffing himself. Then I woke, and lay wondering whether this had been the Holroyd pipe of peace.

Gradually my father grew more confused again. His easiest moments now came over tea with Yolande. She had never noticed that there was anything wrong with him, and he no longer recognised that she was paralysed. Whenever they were together, they seemed to shed their injuries and impairments. What he said to her, what she attempted to say to him, had no connection – except an unspoken connection going back years – and neither of them grew irritable with the other any longer. These were occasions of excruciating hilarity over which, with my dual legal powers, I sometimes presided while my aunt's helpers, Jean and Rita, poured the tea.

But soon my father's neighbours were complaining to the landlord. Was he not a fire risk? Did he attract mice? Why should there be so much noise from his flat at night? One night there was a terrible sound of crashing, cries and commotion. Having no close friends, he was not missed next day until dog William's barking attracted people's attention. They found him lying unconscious on the floor surrounded by smashed crockery, blood, excreta, chaos. No one knew exactly what had happened.

But he was still alive and in the Sutton Hospital he began recovering physically, though not mentally. He imagined it was wartime again and he was back in the RAF. Looking round the ward at the patients walking on crutches, suspended in slings, caught in odd shapes by plaster of paris or attached to pulleys and plasma drips, he whispered to me: 'I don't think much of the new recruits.' After some months, I was asked to find him a residential home. He was obviously confused by the move and on arrival in Epsom kept calling the staff 'Mein host', as if on holiday in Bavaria. Forty-eight hours later, they telephoned me to say that he was far too ill to be in such a place, or even in one of the private nursing homes which I had been reconnoitring. He was afflicted by persistent hallucinations, believing himself to be under attack from people crawling across the ceiling to his bed. Fighting back as best he could, he was spreading alarm among the elderly residents. I drove him away, with his suitcase of clothes and bundle of medical records, to Sutton Hospital, but the ward he had been in only a couple of days before was now closed and there was no bed for him. We sat in the car. I did not know what to do. Eventually I had him certified under the Mental Health Act and he was then admitted to West Park Hospital.

Somehow my aunt's helpers conveyed her to this hospital and she sat happily by his bed. He did not recognise her. 'I can't think why they're keeping him there,' she later said to me. 'There's nothing on earth wrong with him.'

The specialists at the hospital thought they could bring my father some way back to normality, but their treatment was unavailing. He went on believing he was being assaulted, especially at night, by figures on the walls and ceiling. When I arrived one afternoon I saw him poised with a stick suspended in his hand, half-dressed, crouching but not moving. I tried reasoning with him. Who were these people? Why should anyone want to hurt him? He did not know. But it was impossible to reason with someone who had lost his reason. Then I entered his world of fantasy, assuring him his enemies had been vanquished and would not come again. This worked for as long as I stayed with him and could repeat it, but I could not calm his fears for long because he had no memory.

He was rescued from these harrowing assaults, this harrowing of hell, by pneumonia, sometimes called 'the old man's friend'. That, and senility, were given as the causes of his death.

My mother had died of 'disseminated carcinoma of breast' on 22 January 1986 at the age of sixty-nine, her occupation being given simply as 'Retired'. From life, as it were. My father, a 'Businessman Retired', was eighty when he died on 27 July 1988. Medical records are now kept for twenty-five years, but in the nineteen-eighties they were destroyed after only six years. No records therefore remain. I wrote to my father's doctor in Ewell where he lived his last thirty years, but his doctor cannot remember him. The Patient Affairs Officer at West Park Hospital cannot help me, since releasing medical case-note data would contravene the codes of confidentiality laid down by the Mental Health Act; and the Record Department at the Royal Marsden Hospital, though several times promising to send me clinical information about my mother, never does so. The waters of oblivion have quickly closed over them both.

This surprises me because for most of the nineteen-eighties I was engulfed by the bureaucracy of illness and death. Over this decade, on behalf of my parents and my aunt, there were hundreds of letters to write, documents to send back, telephone calls to make. I had to ensure I was doing the best for them, to understand the support systems and confirm that they were dying properly. I corresponded with a Citizens' Advice Bureau in London, the Department of Social Security in Newcastle-upon-Tyne, the Review Section of the Disability Benefits Unit in Blackpool, a benefits agency in Surrey; I wrote to Age Concern and Willing Hands, to nursing groups and homecare services and health centres; also general practitioners, consultant geriatricians, nursing homes, hospitals and undertakers; I was in communication with landlords, residents' associations, the taxation department of banks, the Inland Revenue, the Post Office, solicitors, accountants, estate agents. Much of this exchange, ingeniously obfuscated by developing information technology, was hardly interrupted by my parents' deaths. 'I keep writing to say that my father, Basil Holroyd, is dead. British Gas insists he is alive. If you have any information I should know, please give me access to it.'

The files that blossom round my aunt's simple life are the most voluminous and complex of all, partly because she lives on into the late nineties, and her late nineties. The number of forms

I must tick and cross, denying she is pregnant or divorced, the quantity of pages on which I must go on copying the words 'Not Applicable' leave me with the sense that I am giving evidence against her, invalidating her life, with these reiterated denials. No. None. Never. My answers cover the pages. Each time she has an extension of her stroke or an ischaemic attack and goes into hospital, each time she makes a partial recovery and comes back to her flat, a 'change of circumstances' is electronically signalled and the interrogation begins again. No. None. Never. I must refer to her as if she were a conscript in the army, a number, not by name, so that she can become compatible with the Social Services computer. That someone whose life was essentially so straightforward (who has no income beyond a State pension and the drops that still trickle through that old Heath Robinson machinery, the Holroyd Settlement), that she, at her age, should be forced into a world so alien goes beyond a joke, beyond my irony. I long to murder some of the courteous, patient, well-meaning officials from these departments, units, bureaux, centres.

My aunt was shocked by my father's death. It came as a total surprise to her and she misses him dreadfully, frequently calling me by his name. She has only happy memories of him, his kindness, his generosity, his fun. All their past furies have evaporated. She now resembles to a startling degree her mother Adeline whom she hated, but hates no more. Her temperament is perpetually sunny – no falls, no fractures, can cloud it. Her doctor recommends that she be removed to 'correctly structured' sheltered accommodation. He puts the facts as my father had once done, encouraging me to get my aunt to 'gracefully accept' them. Otherwise, he warns me, 'serious illness or death' might one day ensue. My aunt is ninety and does not want to move, and so I follow her wishes rather than her doctor's, employing more people to care for her in the flat she never wanted to go to, and now does not want to leave. To Jean and Rita and the others she owes the happiness of this period and the prolongation of her life. They keep her going, and going well, for over six years following my father's death.

After a fall in the autumn of 1995, she has to be moved from hospital to a nursing home at last. By then it no longer matters where she is because she cannot tell where she is. Sometimes she says that she has just come back from Ascot or Wimbledon, but as she retreats further into the world of her imagination she communicates less, then almost nothing.

But who is this coming to see her on her ninety-sixth birthday, this person in his sixties who, aiming a jovial wave at the doctor, a barking laugh at a nurse over the raucous lullaby of moans and shouts, steps so cheerily through these heaps of the half-dead, balancing a miniature cake marked 'Yolande' in red icing? Surely it must be Basil Holroyd, man of many businesses. Jean is there. She clasps Yolande's brown and bony hand and shouts, 'IT'S MICHAEL COME TO SEE YOU!' My aunt, bent double in her chair, her hair like fine white silk, her bruised skin thin as tissue paper, does not stir. She is far away, beyond recall. 'MICHAEL!' Then suddenly she looks up and gives that dazzling smile I recognise so well from the old albums, as if to say: Yes, after all and in spite of all, surely this is the best of all possible worlds.

ENVOI

2 0

Things Past

Hugh Kingsmill required of the biographer some account of his or her own life as a passport for travelling into the lives of others. If this, my passport, is stamped with the travels of others more than with my own, it is because their travels determined mine which, by themselves, hold little interest for me. Metaphysical journeys are not undertaken alone, but together *and* alone – at least mine have been.

Here, in vicarious fashion, is my story, my still unsolved mystery. To have a good walk-on part in one's own autobiography, as I have tried to give myself, is as much as any biographer can reasonably expect. For it is not exclusively my life I am telling. The story line I have drawn runs intermittently parallel, I believe, with that of many people who feel the impulse to make some reconnection with their earlier lives. This book, my patchwork, the prequel to my biographies, may seem to present an unusual family saga, but beneath the patina of conventional respectability acquired by many families lie secret episodes and half-suspected dramas, sometimes unacted yet still influential, that grow invisible over time. My purpose has been to pare back a little the cuticle of time and to apply the research methods I have learnt as a biographer to my own life for a while, letting the detective work show through the narrative at some places for those who have a similar curiosity in human nature and its reworkings on a family chronicle. Echoes of what I have forgotten, as well as memories of events I have been unable to forget, linked where possible by discovered facts, have been my signposts.

There are, of course, many unexplored trails: the legend of my Swedish grandmother's purloined diaries and the rumoured disappearance of the sketchbook Picasso gave her with its outlines of *Guernica*; the continuing adventures of Agnes May Babb, my grandfather's *femme fatale*, and other inviting sidetracks. These are different stories, other histories.

I have made journeys to places known and unknown – from the weather-beaten expanses of Barkisland to the fixed industrial archaeology of Borås – where the messages were too faint for me to decipher. But there seems to be no holiday restaurant anywhere that is not still playing one of my mother's favourite tunes. At Braywick cemetery, my grandfather's gravestone, some of its letters and numbers now missing, still possesses a surprising resonance. Scaitcliffe, my school, is agonisingly familiar in its every detail – yet is also crucially changed, having become co-educational. Sheffield Place, The Links, Brocket: all these family houses are now owned by public institutions. And then I come to Norhurst.

Outside, the house does not appear greatly altered. But when I step inside, except for a few details (a banister on the staircase, the panelling in the dining-room) all is unrecognisable, though conveying strange hints of the past, and I feel I am walking in a dream (Maidenhead itself, with its convoluted road system, is my nightmare). Norhurst is still owned by the family which bought it after my aunt's stroke almost twenty years ago, and they remember my father coming down to warn them of the submerged air-raid shelter near the end of the garden. This has become part of their own family lore.

All is changed. But in a recess of the attic, behind an old piece of curtain, stands a pile of lost books. Here is my nursery alphabet and my picture history of the United States. Here is *Mumfie*, given to me by my aunt on my sixth birthday: how could I have forgotten the wanderings on which I accompanied this excellent elephant which come instantly back to me when I see the author Katharine Tozer's pink and blue illustrations? The Mathilda stories my aunt read to me by the kitchen stove have gone. But buried away I spy something I have never seen before, a set of designs for glass light fittings drawn and coloured by my father in the distant days of Lalique. Further back, I find a large photograph of my great-grandfather, the Major-General, looking so much more robust and happy than in the Eastbourne family group taken after the suicide of his wife Anna Eliza Holroyd.

Finally, there is her book, my great-grandmother's, she who ended her life at the age of thirty by swallowing carbolic acid. It is an enormous, sombre-brown calf-bound volume with the gold embossed letters AEH at the front and, on its spine also in gold letters, the word FERNS. Her husband must have given it to her while they were in India in the early eighteen-seventies. Into thirty or more of its spacious pages she has beautifully pressed these unusual fern leaves. Then, like a poisoned chalice, the book passes to her daughter, Norah Palmer Holroyd who, in her twentieth year, has had her name tremulously written in it by her father after his stroke above the date 18 September 1896, the time she became so mysteriously ill at The Links. But she adds nothing herself to the volume which after her death passes eventually to my Aunt Yolande. She pastes into its blank pages, between the pressed ferns from India, illustrations of early nineteen-twenties film actors and actresses, scissored from magazines: Mary Pickford, Lillian Gish, Pearl White, Jackie Coogan, and then, suddenly looking out at me, the handsome features of my mother's ex-father-in-law, the 'matinée idol' Owen Nares. At the end there are some unused pages for the next generation, vacant pages left to me. This ill-omened folio volume, tracking the destinies of three generations of women in the family, would have meant nothing to me before I began my own little book in which it finds a final place, and which I must now let go.

> Go little book, go little tragedy,
> Where God may send thy maker, ere he die,
> The power to make a work of comedy . . .
> And wheresoever thou be read, or sung,
> I beg of God that thou be understood!
> And now to close my story as I should.

The Hol

George Holroyd of Crawcroft and his wife Isabella (née Haigh) ma
was the direct ancestor of John Baker Holroyd, first Earl of Sheff
Henry North Holroyd, third Earl of Sheffield (1832–1909), cricke
Isaac Holroyd, the younger son, was the direct ancesto

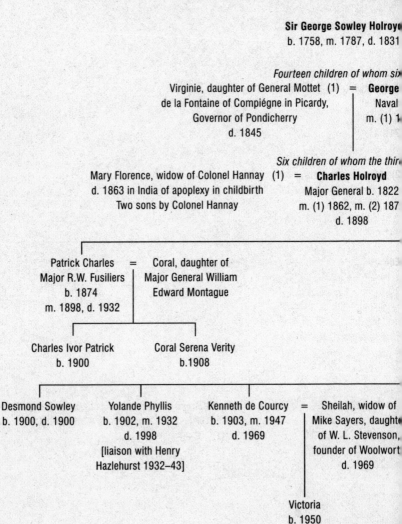

Sir George Sowley Holroyd
b. 1758, m. 1787, d. 1831

Fourteen children of whom six

Virginie, daughter of General Mottet (1) = **George**
de la Fontaine of Compiégne in Picardy,   Naval
Governor of Pondicherry   m. (1) 1
d. 1845

Six children of whom the thir

Mary Florence, widow of Colonel Hannay (1) = **Charles Holroyd**
d. 1863 in India of apoplexy in childbirth   Major General b. 1822
Two sons by Colonel Hannay   m. (1) 1862, m. (2) 187
d. 1898

Patrick Charles = Coral, daughter of
Major R.W. Fusiliers   Major General William
b. 1874   Edward Montague
m. 1898, d. 1932

Charles Ivor Patrick   Coral Serena Verity
b. 1900   b.1908

Desmond Sowley   Yolande Phyllis   Kenneth de Courcy = Sheilah, widow of
b. 1900, d. 1900   b. 1902, m. 1932   b. 1903, m. 1947   Mike Sayers, daught
   d. 1998   d. 1969   of W. L. Stevenson,
   [liaison with Henry   founder of Woolwort
   Hazlehurst 1932–43]   d. 1969

Victoria
b. 1950

...rd Family

...in 1602 and had two sons, George and Isaac. George, the elder son,
...(1735–1821), patron of the historian Edward Gibbon; and also of
...husiast, who founded the Sheffield Shield competition in Australia.
...Sir George Sowley Holroyd, Judge of the King's Bench.

Sarah, daughter of Amos Chaplin
b. 1767, d. 1848

in infancy. The second child was:

...lin Holroyd = (2) Fanny Harrington
...r b. 1790   of Exeter
...n. (2) 1848   d. 1874
...71

2) Anne (or Anna) Eliza, daughter of
Thomas Smith, Indigo Planter
b. 1849
d. 1880 suicide in Glasgow

Edward Fraser Rochfort Holroyd Indian Tea and Lalique Glass b. Calcutta 1875 m. 1899, d. 1961 [liaison with Agnes May Bickerstaff 1926–32]	= Adeline Corbet b. 1876 d. 1969	Norah Palmer b. 1877 d. 1913 in France

Ulla Knutsson-Hall (1) = **Basil Holroyd** = (2) Marie Louise Deschamps-Eymé
b. 1916   b. 1907   (3) Sonia Daphne Reynolds
d. 1986   m. (1) 1934–47
                                 m. (2) 1948–54
                                 m. (3) 1958–67
                                 d. 1988

Michael Holroyd
Biographer
b. 1935

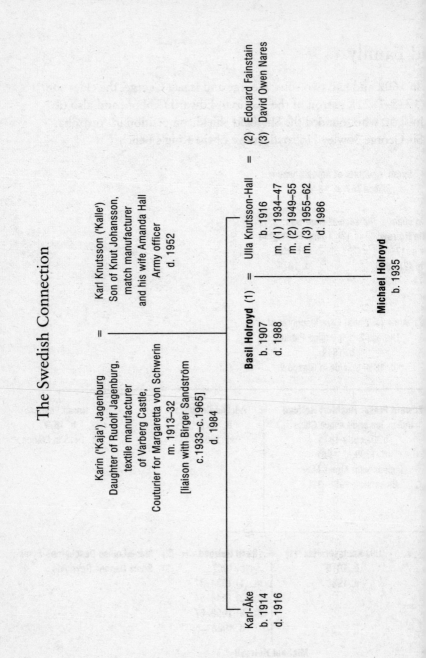

The Swedish Connection

Karin ('Kaja') Jagenburg
Daughter of Rudolf Jagenburg,
textile manufacturer
of Varberg Castle,
Couturier for Margaretta von Schwerin
m. 1913–32
[liaison with Birger Sandström
c.1933–c.1965]
d. 1984

=

Karl Knutsson ('Kalle')
Son of Knut Johansson,
match manufacturer
and his wife Amanda Hall
Army officer
d. 1952

Karl-Åke
b. 1914
d. 1916

Basil Holroyd (1)
b. 1907
d. 1988

=

Ulla Knutsson-Hall
b. 1916
m. (1) 1934–47
m. (2) 1949–55
m. (3) 1955–62
d. 1986

= (2) Edouard Fainstain
(3) David Owen Nares

Michael Holroyd
b. 1935

The Corbet Sisters of Ireland

Three of the twelve children of Michael Augustus Corbet of Sundays Well, Cork, and his wife Maria (née Hudson) died in infancy. The remaining eight daughters and one son were:

Minnie	**Atty**	**Sloper**	**Lizzie**	**Iley**
m. Tom White			'the jolliest'	pianist
			m. Mr Parsons of Bristol	
			three children (including Joan)	

Alice	**Adeline**		**Ida**	**Roland**
m. Stephen	b. 1876		music hall artiste	Hudson Sands
'Nipper' Anderson	m. E. F. R. Holroyd		m. William Temple	De Courcy
	three sons and		of Datchet	Blennerhassett etc.
	one daughter		three daughters,	Flees to America
			Sheilah	
			Betty	
			Joyce	

The Smiths of Glasgow

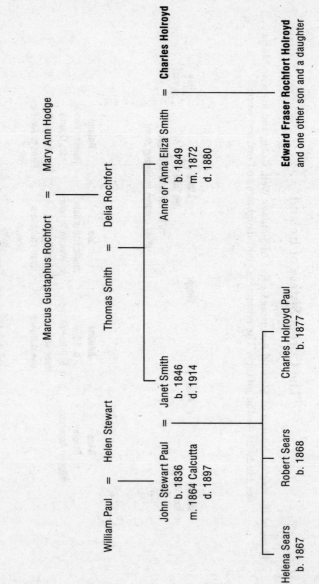

Marcus Gustaphus Rochfort = Mary Ann Hodge

Thomas Smith = Delia Rochfort

William Paul = Helen Stewart

Anne or Anna Eliza Smith
b. 1849
m. 1872
d. 1880
= Charles Holroyd

John Stewart Paul
b. 1836
m. 1864 Calcutta
d. 1897
= Janet Smith
b. 1846
d. 1914

Edward Fraser Rochfort Holroyd
and one other son and a daughter

Charles Holroyd Paul
b. 1877

Robert Sears
b. 1868

Helena Sears
b. 1867

Mosaic

Portraits in Fragments

'These fragments I have shored against my ruins.'

T. S. Eliot
The Waste Land

Preface

OUR FAMILIES, RIGHT OR WRONG

This is a book of surprises – at any rate it has surprised me. Some may think it eccentric: I prefer the word experimental. Initially it arose out of letters I received from readers of my family memoir, *Basil Street Blues*, which was published in 1999. I thought of it at first as a sequel or postscript, even as a 'postmodern interactive' work. Beginning as a requiem, it evolved into a love story, then a detective story: an independent companion volume which I have composed so that anyone can follow the narrative without having read, or remembered, the earlier book.

What it shows, I believe, is the strange interconnectedness of our family lives. We are often reminded that we have only to go back a few generations to find that we are, all of us, approximately related one to another – which is why other people's stories, however puzzling or extreme, contain so many echoes of our own dreams and experiences. Nevertheless, it has been an odd experience learning from strangers about events involving my own relations, as well as finding myself having more knowledge of some fathers and grandmothers than their own daughters or grandsons have. We live in a forest of family trees, and the branches reach out in complicated paths over unexpectedly long distances. In tracing some of these connections and involvements, I have tried to present an anatomy of well-researched, if wayward, family history.

The characters in this book are all ordinary people. But their exploits and adventures reveal how compelling fantasies, as well as mundane facts, guide our lives. It is how a writer mixes these facts and fantasies that divides the historian from the novelist, and determines whether a book is classified as fiction or (that most mysterious category) non-fiction.

1

Illuminations from
the Past

A LAST GLIMPSE OF MY FATHER

I took a postchaise to Uttoxeter, and going into market
at the time of high business, uncovered my head, and
stood with it bare an hour before the stall which my
father had formerly used, exposed to the sneers of the
standers-by and the inclemency of the weather.

Samuel Johnson

'The End.'

After three years I had finished. I had written it all after the old fashion, with a pen and paper, then sent it off to Sarah Johnson. Over many years she has made herself indispensable at this stage of a book – the only person, or so I believe, since she tells me this, who can read my writing and (which is sometimes more illegible) my typewriting. She puts it on to a disk and, after much to-ing and fro-ing, time for second or third thoughts and so on, I have the print-out before me – several copies of it. The time is now approaching for me, in the unconvincing guise of a modern technological man, to edge towards my publisher. But for myself, I believe, I have finished. It is the end. I sit back – then suddenly some words from Samuel Beckett come floating into my mind. 'Finished, it's finished, nearly finished, it must be nearly finished.' And then some more words: 'How often I have said, in my life . . . It is the end, and it was not the end.' Yet surely this really was the end, my signing off.

It was not, of course, quite the end. There would be editing, proof-reading, and then publication. For the publishers that would be the end – and for readers the beginning. But for me, its author, this felt like the end. It was the late summer of 1998, and I was free. Almost free.

As I made arrangements to deliver the typescript to my literary agent, a chieftain amongst agents, the ferociously named, mild-mannered Caradoc King, I began thinking over what I had done. Certainly I had not done anything quite like it before. This was a genuine variation on what I had spent my career doing: writing people's lives. For this time it was my own life I had written. The typescript contained over a hundred thousand words. It sat there on the table. My life.

When people say that everyone has a book in him or her, they usually mean an autobiography – in whatever form it comes: a poem, a quest, documentary, confession, film or play, *roman à clef*. Mine was a family memoir.

Writers are naturally protective over their powers of language. If the magic works, then these mysterious marks we put on paper and send out like messages in a bottle can affect men and women, readers we never hear or see for the most part and do not know, making them laugh or cry, feel and think. Using this ancient technology, even the dead can communicate with us. Like the fabulous garment Prospero puts on in his cell, the writer's art invades our dreams, raises sea-storms and summons kings, makes them excite or entertain us, chasten, enchant. It is a mantle, too, lending writers many disguises which, like the chameleon's ability to change colour, help us find a way through difficulties and dangers.

But we do not always know what we are doing or the effect what we do will have. I didn't even know at the beginning that I was going to write an autobiography and even now had no idea what others would make of it. When I began, I thought I was writing an essay which, following the deaths of my mother and father, might help to fill the gap they had left with some understanding of their lives, and my own. I delayed starting, strangely reluctant, but as soon as I did start I was carried along by a passionate need for those memories which rose up in me as I wrote. Usually a slow writer, this time I wrote quickly, urgently, memory coming to the aid of memory, sinking and resurfacing, as I completed a hundred thousand words and reached my parents' deaths. Then I stopped.

How accurate was my story? That it had emotional integrity I felt certain. But was it factually reliable? Reading through it, I realised that I had pieced together stretches of the narrative from tales I had been told, conversations overheard (perhaps misheard), memories with a haphazard order of events which were themselves blurred by those legends that confuse all our family histories.

So I decided to become once more the professional biographer. Like an enquiry agent who asks questions and keeps watch, and then like a fictional detective who hopes to arrive at wonderful conclusions from a jumble of miscellaneous and apparently meaningless facts, I went back to work. I checked birth, marriage and death certificates, hunted for wills and probate information, examined street directories and census returns, travelled to places my parents and grandparents had told me about, and revisited places I had known when a child. I also wrote to people I had not seen for up to fifty years, asking for their recollections.

Gradually an alternative family history began to emerge, a sadder one than I had known. I began to notice how, to compensate for disappointments, men raise their status and the importance of their occupations on passports and marriage certificates, and women lower their ages. And there were more significant discrepancies moving through every phase of life: examinations never passed, money lost, illicit marriages and illegitimacies, breakdowns, secret elopements and liaisons, inexplicable deaths.

I hold the view that the lies we tell ourselves and others, the half-truths that through repetition we almost come to believe, the very fantasies that follow us like our own shadows, become part of our actual lives. Biographers are cursed by an 'irritable reaching after fact and reason'. You have only to look at the enormous process of verification we have developed in modern times. Never has there been such a colossal apparatus got ready – such an array of scaffolding, cranes, pulleys and tackle – to raise into place, with much pomp and sometimes the trumpeting abuse of lesser scholars, one quotation, complete with its groundwork of notes to inform us who else has used it, where, and to what inferior effect. Despite all this, the best biographers, I believe, must also 'pick about the Gravel' with their subjects and come to feel that intense connection with them that Keats called 'negative capability'.

Biographers walk a tightrope between passionate involvement that lures them into sentimentality, and historical detachment with its arid wastes of information. Those who write autobiographies walk the same line, though in an opposite direction, seeking not intimacy with another past, but some perspective on their own.

What I decided to do was to combine my two narratives, fact and emotion, memory and hearsay, what had been so often spoken and what remained silent. And then I added my discoveries – of events which, though never communicated, soon forgotten and eventually unknown, still formed an undetected pattern within my family. For example, I had discovered that my great-grandmother committed suicide at the age of thirty, leaving her husband to look after their three small children. One of those children was my grandfather, in whose house at Maidenhead I had passed my own childhood. I do not think he ever knew that his mother had killed herself in such an appalling way – swallowing carbolic acid and burning internally to death. Why would you tell a four-year-old boy such a terrible thing about his mother? And not having told him at the time, it would grow increasingly difficult, even pointless, to tell him later. Certainly no rumour of this tragedy reached me, and I feel sure that my father too knew nothing of it.

Yet once I discovered this unexplained suicide, I came to see it as a symbol that spoke for three generations of my family and, by implication, women from other families too: women in the attic, women with undiagnosed neuroses, suspect and unstable and a danger to themselves, women of no importance of whom little was thought or expected, women without self-esteem or occupation outside the family, solitary women who were unmarried or who sought death in marriage. I tried to tell their stories through the story of my aunt, the only one of those women I knew. Searching back for an origin to her predicament, I ended my memoir with my great-grandmother's beautiful Book of Ferns which I had found hidden away in an attic when, during my researches, I went back to my grandfather's house in Maidenhead. Into this massive volume, which had been presented to her in the early 1870s following her wedding in India, she had sewn and pressed, with great delicacy, arrangements of Indian ferns. After her death, this ill-omened volume passed briefly to her mysteriously ill daughter, and from her on to her niece, my Aunt Yolande, who began pasting in pictures of film stars from the silent 1920s, but left its final pages blank, as if a light had suddenly been switched off.

Basil Street Blues was, metaphorically, written on those last empty pages. But only when I had sent it off to my agent and publisher did I turn to a second volume that had lain many years with the Book of Ferns behind a curtain in that attic of my grandparents' house. This was a Book of Lights, drawn and coloured by my father in the 1930s when he had been an agent in London for Lalique Glass.

It was a less imposing volume than the vast, sombre, calf-bound Book of Ferns. Its boards, some twelve by fifteen inches, were covered in a dull, slightly stained canvas, gripped at the spine by a pair of steel rings. But when I opened this rather drab, uninviting exterior, my father's lights, drawn on French grey paper or on white sheets carefully pasted in, suddenly shone forth brilliantly. There were thirty-five of them, done mainly in greens and browns and yellows, all with their notes of scale and full size, none of them exposed to daylight for over sixty years. I was dazzled. Why had I not examined this book more carefully?

Every child's progress depends on parricide – so Isaiah Berlin remarked – which is to say that we must kill off our fathers' ideas and replace them with our own. My father had greatly strengthened the stubbornness I needed to survive as a biographer by pointing me towards almost any career, however ill-fitting, rather than writing. Reluctantly abandoning his vision of me as a tea-planter in Assam (a figure, as I saw it, from a Somerset Maugham story), he insisted that, despite a glaring deficiency in mathematics, I apply myself to the sciences at school, and when this petered out, he had me articled to a firm of solicitors where I languished for a year or two. Eventually, with a gesture of despair over my chronic lack of success, he recommended that I join the regular army and dig in for my old-age pension. But at this point I rebelled.

The reason, I fancy, he set me stumbling over such a steep and unnecessary obstacle course was that his own life when young had appeared so deceptively easy – only to become impossibly difficult after the war. He probably should have been an architect – that's where his talent lay. But it lay hidden. The closest he came to being an architect was during his last years when he worked for a series of building companies. Unfortunately, through one disaster and another, then another and again another, these companies all went out of business.

Officially my father was their chief salesman. He had the reputation of being able to sell anything to anyone. But first he had, as it were, to sell whatever it was, however improbable, to himself – as he had tried to sell tea-planting and mathematics, the law and a military career to me.

Over the years, in brisk succession, glass, steel, concrete, wood, bricks and mortar became magical substances in my father's imagination. They glittered and shone for him as he spoke of them, stood tall and proud as he praised their luminous virtues. Like a conjuror at a children's party, he appeared to perform miracles, amazing everyone with his eloquence. But as soon as he stopped talking, the light seemed to fade; and when he left, his audience would go into a decline, dismayed by their own credulity and, like men betrayed, resenting my father's hypnotic spell over them, his salesman's bag of tricks.

During his sixties and seventies, like a shipwrecked sailor frantically repairing a small raft in a rising storm of bankruptcy, my father would sit long into the evenings bent over his drawings. He wasn't meant to be drawing buildings, but selling them. Yet he loved plotting their contours on squared paper as if, through the sheer enthusiasm it generated, this devoted labour helped him to sell them – especially to people who sincerely, even desperately, didn't want to buy them.

Occasionally he would show me these drawings, but I never took much notice. I do remember, however, how handsome, almost palatial, some of them looked, though they were no more than extensions to golf clubhouses, modest conservatories or additional changing rooms and lavatories. Still, he derived much satisfaction, almost happiness, from drafting everything with accuracy and making it look good on the page. I know the feeling. It is, I now think, a very English characteristic, this potent combination of aesthetics and usefulness, this draftsman's contract.

It is a pity my family made such a habit, even a speciality, of misadventure. While the women seemed grounded in lives of miserable frustration, in strange maladies and unreachable loneliness, the men would float up into silver clouds of fantasy, and hang surreally suspended there. My grandfather, cutting loose from a legal career, sailed unsuccessfully into the tea business. My uncle, rather than my father, studied architecture before, finding himself miscast, he drifted vaguely into farming. My father, I suppose, was the most consistent: having studied nothing, except possibly gambling, he was optimistic about everything but ended up with nothing. We were all amateurs in an age of increasing professionalism. Innocents at home.

Yet there was a brief, bright interlude in this chaotic decline when, from the late Twenties to the late Thirties, the three of them had come together as directors of a company my grandfather founded called Breves, which was appointed the agent in Britain for Lalique Glass. Like the legendary King Canute, standing on the very shores of bankruptcy with his two sons, my grandfather commanded the waves of recession to retreat. But 'what care these roarers for the name of king?' – let alone the name Holroyd. No matter: this happy band of Holroyds grew convinced that a spectacular business boom was about to sweep through the Thirties leading to a decade of peace and prosperity in the Forties. They seemed mesmerised, my grandfather and his two sons, by this beautiful French glass: the goblets, flower vases, car mascots, paperweights and decanters deliciously decorated with sunflowers and gorgeous peacocks, dragonflies and swallows for ever held in flight, cupids and water-nymphs eternally playing. How could anyone look into such wonderful objects and remain a pessimist?

Certainly they couldn't. My grandfather sold everything he possessed and borrowed more than he could repay in order to create a brilliant future in the West End of London. My father's own speciality in all this marvellous enterprise was glass lighting. He hoped to astonish the world with his ingenious table-lights ornamented with opalescent shells, his wall-lights with their flared frames of frosted or tinted glass, and his hanging lights which were sometimes constructed from inverted fruit bowls suspended from the ceiling by ropes. Some of these lights were briefly installed in transatlantic liners, and others used by fashionable restaurants. Unfortunately ornamental glass was going out of fashion in the Thirties. Besides, there were catastrophic breakages when drilling this glass to the metalwork of his lights.

My father seldom spoke to me about this early period of his life. His expectations, I believe, were set too high and his disappointment grew too painful. After the war, when I got to know him, he was struggling to find other employment. Almost anything would do. But the world was now a dark and hostile place, and his days and nights became increasingly uncomfortable. Life, which had seemed such fun, was actually bristling with traps and obstacles, he liked to remind me, and he was eager to see that I got my own quota of difficulties over and done with as soon as possible. With my own best interests ever in mind, and using deep parental ingenuity, he marshalled these hardships, both real and imaginary, all sharp and blistering, and triumphantly presented them to me like an armful of barbed wire that I must immediately embrace. This was his fatherly duty.

I did not find it easy to feel gratitude for this intimidating gift. On the contrary, I felt irritation, anxiety, disbelief – all symptoms of a necessary rebellion that, since my father's death, has been in retreat. A change is coming over me – I feel it as I write. I sense it too every day as I sit frowning over the newspapers, glare critically at the weather, complain about radio and television programmes, raise a judicious glass of wine to my mouth (is it the *fuissé* or the *fumé*?), press furiously down on the accelerator when approaching the amber lights, or simply look in the mirror each morning and see myself beginning the serious business of shaving. As I do all these ordinary things that are second nature to me, I seem to recognise my father, and can hear his voice once again paradoxically warning me: 'I wouldn't do that, Michael, if I were you.'

But, of course, he could never advise himself in this manner or escape his own second nature. He said nothing to me when I took such little notice of his architectural drawings and I regret my indifference now. As an exercise of atonement, I look carefully through the pages of illuminated glass I have found, his glass.

This Book of Lights reveals someone I barely recognise – someone with an optimism and confidence that were fading when I got to know him, and which were altogether extinguished at the end. As I turn these pages from his youth, looking at the array of lenses and beaded bowls, the feather and flared pendants, the multicoloured spheres, the Louvre lights, cylinders and cubes so much of their period which my father designed more than seventy years ago, and that do him honour now, I can see him again, an old man, bent over his drawings of brick or wooden buildings, concrete or steel. I see him through his window in the evening, see him suddenly look up as if some flickering hope momentarily touches him. Then his head goes down, and he is back at work.

2

Quiet Consummation

DEATH OF MY AUNT

The leave-taking is a very, very great source of consolation ... but before we part may I interest you in our Before Need Provision Arrangements? ... Perhaps you think it morbid and even dangerous to give thought to the subject?

Evelyn Waugh, *The Loved One*

Costs is the only power on earth that will ever get anything out of it now, or will ever know it for anything but an eyesore and a heartsore.

Charles Dickens, *Bleak House*

THOMAS. I have come to be hanged, do you hear?
TYSON. Have you filled in the necessary forms?—

Christopher Fry, *The Lady's Not For Burning*

The end came suddenly: a shock but no surprise. On Christmas Day 1998, among the buoyant bright balloons, the carols, cake and holly of the nursing home, my Aunt Yolande finally gave up, and died. Over her years there she had gone downhill very gently, hardly making any noise or movement, seldom noticing the well-intended festivities, the brisk comings and goings, the shouts and cries all around her, occasionally smiling at something but never joining in.

The nursing home telephoned me that evening and I went down a few days later when the holidays had abated. It was a blue day, sunny, clear and cold. The country appeared frozen in beauty as I drove along, sealed from reality in the warmth of my car, cheerful radio-music singing out.

I felt saddened not so much by the fact of my aunt's death as by the contemplation of her life. For the last half-dozen years or so, since her last stroke, she was largely unaware of the hospital or the nursing home, and retained few memories of the past. Occasionally I would take her some old photograph albums, but she no longer seemed to recognise anyone. The past was dying for her, even as it was coming alive for me.

She was not, however, in pain, and seldom seemed distressed except when she fell ill. Towards the end I had tried to let the doctor know that I would be happy for him to assist her in dying, if dying was inevitable – not simply by allowing her to die slowly, but by positively taking her out of unnecessary anguish, as I believe I would wish for myself, and as I knew she had done for her much-loved dogs. But this kindness could not be granted her, and since she and I had never discussed the subject of voluntary euthanasia, I did not try to insist.

I rather dreaded the business of the day. At the nursing home I was handed my aunt's meagre belongings. I could hold them in one arm: a small broken mirror, a few photos, some picture postcards and a bag full of odds and ends – a powder compact, lipstick, purse, comb, handkerchief and hairpins. 'Is this all?' I asked. It was. All that was left after more than ninety years. We agreed that her clothes could be of no use to anyone now and should be burnt. I signed a form, and we exchanged compliments on my aunt's behalf: what a very polite patient she had been – never a complaint, indeed hardly a sound, over her five or six years there.

I felt grateful for anything the nursing home offered to ease the bureaucracy of death. But some things – making the funeral arrangements with an undertaker, notifying the death with the Registrar, helping a solicitor prepare probate – you must do yourself. I had done all this for my mother and father. I was a veteran. I knew what to do. Or believed I did.

At the nursing home I was given a formal notice stating that the doctor in charge had signed a medical certificate. I presented this to the hospital where the doctor worked, and received a sealed envelope containing the medical certificate itself on which was written the cause of my aunt's death (bronchopneumonia).

Adding this to the bulging file of family papers I had put together while writing my recently completed memoirs (papers which were travelling with me, my passenger on the back seat of the car), I drove on to the General Register Office at Epsom. I was supremely well-equipped, able to prove with the aid of this file that I was truly my aunt's nephew, executor of her will, next of kin; and also (should anyone ask) that she had been my father's elder sister. Among these papers was her birth certificate recording that Yolande Phyllis Holroyd was born at 29 Victoria Square, Bristol, on 22 April 1902. So she had died aged ninety-six.

'A long life,' remarked the Registrar as she quickly transferred these facts from the red certificate to a black one, birth to death. But had it, I wondered, been a happy life? I could not believe it had been. I remembered sitting beside her crippled figure only a fortnight before and thinking that no one seeing her in this condition could have guessed at her privileged beginnings.

Her first twenty-five years must have been the best, living with her two brothers in a large, comfortable, Edwardian house just outside Maidenhead, a smiling, attractive girl whom I could still see in family photographs, playing tennis, going riding, bathing and water-skiing in the south of France during the long summer holidays. I had not known her in those days, and had only recently discovered a more sombre story behind the bright surface of this family-album life. She never married, though she had been unofficially engaged, apparently, for ten years or more. The love of her life, I was told, was a dashing yachtsman and soldier called Hazlehurst. The only letters she had kept over seventy years, which I accidentally came across in the lining of an old evening bag after she moved from her flat to the nursing home, had been signed 'H'. They began as passionate love letters written mainly in the mid-1930s, and then subsided into an affectionate correspondence. But afterwards, in the Second

World War, Hazlehurst was posted to Italy, and my aunt learnt that he had married a young Italian girl . . .

'And what was your aunt's occupation?' asked the Registrar. I hesitated, as she waited to type my answer on to the black form. In the years I knew her, under increasingly difficult circumstances, my aunt had simply exercised the family dogs and looked after her ageing parents. Her father, having inherited a fabulous Indian tea fortune, allowed it to leak away through cautious investments in the City and then a highly incautious liaison in the bedroom. Both her parents naturally expected Yolande to marry, yet between them they had imprisoned her in spinsterhood. How could she leave her clinging, hysterical mother after her father, at the age of fifty, picked up a young married woman in his car, set her up in Piccadilly as his mistress and did not drive back home for almost eight years? – all this while his daughter was in her twenties. And what respectable man would happily marry her after such a scandal – a scandal that had left the family almost penniless? She was stranded.

So what had been her occupation? On her birth certificate there had been space only for her father's occupation which he had given as being 'of independent means', though in later life he would, in so many ways and means, become dependent on his daughter. On her parents' marriage certificate he had written 'Gentleman' as his 'Rank or Profession', while her mother left the space blank.

I quickly shuffled through these certificates and we decided to put a dash against Yolande's occupation, as we had against her married name. We gave the nursing home as her 'usual address', and I filled in my 'qualification' as being that of 'nephew'. Then I was handed a copy of the entry. Our business was complete. I was free to go.

I went next to my aunt's bank and, brandishing the Registrar's certificate, smoothing it against the glass window, mouthing my instructions, put a stop on my aunt's account. I felt rather pleased with myself for having remembered to do this. Then I drove on again to the undertakers who, ten years before, had arranged my father's cremation.

Both my parents had been cremated. I vividly remember walking at tremendous speed, as if trying to outpace the onset of grief, from the hospital in London where I had just seen my mother die straight to the undertakers half a mile away. It was a macabre place. As I strode briskly in, setting off a bell, there was a sudden commotion. Everybody stopped doing whatever they had been doing, hushed their laughter, adjusted ties, buttoned jackets and hastened to what appeared as formal positions appropriate for the bereaved. I remember sitting down opposite an official who, leaning reverently towards me, coming very close, whispered a stream of euphemisms on his pungent breath. By contrast, I was terrifically quick and cool, dry and businesslike, a very parody of efficiency, examining my watch and my diary, coughing importantly, as we made arrangements for my mother's coffin and hearse. During these proceedings we were looked down on by two burly men in dark, shabby suits who stood with their backs to the wall, lined up like soldiers, at ease but still uneasy. They would be my mother's pallbearers. Behind the taller of them a wisp of white smoke rose gently into the air. For a moment, in my heightened state, I wondered whether he was Satan risen from the underworld. Then I realised he was holding a cigarette in one of his hands clasped behind his back. When I looked down at the desk to sign some documents, he deftly moved this cigarette to his mouth and back again out of sight. I accepted an invitation to see the Chapel of Rest into which my mother's body was soon to be moved, and the flowers gathered, before her cremation service. It was really no more than a shed in the back area given a covering of paint, and in one corner, I unhappily noticed, there stood a tin of fly spray. Then, as I drove back home, the tears suddenly came and went on coming. I sat in the car outside my home waiting for this fit of crying to cease, and when it finally did, I went indoors, apparently composed again.

My father's cremation had been better, but it had disturbed my aunt. I had a rose planted in his memory, but there was no proper grave she could visit and no gravestone identifying him. He had simply vanished. She felt empty and unsatisfied when she was taken to the Garden of Remembrance after his death. Of course his name was in the Book of Remembrance – but where exactly was he? The word 'scattered' was, to her ears, nebulous and wrong. Neither my mother nor my father had spoken against cremation, and I favoured it. But my aunt did not like the idea. It smelt of hell to her. Those flames. So, I decided, she must be buried.

We arranged at the undertakers for her interment to take place in nine days' time at the annexe or extension of St Mary's Church, some two or three hundred yards from the flat where she had lived before moving into her 'usual address' at the nursing home. I had also come to look through pretty pictures of coffins. The plain pine, the élite elm, the patriotic oak. What would best suit my aunt? Here, it was indicated, lay an opportunity for my aunt to make her final statement – a statement beyond words, something inspiring, perhaps, to encourage others. What should my aunt say? What would she want to say? She who had said so little in her last years. This was an awkward decision. There was such an extravagant choice. Would she rest easy in the Class 9 with brassed handles, polished mahogany veneer and a cover of maroon velveteen; or wait more comfortably in the heavy-style Brocklebank containing special satin drapery? Might she enjoy the Last Supper with press-panelled sides and swing-bar handles, corners patterned after Michelangelo's Renaissance works and a scene of the Last Supper depicted on the lid? I glanced hesitantly at the hermetically sealed Trojan; the Lincoln, boasting a champagne interior; the Equinox with its adjustable bed; the solid timber Provincial, featuring pleated sunburst drapery; and the Tea Rose with its delicate lilac and copper shading. Eventually I picked the simple Windsor coffin for her to lie sightless in, with its gold plastic fittings, white side sheets, frillings and pillow. My aunt had lived most of her life a few miles from Windsor, I reminded myself, while also noting with satisfaction that this coffin was rather less expensive than many of the others.

Prices had certainly risen and the repertoire of euphemisms expanded since my grandfather's death at the beginning of the 1960s. But there was less Disneyfication than Jessica Mitford predicted in her famous book, *The American Way of Death*. I was never entertained with a 'Have a Nice Death' video, or warned about cartoon 'bugs and critters' entering receptacles that were too cheap, or told stories of lamentably inexpensive caskets that blew up from an accumulation of methane gas. I can recall no invitation being made to render my aunt's natural carbon into a gemstone. Nor was I given a caged dove to release into the sky. The funeral directors never presented themselves as belonging to an exalted class – messengers from the Beautiful Beyond. The English Way of Death still retained a Dickensian aroma.

It was now mid-afternoon and, quickly eating a sandwich, I drove over to look at the churchyard. The name of the church was actually St Mary the Virgin, but to avoid embarrassment when speaking or writing, St Mary's rank or condition is never mentioned.

The extension of the garden cemetery, which must once have been a rough open field, perhaps belonging to a farmer, had evidently been made into a churchyard at the beginning of the Second World War. The difference between the gravestones here and in the main cemetery reflects a change in English life. A hundred or more years ago it was the custom to perpetuate men's (and to a lesser extent women's) exploits and achievements on great slabs of blistering Aberdeen granite or solid Portland stone. Ranks and titles, wealth and potency, were proudly recorded, family crests sculpted, grand pretensions conveyed by tall obelisks, cupolas and pomegranates, imposing sarcophagi, Egyptian extravaganzas and elaborate neo-classical canopies. Whole paragraphs were sometimes cut into the marble to remind us of fashionable addresses, political and military eminence, terrible battles and shipwrecks, and, failing these, even honourable employment for distinguished societies and on charitable committees. To walk two hundred yards past such notable monuments is to absorb an extraordinary narrative of imperial history. But the ground is now uneven, the bulbous urns split, the heavy slabs of stone and marble rent asunder, the very angels, horsemen, saints, crazily tilting in the silence, as if an earthquake had shaken the solid ground on which that imperial past had stood. These vast congregations of the dead, united by solitude and stretching to the horizon, are like arenas where at night old friends can steal out between the upturned roots and branches and be reunited, or battlefields for lifelong enemies to re-engage in mortal combat.

But after the Second World War, it is the domestic virtues that are more modestly celebrated: beloved wife, kindly grandfather, much-loved husband, daughter, mum and dad. No one actually dies: they are 'called to God', they 'fall asleep', they 'enter into rest' – and they live on 'for ever in our hearts', 'always in our thoughts', 'until we meet again'. But, as the writing of a family memoir has taught me, in a few years almost all of us are forgotten, and it is the indecipherable inscriptions, worn away by the weather, that tell the true story.

Walking through these ranks of stone, reading their words of farewell, I feel a surprising poignancy over the enigma of departure. Here is genuine massed sadness, like a vast chorus, but inscribed without the language to express it. And this, it seems to me, conveys very well our inability to understand life and death, our need to cover the mysterious tragedy of our condition with simple conventions. As I drove back to London, I resolved to do better for my Aunt Yolande.

In the week before the funeral I opened up negotiations with the solicitor, sending him anything I imagined might be of use: the certified copy of my aunt's death, and a copy of her will; a note of the money in her bank, the addresses of the nursing home, funeral directors, Department of Social Security and tax offices – to all of which I also wrote. Everything seemed to be in order.

Then I turned my attention to the flowers. Would I like a spray or a wreath or something more sophisticated, such as an arrangement of blooms shaped after the hesitant outline of Surrey, the county she was to be buried in? I chose the wreath.

The day of the funeral opened under a brilliant blue sky which, by midday, had turned to furious rain. I was shown into the Chapel of Rest where my aunt's body lay, rather grandly, on the frilled white sheets and a pillow in the Windsor coffin which, her name plate on its mount, had been placed on a table under a series of pink-shaded lights. I remember thinking that this coffin was too small to have contained the streams of red tape that had festooned and entangled her final, quiet years. I sat there somewhat vacantly, looking at the crimson carpet, the Regency wallpaper, the pictures of heroic Scottish landscapes, while the rain hammered on the roof. I was glad to be alone. Margaret, my wife, had wanted to come, but she had not known my aunt – indeed my aunt had known no one besides myself in these last lost years; no one except, in an undifferentiated way, those who had professionally looked after her. She had outlived her two brothers and all her contemporaries, and, even before her first stroke, was fencing herself off from friends. It seemed to me proper that this isolation should be marked at the end, and that I should be her solitary mourner.

I remember feeling grateful that the nursing home, when

writing to me, 'Mark Holroyd', a personal letter with 'sincere
condolences for all the family', had regretted being unable to
send a representative to the funeral due to 'prior commitments'
(did they mean prior committals?). So I am surprised when the
door of the Chapel of Rest bursts open and a rather plump
young woman in black, whom I have never seen before, runs
in out of the wet. She is swiftly followed by the 'funeral
arranger', who introduces her to me. She has that very week
joined the staff at the nursing home and, though she has not
'had the pleasure and privilege' of meeting my aunt until now,
wanted to come to her funeral in order to gain work experience. At that moment the minister arrives and further introductions take place. We laugh and chat, and suddenly it seems
as if we are at a cocktail party. The minister is retired, he tells
us, but always happy, even in atrocious weather (he laughs and
we laugh) to turn out and lend a hand. In his hand he carries
an authorised edition of the Bible, a battered and creased copy,
in which some passages are illumined with an orange high-
lighter.

I get into my car and follow the hearse from the undertakers
to the churchyard, peering through the steamed-up windows
between the whizzing windscreen wipers. Next to me sits the
young woman in black from the nursing home. The cemetery
looks swollen with water as we get out and watch the coffin
being unloaded and hoisted on to the pallbearers' shoulders. We
form up in military fashion – a sort of Dad's Army – raise our
black umbrellas and, as I walk slowly behind the coffin along
the green darkness of the pathway, I see several covered trenches
dug for other new bodies, with pyramids of dark brown soggy
earth beside them. What a forlorn group we must look, a sad
remnant, as we pass along the track, and then straggle diago-
nally across the wet grass, picking our way cautiously between
the gravestones. We are heading for a hole on the edge of the
field, covered by two wooden planks that are lifted off as we

approach. Despite the rain, a gravedigger is at work in a corner of the field and, thinking of the First World War, I suddenly feel an urge to hum that song the soldiers sometimes sang on the march:

> '*The bells of hell go ting-a-ling-a-ling*
> *For you but not for me . . .*
> *O Death, where is thy sting-a-ling-a-ling*
> *O Grave thy victor-ee?*'

Of course, I don't. But all at once I hear some humming from the probationer beside me and, glancing across at her, see that she is crying volubly, luxuriously, her tears mixing with the rain, while I, apparently quite unmoved, a prey to all sorts of unlikely, out-of-season thoughts, walk silently under the same umbrella. Anyone seeing us must have concluded that she is the sorrowing relative and I the bland official.

We stand by the deep watery trench, and the coffin with my aunt's body is lowered, swaying, into it, while the minister reads passages from one of the Epistles to the Corinthians, from St John's Gospel and Psalm 23. They are words of miraculous comfort, hope and confidence: 'If it were not so, I would have told you.'

As we wander back, amiably chatting, I tell the minister what a good choice I think he made, and hear myself sounding as if I were reporting on a British Council reading. Then we emerge on to the road and are in another world. I discreetly tip the minister, and it is over. But not quite over. There is a moment of embarrassment, a pause, no one liking to say that he or she looks forward to seeing me again in case it should be taken as referring to my own funeral. Silently we shake hands and go our ways.

I had been managing my aunt's affairs for fifteen years, even before I was formally granted Power of Attorney in 1985. I had sold her flat, next to the cemetery, after she finally moved into the nursing home in the mid-1990s. The £50,000 it went for became her capital, though it was very much reduced by the time of her death. I and my cousin Vicky paid irregular sums into her bank account so that they would legitimately count as gifts and not income. I was particularly pleased by what I felt to be an ingenious strategy, not realising until too late that had we allowed Aunt Yolande's capital to fall below £8,000, and even in due course below £3,000, the state would have been obliged to step in and help pay the nursing expenses. This was typical of my imperfect understanding of the maze-like benefits system.

Cousin Vicky is my Uncle Kenneth's daughter, a bright, blue-eyed, blonde girl much younger than I am, now married with two children. Her life has been very different from mine and we have few interests in common. Yet when I see her I feel an instant affinity. This is all the more surprising as I have met her only a few times in my life, and so had Aunt Yolande. But Vicky is Yolande's niece, as close a blood relation as myself, and she generously volunteered to contribute some of this quixotic financial help.

The best way of dealing with my aunt's affairs, I had resolved, was to make them as simple as possible. But simplicity is a more complex matter than I imagined. I sold her few Indian Mutiny tea shares, put an end to her small building society account, and placed everything she possessed in her bank. But the solicitor now needed evidence of those long-ago-sold shares, that ancient cancelled account, to smooth away the prickly problems of probate. Searching through the large cupboard where my aunt's records, fifteen years of them, were piled up, I grew once more baffled and appalled to see how her single, straightforward life became weighed down by such a density of paperwork. It lay, like a thick geological layer covering an immensity of time, above the forms, the statistics, the charts of my parents' illnesses and deaths: my private registry, an archival incoherence of ageing papers, with their faint, sickening smell of dust and despair. How could all this have happened? And why had it needed to devour so much of what people call 'spare time'? I suppose that, in a small way, my aunt and I had strayed into that obscure world, clouded by labyrinthine 'account-ability', by opaque 'transparency' and the ever-circling prevari-cations of 'efficiency', which blights the careers of doctors, farmers, teachers and other professions. After its benign begin-nings, this inhumane bureaucracy has been engulfing us all like a monstrous organism. Conceived originally as a method of helping everyone, it has been programmed so as to prevent the cheat from benefiting, and then re-engineered so that we are all identified as potential cheats. I remember how depressed I was made to feel by a language that no ordinary person speaks, an incomprehensible totalitarian language of computer-talk and committee-speak, reinforced by the convoluted jargon of local government loquacity. It seemed as if little of what I wrote to them was 'applicable', and little they sent me made sense. I communicated in paragraphs, they sent me boxes to fill in. But my lines would not fit into their spaces. We were continually at odds. All the evidence of this non-communication I had been advised to store. I tended it gingerly, gave it quantity time.

Some weeks most of my mail was actually for and about my aunt: a voluminous puzzle of papers from the Health Centre, Twilight Nurses, Age Concern, Willing Hands and the Homecare Service; from the Residents' Association, the Citizens' Advice Bureau, the Locality Team in the Social Services Department of the Surrey County Council, and the Treasurer of the Borough Council; from the Caps Central Data Team in Room 82E of the Department of Social Security office in Newcastle-upon-Tyne, the Review Section of the Disability Unit at Blackpool, the Benefits Agency at Epsom, the Inland Revenue offices at Leicester, and something called Taxguard in Peterborough; from the solicitor in Greenwich, the estate agent in Ewell, two banks, three hospitals and eventually the nursing home. Are matters as convoluted as this in other countries? The people in these places were usually patient and kind, but I often felt that I was in a surreal festival of circumlocution.

And here it all was, the awful evidence, the remnants, a mad litter of vacuity filling my cupboard, tumbling out of it, such a macabre debris of paper trailing over the years. I picked up a small bundle and read through it. What had I got? Here I was writing to my aunt's doctor asking for a report on her medical condition following what I believed to be a small stroke while she was still living in the flat we had had adapted for 'a person with disabilities'. He replies that 'it would be extremely unethical to disclose details of her medical care to you or to anyone else without her formal permission'. But formally she has no permission to give. She is too ill and besides, with Enduring Power of Attorney, I am, for such purposes, my aunt. I remind the doctor of this and, to circumvent the ethical blockage, allow some common sense to flow, I provide him with formal permission on my aunt's behalf to speak to me. Once this topsy-turvy act is performed, the doctor is able to disclose that although all the support services including consultant geriatricians have been mobilised, my aunt's 'living circumstances are unsatisfactory'. She should be moved 'as a matter of urgency' to 'correctly structured sheltered accommodation'.

The trouble is that my aunt does not want to move. Anyone who advises her to do so is seen as a messenger of death. Against her will, she was made to leave Maidenhead following her first paralysing stroke in 1980, and has never been well afterwards. She is determined not to make the same mistake again. The doctor, gravely putting all the facts in front of me, hopes I will persuade her 'to gracefully accept them'. His split infinitive reflects a split in our understanding. I cannot persuade my aunt. No one can. And she doesn't feel in the least graceful. She clings to where she is, what she knows. But the doctor feels he has now been placed in an exposed position since I will not use my power of attorney to force my aunt to accept his advice. It is all most unprofessional and he risks being implicated in the mess. He must therefore protect himself. If there is no practical way of doing what he has recommended, he warns me, 'serious illness or death' might eventually ensue – and it will be the wrong sort of death, an unstructured event. My aunt is then on the verge of her ninetieth year. I decide to follow her wishes and continue employing a private army of nurses to take care of her at home. It seems to me a question of whether she dies correctly soon or incorrectly later on.

I picked out another file from the cupboard. What was this? My aunt is now in the nursing home and I am trying to make sure she receives the financial help to which she is entitled. As I interpret it, the law says that she needs £128.65 each week. She has less than half of this coming in, and the difference is made up from Income Support. But the cost of the nursing home is approximately three times what the law says she needs to live on. The social services are not able to pay any of this until I have sold her flat. Increasingly I need the help of several organisations. One of the most difficult is Barclays Bank Taxation Service. It is not beyond them to take more than a year obtaining a small tax repayment from the Inland Revenue. When I urge them on, explaining my aunt's condition and the need for money to pay for her care, I receive an acknowledgement beginning, 'Dear Miss Holroyd' and assurances that my correspondence is receiving attention. During the financial year I am looking at, the Barclays Taxation Adviser obtains a repayment of £184.70 which is good news – it will pay for two or three days' nursing and upkeep. Unfortunately I am also advised that Barclays' fees amount to £169.40, leaving my aunt with £20.30.

In order to understand how anything works, to bring it under control, I must put it on paper and make a narrative. Fearing that my aunt will soon be unable to afford tax repayments, I send a letter to the Taxation Adviser, telling him that I am writing it all up and asking whether they have any objections to my quoting Barclays' financial calculations. This provokes panic. For once I get an instant reply from the Adviser, saying that she cannot reply. Someone else will reply instead. My request is being referred to her 'immediate superior', a Senior Taxation Officer. In due course he writes to explain that the matter must be put before Barclays Marketing Department. But I am not seeking to promote the business of the bank, I answer, I am trying to manage my aunt's welfare, and have merely notified the bank out of politeness. By way of reply, the Senior Taxation Adviser incomprehensibly suggests that 'you develop your request at this stage . . .'

I flung the file down in exasperation. The essential part of my aunt's life was never touched by this abominable accumulation of forms, brochures, leaflets, letters that came from an alien world, utterly foreign to any she would have recognised. Years ago, I remembered, she used to worry about money, but long before the end she escaped into a happier world of fantasy and imagination. There was nothing of her present in this cupboard. I hated these papers, this awful masquerade of controlled caring.

But as I closed the door, a bundle of handwritten correspondence on coloured paper fell out. These are letters from Jean and Rita, who looked after her for over ten years. I glanced through them: and suddenly my Aunt Yolande was alive again.

I hope you are not worrying about your aunt. She is fighting fit. She is always laughing at me. Saturday we were out for coffee, our walk round the park to feed

the ducks and shopping in her wheelchair & this man
was very rude to her so she put her walking stick round
his leg & down he came. She said he won't be rude to
me again. Well, she laughed so much she cryed . . . She
sends her love.

That was towards the end of 1993 when she was in her young
nineties and, for brief periods on good days, full of spirit. Jean
and Rita continued visiting her when, eighteen months later,
following another stroke and a period in hospital, she went
into the nursing home.

Miss H said that she hoped she wouldn't have to stay
at the place long. But it is a lovely place and she has
settled down very well. It's a long time since I've seen
her so contented. She even asked for her lipstick, so is
her old self once again. There was a lovely birthday tea.
The staff brought in a birthday cake with candles on it,
Miss H blew out the candles and made a wish, and the
staff and residents all sang 'Happy Birthday'. Miss H
was on very good form. I had to wake her up and she
was very chatty – it was a real treat to see her so
well . . .

But then:

I'm afraid her mental state has greatly deteriorated. She
is talking a lot about her mother and father, and says
she doesn't like Slough, tho' it's alright for shopping.
She is always pleased to see me but doesn't know who I
am which I find very sad. She is not capable of doing
anything at all for herself and has to be fed. They
had roast beef for lunch so I fed her. She has to be
encouraged to eat or she forgets what to do with it.

Not wearing her dentures doesn't help much. I was told
her mouth had shrunk and it is better to take them
away altogether as she might swallow them. I take her
in some odd bits and pieces now and again. She hasn't
had her hair cut, but is fine in herself, clean and tidy,
and looks very nice. I will always be there for her.

Here, in simple living language, is a glimpse of what may
await any of us, and a sense of the reality obscured by the
cloud of departmental papers that was raining upon us both,
my aunt and me. Under that downpour she was transformed
from a patient and human being into a robotic consumer of
health which must be perpetually checked to see if it were not
being fed too much health, more health than its proper entitle-
ment. Jean and Rita were irrelevant to them, an anecdote,
never a meaningful statistic. Yet they became, as it were, adopted
by my dispersed and disunited family. Their indefatigable
optimism held things together. When my aunt sits mutely in
her chair, bent and bandaged, apparently seeing nothing, they
describe her as being 'in the pink'; when she is almost dead,
they acknowledge that she is 'off colour'. Of course they were
paid. But money was merely an essential, never the motivating
part of our agreement, a means and not an end – which was
the continuing welfare of their friend, my aunt, Yolande.

But none of this was of use to the solicitor. Though I had
struggled to make my aunt's affairs agonisingly simple, probate
reintroduced complications. The nursing home suddenly discovered a bill, over three years old, that had never been paid; the
Benefits Agency somehow paid an extra instalment into my
aunt's closed bank account after her death, and then set about
the infinitely complex business of reclaiming it; a new branch
of Barclays Bank, the Operations Centre at Haywards Heath,
issuing sincere condolences, presented itself as if for a party;
and my accountant entered the stage, asking to be put in touch,

as though for a dance, with my aunt's solicitor, so that together they could begin calculating what interest would accrue at the bank after her death – interest which must now be added to my own taxable income. This, I thought, is how many people pass their working lives. It is called 'the real world'.

It was around this time that, reading through a long, obtuse and deeply unhelpful letter from her publisher, Oxford University Press, my wife Margaret suddenly looked up and exclaimed abruptly: 'I wish I were dead.' And I heard myself pitifully cry out: 'For God's sake, don't say that – I couldn't cope with the paperwork!'

All the bodies, teams, departments, bureaux, agencies and offices that I had laboriously choreographed into a stately waltz, now quickened their steps. The music changed and they began tripping over one another. Whatever documents were sent off to one of them were immediately demanded by another. There was much irritated jostling. New partners, too, joined the dance, such as the 'Recovery of Estates' at A Wing, Government Buildings, in Leeds. I had been in communication with Blackpool, Epsom, Ewell, Greenwich, Guildford, Leicester, Maidenhead, Newcastle and Peterborough, but never Leeds. What Leeds wanted were my aunt's bank statements going back three and a half years, also Inland Revenue documents, pass-books, share certificates for the same period, together with what they called other relevant 'personal details'. I entered the cupboard of papers once more and by the end of the day, dark with dust, held triumphantly in my arms everything that Leeds urgently needed. It was so gross a bundle that it could not fit into the extra-large fortified envelope they had provided.

My spirit of self-congratulation at this feat of recovery faded when, a few weeks later, Leeds wrote to inform me that I owed them exactly £10,559.25. The calculations attached to this precise sum, this most untidy precise sum, were copious. I was urged to disregard the 'Capital Assured Tariff Income' from 28 November 1966 to 16 November 1975, and did so very willingly. The 'Adjudication Officer' had concentrated his attention on eight sections of the Social Security Administration Act of 1992 and identified a 'relevant change of circumstances' covering 151 weeks for 'JC 17 78 73B' (which is the code name he uses for my aunt). These figures are entered in a series of boxes on form QB16. The grand total impressively fills the final box. Over ten thousand pounds. I stare at it. I had read all the leaflets and brochures, gone through the documents, frowned over the instructions. But I had never mastered what they call 'the literature'. So what is it I am staring at?

It is, I begin to see, something to do with the sale of my aunt's flat. Could anyone have believed it remained empty, year after year? Apparently, yes. Knowing I had informed everyone of the sale, I wonder whether it is worth my returning to that infernal cupboard yet again and, like a character from Narnia, coming back with some splendid proof. But proof is useless, the solicitor explains, because we are not dealing with a question of fault, merely of fact. The fact is that my aunt's payment of £130 per week has been too much according to the computer, and the accumulated excess must be paid back at once or else it will attract interest. Interest! What a word! I look unbelievingly at the papers. I cannot credit it – indeed it is pure debit. I write out a cheque.

But to offset this there was an odd bonus to balance the books. While writing *Basil Street Blues*, I discovered that after my grandfather left home in 1926 and established his young mistress, Agnes May, in Piccadilly, he made a legal settlement for the benefit of his wife and three children, which was amended in 1932 by a Supplemental Deed drafted to ease his passage back to the family. The language of these trusts and deeds is marvellously obscure to me. I remember, from my early days as an articled clerk, having the famous seventeenth-century jurist John Seldon's aphorism recited to me: 'Ignorance of the law excuses no man.' But he must, I thought, have had criminal law principally in mind. The reason he advanced was 'not that all men know the law, but because 'tis an excuse every man will plead'. By the twentieth century, the language of the law had grown so complex as to impose ignorance on all ordinary men and women. We are foreigners in our own country. The land is reverberating to the sound of competing languages, and becoming filled with expert interpreters – business consultants, financial advisers, internet teams, text-talk specialists, scientific popularisers, literary critics, political columnists and 'spin doctors' – translating one English language into another, trying profitably to treat layers of verbal ignorance. The impenetrability of legal language, with its sidesteps into Latin, remains one of the most formidable. Read, for example, any small extract from my grandfather's Supplemental Deed of 1932:

> The Trustees shall hold Basil's share upon the like trust
> *mutatis mutandis* as are hereinbefore declared
> concerning Kenneth Holroyd's share as if the names of
> the said Kenneth Holroyd and Basil Holroyd were
> interchanged in paragraph (b) of this clause . . .

And so on for some six thousand words, covering three generations, over seventy years. These trusts and deeds, all signed, sealed and delivered God knows where, became part of a debtors' dance to which dismal rhythm my family was obliged to move.

I needed a lawyer and a professional financial consultant at each elbow to break this legal code and understand its implications. Briefly stated, the Trust tied up sufficient capital so as to produce £2,000 a year income while my grandfather was alive and, in the event of his death, £2,500 to be divided between his widow and three children. The yield in 1932 was 4.7%, which suggested that there must have been some £50,000 capital involved (slightly more to provide £2,500, rather less for £2,000). Sensibly but not sensationally invested, following the index, taking inflation into account, such an income at the beginning of the 1930s would have come to £150,000 by the end of the century, while the capital itself should have risen over seventy years to something approaching eight million pounds. These were dizzying sums that might actually have existed had we succeeded in breaking the Trust. But by law one quarter of the original capital of a Trust would have had to be invested in 'narrow range' gilts and three quarters in 'wide range' equities. Even so, I speculated, it would surely not be unreasonable to hope for half these sums, an income of £75,000 from a capital of, say, four million. Was I on the trail of a lost family fortune? Could I track it down?

The track led me to the Brighton Branch of NatWest Investments, which brazenly changed its name during our negotiations to 'NatWest Wealth Management'. The wealth of the early 1930s had shrunk dramatically. There was no eight million pounds, not even four million pounds capital now. Over fifty years of wealth management had reduced the sum to £16,000, yielding my aunt a little over £300 gross annually – minus, of course, the NatWest management fees. This £300 or so was an annual nuisance partly because no bank, apparently, likes to communicate with any other bank (the NatWest and Barclays did not seem to be on speaking terms), and partly because though my aunt (since the death of her two brothers) was the sole beneficiary of the Trust's income, the assets did not actually belong to her and could not be traded.

Only when Yolande died, the last of her generation in the family, could the Trust be ended and the dwindling shares finally sold. Vicky and I decided to sell everything immediately before the capital was reduced further by additional wealth management. Each of us received about eight thousand pounds. For

Vicky, who had never heard of my grandfather's mistress, Agnes May, and the legal complexities arising from his extended leave of absence from the family, this money came as a total surprise which repaid her for the generosity she had shown Aunt Yolande over her last years. For me, it went a long way to paying off the 'Recovery of Estates' bill from A Wing in Leeds.

At the same time I asked the NatWest to send me all other documents they held connected with the Trust. From these I can now piece together a little more of what happened. It appears that in 1941, when my parents separated, my father made me a ward of court – probably to prevent my mother carrying me off during the war to the safety of a neutral country, her own country, Sweden. I was then five years old and, as 'an infant' represented by my 'next friend', came before the Chancery Division of the High Court, the plaintiff in a case against the Holroyd Settlement trustees. I have no memory of this and probably had no knowledge of it at the time. I am like the 'infant prodigy' from *Nicholas Nickleby*, led by this legal friend into the foggy atmosphere of *Bleak House*.

The case came before Mr Justice Simmonds, a man famous for his prominent eyebrows and bright red face. I remember my father telling me that obituaries of eminent lawyers should generally be read in reverse, so that if a Lord Chief Justice, for example, were to be described as 'humane and witty', you could be reasonably certain that he was a keen advocate of capital punishment and a notorious bore. In *The Dictionary of National Biography*, Mr Justice Simmonds is described as having a nature that was 'essentially sensitive and compassionate' (though the contributor admits that this was 'not always apparent') and that the 'clarity and speed of his decisions' were 'ranked high, particularly in Chancery cases'.

It is difficult to recapture, among the Deeds of Appointment, the trustees' affidavits, the note on exhibits, the faded Case for Counsel's Opinion arriving from the bank the essence of that clarity now. This may partly be because, voluminous as these papers are, they are only a fraction of the entire paperwork given birth to by my infant case, the main body of which has been consumed, evacuated and discarded by the Chancery Registry at the Royal Court of Justice. Nor can anything now be located by the solicitor through whom I acted. Some notion of the speed of this case, however, may be apprehended, and by the standards of *Bleak House*, it is indeed quick. Our floundering in Chancery does not appear to have lasted beyond 1945 – that is, a little over four years – by which time Simmonds had been created a life peer ('finding the serener and more intellectual atmosphere of the Lords and Privy Council much to his taste'). Soon afterwards he was appointed Lord High Chancellor of Great Britain.

I was obviously no match for him. I lost my case, or at least did not win it. Or possibly it is still pending. Who knows? As to Lord Simmonds's compassion, its results could be seen in the rapidly dwindling fortunes of my family after the war.

By the time I had worked this out, probate was completed and Aunt Yolande had settled into her grave – which is to say the dark brown earth surrounding her coffin had settled and I could make arrangements for her tombstone. I was sent a brochure by the undertaker headed 'Timelessness. A Price List'. Fashions have changed since architects and sculptors chiselled vast unseated horses, veiled angels, upturned flambeaux, mantled urns and groups of pathetic mourners, kneeling, supine, into the living rock. I was offered instead various smaller designs: of a footballer, a rabbit, a shepherd, a marble teddy bear; there were rose and chamfered vases; granite memorials shaped with the outline of a heart or decorated with a couple of gliding swans. I went for simplicity: what was called 'The Wheeled Cross' headpiece in Nabresina natural stone on which my aunt's name and dates were cut in flush lead lettering. I was impressed by the skill and aesthetic seriousness of the stonemason of whom, I thought, the undertakers themselves were rather in awe – they appeared to tremble at the sound of his name, Mr Robert Kacmarczyk. Like Mr Joyboy, the venerated mortician and restorative genius of 'Whispering Glades' in Evelyn Waugh's *The Loved One*, who cleverly manipulates the expressions of his unresisting customers, he was an artist, recognised as such and deferred to by everyone.

I wanted to choose a short inscription in a language that, among all the Babel of tongues that had so jangled and upset my understanding as I grappled with my aunt's affairs, I had never heard; a language I did not see on any of the headstones in the churchyard, but which could now come to her rescue.

> No exorciser harm thee!
>> Nor no witchcraft charm thee!
> Ghost unlaid forbear thee!
>> Nothing ill come near thee!
> Quiet consummation have;
>> And renownèd be thy grave!

From this song, its lines in this third verse spoken alternately by Cymbeline's two sons, Guiderius and Arviragus, before they carry off the body of Cloten, I chose for my aunt the single line without a mark of exclamation.

3

Private Faces

A POSTBAG OF READERS' STORIES

Private faces in public places
Are wiser and nicer
Than public faces in private places.

W. H. Auden

While I was in the eye of this impenetrable language storm passing over my aunt's remains, the proofs of my family memoir arrived. There was not very much to correct, but I became aware of several mysterious and frustrating gaps in the narrative, event-plots that I had been unable to develop as a novelist might have done because my researches had led nowhere.

Basil Street Blues was published during the early autumn of 1999 in Britain and the Commonwealth and the following spring in the United States and Canada. I awaited the reviews with a trepidation that was rather different from what I normally experience before the publication of my books. My biographical subjects have been figures whose professional careers and achievements belonged to the reading public. Critics had already formed their opinions about Lytton Strachey, Augustus John and Bernard Shaw – often strong opinions, involving their attitudes to homosexuality, promiscuity or socialism, that had been hammered into their ideologies, sometimes their very identities.

Whatever I had written would initially collide, or perhaps coincide, with those opinions and, for the time being, produce little change in public opinion. In any event, though it is all too easy for biographers to grow sentimentally protective of their subjects and to aggrandise them, my biographies were not really intended to be vehicles of propaganda or promotion. They were non-fiction stories. Even when the secrets of their private lives were posthumously exposed, such public figures could largely take care of themselves.

But it was quite a different matter for my family. None of them were known to the general public, nor had they grand achievements to parade – quite the contrary. I began to wonder whether I had unwittingly presented their financial and emotional disasters as the entertainments of a travelling circus, goading my parents, and even my bewildered grandparents, through acrobatic hoops of fire, shutting them cheerily into cages with the lions. Glancing through an early finished copy of my family memoir when it came in the post, I seemed to see, clambering through its pages, a troupe of ungainly, poignant, gesticulating clowns whose griefs and disappointments, as they tumbled over one another, rang out in sidesplitting farce. I shut the book, shuddered and waited . . .

. . . and suddenly, as if in a dream, remembered Margaret advising me, while on a journey to the Far East, our plane being boarded by what looked like a band of cut-throat freedom fighters, that, whatever happened, however desperate, I *really must not* attempt to disarm them by reading aloud my lecture. This would only irritate everyone and lead to my being shot or flung overboard. It was a surreal memory signalling my uncertainties over the tone and attitude of my book.

But when the book was finally published and the reviews came in, I found to my relief that it had not been shot down. The critics on both sides of the Atlantic, in Ireland and Australia too, were generous, deciding that I had balanced 'high comedy and desperate sadness', as one of them wrote, and treating my researches when translated into narrative as a detective story. Perhaps there was some thankfulness too (reviewers being paid for the number of words they have to write rather than read) that I had at last come up with a book of moderate length.

Fifty years ago, I believe, many critics would have questioned the validity of writing a memoir of such extravagantly humdrum people. But then, over this period, our sense of blood snobbery has diminished. There were, it is true, one or two reviewers who fastened their attention further back on my remote and more distinguished ancestors (they occupy less than twenty pages of the book) – the great lawyer painted by Sir Joshua Reynolds, the noble patron who edited Edward Gibbon's *Memoirs*, the intrepid general who saved the Assam tea-planters from death during the Indian Mutiny, the eccentric cricket enthusiast who founded the Sheffield Shield competition in Australia – and then felt let down by the rapid decline and fall of the House of Holroyd. But this was rare. Most readers seemed at home with the more recent past, the period belonging to their own parents. One critic concluded that I had 'done them proud!' and I remember feeling a surge of relief.

After the reviewers came the readers. Our sense of blood snobbery may have diminished in the twentieth century, but our fame snobbery has risen and supplanted it. How would my family weather this change? I was astonished by the quantity of letters I received. After all, none of the people in the book was famous – they were as unknown as are the characters in a novel before its publication, as unknown and, I hoped, as recognisable. With all this attention, suddenly, momentarily, I was a marvellous proper person, invited to be patron of a church, a member of a racquets club, to purchase a National Service tie, to attend an old school dinner, to speak at the

Guildhall, contribute to a Long-Term Care seminar, address an
adoption society. Among the more unexpected communications
was an astronomical chart of amazing complexity which
revealed 'several synchronicities' with a notorious bishop and
gave prominence to my 'natal Dragon's Head'. I could not
decide, and still cannot, whether this was vastly good or bad
news.

Many of the letters I had grown used to receiving from
readers of my biographies were, it seemed to me, responding
to books I had not written. They would highlight points I had
missed (which is to say details I had thought not worth putting
in), identify misprints as scholarly symptoms of an unconscious
attitude, or concentrate over several pages on a footnote here,
the absence of a reference note there. One reader of my *Augustus
John* felt saddened when, on the very first page, he read of
Augustus's parents travelling from Haverfordwest to Tenby in
1877 without any mention of the fact they would have had to
change trains at Milford Haven. A reader of my *Bernard Shaw*
could not get past the first sentence in which, he felt convinced,
I had given the wrong date for Shaw's death (a mistake occa-
sioned by the fact that he had filed his own obituary of Shaw
for *Time* magazine a month early). And why, a reader of my
Lytton Strachey indignantly protested, had I failed to mention
in any single chapter the role of the pancreas to which so many
of our predicaments can be traced?

The letters arising from *Basil Street Blues* were less arcane
and the responses more spontaneous. People, as it were, took
some of my clothes and tried them on themselves – sometimes
with surprising effects. On emerging from behind the beards
of my biographical subjects I was occasionally stopped in the
street by men of the same age as myself. These encounters were
bizarre parodies of fame, unfocused happenings, moments of
frank bewilderment. I made some notes of them, and now run
them together.

'Hello! It's Michael Holroyd, isn't it?'

'Yes, I think it is.'

'I thought it was. I'm Paul/I'm Nicky/I'm Leonard . . .'

'Oh.'

'You haven't changed at all.'

'I haven't! Really?'

'I read your book in the library. What you wrote about Mr Bailey was spot on.'

'Remind me.'

'How he watched us all in the swimming pool at school.'

'He wasn't a major character, as I recall. And it's a long time ago. We were only ten.'

'Did you go to the reunion?'

'I must have been away, out of town, abroad . . .'

'It was a good show. Lots to drink. I never realised how many of us had become clergymen.'

'Clergymen!'

'Yes. I went to Matthew's/Mark's/Luke's memorial service the other day. Remember him? It was a very good show. Lots to eat and drink. But he'd become a Catholic, you know. Told no one. Not even his wife. What are you doing now?'

'I'm standing in the rain talking to you.'

'No, I mean what are you writing about next?'

'I'm not sure. I'm trying not to think about it.'

'I do a lot of jogging these days – since I retired. Lost tons of weight. Over twenty pounds, would you believe?'

'Extraordinary. There must have been much more of you.'

'So what's your news? What did you say you were writing?'

'Not much. Saw Leonard/Nicky/Paul round here last week. Remember him?'

'I don't think so. Was he in the clothing business?'

'Don't know.'

'I went round to his place once – if it was him – full of models. Wonderful.'

'I wish I'd kept up with him – if it was him.'

By now we are both staring frantically down the street wondering how to disengage ourselves from this vacuous embrace. Then, waving energetically towards imaginary friends, we plunge off suddenly, gratefully.

Other readers tackled my book more psychologically. One, blaming me for her nightmares, telephoned in the middle of the night to discuss them. A good many readers asked for advice with their own autobiographies and family memoirs – and sent me typescripts; one of them, like John Betjeman's, I remember, was in verse. Opinions seemed to differ as to whether I had written a tragedy or a comedy. When I gave it to my wife to read, I explained that it was a comedy – a black comedy in places; when she finished reading it she told me it was a tragedy – with some very good jokes. 'Oh, the familiar pain, the dreadful laughter,' exclaimed another writer on finishing the book. That sounded like tragedy. A novelist, hearing me read some passages on the radio about my parents' deaths, had sat crying in her car, unable to get out – until rescued by a handsome stranger in a corduroy suit. Was it, after all then, a romantic tragedy? But in the video shops, which are an index of our times, there is no category called tragedy.

Other readers had cried with laughter. 'I fell off my chair,' one of them, an actress, complained. She was not demanding damages, but wrote again the following week to report that she 'was crying so much I had to clean my glasses. Thank God for Optrex!' She went on to recommend my publisher to get some eye sponsorship for the book – a suggestion rather ahead of its time.

The travels and adventures of my book, like those of a satellite sending back signals from the unknown – momentary sightings of strangers' lives – began to fascinate me. Two people took *Basil Street Blues* on trains and missed their stations. One, in Italy, was hustled off early by his wife, embarrassed by the loudness of his guffawing. The other hurtled obliviously through Sussex on to Eastbourne – an episode that, since my great-grandmother mysteriously committed suicide while living at Eastbourne, could, I thought, be made into a compelling ghost story.

I had tried to move the narrative of *Basil Street Blues* through several gears, passing from something researched into something experienced, from history towards biography, formality to intimacy, a farce into an elegy. The most amusing piece of lit. crit. I received came from my stepdaughter, who described the book as an unusual mixture of *Cranford* and *King Lear*.

'I never knew you were so foreign,' protested Beryl Bainbridge, who went on to describe the book in a newspaper as a peculiarly English comedy: 'We must all keep a straight bat.' Somewhere between her novels on Hitler and Scott of the Antarctic, Beryl had once contemplated writing a fictional biography of me as the 'Boy Holroyd'. What a place on the bookshelf this would have been! Beryl might have released my dormant self, allowing me as 'the Boy' to hit heroic sixes and score miraculous goals, in a grand Utopia of metaphors. She would have granted me a fantastical new life, as the very Holroyd of Holroyds rather than a Holroyd permanently in waiting. I was promising material since I already possessed a rich, if resting, cast of characters: Swedish mother and French stepmother, a half-Irish, quarter-Scottish father and fully Hungarian stepfather who had, between them, bathed me in a glamorous glow at school. But none of this had distanced me from the other, more regularly derived schoolboys. Born of parents traumatised by two world wars, we were the children of a wounded generation. All of us were being educated, as one of them wrote to remind me, for a world that, by the time our education was complete, no longer existed. It was ripe territory for an imaginative takeover by Beryl.

Guided by my readers, I looked again at the dwindling

fortunes of my family and began to understand how impossible it had been for the men to adapt to new circumstances, and how these new circumstances had come too late to benefit the women. My grandfather haphazardly losing his Indian fortune; my mother for ever travelling the world in search of a glamorous life beyond the horizon; my father, left by all his wives, ending up with only his dog to order around; my aunt with her failing memories of a life unlived. They were all symbols of the peculiar predicament of post-imperial Britain.

Having such varied cosmopolitan influences around me while growing up, I have never been able to see myself as exclusively English. Yet it is shamefully true that, despite my polyglot past, I speak only English. So probably Beryl was right: the book is 'English'. Certainly that was the reason advanced by publishers abroad for not translating it. Because of this, I came to treasure letters from foreign readers for whom, without benefit of translation, the book became part of an inner repertory. 'It is (from my vantage point) a remote world you are describing,' one of them wrote, explaining how, nevertheless, the tone and perspective had 'allowed me to enter it more fully than most guides'. I have kept these few letters from readers beyond the English-speaking world, believing that the point of translation is, within a framework of universal human nature, to make remote cultures more familiar.

Like a Pandora's Box, my book caused tremors from many buried memories. Though I believed that I had been portraying a unique group of extravagant characters, I found that they had struck a chord with all sorts and conditions of readers. 'I know just what you were saying. It all came back.' 'There were many faraway echoes of happenings in my own life and that of my parents.' 'I recognised a lot.' 'Your father would have got on well with my mother.' And so on. There were hundreds of these letters, though many of them went on to describe characters and events that were dramatically different from anything I had written. Yet I knew what they meant: we all had parallel pasts which, to avoid embarrassment or pain, had been brushed and combed into polite fictions. Reading these letters, with their curious stories branching crazily out in every direction, I felt that we all came from the same ground, and this feeling gave me unexpected pleasure – as if a sense of belonging had suddenly invaded my writerly seclusion.

Some critics noted that my title, *Basil Street Blues*, was misleading – and it is true that it landed the book in the music department of several bookstores, both in Britain and in the United States. But I had dreamt of creating something comparable to the music of the blues, the sadness sung out loud and long until the note of love breaks through. Could this word-music call up spirits from the deep? That is what I wished. For if they could reappear between the covers of my book and somehow touch other people's lives, then death itself perhaps might be less final.

'It would be nice to know any other facts that will inevitably be thrown up by readers,' a local historian wrote to me.

I hoped that a few of these new facts might fill the various gaps in the narrative I had become more aware of when correcting the proofs. In the event, while some of them were indeed to do this, others fell haphazardly elsewhere, extending the frontiers of my memoir into unfamiliar ground. Did I know that a much-feared headmaster of my school had been murdered by one of the boys after I left? This question came from a woman two of whose three husbands had been at the school. But another ex-schoolboy from those dreadful days of grey-collared sweaters and acute homesickness remembered meeting this fearsome master some years later with a sense of shock: 'I could not believe what a small, nervous, insignificant man he was, away from his patch.' The son of yet another schoolfriend wrote to thank me, after forty years, for giving him a pink elephant when he was a baby: and then to tell me that a few weeks back, 'at the worrying age of sixty-four', his father had 'died suddenly, and unexpectedly, from a massive heart attack, while reading the *Spectator*'. I had not put him into *Basil Street Blues*, though we were good friends in our late teens and early twenties. And now I remember that we once hired a boat whose steering went so catastrophically askew that we capsized some of the Henley Regatta – about which I wrote a short story in the manner of Jerome K. Jerome.

Some of these letters read like first drafts of, or simply ideas for, short stories. The novelist Rose Tremain, who lived when a child in Sloane Avenue, used to look through her bathroom window at the two big mansion blocks where my mother (between husbands) and I (during holidays) lived at one time or another and, staring up at them, at us perhaps, would speculate on 'people's lives in those flats and talk to them in my mind and invent stories about them ... this was very important to the way I came to value and need a complex imaginative life running alongside my actual life'.

I was given some vivid glimpses of minor characters in my book (the novelist William Gerhardie wearing a protective saucepan on his head during an air raid in the war and afterwards, still wearing the saucepan, searching helplessly for it in his kitchen). But more people wrote to me about places, and how they had changed. The Links at Eastbourne, where my great-grandfather had retired, was now becoming a housing estate; the church where I paraded on Sundays in Winchester, while getting through my National Service, had been turned into a cinema; the apartment on Chelsea Embankment where I sometimes stayed with my mother and her third husband, and which was later bought by Sean Connery, had previously been used by Hitler's ambassador in London, Von Ribbentrop, who, by the time we got there, had been executed following the Nuremberg trials. But the oddest news of all came from Matisse's biographer, Hilary Spurling, who offered some curious speculations over Picasso's biographer, John Richardson.

> The proprietor of the Basil Street Hotel – where you may or may not have been conceived – was the Rothschilds' [or Roseberys'] butler from Mentmore and uncle of John Richardson (himself the son of a Mentmore housemaid who married Sir Garnet Wolseley's piratical quartermaster, afterwards founder of the Army and Navy stores) – so young John may well have presided as bellboy over the Holroyd honeymoon.

My mother had enjoyed many honeymoons since then – more perhaps than I knew. 'How did you survive?' enquired a friend of one of her lovers. 'To have a beautiful mother who was in effect a *poule de luxe* must have been searing at times, yet you seemed to give the impression of being an acquaintance just looking on, and that Ulla's affairs had little to do with you.'

How can I account for this? 'All those years ago,' wrote Beryl Bainbridge, 'I wanted to throttle the Ulla of my memory for bouncing you about like a tennis ball.' But this was never how I felt about my mother. Because of my parents' separation and divorce when I was five or six, and the fact that I lived with my father's parents while growing up, my mother had in some degree seemed to leave me. So, although I remained emotionally attached to her, there was also some distance between us. Did her escapades bring out my prudence, or was I attracted to her way of life? A little of both, I believe. But perhaps of all my family, I most resemble my grandfather Fraser. Somewhat apprehensive, I was without the sting and excitement of aggression, a dreamer who (as the handling of my aunt's financial affairs shows) is maladroit over money. Fraser, his youth like mine 'much delayed', lived in a non-permissive age, yet after an exemplary thirty years of marriage, suddenly, aged fifty (approximately the age when I got married) drove off with a much younger woman. He retained, as I have explained, that special sensitivity to women of men whose mothers die early. My mother did not die early, but our separation may have produced a similar reaction – a few women have been all-important to me. I had not reflected on the possibility of such a pattern before reading this letter, which goes on to describe how the wife of one of my mother's lovers took him back after he had 'recovered his senses', helped him to keep his job, and paid off the debts he had accumulated entertaining my mother. This, like the other side of the moon, was a story that lay hidden from me – a cautionary tale that appeals to my prudence more than to my romanticism.

But if, as several correspondents point out, my book reinforces the view that our patterns of behaviour are genetically programmed, I must also call in evidence from my Swedish grandmother Kaja to account for my mother and myself.

One evening the telephone rang and I heard the voice of Sacha Kardo-Sessoëff. He is a Russian sculptor, aged about ninety now, whom I had not seen for thirty-five years. Between the wars he had made an animated appearance as the youthful friend – '*beau garçon, sportif, flambeur et sans le sou, personnage séduisant*' – and a fellow emigré in the Life of the novelist Romain Gary.* He reintroduced himself on the telephone by reminding me that he taught me to swim in the south of France, where I spent several summer holidays with my mother. I remember him well: a romantic, wiry, outdoor man with a strange accent, a dark-skinned White Russian who obviously attracted my mother, or was attracted to her – it was difficult

---

*Dominique Bona, *Romain Gary* (Mercure de France, 1987), p. 46.

to tell which as a child. I liked him, though he didn't make much of a job teaching me to swim – I retain a tendency, very slowly, to sink – and he did not make much of a living either as a sculptor. Yet he always seemed happy.

When I went over to see him he was almost blind, the complete indoor man, an elegant art dealer, living in some luxury near Marble Arch. We sat in a sombre, comfortable room, paintings by French and Italian masters on his walls, stories of pictures by Raphael and Géricault he had discovered (he wanted an introduction to Anita Brookner). He told me how indignant he used to feel whenever my first stepfather, Edy Fainstain, was rude in public to my mother. He was not a chivalrous man, Edy, I was told, but a bully. He bullied women. Rising slowly, painfully, to his feet, staring back across time, Sacha declared that he sometimes felt like challenging Edy to a duel. Had they been in Russia, he would have called him out. At dawn. But thinking such a gesture might embarrass my mother (she was never an early riser), he did nothing. He regretted that silence now. Then, sitting down again, relaxing, he began speculating as to why my mother had put up with Edy's bad behaviour and, parting his hands in a gesture of despair to the room, concluded that she must have loved him. This was presented not so much as the solution to a mystery as another piece in the insoluble puzzle of why we love some people and not others.

But, he quickly added, this was not the reason why he had invited me over to see him. Did I know that my Swedish grandmother, Kaja, was the lover for a brief period of that amiable anarchist Jacques Prévert, author of *Les Enfants du Paradis*? Prévert had sometimes taken her to see Matisse and she enjoyed playing with his collages. Of course Kaja was dead now . . . He paused, then began again. Had there been anything resembling a Matisse, he asked, among Kaja's belongings? I replied that I had been told Kaja knew Picasso. 'That too,' Sacha answered. I could look for that too. Then suddenly we both laughed as if this were not actually the purpose of my visit, merely an excuse of a shy blind man to meet his swimmer again.

No one writes to me about my mother and father together. The letters I read about my father are separate: how he came into the office one morning 'in a great panic' as he should have been meeting 'one of his wives' flying in from abroad – but he couldn't be sure 'which wife it was'. Another employee wrote of the bewilderment he caused in the office with his jokes. 'He was always looking for a dream,' she concluded. 'I was not sure whether he was ever really happy.' I have described him travelling all over Britain after the war trying to revive his pre-war dreams of prosperity. What I had not known, or remembered, was that he went much further in pursuit of these dreams – as far as Australia, arriving there in 1950 and attempting to restart the agency for Lalique Glass. I think he believed that life in a younger country might bring back his youth. But he achieved this mainly through giving one of his small cousins 'my first tuition at cricket under the clothes line in our backyard' at Double Bay. As for Lalique Glass, that got nowhere and he soon returned.

But one reader, Merle Rafferty, remembers him in the great days of Lalique before the war, when he worked more lack-adaisically, sometimes arriving as late as 11 a.m. at his basement office at the back of Bertorelli's Restaurant in Soho and taking robust charge of the breakages. His older brother, my Uncle Kenneth, turned up at the elegant showrooms in Basil Street far earlier – which was unfortunate since he always seemed in a terrific hurry, slamming doors in the faces of the staff as he rushed from room to room. They knew what was the trouble. 'Kenneth appeared to be ruled and regulated by a married lady who rang frequently to complain about something he had, or had not, done (the phone was very close to me). This upset him terribly and he was full of remorse, but impossibly rude ... He was always in a state of agitation.' So, in his quieter way, was my grandfather, Fraser, as he gazed vacantly round the fabulous Lalique shop with its curved, 'invisible', front window in Bond Street. Fraser relied entirely and for everything on his secretary. She was 'a Mrs Booth, who insisted on being called "Miss". When she went on leave to have a baby, he was absolutely lost and unable to settle anything, ringing her at intervals to find out what he should be doing, and asking "How is the rising generation?" She was not long away, and I wondered what happened to the baby.'

But not even Miss Booth could save Lalique, though the amalgamation with Kosta Glass in Sweden and the American Corning Glassware, which produced glass bricks used by Frank Lloyd Wright, delayed its bankruptcy until 1939. As another correspondent summed up these twelve years: 'I don't think the Holroyds ever made a penny profit.'

Of all these stray pieces of mosaic, the most interesting comes from Ronald Stent, a German Jew whom my father, with the ingenious use of a huge glass elephant, helped to escape from Nazi Germany in 1935. He came to work in my father's basement office and most days 'we had beer and sandwiches at the local pub', he remembers.

Not long after my arrival, we were standing at the bar with other chaps where your father entertained us with corny jokes. One was about some Shylock-type, money-grubbing Yid. It hurt me badly. Once the others had gone I berated your father. 'I hope,' I said, 'that you know I have a reasonable sense of humour, but after the rampant anti-semitism now in Germany, this type of joke is for me beyond the pale.' Basil looked flummoxed. 'If it hurts you,' he replied, 'I will in future

refrain, but that will only make me self-conscious and
wary. Why don't you reciprocate by running my
Scottish and Irish ancestry down? Tit for tat.'

In his generosity, Ronald Stent accepted this as useful advice
about how to get on in English society. But it also reveals, I
think, how by the mid-to-late 1930s my father was already
beginning to fall behind the times. A few years before, Gustaff
Renier had published a bestseller entitled *The English: Are They
Human?*, a precursor to George Mikes's popular *How to be
an Alien* (1946) and Stephen Potter's *One-Upmanship* (1952),
which were read in exactly the amused spirit my father recommends. But when, in 1939, Wyndham Lewis brought out his
book on racial stereotypes, recommending assimilation and
calling it *The Jews: Are They Human?*, the joke was not funny
and (despite favourable reviews in *The Times Literary
Supplement* and the *Jewish Chronicle*) the book had to be
withdrawn.*

When Ronald Stent joined my family in London, his brother,
ten years younger than himself, was still at school in Berlin.
One of the few concessions on transferring money out of Nazi
Germany was for 'educational purposes'. Ronald went to visit
a minor public school in Epping Forest where the headmaster
agreed to take Gunther – on one condition. Having had some
bad experiences with boys from abroad whose fathers had
suddenly been unable to transfer fees, he asked for an established British citizen to guarantee the monthly payments. 'When
I told your father what the problem was, he spontaneously
offered to furnish such a guarantee,' Ronald Stent wrote to me.

---

*In the British Library, perhaps to avoid embarrassment, Wyndham Lewis's
book has been bound so that only *The Jews* can be seen on the spine, whereas
on the spine of Renier's rather indifferent volume the whole title is visible.

I declined, explaining that in Nazi Germany such sudden bans on currency transfer were a real possibility. Basil had an alternative: 'Why don't you take out an insurance policy?' I had never heard of such a possibility. All you could insure as a private person on the Continent was your home, your life, and your bits and pieces. Basil phoned a cousin who was a Lloyd's underwriter: 'No problem,' he said, 'I will get you a quotation.' He 'phoned back shortly. 'Nothing doing,' he said. 'For the first time in my career I have been refused a quote. Hitler's Germany is uninsurable!'

But all was for the best in that worst of all possible worlds. Eventually, in 1940, Gunther reached the United States, where in due course he became well known as co-father of a new scientific discipline, molecular genetics, part of the circle that worked on the structure of DNA, and later editor of the critical edition (1980) of James Watson's *The Double Helix. A Personal Account of the Discovery of the Structure of DNA*. 'If I had accepted Basil's generous offer,' Ronald Stent adds, 'my brother would most likely have become an Englishman, and molecular biology would have lost one of its pioneers.'

One of the most touching letters I received came from an eighty-eight-year-old woman, once an actress, who had played opposite Owen Nares in the London production of Dodie Smith's *Call It a Day* in the mid-1930s. She was then twenty-four and he was forty-eight. 'We fell seriously in love and would have married if Owen could have been free – impossible in those days without a ruinous scandal.' She was suffering from a terminal illness and it 'is very painful' for her to write this letter, but she was moved to do so by a determination not to have her love for Owen Nares, and his for her, which had been fiercely discouraged by the theatrical entrepreneur Binkie

Beaumont, obliterated from the record. So I record it here, with
her maiden name, Mary Gaskell.

Owen Nares was the father of David Nares, my mother's
third husband and the most eccentric of my stepfathers.
Everyone, it seems, has a story to tell of David. A 'most entertaining rogue', one of her girlfriends writes to assure me;
another describes how he would employ his most upper-class
accent when telling low stories on the telephone ('So I told her
to fuck orf'). My great friend at preparatory school when we
were ten or twelve, John Mein, tells me that he came to work
for my stepfather at Crawford's Advertising Agency in the
1960s. 'A certain Mr Nares summoned me to report at 10 a.m.,'
he wrote.

> After [I had waited] 40 minutes, in growing agitation,
> in ambled your stepfather, poured himself a strong
> drink from the boardroom bar, asked a few questions,
> then seemed to fall asleep. To keep things going I asked
> if he was related to the architect Nares who lived near
> my mother. He sprang to life . . . and a few minutes of
> social chat secured me the job.

Over the years John Mein worked at Crawford's he got to
know my stepfather well.

> Fun to be with when things were going well and he was
> not completely drunk . . . I had some good ideas which
> pleased him. I noticed they always became 'his ideas' at
> client meetings . . .
>   He had slicked back hair, Tuscan yellow teeth with a
> ghastly smile, wobbling jowls, and was very portly . . .
> On one flight back from Manchester there was only
> tea, coffee or soft drinks. 'Tell the captain that Mr
> David Nares would like to see him.' 'I can't, sir, he's

flying the plane.' 'Then tell him to fly the bloody thing faster!' I drove him home, longing for a drink myself by this time, but he slammed the house door in my face with no farewell. The true character of the charmer.

About my stepfather's family I made a serious mistake in the first edition of my book. I wrote that, though David was listed in *Who's Who* as Owen Nares's only son, there had been another son, Geoffrey. 'He had been homosexual, was shot for "cowardice" in the war, and then obliterated from the family record.' This sentence provoked what a journalist from the *Daily Mail* described as 'a rare sighting' of Camilla Parker Bowles's father, Major Bruce Shand, who sent an indignant letter to the *Daily Telegraph*, printed under the heading 'Holroyd's "ghastly slur" on a gallant soldier'.

Geoffrey Nares joined my regiment, the 12th Royal Lancers (Armoured Cars), in 1941, coming with us to the Middle East in the latter part of that year ... Early in 1942, he fought a most gallant action in which his troop rescued several British prisoners, subsequently he went from strength to strength, proving a most courageous and intelligent officer, especially in the very dire circumstances that prevailed that summer.

Towards its end, before El Alamein, there was a severe outbreak of a nasty disease called Sand Fly Fever. Geoffrey failed to recover from this when sent back to Cairo, where he died of a tumour on the brain. His obituary in *The Times* duly recorded that he died in active service.

In the last two paragraphs of his letter, Major Shand expressed the hope that measures could be put in hand for removing this slur from a brave soldier, his regiment and the Nares family.

How had I made such a lethal error? I had put 'cowardice'
between inverted commas in order to indicate that I did not take
the charge with moral seriousness, or rather that, for such a
savage lack of understanding, I blamed the military authorities.
But not taking the charge seriously, I did not check and find out
that executions for cowardice had been discontinued after the
First World War. I remember my stepfather speaking of some
shocking event involving Germany in his brother's life that had
led to the removal of his name from his father's entry in *Who's
Who*, and this I did check and find to be true. I also knew that
he had died in the war and, not believing his father would have
eliminated him from the family record simply for a homosexual
affaire (and not knowing of Owen Nares's thwarted love for
Mary Gaskell), I presumed it had been for what was considered
dishonourable conduct in the war. I conflated two stories and
got both wrong. Actually Geoffrey Nares had been seduced in
the late 1930s by a famous German ace tennis player, Baron
Gottfried Von Cramm, a six-foot, green-eyed, blond runner-up
at Wimbledon and in the United States championships, known
as 'the prince charming of tennis' – hence the 'disreputable'
connection with 'the enemy', which was peculiarly unfair because
Von Cramm was imprisoned by the Nazis. Though charged with
homosexuality, and smeared by the FBI as a Nazi, Von Cramm
had in fact criticised the Third Reich and was punished for his
opposition to Hitler. His life was made all the more strange by
a long, unrequited devotion of Barbara Hutton, the glamorous
Woolworth heiress to whom he was briefly married in the late
1950s.

I wrote at once to the *Daily Telegraph* admitting my error
and at greater length to Major Shand explaining how I thought
it had come about. I assured him that it would be corrected in
any reprint of my book as well as in the American edition,
which was then in preparation. He replied immediately,
declaring that his indignation went not a frown further and

saluting me for not blaming the publisher, the printer or a researcher. Then 'with some trepidation' he sent me a copy of his military memoirs *Previous Engagements* (in which Geoffrey Nares appears), inscribed 'In Memory of "The Nares Imbroglio"!'. Later I was able to respond with a copy of the purged American edition of my own book.

But not everyone was so graceful and generous as Bruce Shand, and I continued to have letters of outrage fired off at me by other correspondents that were more difficult to answer politely: for example from 'Yours truly' Major P. J. R. Waller MBE, JP, DL, who concluded: 'Introducing the issue of homosexuality is unworthy and largely irrelevant. What a dirty little turd you are.'

I was on safer ground with my own family. From India I received an invitation to visit the Assam tea gardens and see the legendary curved sword with which my great-grandfather had protected the lives of the tea-planters; from Sweden I was sent detailed corrections to my spelling; and from the United States a story about an Irish great-aunt whom I described as drowning in the Atlantic but who, in this version, reaches America, somehow acquires a title and lives in a terrific castle – eventually falling from one of its turrets to her death. In Britain I was offered an obscure twig from a family tree showing a Martha Holroyd marrying a James Drabble in 1840, and producing a banker son called James Edward Holroyd Drabble. We could have done with a banker. But most surprising of all was the discovery of a large family of cousins, some of them living nearby, of whom I had never heard. They were the descendants of my grandfather's mild-mannered brother Pat, the children of his son 'Mad Ivor' with whom, half a century ago, we had quarrelled and then dramatically parted.

'Is there anything more complex than the family?' one reader asks. 'Shakespeare's tragedies would not have existed without them.' Perhaps the most complex and tragic family story comes from cheerful Sally Anne, a cousin who believes she was misplaced as a child. Our Irish grandmothers were sisters (Corbets of County Cork), but Sally was abandoned by her mother Joyce and adopted by her Aunt Betty. 'Since Betty died I feel free to investigate and search for my Dad, whom I do not remember as I was adopted when a few months old,' she wrote to me.

I used occasionally to see Sally Anne when I was very young. Her 'mother', Betty, would sometimes invite me to parties in Maidenhead. I was terrified by these parties and much preferred seeing Sally's half-brother Dick, who occasionally came to play with me at my grandparents' house. He was the only child who visited us, and I remember picking up the rumour that he was the illegitimate son of Rex Harrison. 'At the age of 20, Joyce [their mother] met Rex in the Nag's Head, Kensington,' Sally explains in her letter. 'They went to Maidenhead for a party, got very drunk and returned to Baker Street. Joyce became pregnant and was whisked away by her sister Betty to Monte Carlo – calling herself Mrs Temple [which was her maiden name] . . . my brother is now in touch with his half-sister. They regularly meet and get on well together.'

Since none of this appears in Rex Harrison's biographies (all of which acknowledge his promiscuity, infidelities and liking for 'wayward girls'), I felt pleased to have got it right and happy to learn it turned out well. I gave Sally what information I had and a year later she reported on her progress. Things had not gone well for her, but the research was advancing and she was heartbreakingly optimistic. Her husband had died, she was alone and, having recently been operated on for breast cancer, was 'at present undergoing chemotherapy', to be followed by radium treatment. Nevertheless, despite these setbacks, she was getting ahead with her researches. Reading *Basil Street Blues* had spurred her on to find out more about her own past which grew ever more interesting to her as her future became more difficult. Her mind was frantically active, the family tree growing and spreading (her great-grandfather, she discovered, had a stained-glass memorial window at Worcester Cathedral) and she was planning to write her memoirs. What memoirs they would be! I imagined them as a film scenario.

Sally Anne and Dick were brought up very respectably at Maidenhead by their churchgoing Aunt Betty who pretended to be their mother. But though all letters from their real mother, Betty's sister Joyce, were confiscated, they began to suspect, even while they were still very young, that they had been adopted. After all, were they not the only two of the five children in the house who were left-handed and had blue eyes? Sally's half-sisters dispute much of what she comes to believe, attributing it to illness. Still, she remembers sometimes pestering their nanny with questions – and one day she blurted out the awful truth: and was instantly dismissed. This chink of light was quickly put out and the children still kept in the dark.

'I could not help being struck by the similarity of my mother's [Joyce's] escapades and your mother's,' Sally Anne wrote to me. After more surgery and chemotherapy, she resumed her researches and came across one of those stories that are said to be stranger than fiction.

A year after the birth of her son Dick, Joyce met a very tall gentleman called Bill at the Berkeley Hotel in London and, not wishing to have a second illegitimate child, quickly married him – Rex Harrison on this occasion taking the role, a vignette, of best man. But when Joyce became pregnant with Sally, her very tall husband Bill fled abroad to neutral Switzerland, soon afterwards petitioning her for a divorce and citing as co-respondent a shorter gentleman called John, whom Joyce later married in Jamaica, while Bill himself retired to Frinton-on-Sea.

The happy couple travelled to Jamaica rather hurriedly, indeed urgently, after Joyce had shot a third gentleman of undiscovered height and name who had entered her bedroom in London at dead of night – and been left for dead that very night.

Joyce's two sisters, the churchgoing Betty and an animal-trainer Sheila, pursued her to Jamaica and pleaded with her to come back to England and face the music. She would not be prosecuted, not seriously, they assured her. They had not read about this murder in the newspapers – not that they read newspapers much. But they had heard nothing on the wireless. Besides, they did not really believe her. And she did not actually believe them. But she did eventually move, for reasons unexplained, to Mexico City. However, the cold winter there was not good for her bones and the rainy season played havoc with her hair – and after all what was there left now but bones and hair? Not much. So, reflecting that she might bloom again for a season in a more encouraging climate, she descended on Acapulco. And here, for a brief, improbable moment (as if to prove the validity of Sally's comparison) she encountered my mother, at that time hitched up with a Viennese manufacturer of motorbicycles. Joyce, who was somewhat older than my mother, must have been in her fifties at this stage in the plot. But she was in her *young* fifties, which is to say that she still dressed as a teenager, aided by a variety of bright wigs and persistent treatment from a plastic surgeon. She had by now spent all her money and was supported financially by her two generous and disapproving sisters, the dog-training Sheila sending her £4,000 a year, and the churchgoing Betty (who was still bringing up her son and daughter at Maidenhead) adding a further £100 a week. With this money, and occasional bonuses extracted by brilliant feats of emotional blackmail, she was able to experiment with more ingenious facelifts, purchase some new jewellery, gather a pack of poodles, and, as she grew older, more wretched and deeply alcoholic, refuse all offers of humiliating help from the International Social Security. The rented villa where she holed up during the day was primitive, and her exotic nightlife in smoke-filled piano bars and garish transvestite clubs increasingly sad. Even so, she found the opportunity to marry once more, this time to a Mexican gentleman with a long name but of dubious moral stature who turned out to have a wife and two children back in Mexico – where an order was issued commanding him never to see Joyce again.

Joyce died of pneumonia and malnutrition in the mid-1990s. 'I have no idea where she is buried,' Sally Anne wrote to me.

But she was still on the trail, adding to her life in retrospect, eager to find out whether 'I too have any half-brothers or sisters'. Nothing could stop her. She had already located a cousin in Tasmania. And despite the cancer, her husband's death, the dreadful shadow of this past about which she was determined to discover more, she was brimming with curiosity, had taken up painting and was beginning to exhibit her pictures. After another dose of chemo, 'I now feel a great deal better,' she ended her letter, which she signed with her married name, Sally Anne Hurt. But in 2002 I heard she had died of cancer.

4

Self-Seeking

THE BEGINNING, A MIDDLE AND SOME SENSE OF AN END

As I was going up the stair
I met a man who wasn't there.
He wasn't there again to-day –
I wish to God he'd go away.

Anon

'You stay hidden,' writes Margaret Forster near the end of a letter to me. She is a novelist who has written two remarkable volumes of family memoirs. So is she right? By training I had learnt to explore others through myself but by temperament I like to explore myself through others. That is what I believed I had done.

All good biographies are intensely personal since they are really accounts of the relationship between a writer and the subject. But biographers also hide themselves behind their subjects, inhabiting those invisible spaces between the lines of print. Had I hidden myself behind my parents and grandparents too, while trying to fix my identity through family echoes and associations?

I do appear, of course, in my book on many pages and at many places: in my grandparents' dark house and on the margins of my schools; stumbling through the army, then starting out as a writer who gains invisibility in the belief that it is the invisible person who tells the visible world's stories. Intermittently, in this manner, I tried to tell my story. So I suddenly appear, first as a child racing up and down my grandparents' garden; then, an adolescent, sitting alone in the garage, an audience of one, listening to my secret concerts on the radiogram; and then again, as my own ghost, waking from a nightmare. There are other sightings of me too: obliged to arrest myself during National Service; and, back in civilian life, corresponding with myself in the guise of my mother and my stepfather.

All these, I now see, are images of solitude. I am the point at which my family's failures peak and end. I exult, apparently, in failure, make a set piece of it, reserve for it my most precise irony. I am not so comfortable with success, not so sure how to present it. But I have had more success, like a mirage that vanishes as I reach it, than I ever dreamt. Being someone who has two birthdays, one for each of my parents, who could not agree on a date, I have perhaps had two chances also. 'Having two birthdays means both that you were never quite born, in the ordinary way,' the biographer Carole Angier writes to me, 'and that you were doubly born, the second time as a writer.' Perhaps that is the best answer for this ambiguity.

But can I bring these two selves, the writer and the subject, together on the page? Can I write about myself not passively as a listener or reader, an echo of others? It seems to me that, whatever I write, I reveal myself, my attitudes and preferences. So why is it so difficult to use the first person singular and centre the narrative on me?

I remember, a few years ago, the uncomfortableness of having my portrait painted. A cocoon of tiredness seemed to shut off the oxygen as the artist's concentration encircled me. When I work I lose myself by concentrating on others, and afterwards I feel revived. But, though I am doing nothing but sitting in a chair as the artist's model, it is an oddly exhausting experience, as if the current of energy is travelling in the wrong direction. I sit up, brace myself, take notice, and generally behave like an animal seeking to please. I smile. At the end I feel no eagerness to look at myself. When I do look, I recognise a peculiar rictus in the glare of life.

Now I must put together a pen portrait of myself as seen by others. But how can I do this? I look down now and see my hand still writing, but little else. And if I look up to face the mirror, there is an amalgam of my parents, and their parents, staring back. What have I added? I must find a story with a beginning, a middle and some end to answer this: a story about myself.

In 1979, at the age of forty-four, I accepted an invitation to teach a couple of courses, one undergraduate, the other post-graduate, at Pennsylvania State University. I planned to combine two days a week teaching (plus half a day of preparation, marking essays etc.) with trips to those manuscript libraries in the United States which held the papers of Bernard Shaw (whose biography I was then writing). This developed into a hectic, sixteen-week programme involving over fifty flights to and from Penn State. If there's a blockbuster to be written round Pittsburg Airport, I'm your man.

I had never taught anything before, indeed never been a student at a university let alone a university abroad. But this seemed a good and practical way of paying for my research journeys – with the bonus of picking up some American culture.

I was to work in the curious-sounding Ihlseng Cottage, an incongruous small building on the large modern campus, named after its nineteenth-century owner Magnus Ihlseng, a white-bearded Norwegian, Dean of the School of Mines in the 1890s. By the 1970s the cottage had become an Institute for the Arts and Humanistic Studies whose director, the well-known inde-fatigable academic and versatile author Stanley Weintraub, with his wife Rodelle, a fine early-autumn rose, entertained me grandly at the university's expense when I presented myself (I was especially impressed by the dishes of meat, fish and poultry from all of which, simultaneously, as in a boy's dream, we were given copious helpings).

My initial nervousness was exacerbated when, on arrival, I was handed with an air of urgency some bulky medical insurance documents. Apparently my predecessor, a scientist who came from middle Europe, had fallen ill and, being improperly insured, did not qualify for proper treatment. The result had been a bad case – or so I gathered – a bad case of death. In the circumstances I signed everything that was placed before me rather eagerly and, after a few questions about my teaching schedule, prepared to enter the classroom. Taking a formidable breath, squaring my shoulders and putting on an expression of authority, I marched in like (remembering my mixed ancestry) the very model of an English gentleman, a Swedish count, a Scottish laird, an Irish absentee landlord: something, at any rate, considerable and impressive. But what impression did I actually create?

'He was disappointing on all counts,' remembered one of my students. She, with most of the others, had been speculating over what this 'mysterious professor' from abroad would be like. It was generally assumed that, having come so far, I would carry round me a prevailing air of importance, would strike them all as indefinably fascinating, and be of course proper and precise in the best British tradition. Indeed, in my fashion, I had tried to meet these expectations. But as I entered, a cup of coffee in one hand and a bundle of books and tapes under my other arm, there was a murmur of dismay.

No bowler, no cane, no pipe, no distinguished beard even.
No 'cheerio' or 'chap' . . . He slouched. As he sat down
and back in his chair, he looked at us and ran his fingers
through his already disordered hair. What a letdown!

I did not know then that most of my students, both in my undergraduate and postgraduate courses, had been dragooned

into attending these classes as part of their literature require-
ments. They were not volunteers. A press release had been circu-
lated round the Humanities Department making me out to be
a very significant person. I was to deliver one or two special
lectures. And this was not all. In the library stood two glass
cases that had been importantly prepared with the credentials
of my career: fellowships and prizes, favourable reviews and
illustrated interviews, manuscript notes, and first editions (which
were in truth less rare than second editions). Standing in front
of it all later that day, I felt intimidated by this glittering array.
Obviously it was the living embodiment of these glass cases that
my students had expected to see entering their classroom.

My one immediate asset was my 'British' voice. 'I may fall
asleep during every session,' wrote another student, remembering how she felt during the first class, 'but at least I'll nod
off to a pleasant sound.' But of course my peculiar accent was
something of a cultural barrier. Was I being funny or was I
serious? It was so difficult to tell. By the second week they had
mostly decided that I was at least *trying* to be funny. It was
probably British irony, that most awkward of all styles to translate. But they had been guided to their decision more by my
appearance and behaviour than by what I actually said, pleasant-
sounding as that might be. I was 'the man who came rushing
into the classroom every week looking a little bit like a curious
mixture of Rex Harrison and Jerry Lewis', another student
wrote. In other words, a blatant comic.

What struck several of them during my carefully structured
course was the informality sometimes reaching into chaos, and
my air of helplessness in the middle of it all. 'Mr Holroyd is
very bad at looking stern.' I was surprised to read this sentence
since I had been practising sternness in front of the mirror until
it almost cracked. But eventually I decided that here was one
student's brave stab at that sophisticated literary device, the
unreliable narrator – and I annotated her essay accordingly. But

I still had, they all observed, that desperate mannerism of running my fingers through my hair every few minutes ('I wonder if his grandmother ever told him that this makes one go bald'). One student drew an impression of my constantly rearranged hair underneath her description of it. 'His hair is rather wild,' she observed. 'It's amazing the way he gets it to stand up and lay flat in such a chaotic pattern. It looks like this.'

To this she added a drawing of me sitting alert and upright in a chair after one of my long research trips – a drawing which everyone happily agreed was very accurate (though perhaps this was a form of American graphic irony, it occurred to me, and with that interpretation I present it here).

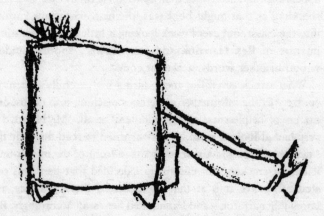

All these comments about me arose as part of (and perhaps in retaliation to) the final assignment I had set my students early on in this course. It was a literary biography and autobiography course, and as their final paper, the very essay that would carry their grades, I had asked them to write a pen portrait-in-miniature of myself. There was a gasp of genuine horror when they heard this. 'I was no longer amused,' wrote one of them, perhaps echoing Queen Victoria. Never had they heard anything so vainglorious. But then perhaps it was some trick, even a British 'joke'. I was often playing tricks on 'the poor students'. For example, among the ten or twelve books I had set for this course were a couple I disliked. Why would I choose 'a bad book' for them to read? The reason gradually became clear. I did not want them to second-guess what I thought. I did not want them trying to please me. I wanted to know what they thought themselves and to make any differing reactions to the texts the basis for our discussions. Should they deduce, therefore, that I did not want them to please me with this final paper too, the pen portrait of myself? How much hostile criticism would I accept without downgrading their papers? How much flattery could I swallow without being sick?

What I really wanted them to do was to use the library in a new way; to find out to what extent I was that person in the glass cases there; to connect the craft of reading with the craft of writing; to read between the lines of a text.

From a number of the essays they wrote, I found out that, during one of the coffee breaks, they had discussed whether or not I was homosexual. After all, I was unmarried. Also I had written a Life of Lytton Strachey and an introduction for the American edition of Quentin Crisp's *The Naked Civil Servant*. Then, too, among the autobiographies I had set them to read was a book by another homosexual author, *My Father and Myself*, by J. R. Ackerley. But there was conflicting evidence.

One of my books had been warmly dedicated to a woman. A quick glance at my recently published *Augustus John* in the library revealed that he was a committed heterosexual. Perhaps it was necessary for biographers to reach beyond their instinctive interests. In the end they decided that I wasn't a homosexual. But how could they be certain? Did anyone dare ask me – and if anyone did, would I answer truthfully? Only one student pressed her enquiries further.

And that last sentence shows you what they were up against. What exactly does it mean? The American language is stronger these days than the English language. It's blunter, ruder, more muscular, demotic, direct. It is pitted, lavishly, with assholes, bombarded with one helluva lot of kicked butt, and does not boast the delicate, smooth bottom of British English. Of course English can be elegant, but its elegance is so often evasive, oblique, polite, ambiguous. It may be prettily enough served up, of course, but where in Christ's name is the big meat? Here was a cultural obstacle my students had to get round to understand my game, decode my language, discover my secrets. Why had I invited them, as it were, to play detectives, only to leave them so few clues? Though claiming to be opinionated to the very edge of libel, I seemed to have no emphatic opinions at all, certainly no emphatic political opinions (it was the time of Three Mile Island about which I appeared wonderfully inscrutable – more eager to hear my students' opinions than air my own). Where was my conviction, my 'passionate intensity'? I sounded infuriatingly cheerful, almost aggressively mild, and had more questions than conclusions – unless, that is, a conclusion may be embedded in a question (was Three Mile Island a signal from the future? I asked). The main difficulty was that I seemed so detached, too detached maybe, detached really from myself (using 'one' instead of 'I' or 'you' or 'we' sometimes when speaking, as if I were royalty, or at least not me). It was a strange and sobering performance. How could they get around it?

One evening, when the students came over for supper, we continued our discussion between drinks and I quoted a sentence written by an autobiographer who, in order to get a divorce, had been obliged to hire a French detective to report on the activities of his wife in Paris. Though her life there was a twenty-four-hour-a-day ritual of trivialities, he found the report in precise, impersonal French so unexpectedly amusing that he concluded: 'If I were a rich man, I would pay to have a French detective's report on my own movements.' My students were less amused by this aside than I was. For it reflected something of our own predicament. Besides, they said, it was taking vicariousness too far.

We sat around pouring out various odd uneven bottles, now one, then another, and I thought that this was the sort of group discussion I had missed when young. Only it was focused on me because of that dreadful paper I had set. One student suggested I was wearing a self-protective mask and wondered why. Or, another student ingeniously argued, there was no mask at all, and what they were experiencing, my temperament, my voice, represented very well a country that was becoming increasingly distanced from history's active, mainstream narrative – the hectic narrative of the United States which, in the echo-chamber of our 'special relationship', we merely parodied. Or whatever. They were teasing me tremendously, getting their own back, enjoying themselves. There was much laughter as their speculations spiralled into fantasy. Or whatever indeed!

I poured myself another drink.

Or perhaps, I intervened, we should jettison that word 'or'. Our lives came to us as a series of 'ands' – one damn thing after another – and the skill of understanding them depended upon an ability to connect all sorts of views and events, not edit them so much as to make a pattern of them.

And, I went on remorselessly, if I was the man in the

self-protective mask, then it would be reasonable to conclude that this mask did not resemble me in any way. Why else would I have chosen it? It must be an act of misrepresentation and as unlike me as possible.

Unless, I added, I had grown into it.

The food came to my rescue – I had by now drunk quite a lot. In this warm social atmosphere, my vague and enigmatic manner was beginning to acquire a flavour of poignancy. 'Where nothing lives, nothing can die.' Somewhere I had written or said this (written *and* said this, for, as my students pointed out, I quite often said what I had written). If I became too attached to life, would I not have more to fear from death? My apartment, they noticed, was bare – no flowers, no pictures, while in London they knew I had no domestic animals, not even a frog or stick-insect. So I was obviously a solitary. And yet, I appealed, from the centre of my crowded supper party, swaying slightly, I was gregarious. I actually liked people, some people; and also various animals. Even so, my students spied a dangerous fate in store for me, and from it they plucked a delightful solution to their problem. I had been keeping company with the dead, my biographical subjects, too long, and had set them the task of rescuing me from those glass cases in the library (even though, they reluctantly acknowledged, it was my glass-case career that had brought me over to them). There were several ways in which they set about this . . .

Next morning I had an awful hangover.

The students' final papers were written in many forms: as a diary, an obituary, a letter to a publisher; as a forward-looking science-fiction pastiche, an autobiography with myself as the significant other character, and as pure literary criticism. I had tried to bring the reading of books out of the glass case, but had also perhaps converted myself into a text.

We met, the eleven of us, Constance, David, Diane, Karen,

Kate, Linda, Maureen, Miki, Terese, Thomas and me, for some three hours a week over ten to twelve weeks. And it was fun. But what they handed in, they reminded me, were merely first impressions. So what I now have are the beginnings of a self-portrait.

For the next stage, I must turn to a book first published in 1936, the year after I was born. It has on its hardback jacket a silver mirror, and it makes bold on its title page to offer 'about three million detailed individual character studies through self-analysis'. Surely this should do the trick, at least help me do it. *Meet Yourself As You Really Are** was constructed by Prince Leopold Loewenstein, a political scientist and philosopher educated at the University of Vienna, who later specialised in the psychology of Nazism and Fascism; and it was composed by his friend – and later mine – the novelist William Gerhardie, who had been educated in Russia and at Worcester College, Oxford. So testing a work did it prove that these co-authors, who had long been friends, split up after writing it and never spoke to each other again. It was, I sensed, a potent book.

I worked from the paperback edition, an old yellow-covered Penguin Book, No. 382, carrying advertisements which urged me to smoke Grey's Cigarettes, eat Fry's chocolates, and then go to the Pelman Institute to have my worries removed (half fees for members of His Majesty's Forces). The advice sounds bad today and the solution dubious. But I persist, tracing my psychoanalytical outlines through the complex framework of questions and instructions. I acquire a colour, yellow. Is it sunlight? Am I cowardly? Then I am given a river, the Neva which flows through St Petersburg into the Gulf of Finland (and also provides

---

*In the United States the book was called *Analyze Yourself* and edited by Victor Rosen (1955).

a link with the Caspian Sea). I take this as a good omen, since Gerhardie himself spent his childhood in St Petersburg. What do I find out about myself as I steer my way through these pages?

> You belong to a type of character which is composed
> of the most contradictory features and ... [is] very
> difficult to understand. People of your type resent
> loneliness almost as much as the company of others ...
> Quite generally it can be said that your type of
> character produces pronounced individualists.

But the River Neva then branches wildly, and I learn that:

> You are probably generous as far as property and
> money go, but we cannot give unrestricted praise to this
> generosity. It is not the expression of a happy and
> well-balanced disposition. You resemble, though it
> might seem somewhat strange to you, your very
> opposite type – the avaricious ... There is something
> destructive in this exaggerated tendency to give.

Reading this, I am reminded of an episode from the 1970s which reveals what it was like to be on the receiving end of my help. I had been asked to write the prefaces for a reissue of William Gerhardie's works, but soon found that he considered my praise of his books insufficiently unqualified. My avariciousness was evidently showing through my generosity and it threatened, he believed, to destroy his posthumous reputation, or at least to impair it. In exasperation, he berated me for being 'a *smilingly* impenitent, pig-headed, bloody-minded, bigoted, intolerant, unyielding, unelastic, *hard*, inflexible, opinionated, fanatical, obsessed, pedantic, rook-ribbed, *unmoved*, persistent, incurable, irrepressible, intractable, impersuadable, cross-grained ruffian – no offence implied'. And none taken.

Eventually I was to solve the problem by reading my prefaces to him over the telephone instead of sending them by post, raising my voice through a magnificent crescendo as I bellowed out passages of unrestricted praise, then dropping to a modest whisper when delivering the lesser sentences. This scheme of orchestration, which worked well, should probably earn me several extra epithets from the thesaurus: cunning, tricky, artful, prankish, *unblushing*, foxy, scheming, Machiavellian, *double-tongued*, unstraightforward, devious, slippery, shameless, fly . . .

A self-portrait, I see, is beginning to emerge. I go back to the book to find out if I have any more luck. The River Neva takes me in my yellow submarine to the next landing stage.

> You are not the type of person whose company is
> sought after by others, except by those you know really
> well. But how does one get to know you really well?
> You do not make it too easy. You do not talk readily
> about your inner struggles and the problems that beset
> your mind. You are rather like a sick person who does
> not want others to know he is ill.

I seem to remember that when I last played this game twenty or thirty years ago, I came out rather better than this. My character is deteriorating. How far can this go?

> You are at war with yourself for being at peace with
> the world. You find it is more than life is worth to
> fight the world, and you are far too frank to humbug
> yourself . . . your capacity for suffering is out of all
> proportion to the use you can make of it.

I throw the book across the room. The trouble has been that I can answer many of the guiding questions with equal accuracy one way or another. But when I attempt to follow other tributaries of my river, I fare no better. No wonder the book was never a bestseller. It does not flatter its readers.

But the process of stitching together these paragraphs to fit myself brings to mind another refitting exercise. This took place in the 1990s at the University of Ulster at Coleraine. Having misread my invitation, I arrived without a dinner jacket. Since my name was to be mentioned in a speech during the dinner, all eyes would be turned on me, the only guest inadequately clothed. This could not be. Alerted to the crisis, the departments of the university came collectively to my rescue. From the Faculty of Engineers arrived a splendid tuxedo; from 'Life and Health', a fine shirt; from 'Informatics' some dazzling cufflinks; and from the Social Sciences a terrific bow tie. But the wonder of it all was that everything fitted me perfectly. As I went through into dinner, I looked smarter, faster, more tailor-made for success than I could possibly have done in my own best clothes. My students at Penn State, and those non-speaking authors of *Meet Yourself*, would not have recognised me.

'It's over. All over. Nearly over.' But hold on. To complete this assisted self-portrait I need an authentic end. How to convey the sense of an ending when it is 'not the end'? Not quite. I call on absence and the blank page to see me out. 'What Might Have Been' is a poem I have kept since I first read it years ago.

> Now that you've really gone
> And not forever bobbing
> Just out of reach
>
> Now that not streets and weeks
> But months and an ocean
> Lie between us

Now that I look
Into a calm grey distance
And see (as you have always done)

What might have been
As not a blue-print or a sketch
But a finished work

That couldn't be improved upon –
Each line we've added since
A weakening – I am beginning

To understand at last
What you meant when you said
'I am best at absence.'

5

Philippa

HER STORY

... I cannot see the flowers so sweet
I cannot smell and I cannot weep
And I cannot wake and I cannot sleep.
For I who laughed and loved am dead,
And laid out on my cold white bed,
With my jaw tied up lest it give offence
And my eyelids closed with a couple of pence ...
It seems a senseless thing to die!

Frank Harris

But Margaret Forster's letter has not yet reached its end. 'I wondered a lot about your beautiful mother, and the effect her beauty had on you as a young man, and on your girl friends,' she persisted. 'You describe how proud you were of her appearance when you were at school, but I wondered about later, when you were, say, 25 or so, and she was an incredibly young looking 43, so exquisitely dressed & lovely – what kind of ideas did it give you about women in general, & how did it influence your love life?'

I do not know the answers to these questions, and feel a great resistance to answering them. But other readers, too, have chided me. So I shall try to fill one more gap in my story.

When I was twenty-five or so, I was having my first sexual experiences with prostitutes. This was not because I preferred sex with strangers, or wanted to feel superior to women, or needed to separate sex from friendship and love, but because it was the only sexual experience straightforwardly available to me. My mother and father, going their separate ways, and so many ways, had not helped to integrate me into any community. Though I still saw one or two schoolfriends, I was a floating figure, incapacitated by all the tedious ineptitudes of youth – shyness, self-consciousness, lack of confidence – that I retained far too long. Yet I was extremely susceptible to women – and many women appeared beautiful to me. Having no sisters, and confined so long within the male worlds of boarding schools and National Service, I had no habit of companionship with women, though in later life I was to find their companionship easier and generally more rewarding than that of men.

I walked all over London in those days and nights – especially the nights. I would walk for hours, anywhere, everywhere, tiring myself out so that I could eventually sleep. Sometimes I would lose myself in strange streets, striding along until I found myself back on course, thinking about all sorts of possibilities – people, usually, and paragraphs. I looked at the places I passed in all weathers, but more intently at the people, and flattered myself that I was like Dickens in his young days (perhaps I was so far as the mileage went).

In the 1950s many streets in London were lined, under the lights, with prostitutes. I would set off for my long exhausting walks, and occasionally, if I had amassed three pounds (a considerable sum), I would go with one of them. In anticipation, I felt a trembling excitement, as if I were entering the first stages of a romantic adventure, but afterwards no French novel was to develop round me and I remained solitary. Nevertheless, I did not regret spending my money in this way. It seemed completely natural and necessary – all the more so since sex before marriage for girls was still rare in those days.

Not having read Bernard Shaw, I did not equate the crowds of prostitutes in those lurid pools of light with Britain's post-war poverty, though I did recognise in it a legacy from Victorian London. When, in 1959, R. A. Butler's Street Offences Act virtually cleared prostitutes from the streets, a new age was launched combining official puritanism with the beginnings of 'free love' – and distancing the language and legislation of Westminster further from actual life, street life. The streets themselves were eventually to be populated by beggars and vagrants (unknown before the 1970s) who pitched their mattresses under bridges, in doorways and anywhere else made available in the expanding ground between rich and poor.

I have described how I later met and fell into bed with my first girlfriend, Jennifer, a ballet dancer from the north, and I quoted her shrewd and vivid comments on my mother and father. After several years together, she gave me an ultimatum: either we married or she left. Otherwise there was no future. But I had no desire to marry, probably as a result of my parents' many unsuccessful marriages and the difficulties these had provided. So we parted, Jennifer and myself, with immense sadness on both sides. I remember watching her walk away to the end of the street and turn the corner out of my life, not knowing what would happen next. She did not look back.

By then, entering my thirties, I suddenly found myself becoming quite popular with some women, and had one or two affaires. I was not stubbornly 'faithful' to anyone, nor (despite the pain of jealousy) did I question anyone's faithfulness to me. These were games of love we were all playing in the 1960s, serious, delightful, with moments of anguish, beauty and farce. As for myself, it was as if I were copying my parents' promiscuous emotional lives unburdened by the complications and formalities of marriage and divorce. Though I said and did many silly things, and was sometimes insensitive through incomprehension, I look back on this time as being vital and necessary. One of the advantages of early low self-esteem and a slow start is that many happenings which others seem to take for granted – driving a car, publishing a book, having a love affair – strike you as miraculous. Certainly for me the late 1960s still has the distant glow of a miracle.

Everything changed dramatically towards the end of that decade, when I became involved with an extraordinary girl called Philippa Pullar. I met her at a dinner party given by the editor who was publishing my *Lytton Strachey* (she was a friend of his wife). A young American writer, Stanley Olson, was to describe Philippa two or three years later as 'the sexiest middle-aged – 30 – woman I've ever seen. Every word is like a mini-orgasm – she's splendid.' Certainly I thought her splendid that evening. The atmosphere around her seemed to reverberate with fantasy, infinitely hopeful yet charged with alarm, even danger – especially danger. Nevertheless, here was someone who, even on the very worst of days, lived under a brilliant sun. Her luminous presence brightened everything near her. She had an oval face, long, blonde hair to her shoulders, piercing blue eyes and a small straight nose – but the truly remarkable feature was her voice. It was highly theatrical, mannered and melodramatic, also rather camp, full of exaggerated emphasis, unlike any voice I had heard. She used it to great comic effect, but initially, like many people, I felt disconcerted, wondering whether it was an affectation put on for dinner parties. Only when I got to know her better did I come to realise what perfect orchestration this voice gave to the expression of seething rebelliousness within her. She took the accents of smart society and sent them up rotten. She made conventional manners sound farcical, speaking with an exhilaration that testified to the urgency of her need – a need to escape the suffocating conformity in which she had been brought up. Her spectacular personality was like some incandescent shell that concealed and protected an acute sensitivity.

Her father had been 'a creature of convention' and 'a victim of respectability', who lived in scowling silent horror of Jews and gypsies, socialists, homosexuals and all other hooligans. Having served in one world war, he passed the next, while

Philippa was growing up, somewhere in the West Country carrying out duties 'suitable to his rank of major'. Philippa herself was moved from house to house avoiding the bombs and scuttling into shelters with her mother, who was of a highly nervous disposition. 'I was a delicate child and a constant worry to my mother,' she remembered. She was also, from the very first, a surprise, her mother having been told that she could never have children – and then conceiving her daughter when in her late thirties.

Philippa did not know that her highly conventional mother was the illegitimate daughter of a free-thinking woman who had left her husband and eloped with the son of a Scottish nobleman. Both died in the flu pandemic of 1918, leaving their only child (Philippa's mother) to be brought up by an elderly governess. It was no wonder then that she longed for Philippa, her only daughter, to be respectable and safe, or that she unconsciously passed on to her a vibrant sense of insecurity. In the mother this took the form of an acute anxiety over the uncertainties of daily life; with Philippa it eventually focused on death.

Her childhood friend, Clare Michell, remembers how, from her earliest years, Philippa longed to escape the protective embrace of her mother, and how wild she would sometimes be when she got away. On a school holiday in Austria, the train having broken down in a deep snowdrift near Innsbruck, Philippa climbed through a gap at the top of the compartment window, ran along the snowbank outside the train, and was later seen being chased back along the top of the carriages by amorous waiters. 'We were all very impressed by her daring,' recalls Clare. Another time Clare remembers how scandalised people were to see her whizzing along on a bicycle beside a French canal pursued by (or was it pursuing?) a wild boar. 'One forgets how staid people were in the 1950s.'

Philippa stood out from her schoolfriends, not being dependent on their company. 'She wanted to run things rather than join them,' Clare Michell wrote, 'and didn't like being upstaged.' Some of these schoolfriends believed she would become a famous actress, like 'the terrific Kemble'. Henry James's description of the 'lavishly décolletée' Fanny Kemble also gives a good and lasting impression of Philippa in her many roles: 'joking, punning, botanising, encouraging the lowly and abusing the proud, making stupidity gape . . . and startling infallibly all primness and propriety'. The great nineteenth-century actress, James adds, 'assisted at the social comedy of her age' with the originality and gaiety of her 'admirable nonsense': and so, in her fashion, did Philippa.

But of course the stage was unacceptable to her parents. Philippa's father wanted her to behave well; her mother wanted her to dress well: and in their opinions she positively did neither. From being a delicate child she grew into a riotous tomboy who was expelled from her first boarding school at the age of thirteen for writing a sexually explicit work of fantasy. It took the form of a correspondence between herself, in the role of a dashing young lover, and her best friend as the beloved, beginning innocently and then blossoming into imagined consummation ('It was lovely to feel a bit of me inside you' etc.). From her next school (which specialised in deportment and embroidery in a house that had belonged to the anti-suffrage novelist Mrs Humphry Ward) she was also expelled following what she called 'a run of bad luck' which began when her pony Chocolate, famous for his extravagant co-ordination of bucking and farting, chased the riding mistress up a tree.

Her parents then decided that she must 'do the Season', find a suitable husband, and settle down. Quickly. Her mother would see to her clothes, dressing her up like a pink doll, while her father, though seldom breaking his silence, would somehow convey the modest behaviour that was required of her. Later on, Philippa was to write a brief history of the London Season, the last chapter of which featured her own debutante exploits while 'coming out' during Coronation Year. She was taught how to curtsey by Madame Vacani, how to put on make-up properly by Hermione Gingold, and how to dance correctly to Tommy Kinsman's band ('you leant slightly backwards, shoulders not moving, the right arm stretched down towards the floor, and if one were in love – or fast – the fingers were linked together').

To her parents' relief Philippa became engaged to Robin, a young man with a beautiful house in Carmarthenshire. 'I was as much in love with the place as the man himself,' she later admitted. His sudden death before their marriage shocked her profoundly. 'Never before had I seen serious illness: the fear, the blood transfusion tubes, the struggling for breath, the vomiting,' she wrote. 'My world had shattered . . . I was distraught.'

Mourning her own pain, she took up and then gave up a succession of jobs over the next three years – as a waitress in Chelsea, a cook in Soho, an air hostess. She became well known for her wild parties and for the impressive quantities of alcohol she drank. In desperation, her parents relaunched her into the marriage market of the London Season. Though social life was beginning to change radically in Britain, the structure of the Season still stood intact (though 1958 was the last year that debutantes were individually presented to the Queen). 'Isn't it sad,' one of the mothers remarked, looking over the banisters in Grosvenor House at the lines of daughters rehearsing their ridiculous 'curtseying to the cake' for Queen Charlotte's Ball. 'They are *en route* to the kitchen sink.'

Philippa (whose maiden name was King) married Robert Pullar because by this time all her friends were married. He had been proposing to her for a long time, enticed, so she believed, by her unavailability – she had been adamant, following Robin's death, that she would never marry. As soon as she accepted him, she knew it was a mistake. At night she was tormented by awful dreams; by day she took herself in hand and carried on with the marriage arrangements.

They went to live in Devon where, having lost his capital in a failed agricultural equipment company, her husband took to raising battery hens, at which he also failed – but which gave rise to Philippa's passionate hatred of factory farming and a crusading kindness on behalf of all animals. She felt imprisoned by this marriage, a prey to Satanic hallucinations, on the very edge of madness. Everyone told her she would feel better once she had children. She had two sons, and felt worse. She accepted responsibility for her children, but was not a good mother, resenting the implication that women who were not natural mothers must be inferior women. 'I would wonder how it was possible to be so miserable,' she later wrote. 'This was hell, that at least I knew.'

In the mid-1960s the two of them left Devon and separated, he going to work in London, she buying a house in Deal (which had once been owned by the judge who convicted Oscar Wilde). It was during this period that I met her at dinner. She wrote down her telephone number that evening on a book of matches and handed it to me. A few days later I rang her and went down to Deal for a weekend. On the Saturday night we slept together in her bed. I remember the softness of her skin, her musky smell and how young she suddenly looked, would always suddenly look, with her head on the pillow. By Sunday, we decided that we wanted to go on seeing each other. There is 'a marvellous cosiness about sex', Philippa later wrote; 'there in the room with the fire blazing you could make someone secure, if only for a brief moment, for it seemed to me that many men were haunted by sadness: they yearned for contact, communication – some even longed for love. And for a brief interlude sex gave them release from their isolation.'

In the Prologue to her book *The Shortest Journey* (1981), Philippa was to give me the name Horace (after Horace

Walpole). I was, she wrote, 'the perfect antidote to my husband: gentle, sensitive and intelligent: an author working on a long biography of an eminent man of letters.

> He educated me, introduced me to music, books and ideas ... gradually and creakingly, my brain began to function ... When Horace and I were together it was as though an electrical spark flew between us, igniting some force that was both invigorating and cleaving. We were both of us stimulated, full of verve, and we *laughed*. I calmed down considerably ...
>   Horace altered my way of thinking. Horace altered my attitude of mind. Certainly I did not want to marry, but I did want to be with Horace.

Philippa was to describe me as her 'second teacher', her first teacher being Chocolate, the exuberant pony which had swerved and bolted with her across the English countryside, taking her everywhere and opening up in her a new feeling for the land: 'the crushed turf of the downs redolent with wild thyme; damp earth mixed with bluebells; gorse; hay; the tarred string of hay nets; saddle soap and the warm sweaty breath of Chocolate himself. Celandines shone in the spring, the ground drummed in winter with white frost.'

What Chocolate had taught Philippa, she taught me. Life grew more tangible and vivid. I began to use my eyes, to see the visible world around me with greater subtlety, enjoyment and understanding. It was as if a veil had been removed. I spent many days and nights at Deal, which I came to see through Philippa's eyes. Her eighteenth-century house faced both west and east. On the west side stood a conservatory, full of the scent of flowers, and a walled garden, with its central quince tree, framed by the tiled roofs of houses nearby. In summer, the vine hung with muscat grapes. Jasmine, tobacco and datura, whose white bells bent over the pond, filled the air with a heavy fragrance. On the east side was the sea over which, at low tides, you could make out the masts of ships that had been wrecked on the Goodwin Sands.

Walking along the cliffs at evening, we appeared to float in the dusk, looking down on the childlike boats below. On late still afternoons, a cricket would sometimes sing in the garden, as if we were by the Mediterranean. This garden attracted all sorts of butterflies – I had not seen so many since I was a boy – tortoiseshells, chalk blues and purple emperors that wandered around the lavender, fennel and savory. Whenever possible we ate in the garden and would watch the moon rise from the sea like some dull, red ball growing gradually into a huge corn-coloured orb that appeared to be attached to us by triangular paths of light along the surface of the water.

But magical as these summers were, it was the autumn, with strange evening mists, the dartings of the swifts and swallows through the air, the mournful serenade of foghorns sounding along the curve of the beach and mixing with the rhythmic chanting of the pigeons, the whistling of the starlings, that held a more poignant beauty. I had never experienced before anything of such lingering intensity. It was as if I had suddenly woken up to all that was around me, as if everything was coming for the first time into focus.

But then there were the winters. As the nights drew in, we fixed storm windows on the front of the house against the icy wind and the rain beating in, sometimes ferociously, from the Straits of Dover. It accelerated along the narrow tunnels of the streets, making Deal a winter fortress under siege. From November to February, no sun reached the garden which lay in perpetual shadow, its trees angrily swaying, like the land-scape of a dark underworld.

Philippa's moods matched the seasons, and there were times when she would feel miserably incarcerated at Deal, with her two

sons, several cats and a parrot as her gaolers. To remedy this I
suggested that we rent an inexpensive flat in London, so that to
some extent she could escape this horror of imprisonment.

We found a rather seedy maisonette on the top two floors
of a house in West Kensington. It was infested with mice which
soon made friends with the free-range, multiplying guinea pigs
which Philippa had unaccountably brought back one night from
a party. 'Meet Philippa, meet her animals,' wrote Mike Foss
who visited us there.

> When her key was in the lock, a rustling of light
> squeals began beyond the door. The guinea pigs were
> welcoming her home . . .
>   I think she liked them because they were droll and
> fat and happy, and that was a good state for any
> animal. There were also some cats, one with three
> legs . . . The three-legged one got no special favours
> but shared the rewards of residence, and the fleas,
> impartially. Philippa was scornful of mollycoddlying, for
> cats or humans. Three legs were plenty for a cat. A
> determination to enjoy life was what counted. The
> accidental loss of a leg was merely an incident, a test of
> character. The cat seemed to know this. It didn't fret.

Mike Foss, then an aspiring writer who contributed reviews
to *Tribune*, first met Philippa in a pub. 'There was something
nautical in her confident gait,' he remembers noticing as she
cleaved her way through the press of noisy male drinkers.

> Planting herself firmly between us, she started
> immediately, as if she had known me for years, to tell
> me an improbable tale that verged on disaster but was
> resolved into a condition of farce and puzzlement. At the
> same time she reached an absent-minded hand into the

sandwich cabinet, extracted a scotch egg, and began to
eat it with much criticism of its texture and taste, though
the egg was unordered and unpaid for. 'If they put these
things on the bar,' she said brusquely, 'what can they
expect?' I saw, for the first of many times, a look of
amused consternation on Michael's face.

On the ground floor of our London flat was Mrs del Rio,
a harmless widow who wandered in all weathers very slowly
round her tiny garden pursued by an elderly cat. Above her,
and below us, lived the formidable Mrs Harvey, an aggressive
old lady who was rumoured to write poetry and to have been
imprisoned in China. She was 'at war with herself and with
everyone else in the world', wrote Philippa, who pictured her
as a twentieth-century London witch.

She wore a strange brown habit, bubbled evil-smelling
concoctions in her kitchen and piped abuse ... in a
terrible quavering wail. She planted wooden cats' heads
in her window-boxes and watered them, their drips
combining with those from the lavatory brush suspended
from the window-sill ... No one was unaffected by
Mrs Harvey's delusions, which were quickened
alarmingly by the full moon – it was rather like living
in a sea resort and being governed by the tides.

Mrs Harvey suspected Philippa and me of being spies. Having
fixed up an emergency notice on the front door reading 'PRIVAT
LETTER CAGE' (an 'E' having gone missing in the heat of her
passion), she would mail our letters back to the Post Office
marked 'NOT Known Here'. This was particularly exasperating
for me as I vainly waited for letters of congratulation on my
recently published *Lytton Strachey*. Once, when we invited a
venerable member of the Bloomsbury Group to lunch and were

saying our polite goodbyes in the street below, Mrs Harvey suddenly loomed over us on her balcony, waving her lavatory brush. 'Vile woman!' she screeched, gaining an immediate audience of builders from the scaffolding opposite, and school-children making their way back home. 'Your morals match your vermin, madam!' Another day, I invited my father to lunch so that he could meet Philippa. Mrs Harvey, who had by then decided that we were running a betting shop to conceal our spying activities, shot out of her door and tried to arrest him on the staircase, roaring out as she grappled with him: 'Pretending to place *another* bet, are you?'

My father was profoundly bewildered by Philippa and every-thing that went on around her. He could never quite get his balance in her company. If he had a slightly risqué anecdote from the Twenties or Thirties up his sleeve, she would have a more outrageous contemporary tale to cap it – and it came from all over her person, never just her sleeve. I remember her telling the story of a party she had gone to with some Russians. Considering the quantities of vodka they had drunk, it was just as well that her car was not working that evening. She caught the last bus back and ended the night in bed with the conductor (it was a number 14 bus, she recalled). Turning to my father, sitting there in his suit, she exclaimed: 'Really, my dear, it's easier these days to get *oneself* serviced than one's car!' My father, who usually enjoyed talking about cars, was speechless. He tried to gain the initiative. When he came down to Deal, he ordered some oysters and, while giving us a rather compli-cated tutorial on how best to open them, suddenly fainted, collapsing with a bang on to the floor. Somehow he could not assert himself. A committed dog-lover, he was never quite at ease among the flocks of guinea pigs and rabbits, the cats and parrot. How could he take a rabbit for a walk? It was frankly impossible. Back in the safety of his flat in Surrey, alone with his dog, he would chuckle with amusement, remembering some of Philippa's eccentricities. But really, he thought, she was a high explosive. Using his special low voice, speaking with paternal gravity, clearing his throat a good deal, he would remind me that she was still married with two sons, and then, his voice descending still further until I could hardly pick up what he was saying, he would warn me against marriage after her divorce came through. He had made this sort of mistake himself. 'So I know what I'm talking about, Michael,' he would say – and then grow suddenly silent as if realising that, had he not made this mistake with my mother, I would not be sitting opposite him.

My mother was also puzzled by Philippa, who struck her as being so extravagantly English that, when they met, she herself became excessively Swedish. I felt as if I were their interpreter. There was a foreignness between them – and a wry understanding. Their early years must have been marked by a good many similarities, including a determination to make up for the remoteness of their parents with a hectic social and sexual life. But Philippa was already finding sources of happiness other than the love of men: in her plants and animals, later in her writing, and finally in the comforts of esoteric religion. My mother, on the other hand, though with lessening conviction, went on playing the same game, as if the clock had never moved on and she had not grown older.

When, aged around sixty and no longer in receipt of a 'pension' from her Viennese ex-lover Egon, my mother began to find life in London financially impossible, Philippa offered her free use of the maisonette that was attached to her house in Deal and which she sometimes rented out. But my mother refused. She still thought of London as offering everything that was attractive and exciting in life, whereas Philippa was beginning to feel that, as she wrote in *Gilded Butterflies* (1978): 'London has always had a disastrous effect on people.'

London certainly seemed to be having a disastrous effect on

us, as if Mrs Harvey was aiming dreadful spells at us through the ceiling, spells that rose with the malodorous fumes of her cooking. Philippa grew seriously ill. One of the causes was her writing. She needed to make some money and it was obviously more practical for her to work at home, as I was doing. She had decided to write a book that would enable her to vent her hostility to intensive farming, and to attack the money motive that seemed to be growing up everywhere around her. It was to be a most ambitious work – a compendium of all she most hated in a world that, she was discovering, concealed so much cruelty under its polite veneer. The main text of this book was the diary of misery she had kept while living with her husband in Devon. She opened it and read once more the excruciating descriptions of the chickens they had kept in tiny cages, some of them blind, all with their bodies raw from constant friction against iron bars, and with their beaks electrically amputated (a harrowing process, 'ghastly with gasps, sizzling and blood'). She heard again what seemed to her their screams of distress from those awful prisons at the end of the garden. She remembered having to drive them in their crates to be slaughtered – 'hauled out and hooked upside down on a conveyor belt and, flapping what was left of their poor wings, they rotated to their death'. At night she dreamt of their dead bodies, limp and dangling, their eyes white, their throats cut – she could hear the knife ripping into the flesh and would start awake screaming. She felt she *was* those chickens, painfully confined, destined for awful death. Her nightmares began to invade the day. She had hallucinations, and saw Satan sitting at a table in the kitchen, grinning at her. The horror and misery of ten years before returned. She hated herself, her malevolent nervous system, and she hated a world that was bursting with such pain. She did not want to belong to such a place. Her moods lurched and swerved violently, unaccountably – she swallowed purple hearts, anti-depressants, sleeping pills, all mixed with alcohol.

It was impossible to tell what effect they were having. I believe she would have come through had her book been accepted. It contained many strong passages, but was uncoordinated, in places incoherent. A good editor might have rescued it, made it acceptable, harnessed its power and originality. But this would have taken time and skill. I could not do it – it was *her* book – and though I could provide bits and pieces of help, I knew I must not trespass. It was a wonder how, in such exhausting circumstances, she had managed to complete it. Like an SOS she sent it out, but no one answered. She felt rejected.

One morning after breakfast, while we were in the kitchen, she casually mentioned that, having watched the chairs and table dancing grotesquely round the room, she had swallowed several handfuls of sleeping tablets. She had had enough. Though she sometimes had delusions, she never told lies. As soon as I felt certain this was not a fantasy, I went to the telephone, dialled 999, and summoned an ambulance. I tried to keep her upright and walking till I heard the siren of the ambulance approaching. The paramedics fought their way up past the yelling Mrs Harvey and took Philippa to the hospital where she had her stomach pumped. Had we been an hour later, I was told, she would probably have died.

And here, as Philippa recovers in hospital, I must pause to consider the implication of what happened. For this was not to be the only suicide attempt by someone I loved. There would be one other that, unintentionally, ended in tragedy. What can I deduce from this? I believe I have sometimes been attracted to women who, in lay terms, may be described as manic-depressive. The manic aspect of their personality eclipses my mother's beauty, and I am mesmerised – to the extent of not comprehending, not wishing to comprehend, the dark hidden side of their personalities to which my intelligence should alert me. I am frightened of depression, nonplussed, made inert. But I have a personality that may, at first sight, attract the manic-depressive. For I am like a tightrope-walker who has had to find a perilous route between the extravagances of my mother's and my father's separate lives. So I appear, on my tightrope, to be miraculously balanced – and this feat of balance has its own appeal for those in danger of plunging, one way or another, into extremes. Also, I know that some women came to feel that I was not sufficiently taken care of by my parents. So, with my two birthdays, I am again two people: the boy whose lack of love can be made good; and the father-figure, with his elevated balance and even-handedness, a figure of tall authority. Yet this authority has its limits and the tightrope its distance.

There is another question that occurs to me and that I must try to answer. Do I have an unconscious wish to punish my mother, who often left me while I was growing up? And have I turned the need for revenge on to other women? The fact that I am completely unconscious of such a motive and do not pick it up even as a faint echo, does not of course invalidate the possibility of an unconscious motive. But the devastation I have felt, the long period of grief, is the evidence I would bring forward to refute this suggestion. In short: I do not believe it to be true.

What I did learn from Philippa's illness was the irrelevance of my good sense, the uselessness of my logic and reasonableness. She was beyond reason. But she also appeared to be beyond the help of her doctors – it was they who had given her those almost fatal pills. She also went to a psychoanalyst but was, she confessed, unable to help him.

One doctor informed her that she was suffering from serious hormonal imbalance aggravated by the contraceptive pills she was taking. In the ensuing muddle of dates and other pills, various sheaths and some medieval-looking devices, Philippa became pregnant. There was no question of her having another child – she was far too unstable. At first, with my aid, she experimented with several ancient recipes for inducing a miscarriage – drinking gin in hot baths and brewing up pungent herbal concoctions laced with vinegar that mingled in the air with Mrs Harvey's venomous boiled cabbages. When all this failed she consulted her doctor. But getting an abortion was not then easy. The weeks ticked on as she went off to be examined by doctors and psychiatrists. She told them about her attempted suicide, described the Satanic hallucinations, her chronic depression, and the fears she had of going insane – all encircling dangers for a baby. It was a matter, as I saw it, of making these doctors more frightened of the consequences of not allowing her to have an abortion than of any criticism arising from the charge of unnecessarily taking a life. Eventually, after some four months, they consented and I drove her to the hospital.

Did I mind not having a child? Not at all. My single thought then was for Philippa's health (on which my own depended). Did I mind later? Do I mind now? The answer is the same. It has never worried me, and I have hardly thought of it until now. Why, then, don't I mind? It has, I believe, something to do with my own childhood and family rather than the fear of seeing more love go to the child than to myself or of my own childish side being eclipsed by a genuine child. I got on quite well, I think, I hope, with Philippa's sons, though I was careful to see that I never came near to replacing their father. Indeed there was no question of that. They spent half their holidays with their father, and were soon going to boarding schools, so I saw little enough of them both. The elder son, sensible, down to earth, began to feel, I thought, that his mother was a bit mad. Sebastian, the younger son, sometimes pretended to be a guinea pig or cat in order to get more loving attention from her. She treated them both in as carefree a way as possible. No doubt they were up to something, something inadvisable, but it was not her concern; no doubt they had their own plans and would not welcome her interference. Had Philippa wanted another child, I would have felt nervous, but would not have objected. And then I would be able to answer these questions with greater validity.

Philippa herself, I thought, took the abortion very matter-of-factly. But when I went to collect her, hurrying her along somewhat because the car outside was parked on double yellow lines, I saw for a moment tears in her eyes. I have not forgotten that.

We had both been profoundly shocked, and recognised the need to review and reorganise our lives together. My plan of living in two places so as to alleviate Philippa's fear of being trapped, though superficially appealing, had not worked well, even after I learnt to drive the car – a stubborn, bad-tempered, snorting old monster that had once been a proud and stately Austin. Much of our time seemed held in traffic jams along the M2, then in the process of being constructed, the car overflowing with bowls of soup, flowers, fruit, typewriters, miscellaneous papers, cats, guinea pigs and grumbling children. Instead of providing freedom, our dual town-and-country life grew into a whirlwind of anxiety, incompetence, exhaustion and irritability. My instinct was to simplify life, Philippa's instinct was to enrich it. Each was a good corrective to the other, complementary in good times but in bad times mutually destructive. How could we make the bad times good?

Our solution was: *rus in urbe*. Philippa sold the beautiful house in Deal, we gave up what we now thought of as our haunted maisonette in West Kensington, and bought a Victorian house on the frontiers of Putney and Barnes. *Urbe* was all round us: in the trains that clattered and rumbled past the end of the garden; and the aeroplanes that flew just above us on the flightpath to Heathrow; and also in new tower blocks of flats that intermittently blocked out the sun in winter. But the house stood in an unadopted private road on the frontiers of the country, next to an open common where cricket was played in summer, fairs and circuses camped in the winter.

And there was space, both in the house and especially in the garden with its mulberry tree at the centre up which Philippa trained white roses. Like the quince tree at Deal, this mulberry tree, with its red and white blooms, gave a strange, fairytale atmosphere to the garden, ever-changing and extraordinary, where you could easily lose yourself. Philippa grew honeysuckle and clematis up the walls (and over some of the windows), made the rectangular shape of the ground appear wonderfully asymmetrical, full of surprises, with curving paths leading to a naked wooden statue, some trickling water, a kitchen garden, much of all this concealed by a rich texture of plants and shrubs. She designed a conservatory, dug a pond in it, and then filled it with enormous fish that were so fiercely tame they appeared, as we sat there in the evenings, to be trying to come out and settle on our laps. Certainly the fish alarmed the cats. Indoors and out-of-doors, jumping in and out through the open windows, there was room for all the animals – to which she added various frogs and a spectacular black cockerel to which, as the writer Andrew Barrow* remembers, she sometimes flung slices of continental cheese.

The house became a wonderful stage for Philippa's dramatic talents. There were heavy, theatrical curtains fitted by an Amazonian young woman whose unusual window-boxes confronted Scotland Yard – years later, after her marriage had been annulled, she became Princess Michael of Kent. These curtains, pinned back but apt to shoot sideways unprovoked, suited Philippa's personality. Her friend, the psychotherapist Andrew McCall, thought of her as a natural actress – how else

---

*Andrew Barrow courageously invited Philippa and Germaine Greer to a celebratory dinner for Quentin Crisp (whose *The Naked Civil Servant* was being shown on television). They 'brought out the worst in each other', Crisp decided after a vociferous argument broke out between them, completely upstaging him and silencing their host.

was one to reconcile the many contradictions of her personality? At one time she would act poor, another time wealthy; she could be fiercely chaste and then again extraordinarily promiscuous. When Andrew observed that none of the bedside lamps in the house worked, she replied that it would be 'inauspicious' to sleep with the electrician – evidently the notion of paying him had not occurred to her, for at that phase of the moon she was poor and chaste. This problem was eventually solved by Eduardo Sant'Anna whom she commissioned to install electrical wiring in the lodger's room and who 'soon afterwards became the lodger myself. We had an agreement where, instead of paying the full rent, I would do the house cleaning for her.' As a foreigner, he instinctively venerated her English eccentricity. 'She never failed to amaze me even when I was supposed to take her seriously,' he writes to me. 'Instead of adding salt and pepper to the dishes she created, she sometimes put in an ingredient like onion or cinnamon to bring the whole thing alive, and it did. Even the weeds in her garden were treated as delicacies.'

She liked shopping in the North End Road market, but would annoy the stallholders by picking up, and making off with, fruit and vegetables that had accidentally fallen from their barrows into the gutter. For clothes she shopped largely at jumble sales, but from time to time would take herself off to some smart shop in the West End. There was no telling how she would make her entry at a party.

We lived on the very edge of chaos. 'It was not straightforward pandemonium,' Stanley Olson observed. In the kitchen, there were no handles on the taps, so we used pliers. Every electrical gadget had developed a life of its own and needed to be coaxed, spoken to gently, as if it were an extra animal. All this was oddly mixed with various family heirlooms, such as the smart, silver dinner service she inherited from her parents. She kept the silver and brass surfaces within the house highly polished, so that their sparkle appeared to light up dark areas

of the rooms. These rooms were often vastly untidy, but full
of idiosyncratic beauty. She had a distinctive style – an eye for
unusual objects, strong colours and striking juxtapositions –
and a liking for comfort that seemed oriental in its indulgence.
We had huge wood fires made of logs, trees, pieces of furniture, odd fencing, all brought back from walks and fed to the
lively flames which, like a many-tongued hydra, reached out
and sought to devour the room. Great urns containing mixtures
of flowers appeared to give out light, piles of miscellaneous
books rose from the floor like stalagmites; esoteric carpets, that
had suddenly taken Philippa's fancy, seemed as if they might
magically ascend. On the walls, covered with green, yellow or
even purple paint or sometimes a blue book linen she had
discovered in France, hung large paintings of birds and unicorns
and, in her bathroom, hung slightly askew, an interesting nude
of herself. This bathroom was next to her study and had a
deep, old-fashioned tub grandly raised on a platform at its
centre, with an easy chair beside it. While the bath was running,
a friend, some historian or painter (Mike Foss, maybe, or Stella
Wilkinson) might occupy the chair for a continuing chat while
Philippa, in a dressing-gown, tested the water and made her
preparations.

I had then begun writing my Life of Augustus John, and it
seemed to me that Philippa possessed a similar instinct for
beauty as that of the legendary Dorelia John. By opening my
eyes to the visible world, she enabled me to write of Dorelia's
houses with their mixed smells of lavender and pomanders,
wood and tobacco smoke, their haphazard piles of apples and
nuts, soft lead tubes of paint, old saddles, arrangements of
flowers taken from her flourishing gardens full of beehives,
vegetables and caravan children, at Alderney Manor and Fryern
Court. I could also write of the solitary landscapes in Wales
and France that had quickened Augustus's imagination.

Philippa herself was now working on a new book. The idea

for it had come to her as the result of a conversation we had over supper in Deal with the novelist Simon Raven. He had been banished from London by his publisher Anthony Blond, and lived in lodging houses at Deal – an outwardly dull, unchattering, regimented life designed to support his writing. But there was nothing dull about his conversation. Like Monsieur Jourdain, he spoke prose – a charming mixture of politeness and indecency, full of gossip, wit, and allusions to his love of cricket and classical literature. He was a big man, red-faced, mild-mannered with a volcanic soldier's laugh and the aesthete's delicacy when referring to indelicate matters (which he often did). His reputation, lit up by rumours of gambling and ambiguous sexual adventures, was lurid, but he maintained a respectable, semi-military exterior and was a martyr to his timepiece. As an outsider with easy access to smart society, he didn't seem to care what people thought of him. He had been to their schools and been expelled from them, ran up serious debts while serving as a commissioned officer in the army, and was 'a very naughty boy' (according to Lytton Strachey's friend, Dadie Rylands) while at King's College, Cambridge. When we met him at Deal he was beginning to satirise this world in his *Alms for Oblivion* sequence of novels (in which he is reputed to have used Philippa for the character of Maisie).

What we said that evening to give Philippa the genesis of her book, I do not exactly know. Nor did we know then, since she could never explain it. She hated being asked what her book was about. 'Actually, I do not know what the book is about,' she would volunteer. It was as if she were working at a gigantic jigsaw without a picture, and would see this picture for the first time in its entirety only when she put in the last piece.

Her starting point was food, the food and other appetites of the Victorians in relation to our own. 'I was unequipped to use standard analytical processes,' she later admitted. But she also thought that these analytical processes, when used by economists, for example, were unsatisfactory because they never followed the arguments into adjacent areas that bordered on their own speciality. In place of this truncated matter, Philippa wanted something all-embracing, which meant that she could not simply begin with the Victorians. 'I went deeper and further back into history until at last I arrived at the Roman Empire . . .'

Each day she set off for the Reading Room at the British Museum, determined to get a grounding in European history. She read and took notes, it seemed to me, on everything under the sun: agriculture, aphrodisiacs, social taboos, religious practices, eunuchs, witches, and of course the facts and figures of modern factory farming. With these researches she combined her own experiences, 'rummaging through hedgerows, wallowing in spices, pot herbs, puptons, pickles, jellies, fritters, ragouts and custards, bubbling mediaeval potions, tasting such rarities as messes of potage, frumenty, civet, charlotte, wild carrot, glasswort and skirret'. Some of these substances appear in her appendix of rare Roman and medieval recipes, others in an appendix about aphrodisiacs (called 'The Stuff of Dreams').

I watched this process with amazement and apprehension. Philippa worked, with terrible energy, to a point of exhaustion and with desperation, as if her life depended on it – as perhaps it did. I could help a little this time, giving her anecdotes and episodes that provided useful connective tissue in the narrative. 'Her study in Barnes, overlooking the back garden, was piled with the notes of her curious researches,' remembers Mike Foss, who had by then become a professional historian. 'Such was her enthusiasm for the ingenuity, and daring, of the human capacity for enjoyment that she drew others into her exhilarating chase. I thought I had no particular interest in her subject, but still found myself willingly digging about on her behalf in the Public Record Office.' He was obliged to gather dictionaries and grammars around him, for she put him and Simon Raven to work translating pages of Latin for her. So there, among the acknowledgements to several learned butchers of Deal, to Lloyds Bank in West Kensington, the editor of the *Meats Trade Journal*, the Federation of Women's Institutes and to Penelope Jardine 'for many scholarly errands in Rome' (where she met and spent the next thirty to forty years with Muriel Spark), stand their two names, Mike Foss and Simon Raven, both masters of Latin texts. '*Consuming Passions,* as the book was called, was my education,' she later wrote. 'My mind must be one of the most cumbersome and corroded that has ever tried to make a book. It was nerve-racking.'

But it succeeded – she succeeded. She reinvented herself in *Consuming Passions*, created a new life. When it was published in the autumn of 1970 (the publisher at the last minute replacing on the jacket a loaf of bread shaped like an extended penis with a respectable Hogarthian orgy), she was invited to appear on television to cook a medieval banquet. Her optimism leapt over the impossibilities, and the studio echoed with everyone's laughter – the crew, even the cameraman, could not stop laughing. At the end, the television presenter Eamonn Andrews sat down to taste her array of dishes – the 'furminty with venyson', 'Sir Kenelm Digby's White Pot', the 'goos in bogepotte' or 'harys in cyueye' – and as the end music began, the credits rose, he could be seen clutching his throat with a cry of 'Oh my God!' Then everything went blank. It was excellent television.

So what is her book about? It is about agricultural fertility rites and Anglo-Saxon drinking competitions, cheeses carried by the crusaders, joke food, severed heads, visions produced by fasting, remedies used in monasteries against ennui, surefire birth-control drugs in ancient Rome, the voluptuous menus of the Hell Fire Club, and Sweet Fanny Adams. You can find birds flying out of pies there, discover the medieval price of poultry and the fifteenth-century attitude to milk, and improve on the art of masturbation using vegetables (do not omit the well-endowed carrot). All this, and very much more, whirls around this extraordinary book. It is like a solar system, apparently chaotic yet with the abiding pattern of chaos, held together by a tremendous force of energy and inquisitiveness. Out of muddle and despair, with a prodigious effort of will, she had produced the most original and macabre creation. 'It is a work of love and care and art,' wrote *The Times* reviewer. 'Never have I come across such a crisp, exciting – such a very feminine history of taste.' Philippa dedicated it to me, and to me it remains a wonder.

Even before *Consuming Passions* was published, she had begun another book, her Life of Frank Harris.* This was at my suggestion, and she wrote it to some extent in tandem with my own work. My first biographical subject, Hugh Kingsmill, had written a brilliant memoir of Harris, who also had a good walk-on part in my *Augustus John* (and would later have a more significant role in my *Bernard Shaw*). I also possessed some Harris material left to me on his death by Hesketh Pearson (who had written two little-known essays on Harris).

All this made for a good start, and we took off on an enjoyable research tour through France, following Augustus John's journeys† early in the century until we arrived at Nice

---

*In 2001 both *Consuming Passions* (with an afterword by Paul Levy) and *Frank Harris* were brought back into print in the Penguin Classic History and Classic Biography series.

†Philippa makes a brief, anonymous appearance in the preface to *Augustus John*, where she is shown enlivening some complicated negotiations at the Musée Rodin in Paris: 'a girl, indispensable I hoped to the pursuit of John scholarship, who was afflicted in several languages with an ingenious grasp of malapropism ("masturbate" for "masticate" was one I remember with affection).'

where, in 1907, John and Harris had an explosive encounter (we offered slightly different interpretations of it in our two books). Then we went on to Monte Carlo. I drove up to see my stepfather Edy's grave on the Grand Corniche at La Turbie and also the tiny villa where my mother had taken me sometimes in the summer holidays from school. Philippa went to the Palace where she hoped to find something significant in the archive about Harris's friendship during the 1890s with Princess Alice of Monaco, an American forerunner to Grace Kelly. Palace protocol appeared strict, but after presenting formal letters of introduction from Captain Simon Raven MA (Cantab), late of the King's Shropshire Regiment, a Fellow of the Royal Society of Literature Michael Holroyd, as well as her well-hyphenated, Old-Etonian publisher, Christopher Sinclair-Stevenson – and finally, as a trump card, her three-guinea membership card of the Royal Horticultural Society – she passed muster and gained entry into the private archive. She was allowed to work there for only two days, as there was to be a royal festivity afterwards and all work must stop. She arrived at the Palace library as it opened and left when it closed, accidentally putting a bulging confidential file in her commodious bag and carrying it off on her last day. The rumpus this caused as, among the prancing horses, the marching soldiers, she struggled next morning to return the secret papers (spilling them over the parade ground in the wind) would make a fine scene were any film to be made of her life.

Readers of her *Frank Harris* will see that there is no acknowledgement or reference made to the Palace Archive at Monte Carlo. This was one of the Palace conditions – they did not wish to court further embarrassments. Those who are versed in biographical subtexts will become aware of an anomaly in Philippa's account of Frank Harris's relationship with Princess Alice and Prince Albert of Monaco. 'Harris's letters to Alice, together with all her papers, were by her wish burnt on her death by her executor Isador de Lara,' a foot-note records. So what were the files on which she was working at the Palace, one of which she had briefly purloined? She makes no direct quotations from letters, but paraphrases passages when describing Harris's sentimental relations with Princess Alice and his dubious financial transactions with the Prince. This indirectness, however, becomes curiously appropriate for a man whose published memoirs, *My Life and Loves*, is so crowded with fantasy women, but who omits from it the women he actually knew.

Frank Harris was a good subject for Philippa. As one of her set pieces in *Consuming Passions*, along with Samuel Pepys's erratic breakfasts, Henry VIII's wedding celebrations and the pretensions of Trimalchio's Feast, she quoted Harris's dreadful account of a Lord Mayor's banquet, full of rotting green meat and accompanied by the pungent evacuations, delivered like pistol shots, of the Lord Mayor himself. But now her brilliant researches revealed much that had been unknown in Harris's miserable birth and upbringing, and which gave a background of pathos to his over-ambitious career. She exulted in some of his more outrageous exploits, but added compassion to high comedy. The man who boasted of knowing the King had actually longed to be invited by Mrs Humphry Ward to the house from which Philippa as a schoolgirl had been expelled – she was sensible to such ironies. She also grew adept at distinguishing between Harris's wayward fantasies and the more modest facts of his life, because, she said, his compensatory stories were so like her own.

Philippa also came to liken Harris in her mind to Simon Raven. Both men, she believed, had once fallen in love, been rejected, and resolved never to be so fearfully hurt again. Neither of them dared to grow up, but inhabited clubs and institutions, like wombs, from which they were reluctantly

ejected. Women they treated as fantasy creatures (Philippa
had been to bed with Simon a few times for sessions of mutual
masturbation but never thought of him as a lover). As they
grew older, they lost touch with reality and came to believe
their own fantasies. A parallel to Harris's lonely and disillusioned last years could, she later believed, be seen in Simon's
last book, a memoir called '*Is There Anybody There?*' *Said
the Traveller* (1990) in which she herself appears as 'a lank-
haired authoress' much given to cooking 'blowflies, vervain
and rabbit's sphincter', who mistakes a bottle of golden bath
essence for some liqueur – a chartreuse, I think.

Philippa did not mind any of this, but she was appalled by
the book's unkindness to her friend Guy Nevill who was dying
of AIDS. Like Harris's last writings, the pages of Simon's final
book seemed to her corroded with the bitterness of male impo-
tence. Though he had enjoyed a new lease of his professional
life by successfully adapting for television Trollope's six Palliser
novels, as well as books by Nancy Mitford, Aldous Huxley and
Iris Murdoch, then writing *Edward and Mrs Simpson*, he did
not appear to value this work. His charm evaporated, leaving
a sourness lingering in the thin air. So their long, intermittent
friendship stuttered to its end.

Cruelty was ever her enemy. Antagonism had entered our
own relationship through the door of insanity. In madness,
and in my sullen opposition to madness (the unhelpful, self-
protective shell where I took cover), terrible things had been
said that still hung mutely in the air we breathed. We had
damaged each other so fundamentally that we could not repair
ourselves. Our wounds remained as painful bruises that came
vividly alive whenever small differences arose. When Philippa
went off to the United States to study the Frank Harris papers
held in several manuscript libraries there, I realised guiltily
how grateful I was for the peace and freedom of her absence.
When she returned, she told me I had missed an excellent

opportunity for leaving and been a fool not to go. So, when she set off on a second tour of the United States, I did go, moving to a small flat in Fulham which I rented from a remarkable Swedish woman, Viveka Stjernsward, a friend of Elspeth Huxley. Here I struggled with the final chapter of *Augustus John*, his last illness and death, which I finished very slowly, feeling shell-shocked and empty. Then the typescript went away to its publisher, and I started a new life, happier at first, though leading to a tragedy.

After Philippa returned from the United States, she did not leave the house in Barnes for a month. She drank a great deal and then became crazily promiscuous. Stanley Olson,* who

---

*Stanley Olson (1947–1989), the biographer of Elinor Wylie and John Singer Sargent (also appointed by Rebecca West as her authorised biographer) was an unforgettably perplexing character. Given up for dead at his birth in Akron, Ohio, by his parents, he later recreated himself in London as a striking English eccentric. Despite his natural awkwardness, dark spectacles and a somewhat cumbersome figure, he got himself up as a 1920s dandy, with clever bow ties, superbly tailored cream suits and startling co-respondents' shoes – in all of which he could be spotted pedalling his tricycle through the West End streets to the Ritz, his black spaniel Wuzzo alert in his special dickey designed at Harrods.

Stanley seemed to me the perpetual student, curious about everything, confusing about almost everything, knowledgeable and naïve, invalidish yet full of energy, generous and demanding, immature, precocious, affluent yet perpetually in debt, secretive, gossipy, a partial dyslexic determined to emerge as a fluent writer. In my imagination he appears as an amphibious creature rolling merrily, tragically, across the land, his adopted land, in thrall to the operas of Wagner and the survivors of Bloomsbury (he had written a thesis on the Hogarth Press). Eventually I found his hospitality too oppressive – I simply could not keep up. Stanley never seemed to sleep: then, at the age of thirty-nine, he suffered a paralysing stroke from which he eventually died. His biography by Phyllis Hatfield, *Pencil Me In*, was published in 1994 (André Deutsch).

reported her as being under sedation, blamed my timing which, he told Frances Partridge, was a sign of my being 'emotionally immature'. There is perhaps no perfect moment for such a painful wrenching apart, and I do not think the timing was specially insensitive. But in so far as I felt unable to prolong the emotional battery, to move through the storms into calmer periods, the charge of immaturity may be true.

Six months after I left, Philippa went down with an un-diagnosed illness. 'My temperature rose and stayed at about 103 degrees for about three weeks,' she wrote. 'Pints of sour yellow sweat poured out of me, day and night. The sheets were so wet they could literally be wrung out. When I recovered, my depression had more or less left me for ever . . . I felt light and euphoric.'

She was looked after by the improbable, larger-than-life figure of Paul Levy, the American writer, apricot-coloured, curly-haired, clever, secretly vulnerable, an out-to-lunch Kentucky Falstaff, bursting with generous fantasies, whom I had first met at Harvard in 1968. He had come to me after a lecture I deliv-ered there and asked whether I could give him introductions to some surviving members of the Bloomsbury Group. Within a year, he was living in England and knew more people in and out of Bloomsbury than I did. One evening at dinner, he explained to me that his career stood at an agonising cross-roads: should he write a masterpiece or become a professional gigolo? It was a knotty decision which he ingeniously untied by publishing his biography of the Cambridge philosopher and guru of Bloomsbury, G. E. Moore, and then changing course to become himself a philosopher in the kitchen. Living on a duke's estate, his raw fantasies were trodden into intoxicating fact.

During his first few years in England, Paul's life seemed to be shadowing my own so faithfully that Philippa suggested, as a joke, that he was secretly in love with me. In the early 1970s, after my *Lytton Strachey* was published, Paul edited Strachey's occasional writings in a volume called *The Really Interesting Question;* and while I was working on my biography of Augustus John, Paul hitched up with one of Augustus's grand-daughters whom he would bring to Philippa's parties. Then, when I left her house in Barnes, Paul stepped in temporarily and, with his great energy and generosity, helped Philippa over a critical time. Later I was able to repay some of his kindness by facilitating his marriage to the art editor Penny Marcus, whom I had known quite well when she worked for the Tate Gallery. At their wedding party near Oxford, a splendid affair of tents, fireworks and celebrities, Paul appeared dressed entirely in white, while Penny, famous for her beautiful bones and soft voice, was in deepest black.

Philippa and I kept away from each other, not from enmity so much as cautious self-preservation. Soon I went west to live in Ireland (strategically placed between a convent and a barracks) to begin writing my biography of Shaw, travelling to the United States to work on Shaw's papers; Philippa went east on the first of several long journeys to India, where she fell under the spell of the boy guru Sai Baba, about whom she wrote in her 'spiritual travelogue', *The Shortest Journey.* She went on to study yoga and Sufism, began training with the National Federation of Healers and became an intuitive therapist, employing a bewildering range of techniques, from drumming to the laying on of hands. With the psychic teacher Lilla Bek, she was to write books on spiritual and lay healing, and also study Egyptian hieroglyphs with the passion she had previously brought to the study of European history in the British Museum. But she 'never fell for the whole spiritualist package', Paul Levy observed. Indeed she seemed incapable of treating any religious enter-prise with solemnity. She diverted an expedition to find the resting place of Noah's Ark on Mount Ararat with an excur-sion to see the swimming cats of Lake Van; she broke off her

astrological researches into the Hindu religious fair, the
Kumbha Mela, to write an article on dustbins; and she several
times interrupted her studies in Egyptology at the University
of London by leading parties of Temple Medicine Tours along
the Nile – in the wake of which came streams of improbable
'Carry On' stories.

At last we began to see each other again. From time to
time from the early 1980s onwards, Philippa would telephone
me, ostensibly on matters of grammar: how to give linguistic
support perhaps to some intimations of immortality arising
from her transcendental meditation. Using many full stops, I
would try my best. Then we would relax and have supper
together. She was an inspired if eclectic cook (her curious
green tomato crumble was well known for its psychedelic
side-effects), and she still drank plenty of wine, some of it
homemade. Was she using these exercises in transcendental
grammar to release me from my male prison of rationality?
Not seriously, I think, though she enjoyed making fun of me.
She knew that I believed her to be advancing, like Frank
Harris, ever further into make-believe. Instead of denying this,
she would point out that fantasy was an everyday ingredient
of our lives, and therefore part of reality. She also quoted
Hugh Kingsmill back at me, to the effect that incredulity was
no more adequate as a response to life than credulity. She
lived somewhere between the two.

In fact I believed something rather different about the nature
of her quest. She did not look after herself, fearing illness, doing
nothing, simply waiting for it to pass, as men do. She preferred
the idea of psychic to surgical operations. While travelling in
the Philippines, she had fallen ill but ignored the symptoms,
drank a lot until at last she lay dying on the beach, almost
unconscious, finally it seems reconciled to death. But then she
was rescued and taken to hospital, revived, operated upon (having
her cancerous womb removed) and, regaining consciousness,

was suddenly terrified of dying. She attributed the shock of
this experience to a combination of alcohol and anaesthetics.
In any event, the sudden apprehension of death, intense and
awful, brought back to her, I believe, the feelings she had tried
to suppress after her fiancé Robin died. This time she reacted
differently. Much of what she hoped to find in her searches,
and to give others, was a magic cocktail, inducing the courage
of acceptance rather than forgetfulness, and lessening the horror
and sadness of death. For unless it could be appeased, death
came to us like a monstrous dragon from a child's nightmare.
She had seen the devil in her madness; she wanted to become
aware of a primordial and beneficent presence in the days of
her well-being. What she possessed, and suggested that other
people possessed, was a remarkable ability to change. At her
house in Barnes, she created something like a temple to which
all who were afflicted as she had been, all who were heavy-
laden, could come: there was a priest, an analyst, a vet, an
Irish painter, a secret drug-taker from the United States, a
duchess, a harpsichordist, a transsexual, an astrologer, a
divorcée, a man found nearby in a gutter, a woman who had
made a comparative study of communion wines; there were
alcoholics, men and women who were bereaved, the lost and
fearful, wounded souls of all ages, classes, nationalities, conditions. She had lost her own womb, but made her house into a
womb where these people felt they could be reborn. She was
their Mother. Someone special. Some of them were excruciating bores, but it didn't matter. She lit candles and set them
drumming, dancing, singing, praying, drinking, meditating,
laughing. She gave them concerts and counselling. She gave
them a good time so that they could gain more confidence,
learn or remember how to take pleasure in life. They talked of
Tantra, sorcery, Satanic possession, vasectomy, schizophrenia,
magic mushrooms, garlic and samphire, magnetism, illusion
and delusion, and the need to discover a synthesis of fact and

fantasy, death and life within the great paradox of time. It was a house of imagination and healing pantomime.

Of contemporary politics Philippa knew almost nothing. Her world and that of party politicians had little in common, and what little there was they saw differently. Most politicians would not have liked her attitude, which was a form of *noblesse oblige*, while she deplored their tendency to narrow careerism, their poverty of imagination. In her own work she was helped for a time by a peer of the realm who performed some secretarial duties for her (and after whom, title and all, she named one of her cats). 'Like many with a naturally aristocratic temperament, she was egalitarian at heart,' observed Mike Foss. 'I think she would have agreed with Mandeville's *Fable of Bees*, liking not only the ironic mockery of the economic analysis but even more the wit and verve of disreputable ideas. She was nothing if not an iconoclast.'

Some people, such as Frances Partridge, always felt Philippa to be 'maddening' – and certainly she could be provocative. But Frances, I believe, resented the fascination Philippa exerted over several male friends they had in common – Paul Levy and Stanley Olson, besides myself. In much the same spirit she castigates in her diaries that other Bloomsbury translator from the French, Lucy Norton, a splendid Grand Duchess of a figure whom Frances casts as an 'arch-spider' weaving her web around me and Paul Levy. 'How can they bear to be deluged in the thwarted maternal feelings from that vast, cushiony bosom?' she asks with disgust.

Philippa must have sounded more purely eccentric to Frances, less easy to cast as a thwarted mother or malicious daughter, but whose irrational lurches towards self-destruction might destroy us all. She was undoubtedly a complex and difficult girl – that is what her parents thought, and also what others who knew her, cared for her, loved her, were sometimes driven to feel in her twenties and thirties. But then, at a point of crisis, she had turned and found a way of coming to terms with these threatening complexities. She, who had been rejected by her father, was to welcome the world's rejects into her home, turning conventional failure into a story of eccentric success. Her very difficulties became the source of her strength. She appeared to be congratulating people on their problems and disabilities, as if they were special gifts that added to the rich variety of life and the entertainment of those parties that raged through the beautiful chaotic rooms of her house. The vitality of these amazing evenings buoyed everyone up. It was all right after all. Everything was all right, after all, in the end. Everything.

Philippa did not eliminate her riotous past, but added objects from this new phase in her life, her last phase, to the décor of her house which reflected all the stages of her strange pilgrimage.

A few of her old friends found it difficult to keep in step with her. 'Her stride was wayward. She went where she wanted. I drifted away not for lack of affection, but under the tyranny of circumstances,' recalled Mike Foss. 'I never saw her again.

But from time to time, returning to south London, I cut across Barnes Common and passed the end of her old road. It looks much the same now as in those cheerful days – a slightly dingy tunnel of untrimmed vegetation leading to the abodes of the professional classes. Then, remembering Philippa, I cannot help but smile as I think of that unconstrained package of vivacity and candour – a radiant cuckoo in those nests of dullness.

My own life, which had been deeply thrust down, was then beginning a new and better phase. I read about it – and so later on did Philippa – in a newspaper one Sunday in the autumn of 1982. What I read appeared highly unlikely. The newspaper reported that I had secretly married the famous novelist,

Margaret Drabble. Could it possibly be true? This was what people telephoned all week to ask. At my publishers they were taking bets for and against, and my editor (who knew me well and betted against) rang me to find out whether she had won. I hesitated to tell her the truth.

The truth was that I had returned from Dublin in the late 1970s to live in the badlands of Ladbroke Grove. It was an awkward journey back. The banks in Ireland had gone on strike and closed for several months. My bank had thoughtfully presented me with a piece of paper that, they explained, would enable me to transfer everything in my account, pretty well all my capital, to a bank in England. Unfortunately this piece of paper, though quite large and rather impressive in appearance, had been drafted inexactly (the number not agreeing with the figures as spelt out) and in consequence no English bank would honour it. I felt like Neville Chamberlain waving that fragment of paper signed by Hitler and proclaiming in 1938, 'Peace in our time.' Suddenly, in my own time, I had no money at all. And I had no peace of mind. I was bankrupt. I remember ringing the Dublin bank from London and speaking at some length to a woman there. She was very understanding, but could not help because, she eventually revealed, she was merely the cleaner – no one else was coming in during the strike.

Then there was my car. In Dublin, whenever Ireland played England, the Irish crowds would celebrate or retaliate by dancing jigs and tangos on the top of my car which, as I looked out at it next day, resembled a new form of low-slung sports model. Eventually I managed to get round this hazard by replacing the English numberplates with Irish ones. This meant, however, after I drove back to England, that I would be stopped every few miles by the police who insisted on searching it and me for IRA weapons. My progress through the streets was curiously intermittent until, through lack of money, I came to a halt.

As if this were not enough, there was also trouble with my trousers. Before leaving Ireland I arranged for almost all my clothes to be cleaned, packing them straight into the car as I left – only to find when unpacking in England that I had the jackets of my suits, but that was all.

I was cutting a poor figure on my return. Taking pity on me, not for the first time, the novelist Angela Huth carried me off to dinner at the Ark Restaurant in High Street Kensington and hearing a couple at the next table talking about a flat they wanted to sell, I walked desperately over to them and bought it. Of course I went over to see it the next day. I think I would have bought whatever I had seen, but what I actually bought was what I wanted. It was what estate agents call a 'maisonette', and I acquired it without benefit of estate agents. How then to pay for it? Nineteen thousand pounds. I partly solved the problem by taking my piece of paper to an Irish bank in London where I had no difficulty in retrieving my approximate money. A few days later I was hanging up my jackets in my new home. And I was soon joined by Bernard Shaw, whose papers, books and other scholarly baggage arrived by truck from Dublin. I settled down for life, as it were: Shaw's life.

The area around Notting Hill was not then generally fashionable or expensive. No one had thought to make a glamorous film there – the only Notting Hill films I had seen were *Ten Rillington Place* about the celebrated murders of seven women (round the corner from my new home) by John Reginald Christie (excellently played by Richard Attenborough), and *Pressure*, about kids squatting in derelict houses. The place had made brief appearances in literature – as Arthur Machen's nightmare country, where all roads led to Goblin City, the ancient cemetery of Kensal Green with its white gravestones and shattered marble pillars, the birds above circling like vultures, a detested habitation of the dead; and as G. K. Chesterton's wilderness of bricks and mortar dominated by the tower of Campden Hill

Waterworks, a kingdom to be defended by the Napoleon of Notting Hill against the advance of progress.

But it was Colin MacInnes, with his novels of the 1950s London underworld, who was to make the place truly noto-rious. He saw it as a drug-laden suburb of stagnation, bisected and enclosed by concrete precipices, sinister culs-de-sac littered with smashed bottles, truncated crescents going nowhere, and crossed by random lines of railway scenery and the dark margin of the canal 'where nothing floats except cats and contracep-tives'. These crazy intersections created mean and awkward slum islands and brought them perilously close to the tree-lined streets of respectability, graded Victorian mansions with their trim tended gardens. Rising above all this uneasy habitation stood the grim fortification of Wormwood Scrubs (the awful, Dickensian-named prison), also a neo-gothic, nineteenth-century hospital with its turret of discoloured brickwork, the monu-mental gasworks rising and falling like some vast lung machine, and the hopeless ugly tower blocks – vertical traffic jams of stacked-up people.

Twenty years after Colin MacInnes's *Absolute Beginners* was published, when I moved in, many deliberate improvements had been introduced – brightly coloured sports facilities, neat new housing trust villages, symmetrically planted roundabouts. Notting Hill riots were reorchestrated into the Notting Hill Carnival, though violence still haunted the atmosphere under the fresh paintwork, between the bursts of repetitive music, in the shadows late at night. Martin Amis was now our laureate. I occasionally saw him wheeling his baby from the off-licence. He found the sub-motorway culture, with its dense, haphazard tattoos of competing graffiti (the angry scrawls in Arabic lettering through which could still be seen the glimmering commandment of the Great Beast 666: 'Do What Thou Will Shall be the Whole of the Law') a rich hunting ground for his exultant scenes of moral anarchy. In his pages everyone is out at night robbing everyone else in primitive exercises of financial redistribution. I was robbed three or four times, though the burglars, adding injury to insult, found almost nothing worth the stealing (who, after all, wants books?). They fell back, like tired children, into pointless disorder, scattering Shaw's manuscripts, like random clues in a paperchase, from room to room. By the time Margaret came visiting, my maisonette was barricaded with locks and alarms.

I take credit for introducing Margaret to the wastes of Ladbroke Grove. We used to go on walks between the caravan people and snooker players under the motorway, passing mountains of burnt-out cars, and the bones of bicycles lying, like dismembered skeletons still tethered to the lamp-posts, along rows of dying pigeons in the gutters, to the violently painted, half-demolished Apocalypse Hotel (from which no traveller returns), its desperate customers in the *trompe l'oeil* paintings hanging crazily from its windows, never to escape. Some evenings, to the distant beat of reggae music, we would stroll across the dark patches of communal gardens, avoiding their slippery puddles of vomit, their glinting patches of shattered glass, reading the plastic police notices politely requesting information about local murders, the trees stuck with children's appeals for lost dogs or cats – hazardous landscapes of evil-smelling rubbish that moved menacingly in the wind. For anyone keen on observing social change in Britain in an extreme form, this was compelling territory, and Margaret was to use it dramatically in *The Radiant Way*,* the first novel she wrote after our marriage. Here, with its cramped and dismal terraces, its underpasses and tunnels lit with flickering neon lights, Notting

---

*Fifteen years later, in *The Seven Sisters*, she gave the place, now with its modern oases of health clubs and silver Eurostar sheds, another, more contemporary, going over.

Hill became a place of desolation and danger, patrolled at night by foxes and wild cats, and rat-faced people watching invisibly from their holes as you hurried along the shabby streets past those vandalised cars in any one of which, perhaps your own, may rest a dismembered head, wrapped in a piece of mutton cloth, its eyes staring, threatening to petrify you. To such a ghastly region had she been serenaded from the sunny uplands of Hampstead Heath, with its innocent children flying kites, its healthy joggers and keen footballers, its romantic memories of Keats and Shelley. I did this.

I had known Maggie, as I shall call her from now on, over many years, meeting her at parties as a casual friend. But all this changed one day after she saw me lunching near the British Museum, the table piled with proper vegetables, opposite the imposing atheist and secretary of the Shaw Society, Barbara Smoker. We sat at our meal serious-faced, correct, like two chess players, intent, bent forwards, occasionally moving a bowl of curry, some proteins or a glass of tap water, concentrating on matters secular and alphabetical. Though we were way beyond reproach, something about this scene sent a pang of pity through Maggie's tender heart, and that evening she telephoned and invited me next week to join a dinner party she was giving at her house in Hampstead. I eagerly accepted, and when I drove away that night, I apparently left my raincoat in the hall – an act which may be seen as the equivalent, literary critics tell me, of the Victorian lady carelessly dropping her handkerchief.

By the beginning of the 1980s I was living quietly islanded off Ladbroke Grove, still with Bernard Shaw, behind my double glazing and grilles. And though I still invited emotional complications, in some ways I lived simply and, despite the paraphernalia which made it more difficult for me to go out than for burglars to get in, I had little of the siege mentality of some war children. 'Apart from books,' Maggie reported after an early visit, 'there wasn't much else in his house. The fridge contained a lemon, bottles of white wine, vodka and mineral water. There were withered walnuts in a jewel box, a small can of baked beans in a cupboard, and an oven without a door . . . I know Michael can survive on bananas.' With these bananas, and little else, I apparently resembled the eponymous figure in *Krapp's Last Tape*. But I had a future.

The marriage took everyone by surprise. After all, was I not a happy-go-lucky bachelor, more eligible for affaires than weddings? By then I was getting on for fifty, and could go no more a-roving. And hadn't Maggie sworn never to remarry following her divorce ('a painful process best forgotten') from the talented actor Clive Swift? But like Philippa, she was one of the last of the Early Marriage Generation who married to get away from their mothers. Up to the mid-1980s, a woman's career was not generally accepted as a fit reason for leaving home. But marriage, however implausible, had to be accepted.

It was reported, our marriage, as a very bold enterprise, but it was in fact more of a tentative experiment. We experimented first by taking a trial-and-error honeymoon well before the wedding, setting off together for a week in Hollywood where we saw the first night of Christopher Hampton's play *Tales from Hollywood*. Back in London we continued going out and staying in together and then spent an enchanted summer in Somerset, where Maggie had rented a somewhat derelict Dower House (the bed we slept in collapsed in the first week and we passed the following weeks sleeping on the floor). The house lay in a lost valley where the sheep were all pink from the red earth, the sun sank early behind the tall hills, and time itself seemed magically suspended.

Our experiment in courtship continued that summer in my blue, automatic car in which I taught Maggie to drive, chiefly by falling asleep in the passenger seat next to her – a gesture of confidence in her ability to steer us safely home at night.

She always did. 'I must have been in some kind of trance all that summer,' she admitted. 'We were captives to one another and the driving lessons were our alibi.'

We were married in September 1982 at the Chelsea Register Office in the King's Road. Beryl Bainbridge acted as our 'best man', and the function was conducted by a forbidding lady in black whose bunch of keys, jangling from her waist, brought unpleasantly to mind the word wedlock. When she told us we should have gathered more witnesses, I brightly suggested going to the romantic fiction shelves of the public library next door and recruiting a few devotees there. She was severely unamused.

The most shocking ingredient of the marriage, to judge from later press coverage, was our decision to keep our two homes. Maggie's house in Hampstead was full of the coming-and-going of teenage children (she had two sons and a daughter), a visiting mother, and an assistant who was working with her every weekday on the commodious *Oxford Companion to English Literature*. As for me, Bernard Shaw now occupied two of my three rooms and the avalanche of his words was leading to the subsidence of the building. So our arrangement was really one of romantic common sense. We spent weekends in Hampstead and had dinner together two or three times a week, telephoning each other whenever we were apart. We also took holidays and went on lecture tours abroad together. Had we not been married we would have been described as 'living together' by journalists who, since we were married, reported us as living apart.

We had hoped to keep our marriage relatively private so that, as stale news, it became no longer 'newsworthy'. But after two or three weeks, it was reported in the *Sunday Times*. What exercised journalists, then and thereafter, was these *deux ménages*. What could it all mean? What it meant was that the institution of marriage was changing, becoming more varied and less constraining than it had been thirty years earlier.

Privately people understood this, and many couples envied our freedom and intermittent distance. But publicly our arrangement was represented as deeply unconventional, dubious and eccentric. In vain did I try to explain that most couples had homes from home that were called offices, whereas we worked at home and needed more space there. As eminent predecessors I cited William Godwin and Mary Wollstonecraft living as near neighbours after their marriage. Eventually my statements grew more whimsical. I explained that I had been studying Hugh Kingsmill's famous panorama on marriage, *Made on Earth* (1937), and been influenced by Milton's good-natured views on divorce. I very much liked too, I added, the Shavian notion of limiting the marriage contract (easily obtainable from the drugstore) to one year, with a joint option to renew it every twelve months. It was left to Maggie to translate my concoction of references and quotations into understandable language. Marriage did not suit everyone, she reminded astonished listeners, and it had to be handled with care. It should no longer be an expectation or an obligation. Perhaps the only odd feature of our own marriage, it occurred to her, was me. 'He invents things as he goes along. This is very liberating.' It was also a great compliment, I decided, for a non-fiction writer.

Though I had told some friends about our marriage, and also my parents (who had never met Maggie), I had not yet told Philippa, who eventually read about it in a newspaper. Our own stormy relationship ten or twelve years earlier had made me wary of letting anyone know much of my sexual and emotional life. I kissed and did not tell. For how could you tell anything of significance without introducing betrayal? The answer to that perhaps is that it can only be done in the calm distance of retrospect, as I am attempting to do – and even then the telling is like a difficult translation from another language, from privacy into print.

Philippa did not compartmentalise her life as I did. She packed everything and everyone together – and let them all sink or swim. In her more riotous past people had sunk, and there were genuine regrets. But now, by whatever inflatable means, they stayed afloat.

Philippa wanted to meet Maggie and in due course invited us to supper in Barnes. As we drove across the Common and along the pot-holed private road to the house where I had lived in the very late 1960s and early 1970s, I attempted to carry on introducing her to Maggie before they met. Their personalities, background, lives and careers were so thoroughly dissimilar that I could not imagine what they would make of each other, how they would get on. Yet I very much wanted them to get on, rather in the manner of the dying Edward IV in Shakespeare's *King Richard III*, urging those around him to be at peace so as to facilitate his own passage into heaven: 'Hastings and Rivers, take each other's hand/ . . . Dorset, embrace him; Hastings, love lord marquis/ . . . And make me happy in your unity.'

We parked between the pot-holes, struggled through the over-grown front garden past an enormous wooden statue of a naked woman, knocked and pressed bells, and heard the collective mewing and scampering of the animals within. Then footsteps, some rattling of the doors, cries of despair over keys – and we were in. I immediately put on an abstracted air as if I were partly elsewhere, at least not all there, wandering vacantly around and bumping into misplaced furniture until given some-thing useful to do: the pouring of drinks. Then I waited to see what course the evening would take.

Philippa and Maggie had only one thing in common that they knew – and that was me (though perhaps I was a slightly different person with each of them). Since my return from Ireland and move into Ladbroke Grove, Philippa had devel-oped an attitude of affectionate teasing towards me. Maggie at once picked up on this, and in relief perhaps I played along

with it. But what on earth did Maggie really think? 'I liked
Philippa immediately,' she later told me,

> though I could not have said why, and liked her more
> and more as I got to know her better. Indeed I think I
> came to love her.
>   I can hear her voice now – she had pronounced and
> endearing vocal mannerisms, a kind of lilting precision,
> a strange and musical distribution of emphasis that I
> found very attractive. Her manner was calm, but at the
> same time intense and attentive . . .
>   She was full of stories – about handsome men and
> Arab stallions in Egypt, about Egyptian mythology,
> about stars and flowers and potions. I suppose Philippa
> was whimsical, in that she was full of whims, but she
> was sharp and witty, not sentimental. She was a
> risk-taker with a great and fearless openness, and a rare
> adventurousness of spirit. Most people who talk about
> calm and healing (not that she did, much) make me feel
> very tense, disbelieving and irritable, but Philippa had
> the reverse effect. She did calm and heal people. She
> was the real thing.

I could see, too, that Philippa warmed to Maggie, who was
far from being the didactic literary intellectual she had feared,
and in fact something of an open-minded bohemian herself
with a soft spot for risk-takers and romantics, the dishevelled,
even the destroyed. Philippa invited us to a tumbledown house
she had rented on Valentia Island off the west coast of Ireland
while we were over there one year. I remember her giving us
strange, delicious, green drinks that produced, over the following
week, unfortunate effects on my driving. Not a day passed
without my losing, by some infinitesimal miscalculation, a
couple of wing mirrors, some bumpers, the aerial and so on

until, by the time we reached mid-Wales on our way back to England, I was driving a skeleton car as if in a cartoon. But mostly I remember our visits to her house in Barnes. And so does Maggie.

> She seemed to lead a charmed life, in a charmed place.
> I was very impressed by the beautiful and luxuriant
> disorder of the house – large high rooms, with large
> paintings, and large mirrors and dark comfortable
> furniture. There was a feeling of faded grandeur, as
> though we were in an old much-inhabited country
> house in town, where the same people and animals
> had been living for generations . . . There were cats
> everywhere, weaving their way along mantelpieces,
> sitting toasting themselves on the Aga, curled up before
> log fires, disappearing crossly down dark corridors.
> There was one particular cat called Mr Parsley whose
> name gave me much delight. There were also fish.
> Philippa had made an indoors-outdoors fishpond
> conservatory, and in the pond large golden fish teemed
> and proliferated. They came to her call, like chickens.

It is hard to make friends later in life, but here, it seemed to me, was a genuine late friendship. To some extent I was its catalyst – they both put themselves out for my sake – but then it developed its own momentum irrespective of me. They held unlikely interests – I remember them one dark night in the middle of Barnes Common, their heads raised to the heavens, identifying clusters of stars. Another night, after they had been out walking, Maggie fell asleep on the hearthrug. 'I am not very good at falling asleep on other people's hearthrugs, so Philippa must have cast a spell on me,' she later explained. 'She did have a magic quality.'

They trusted each other, made the other feel she was doing the right thing, were discerningly uncritical, spontaneously generous, and made me happy in their unity. That was the magic. At Christmas, or on a birthday, Philippa would sometimes lead small troops of her friends on rustic-suburban walks, animating the landscape around them with surreal visions. I remember Maggie coming back and telling me of a field of llamas near Guildford, and a red-haired woman praying on her knees near a chapel. These walks would end in celebratory parties at Barnes, where I had been left in charge of the oven and cats.

There were many gaps between our meetings, since all of us were working hard and quite frequently travelling. After her mother died, Philippa became rather more secluded, listening to her radio in the evenings and working on her patchwork quilt. In some ways she was not so unlike her mother, possessing a similar stubbornness and individual tastes (Mrs King enjoyed drinking a bottle of stout over a meal, followed by some sweet wine). She had by this time reached the age at which the thoughts turn lightly towards family history. She was delighted to find, hidden in the dark past, a spirited ancestor called Dolores, a dancer from Spain, her great-great-something-or-other, who married an Irishman and produced a daughter who had connections with Edinburgh Gaol. Much encouraged, she travelled north to pursue her investigations and was rewarded by the discovery of a scandal involving 'the MacDonald of Sleat'. It was all most promising, though it took her out of London a great deal. One summer – it was in 1997 – we noticed that we had not seen Philippa for more than six months, and I rang to invite her over to Ladbroke Grove. She answered hesitantly, saying that she expected to be off on a long journey soon, a sort of holiday. I told her she must see us when she came back.

Six weeks later she was dead. She had told almost no one that she was suffering from terminal lung cancer. She was looked after by a homeopath doctor and a practitioner of aromatherapy and reflexology who gave her massages to relieve her laboured breathing. She was determined not to die in hospital. In *The*

Times obituary, Paul Levy wrote: 'She refused treatment, saying that she would take upon herself the responsibility for her illness – either healing it or managing her own death. In either case she intended to set an example for the many people she had nurtured and helped, and with the minimum of drugs she did just that, fortified by the essentially comic view of life that is evident in all her books.'

With this obituary appeared an extraordinary photograph of her taken in the last year of her life. It shows a face of confrontation and acceptance, with signs of pain absorbed into it, as she sits, a shawl round her shoulders, waiting. She has a determined expression, not grim but with nothing weak or trivial in it. I find it almost unbearably moving.

Her younger son Sebastian, whom I had first got to know in Deal, telephoned to tell us the news and we went over for the last time to her house in Barnes. Brilliant sunshine filled the garden and gave a dusky warmth to the rooms. Her body still lay in the bedroom upstairs before eventually being taken to Shropshire for its dedication and green burial in 'a lush green valley, full of bird chatter and animal life'.*

Her friend Stella Wilkinson had noticed how her corpse had been changing over the days. At the beginning it had looked

---

*Philippa had made it clear that she wanted her body to be put in a card-board coffin and buried in a place of natural beauty. The Natural Death Centre (to which she was attached as a spiritual healer) held a list of approximately seventy such sites, and was able to help her son Sebastian find a cardboard coffin and also give him the information he needed for an embalming service. The site he chose outside Ludlow belonged to Ann Dyer, who was offering her ancient orchard for private burials and who intended to plant it with memorial apple trees whose species were under threat. An additional advantage to this site was the Dyer family chapel, on the edge of the orchard, where Philippa's Celebration of Life service was held on Sunday 14 September 1997.

extraordinarily ancient, almost Egyptian, then more like a bird, and then again like a girl, an Ophelia, with long dishevelled hair spread out as if floating on water. 'I had never seen an unembalmed corpse before or experienced the shocking difference of flesh tone after life,' Stella said. 'It was part of her generosity not to have been a frightening corpse.' It was also perhaps due to the manner of her death. Many people, as the doctor confirmed, die in fear, leaving dreadful, contorted expressions on their faces. But Philippa had not died like this. The atmosphere in the house, though peculiarly intense at the start of her final illness (she did not like being nursed by her son), had, I was told, grown easy and serene as her strength evaporated. And that tranquil atmosphere persisted after her death.

About twenty-five of Philippa's friends wanted to go to this burial ground, and her aromatherapist, Viv Knowland, took on the job of getting a coach company which would be prepared to take them, along with Philippa's body in its cardboard container, into Shropshire. 'There were some very strange reactions to my request,' she recorded. '. . . [and] mutterings about the Health & Safety Act.' Eventually she did find an owner and driver who, for £500, was prepared to drive everyone the three hundred miles or more from Philippa's house in Barnes to the orchard near Ludlow and back, with the coffin, now decorated with Egyptian symbols in shades of blue, terracotta and gold and lined with a roll of muslin, placed in the luggage hold underneath. Viv Knowland has described the day of 'Philippa's green and final journey'.

'We set about decorating the Chapel with flowers and candles in preparation for our service. Philippa's coffin was laid out in front of the altar with an amethyst crystal and her handmade drum placed on top of the coffin. The service was almost spontaneous with everyone taking part – there was chanting, prayers, remembrances, poetry, Irish flute music, Bible reading, a song specially composed and sung for Philippa, a period of contemplation and meditation – a wonderful mixture of happiness, sadness, smiles and tears . . .

'The coffin was then carried slowly across the orchard to the prepared grave. Bay leaf branches and rosemary sprigs were strewn over the bottom of the pit and then Philippa in all her splendour was lowered gently into the grave.'

We sat in the garden, the unseen trains clattering by from time to time. This intermittent noise made a strange juxta-position of two worlds, as Maggie later remarked, the muffled sound of the trains reminding her of another timescale, yet somehow intensifying the remote and rural quality of Philippa's world. I was touched by Sebastian's mild unworldliness. He seemed unprotected, but Philippa's spirit lived on in him, I felt. They had been peculiarly close over her last year and the sweetness of his temperament, reflecting this closeness, was very appealing. It looked as if he had got her love at last. He told me that his mother had finished her dissertation, *Magic and Mysticism in the Ancient Egyptian Pyramid Texts*, for an MA course at Kent University – she had corrected the proofs the day before she died. Then we relapsed into stories of Philippa's boisterous séances, and the time she had been likened to Joan of Arc after falling into Lord Montagu's fire at Beaulieu.

But her death had been untimely in many ways. There was much unfinished business especially in relation to her sons. The elder one, whom she had considered conventional, was to become a part-time chimney sweep. How she would have liked that – liked that in him.

While I talked with Sebastian, Maggie went and lay in the long grass under the mulberry tree. 'I felt a sense of great loss, as though something irreplaceable had been taken away – as indeed it had. The sun shone gloriously, the garden was still beautiful, the cats still weaving their way around, the flowers still clambering through all the open windows, and I knew that we would never enter this small paradise again.'

Then we left.

When first hearing of Philippa's death, Maggie had burst into tears, lamenting the loss of a friend in the future, the friend of old age she would miss. I sat with that numbness which is a refusal to believe, the first stage of a familiar grief which woke me early each morning, sat on me like a stone even before I had remembered the death that was its cause.

'It seems a senseless thing to die!' That line of verse which Philippa had used as part of an epigraph for her biography of Frank Harris came back to me. I got the book down and began reading. What particularly struck me was the last paragraph of her preface which is a restatement of Samuel Johnson's declaration in his *Life of Savage* that no one who has not suffered the same misfortunes and persecution as Savage has the right to judge him ('nor will any wise man presume to say, "Had I been in Savage's condition, I should have lived and written better than Savage"'). Philippa wrote:

> It is tempting to feel ourselves more worthy, sympathetic
> and serious than Harris, to be disappointed with the
> facts of his life since they do not support the notion of
> him as the anti-Puritan hero that he longed to be. In this
> biography I have tried to show Harris as someone more
> human and complicated than either a hero or a villain.
> He was a man whose ambitions exceeded his talent and
> his energy. This is a condition that at one time or
> another has afflicted most of us and calls for the kind of
> understanding that we would wish for ourselves.

That is the spirit in which I have tried, in response to Margaret Forster's challenge, to write about Philippa in this chapter. Have I answered her question? Perhaps not. But I have, I hope, imbued these pages with some of Philippa's talents and shown what she gave me – what I needed to be given.

Maggie and I do not speak much of Philippa now: she is part of our known and accepted pasts – part of our unspoken selves. But occasionally something will prompt another memory, make us speak it aloud. In *The Literary Companion to Cats*, Clare Boylan quotes some lines by Francis Scarfe:

Those who love cats which do not even purr
Or which are thin and tired and very old,
Bend down to them in the street and stroke their fur,
And rub their ears and smooth their breast, and hold
Their paws, and gaze into their eyes of gold.

I know those cats. They found sanctuary in Barnes and somehow they survive in the dangerous streets of Ladbroke Grove. Maggie waits patiently, with understanding, as I stop to stroke one of them. But then I hear Philippa's voice warning me not to deceive it into trusting all human beings. 'You don't want it made into gloves!' So I content myself by whispering this warning before going on.

In the garden at Somerset, Maggie suddenly recalls what Philippa said of a plant there (Teucrium maris) tumbling down a wall. 'It has such a pretty habit.' It is a phrase that regularly comes back to her now, 'because she herself had so many pretty and graceful natural habits'.

A more sombre note came from Robert Skidelsky. Relishing Philippa's 'great presence and many changes of style', he remembered last seeing her 'sitting, as it were, on a throne, improbably dressed like the Queen Mum'. But if Philippa, who called to mind such a symbol of longevity and was herself always fizzing with eccentric energy, could die so unexpectedly, and so comparatively young, then for the rest of us 'it's choppy water from now on'.

A tree was planted above her body in Shropshire. 'I sometimes pause and think of this tree,' writes Eduardo Sant'Anna, 'firmly rooted in the ground with its branches spreading through mid air, swaying from side to side almost in a frenzy, almost like someone I used to know.'

6

The Search

FAMILY STORIES

Pilgrim's Progress, about a man who left his family, it didn't say why.

Mark Twain, *The Adventures of Huckleberry Finn*

. . . here, where the living and the dead share the same space, sometimes, in order to find one of them, you have to make a lot of twists and turns, you have to skirt round mountains of bundles, columns of files, piles of cards, thickets of ancient remains, you have to walk down dark gulleys, between walls of grubby paper which, up above, actually touch, yards and yards of string will have to be unravelled, left behind, like a sinuous, subtle trail traced in the dust, there is no other way of knowing where you have to go next, there is no other way of finding your way back.

José Saramago, *All the Names* (translated by Margaret Julia Costa)

Among all the stories I was sent, there was nothing of the person about whom I was most eager to learn more: my grandfather's *femme fatale*, Agnes May. As I toured the country giving readings and talks about family memoirs at festivals, I would ask the audience if they knew anything of her, but answer came there none, and we usually settled for putting all our families into fierce competition as to which was the most dramatic, secret, dysfunctional, strange. Even abroad, in Chicago or Montreal, my own family performed very well in these contests.

After three or four months, I thought of a new way to elicit information, and drafted an article which I called 'A Tale of Two Women'. The two women were Agnes May and my Aunt Yolande. Looking closely at their very different lives, I saw that they represented a dramatic shift in the moral and sociological landscape of Britain. When things go wrong, as they did for my aunt, I wrote,

we are tempted to ask who is to blame. But perhaps this is not the right question. In retrospect my Aunt

Yolande's fate appears inevitable, as if it were locked
into a national predicament, its narrative keeping pace
with the decline in imperial and class confidence. The
other side of that story is the wonderful rise in the
fortunes of my grandfather's ex-working-class mistress,
Agnes May.

I went on to expand this article into a public appeal for
information about Agnes May, using facts I had discovered but
been unable to work into the published narrative of my book.
Perhaps it was not surprising that my grandfather's mistress
had been only seven years older than his daughter. As I had
presented her to the reading public, Yolande appeared like
the character in an Anita Brookner novel, limited by cultural
conditioning, perhaps also by loss of nerve or an excess of
sensitivity, disappointed in her romantic expectations, left alone
before the end. Agnes May, on the other hand, was far from
solitary and had the makings of a twentieth-century Becky
Sharp. I longed to find out more about her.

'She had been born at 56 Hardshaw Street, St Helens, in
Lancashire, a daughter of the glass-grinder Joseph Bickerstaff
and his wife Robina (whose maiden name had been Laurie),'
I explained in my article.

Unlike Yolande, who stayed so dutifully with her
parents, she must have left St Helens before she was
twenty – she was not yet twenty-one when she married
Second-Lieutenant William Reynolds Lisle, at Oxted,
near Godstone; and only in her twenty-fifth year when,
eleven days after having been divorced, she married
Captain Thomas George Symonds Babb, the son of a
hotel proprietor in Minehead, Somerset . . .

Eight years later, Thomas Babb cited my grandfather
as co-respondent in his divorce petition. Agnes May

immediately married a wealthy businessman, Reginald
Alexander Beaumont-Thomas, and went to live in
Duchess of Bedford Walk, Kensington. *The London
Street Directory* shows them living there for a couple of
years. Then they vanish and the trail runs cold.

It had taken many weeks of research to trace her this far. I
went to Minehead and advertised in the local paper there to
find out if anyone remembered her or her second husband; I
went to Oxted, had tea in Rose Cottage, Barrow Green Lane,
where she had briefly lived with her first husband, and examined the deeds of the house (which appeared to belong to a
railway company). But nowhere could I pick up an echo of her
presence, the ripple of a distant memory. From all these places,
including Kensington (where I examined old telephone books,
the electoral register and street directories at the local studies
centre) she had quickly moved on leaving, as it were, an empty
page.

I consoled myself by reflecting how fortunate I had been to
locate her at all. Initially I knew nothing except what I learnt
from a Deed of Covenant my grandfather made in the early
1930s when granting her a quarterly allowance for 'past services'.
I came across this document at the back of a chest of drawers
after my father died and saw that her name was then Agnes
May Babb and that she was a married woman (the allowance
ceased if she returned to her husband). With this meagre fact I
went to the Registry of Births, Deaths and Marriages, then at
St Catherine's House in the Aldwych, and began trawling through
the apparently endless lists of marriages in their heavy alphabetical volumes. Had her husband's name been Smith or Jones,
the hunt would have been impossible. But the surname Babb is
comparatively rare and so, even if I did not then know her
husband's first name, I always felt there was the prospect of
discovering her. I looked backwards for the Babbs' marriage,

and then I looked forwards to see if by any chance she had married again. Altogether I covered almost fifteen years of marriages throughout England and Wales: and then one afternoon I found her. She had married Reginald Alexander Beaumont-Thomas in 1934. Luckily their marriage certificate was crammed with information. It gave me her father's name, her age, the full name of her ex-husband and, then a surprise to me, the fact that this was her third marriage. A month later, by laborious trial and error, I had in my possession her three marriage certificates, her divorce papers from Somerset House, and her birth certificate. Yet I felt she was fighting me all the way. By continually experimenting with her age, changing her first names as well as her last, haphazardly inventing addresses for herself and wide-ranging professions for her father who regularly dies and miraculously comes alive again on these official papers, she had laid down such a thick smokescreen that I finally lost her. Had she married a fourth or even a fifth time? Had she gone to live abroad, perhaps in the United States or France, and then died there? She could not still be alive or, if she were, then she was nicely over one hundred years old. All things seemed possible, but the fact was she had given me the slip.

I switched my lines of enquiry first to her father's family, the Bickerstaffs, then to her last-known husband's family, the Beaumont-Thomases. Sometimes the quickest way to find the date of a death is to search through the inventory of Wills and Letters of Administration. I discovered that Joseph Bickerstaff, who died in Hampshire in 1942, left an estate valued at £207 which automatically went to his widow Robina. There was no mention of their daughter Agnes May, and Robina Bickerstaff herself left no will when she died the following year at Myrtle Cottage, Brockenhurst – probably, I thought, because she had no money. 'Like a bird, Agnes May appears to have freed herself from her family cage,' I concluded, '... [and] was moving in wealthy circles by then, in contrast

to my Aunt Yolande who never married and remained financially dependent on her family all her life.'

I surmised that Agnes May must have been quite wealthy
because of my investigations into the Beaumont-Thomas family.
One of the more infuriating obstacles in research is the hyphenated name. Sometimes this family appeared simply as Thomas,
at other times they shot up the alphabet and attained Beaumont.
In the hope that someone might remember them and respond
to this appeal for information, I put into my article all I had
discovered about Agnes May's third husband since finishing my
book. The second son of a successful steel manufacturer, Reginald
Beaumont-Thomas was educated at G. Davison Brown's preparatory school in Brighton, and went on to Eton College. His early
years were deeply unmemorable. Despite getting through three
tutors at Eton, 'he won no prizes, played no games, and left
after only two years', I wrote after consulting the archivist at
Eton College Library.

> He was almost eight years younger than Agnes May,
> and this was not his first marriage, either. In Paris, at
> the age of twenty-two, he had married Germaine
> Blanche Aimée Dubor, who seven years later petitioned
> for a divorce on the grounds of his desertion. That year,
> 1932, he gives as his address the Junior Carlton Club in
> London. His name appears in the 1937 edition of
> *Burke's Landed Gentry* as the younger brother of
> Lionel Beaumont-Thomas, then living at Great
> Brampton, Madley, Herefordshire. But Reginald's
> marriage is not mentioned, and all the Beaumont-
> Thomas family disappear from future editions.

This article appeared in the *Sunday Times* in Britain, and
Threepenny Review in the United States. I waited, apparently
in vain, not knowing that it would eventually lead to an

extraordinary discovery transferring my aunt from the solitary pages of an Anita Brookner novel to the crowded text of Iris Murdoch's fiction with its formations of elaborate coincidence and its complex infrastructure of relationships.

The first intimation I heard of something strange was during a telephone call from my friend Carmen Callil. She had dined earlier that week with some friends of her family, one of whom had seen my book and told her I had got everything wrong about my aunt's lover and fiancé, Hazlehurst. She had known him for the best part of forty years and never heard him speak of a Yolande Holroyd. Either I had got hold of the wrong man, or else my Aunt Yolande had been living in a fictional affaire. On the whole it was probably the latter, she thought, since Hazlehurst was certainly a most fascinating man who mesmerised many people. But he was also a married man, eventually a much-married man. In these circumstances, it was highly unlikely that he had been so closely attached to my aunt and for such a long time – over ten years. Besides, it was not as if he were afraid of mentioning the names of women, particularly a woman called Iseult. Could this Iseult have been by any chance his pet name for Yolande?

I remember laughing at this far-fetched notion. After all, I had Hazlehurst's letters to my aunt spanning almost ten years, and in none of them did he call her Iseult, or anything but Yolande, his dear and beloved Yolande, the woman he hoped to marry once he had made enough money to propose and be accepted by her parents. On the envelope of an early letter my aunt misspelt his name. He wrote back at once from his yacht to correct her, spelling out his surname in capital letters at the top of his reply.

But because he signed his love letters with a simple 'H', I never got to know his first name (everyone called him Hazel), and I was unable to find his birth certificate. So he remained

HAZLEHURST
~~NOT~~ HAZLEHURST
~~CHISWICK 5845~~   YACHT FROTHBLOWER,
            ~~CUBITTS YACHT BASIN,~~
            ℅ Toogs Bros   CHISWICK, W.4.
            ~~Teddington~~
            ~~Saturday~~   9/9/33

Dearest one.

I was so very glad to get your
letter. You were such a time answering
mine that I almost thought you were
talking me literally when I asked you not
to waste valuable time writing to _me_. As
you probably gathered from my last letter
not being frightfully full I was a bit
depressed & the actual writing the
postman still further depressed me. As
then I am I imagined all sorts of
things such as you finding someone
else, & it wouldn't be difficult for you
you know. at any rate in men though

something of a mystery to me – but not so mysterious that I could credit the stories of Carmen's friend.

Shortly afterwards, I received a rather impatient letter from a reader of my article, 'A Tale of Two Women'. She wanted to know whether the memories of my grandfather's mistress, Mrs Beaumont-Thomas, which she had sent me were of use. 'I should be most pleased to hear as naturally I am now very interested myself and could maybe help you further.' I was not surprised to find that the newspaper had failed to forward this correspondence. It had not treated my contribution as a genuine appeal for information and, greatly thickening the confusion, had shown a picture of my Aunt Yolande as if she were my grandfather's mistress, Agnes May. Fortunately, my correspondent had kept a copy of her original letter, marked 'Private and Confidential', which she now posted to me. This, too, questioned and pretty well refuted the story I had told in *Basil Street Blues*. 'My mother was a great friend of the Beaumont-Thomases,' my correspondent explained, remembering her visits to them in Brighton.

> On occasions I would be taken to visit them on a
> Sunday morning for cocktails. She was called Vera and
> appeared far from a 'scarlet woman'. Slim, attractive,
> sophisticated with great style, always kind and warm to
> a gauche 16 year old boarding school girl. Reggie
> [Beaumont-Thomas] was a paraplegic from an injury he
> sustained playing Rugby at Eton (I believe). He was
> tall, good looking, hospitable and charming. He was
> always in a wheelchair and she was caring and
> attentive – they seemed very fond of each other. They
> had no children and lived in a bungalow (for Reggie's
> chair, I assume). Vera drove the Rolls . . . She was a
> delightful woman who obviously had to re-invent
> herself to escape the dreary working-class north and,

after sorting out a few early mistakes, found happiness
with Reg for around 40 years. And with a paraplegic,
that has to be love.

Though this letter was full of oddities (such as playing
'Rugby at Eton'), I felt certain that here was the Reginald
Beaumont-Thomas who married Agnes May in the mid-1930s.
She was continually calling herself new names and inviting
others to do so. But what did surprise me was the dramatic
way in which she had continued to reinvent herself. That the
daughter of a working-class glass-grinder from Lancashire
should have fled south while still in her teens, married two
husbands and lived with my grandfather (one of her 'early
mistakes') in her twenties and early thirties, then landed up,
while still in her thirties, marrying a millionaire was remarkable enough. But that she should then have changed from a
'scarlet woman' to this knitted figure of domestic virtue and
connubial stamina – a very model of matronhood – took me
aback. I had difficulty picturing her as a devoted nurse. Yet
it appeared to be true.

The next letter from a reader was more contradictory still.
Thomas Lyttelton remembered very well the phenomenal Mrs
Beaumont-Thomas (known locally as 'Mrs B-T'). She was living
in Highgate Village during the 1940s and until the early 1950s
when she left London for East Anglia. Hers was an 'unforgettable name to me, so often was it repeated by my parents in
my teenage years', he wrote.

By no means devoid of 'character' themselves, my
parents clearly saw their equal in Mrs B-T ... A large,
robust 60ish year old, as I just remember meeting her,
living apparently alone in this huge house [where] ...
her name, perhaps spirit, lived on.

He then gives me that name (which she signed on the contract of sale for the house): Iseult Marjorie Beaumont-Thomas.

All at once the country appeared to be teeming with Mrs Beaumont-Thomases of various heights and widths, robust, scarlet or nurse-like, and in different places at the same time – all of approximately the same age. Yet I knew from my researches that there was only one Beaumont-Thomas family in Britain. I simply could not make sense of it.

Finding some sense in it all was made no easier by the number of false trails that were opening up, such as a picture of a high-spirited dancing lady, apparently in Hungarian costume and allegedly Agnes May in full bloom, that was sent to me from Dublin. Was this herself? On investigation, it turned out to be the likeness of a Dun Laoghaire housewife who in the 1940s had (obviously with some abandon and allegedly for charitable purposes) entered a fancy-dress competition. 'It just seemed to have the right feel!', explained the Irish archaeologist who sent it.

By now, as if using a type of instinctive litmus paper, I was becoming adept at sorting out these false trails from the true leads. When a woman in Suffolk wrote to tell me that follow-ing the early death of her husband's uncle, a surveyor called Ignatius Dracopoli, his widow Isolde had married Beaumont-Thomas, I knew at once that this 'Isolde' must actually be the peripatetic 'Iseult', and felt for a moment I was on the verge of catching her up. I suspected that Iseult Beaumont-Thomas was probably the wife of Reggie's elder brother Lionel. At this point another member of the Beaumont-Thomas family (actually a rare Treherne-Thomas) wrote to introduce himself, claiming that 'as both your grandfather and my father's first cousin Reggie Beaumont-Thomas enjoyed Agnes May's favours – at least she was married to Reggie! – we seem to have a tenuous connection'.

The Beaumont-Thomases (including their several mutations

into Treherne-Thomases, Spence-Thomases, Massey-Thomases, Wyndham-Thomases, etc.) were, he reminded me, a very wealthy family. Their great fortune had been created through the steel industry in Wales during the nineteenth century, initially by the son of a Somerset coal merchant and then enlarged by his son and two grandsons, the elder of whom was Reggie's and Lionel's father. My correspondent sent me some pages photocopied from a privately printed history of these variously prefaced Thomases, *Men of Steel* by David Wainwright (Quiller Press, 1986). I had never heard of this book and read the enclosed pages with interest.

There was only one mention of Agnes May's Reginald Beaumont-Thomas – simply recording his birth as Lionel's younger brother. In commercial terms Reggie was obviously a man of no importance. But I was able to learn much about this family so curiously entwined with my own. His brother's life appeared to occupy a whole chapter.

Lionel had been born in 1893, was educated at Rugby, and later served in Belgium and France during the war. He had been married twice – to the same woman: the daughter of an officer in the Colonial Service. The first time, in June 1913, they had married in secret at the Paddington Register Office, Lionel (as I later discovered) adding a year to his age to make him a full twenty-one, the same age as his wife. The reason for this secrecy was the violent opposition from Lionel's mother, Nora, who disapproved of love matches, having herself married for reasons of pure wealth and position. She was extremely ambitious on behalf of her elder son and wanted him to make an advantageous marriage, perhaps into the aristocracy. To separate him from his girlfriend, she arranged for him to be sent to Luxembourg for a year, ostensibly on steel-making business – a move which actually precipitated their marrying in secret. When Lionel returned, in the summer of 1914, still in love with the same girl, his mother at last gave her grudging consent to their union –

only to be told that they were already man and wife. This prompted a monumental rift in the family that was finally settled by the First World War, at the beginning of which, on Nora's insistence, a second wedding ceremony, this one at Holy Trinity, Brompton, was performed.

Lionel was to take part in almost all the major military engagements of the war along the Western Front. At the beginning of 1917, he was awarded the Military Cross. But his father Richard, attending the investiture at Buckingham Palace to see King George V confer this decoration on his son, caught a chill that led, a fortnight later, to his death at the age of fifty-six. Lionel then became a director of the steelworks while still a serving officer. There is no mention of Reginald because he was ten years younger than his brother and still at school – suddenly a very wealthy fifteen-year-old.

In any case, all their mother's ambitions seem to have been channelled through the active brother, Lionel. In the early 1920s he stood as a Conservative candidate in two safe Welsh Labour seats and on one occasion, his car being trapped by angry miners, he escaped on foot across the hills. Impressed by his resolution and speed, the Conservative Party adopted him for the more promising King's Norton division of Birmingham which he narrowly won in 1929 against the national swing to Labour. 'I have had to write so many letters of condolence to-day, that it is a real pleasure to be able to congratulate you on your magnificent win,' the future Prime Minister, Neville Chamberlain, wrote. He won the seat again in 1931, was given a junior post in Ramsay MacDonald's National Government, and tipped for a powerful political future. Then suddenly, in the spring of 1933, he announced his resignation 'owing to ill-health'. This somewhat baffled me. Neville Chamberlain's letter, reluctantly acknowledging his resignation, seemed to hint at other reasons, hidden reasons, for abandoning such a short-lived and promising political life.

I am naturally very grieved to hear that you feel you
cannot continue to remain a member; and while I fully
realise your difficulties and appreciate that it is only the
exigencies of the situation which have led to such a
decision, I shall always be very sorry that you have had
to cut short your political career.

Such language did not seem quite appropriate for serious illness.
Besides, Lionel was healthy enough to be accepted for renewed
army service six years later, and in 1942 was appointed head
of a British Military Mission which set off for the Middle East.

On the last photocopied page, I learnt a little more about
him. The life of a Member of Parliament, David Wainwright
ominously wrote

is time-consuming and a heavy strain on personal
relationships . . . Social life is liable to be disrupted,
and the effect on family life can be devastating. Lionel
Beaumont-Thomas was approaching 40, tall (he was six
foot five inches), balding but fair-haired and fair-
complexioned, with a 'good war record', and wealthy.
When in London, he lived on his yacht moored on the
Thames opposite the Houses of Parliament, to which he
was ferried by launch. It was an impressive setting even
for a period when rich men would be admired for
demonstrating their wealth in outward show. Devoted
to his wife and family, he nevertheless had an eye for
pretty women.

What this seemed to tell me was that I had been wrong in
assuming the mysterious Iseult to have been Lionel's wife. In
the account of his career I was reading, she was named as
Pauline, and her maiden name was not Dracopoli but Marriott.
As for his brother, 'I do not think Reggie had any children,

and I doubt that he ever married again,' my correspondent
ended his letter. 'He was always going on sea voyages and
breaking his legs.' The copyright line in *Men of Steel,* he pointed
out, named Pearl Brewis along with David Wainwright. 'The
person you really need is Mrs Pearl Brewis – Reggie was her
uncle.'

News of my book must have been travelling among the
family, though they were not, I later discovered, normally
fond of communicating with one another. A few days later I
was opening a letter from Pearl Brewis, Lionel and Pauline
Beaumont-Thomas's daughter. She had been reading *Basil
Street Blues* and had found the chapter about my Aunt
Yolande and her relationship with Hazlehurst particularly
interesting. She had immediately recognised the photograph
of Hazlehurst. In the early 1930s his yacht *Frothblower* used
to be moored next to her father's yacht *Pauline* in Cubitt's
Yacht Basin at Chiswick (when it was not stationed opposite the Houses of Parliament), and it was on *Frothblower*
that Lionel had met Iseult – and her two children. But the
photograph I had reproduced came from the late 1930s on
board a yacht called *Llanthony*, which I had also mentioned
in my book (Hazel wrote a series of love letters to Yolande
from it).

'My father had extreme money worries during the early
'thirties, & was very vulnerable at that time to be attracted by
Iseult who, as my mother used to say, "set her cap at him",'
Pearl Brewis wrote.

> He insisted on leaving my mother to marry Iseult &
> made the necessary arrangements by paying someone to
> spend the night with him. This ended his parliamentary
> career, and he had to excuse himself on grounds of 'ill
> health'. My father sold the yacht 'Pauline', named after
> my mother, & bought the 'Llanthony' . . .

I have several albums of photographs showing
yachting in the canals & the South of France, but am
unable to identify many of the people. These date from
1930–1940. Maybe your aunt and Hazel are among
them. Hazel and my father certainly remained friends.

Having read this, I did something obvious which I should
have done very much earlier: I looked up Lionel Beaumont-
Thomas in *Who Was Who*. I had been unable to find his death
certificate, but nevertheless saw his name listed in the 1941–50
volume, where it is noted that he died in December 1942.
Diplomatically, no date is recorded for his marriage to Pauline
Marriott, and therefore no confusion is created round their two
weddings. But a date is given for the dissolution of their
marriage. It is 1934, the year he later married his second wife.
Her name is Iseult Hazlehurst.

But who *was* Iseult Hazlehurst? I still hadn't pinned her down.
Possibly, I thought, she was Hazel's sister. That would fit the
facts in so far as I knew them, and explain how Lionel
Beaumont-Thomas had met her on his yacht and became a
friend of her brother. Having two children meant, of course,
that she had probably been married and then, after the death
of, or divorce from, her husband, reverted to her maiden name
as many women did and do. Certainly she could not be either
of the two women in my article, Agnes May or Yolande.

I had enough new evidence now to do more checking of
births, deaths and marriages. I also planned to visit Pearl Brewis
in Hampshire, and made arrangements to meet Carmen's family
friend who had known Hazlehurst and now lived in Chelsea.
But first I read again carefully through Hazel's love letters to
my Aunt Yolande.

There are several references to 'the family', but all of them
turn out to mean the Holroyd family – there are no other

Hazlehursts mentioned in any of the letters. These surviving letters begin in the early summer of 1933, that is not long after Yolande's father Fraser, my grandfather, returned from his six-year fling with Agnes May. Already Hazel and Yolande seem very close, and have discussed, even argued about, their previous relationships. 'I know why I failed before, and yet I refuse to learn,' Hazel writes by way of apology after one of these arguments. 'In both cases I was so damned inferior to them, and they naturally couldn't stick it, & moved on. Bobs so aptly expressed it one day – "The Starling after the Eagle" – & it quite confirmed my own private opinion. Now what's the answer to *you*. You are so very much superior to both before, then I must of necessity be found that amount worse off.'

This is unusual: a man claiming so much convoluted 'inferiority' to his previous girlfriends as well as to his present love. Perhaps he is genuinely distrustful of himself, or else simply using this device to defuse more damaging emotional arguments from Yolande. She, though obviously in love, is cautious, and slightly suspicious of Hazel, who reassures her: 'As for naughtiness & wickedness, no. There has been no temptation, & if there was, I would be quite sufficiently unmoved . . . I never missed anyone so much & never felt so completely dependent upon one person before. All feelings I had for Bobs were water compared with what I feel for you. I never hope to be fonder of anyone, for it really hurts, & I'm afraid, so very afraid . . . All my love my one own darling Yolande. H.'

There is a further mention of Yolande's predecessor, the curiously named Bobs, in another letter that year, also written from the yacht *Frothblower*. 'I had a letter from Bobs,' he writes, 'and she said she hopes Yolande is sweet to me for I am a very dear person in some ways & she is so glad I am completely cured of her. She is so happy.'

Otherwise, though there are descriptions of yachting trips, there is no identification of the other people who are on board.

He mentions that he is starting a new business and asks permission to make Yolande his nominee on the board of the company – a preliminary, he hopes, to their names being joined, once this business is successful, in marriage.

I can make better sense of my aunt's caution and Hazel's self-deprecation once I have spoken to someone who knew him. Myfi Heim, whose name Carmen has given me, appears immediately to solve one of my intractable problems: why I had been unable to find any record of Hazlehurst's birth. 'He told me he was born in Ireland (his mother's name was Nelly) and that both his parents had been killed in a car accident there,' she says. Hazlehurst himself, apparently, was very keen on racing cars. She approves of this, being herself an outdoor woman who hunts, fishes, and is a crack shot. To ease our conversation indoors, she pours us each a hefty glass of champagne.

I tell her of my Aunt Yolande's long attachment to him, and how devastated she had been to hear of his sudden marriage in Italy during the Second World War. Myfi Heim knew about this.

'He was stationed in Salerno,' she tells me, 'and commandeered an apartment belonging to an Italian lady who lived in the house with her two daughters. He married the elder daughter, Palmina Abbagnano, who was nineteen, and brought her back to Cheshire where he had been posted at the beginning of the war – several ladies there were very disappointed to see him return with a wife (he always, by the way, called her "Prunella"). Everybody loved his company – he was lively, quick-witted, good fun. He owned a tough little naval schooner then, called *Black Pearl*.'

'What was his business?'

'He was a consultant engineer – and very good with boats. He would take everyone out on *Black Pearl* – dogs and children too.'

'Did he have any children of his own?'

'No, he didn't. His marriage to "Prunella" didn't last very long. They were divorced quite soon after the war.'

'Did you ever hear him speak of my Aunt Yolande?'

'No. Never. He used to speak of Bobs or Bobby rather bitterly sometimes. She was an earlier wife.'

'He was married to Bobs?'

'Yes, I think so. He told me he was married at seventeen, but quarrelled with his wife over a game of croquet on their honeymoon, and never saw her again.'

'I'm astonished.'

'He was full of stories like that.'

'Did he have a sister?'

'Not that I heard of. I can't remember a sister.'

'Someone called Iseult?'

'I think that was his wife, Bobby. He was always giving people new names.'

Each new name I heard added to my confusion, as if I were playing a complicated game – the Parting of Names – the rules of which, as in a worrying dream, hadn't yet been explained to me. Hazlehurst had no first name as yet, but the women had so many: Agnes May, Vera, Bobs, Iseult, Isolde, Nelly, Nora, Yolande, Pauline, Palmina, Prunella, Pearl – my head was spinning with them. We had, I discovered, finished the bottle of champagne. And I was coming away with one extra name, that of Palmina's younger sister. Her name was Mariolina.

Mariolina, who lives in Chelsea, remembers Hazel very well. For a brief time, she had been his sister-in-law. 'He used to drive sports cars, and spoke quite a bit of his hunting days. He'd also won a wonderful lot of silver cups in yachting races. Altogether he was a very dashing figure, amusing, highly attractive and of course athletic – also very good with children. My daughter Tessa worshipped him, though I remember him telling her off for eating too much, and scolding her severely for reading *Lady Chatterley's Lover*. He could be rather strict – especially with anyone who was sick on his boat when he took them out to sea. Occasionally, too, he could be quite snobbish. He objected strongly to my son being sent to Harrow. He himself, as you know, had gone to Eton – though he admitted to having run away! Incidentally, he was decorated by the King at Buckingham Palace. But you can see all that in his *Who's Who* entry.'

'He was in *Who's Who*?'

'Definitely. I remember him telling me so.'

I feel doubly stupid, having also failed to look up Lionel Beaumont-Thomas. But later, when I hunt through the volumes of *Who Was Who*, I cannot see his name; and when I write to the archivist at Eton College Library, she cannot find him in the Register of Old Etonians. 'In my experience boys said to have run away from Eton were rarely here in the first place,' she wrote, 'so I am not altogether surprised.'

I had one more person to visit, Pearl Brewis, who united in my mind the Hazlehurst, Holroyd and Beaumont-Thomas stories, being Lionel and Pauline Beaumont-Thomas's daughter, a one-time stepdaughter of Iseult, and niece of Reggie Beaumont-Thomas. Surely she would be able to bring clarity to this dense plot.

By one of those coincidences that mean nothing and lead nowhere, but suggest the interconnectedness of all life, I saw with surprise that Pearl Brewis lived only a mile or so away from Myrtle Cottage, on the edge of the New Forest, near Brockenhurst, where Agnes May's mother, Robina Bickerstaff, died in the summer of 1943. Pearl knew nothing of Agnes May's mother, but she did meet Agnes May herself shortly before the war. This was the first person I had met who had seen my grandfather's inamorata. I felt I was taking one step closer to her.

Previously I had been unable to take this story beyond 1934 when, Agnes May's second husband, Thomas Babb, having divorced her (citing my grandfather as co-respondent), she immediately married Reggie Beaumont-Thomas. For a couple of years they had lived together in Kensington – then they left London and I lost track of them. Pearl Brewis can tell me where they went and what then happened.

They went to a small town in Hertfordshire called Bushey where Reggie bought a house on the heath called The Tubs. It was not far from Pinewood Film Studios at Elstree. He and Agnes May would often invite actors and actresses over for parties – there seemed to be parties going on all the time. The large garden with its splendid swimming pool was perfect for summer gatherings, and at night they would play in one of the rooms on the ground floor that had been made into a private casino or 'gambling den'. One way and another, the house was like a miniature Hollywood. Agnes May herself, with her brass-blonde hair, was known as 'the American barmaid'. People called her 'Maimie' which amused her.

I felt a jolt of recognition on hearing this, and noticed later that on her first marriage certificate (when marrying William Lisle at the age of twenty in 1916) she had given her first name as 'Maimie Archie'.

Pearl Brewis had met Agnes May only once. But among the pile of correspondence, photos and albums she had gathered together for me to examine was a letter written by her father Lionel on 30 October 1942. 'Just seen Reggie,' he writes. 'He is very well and looking a lot better, having got rid of his wife. He has bought a bungalow down near Brighton.'

Though they never got a divorce, Agnes May and Reggie seem to have separated permanently. He made her an allowance (rather as my grandfather had done): it was rumoured to have been a lump sum of several thousand pounds plus an annuity of almost two thousand pounds (tax-free) a year – similar to a financial arrangement he had made ten years before, following the divorce from his French wife, Germaine Blanche Aimée

Dubor. He then went to live with Vera, the ex-wife of a dentist, who took the name Thomas and lived with him near Brighton until his death nearly forty years later.

Pearl did not know what became of Agnes May after 1942, so I asked her some questions about her Uncle Reggie.

'He was immensely tall,' she tells me, 'almost seven feet (Lionel himself was a good six foot five inches). He had a small head and was semi-paralysed on one side (either it was infantile paralysis or else "sleepy sickness"). Decidedly he was very far from romantic to look at. Yet he was a playboy and exercised a passion for fast cars – "one foot on the accelerator, one foot in the grave" was his motto. Unlike Lionel, he never worked, never had a job – except for a brief period when he acted for Rolls-Royce as consultant on their coachwork. He loved cars. He once owned five Packards.'

I then ask her about her father, Lionel Beaumont-Thomas.

'It was a terrible shock when he fell in love with Iseult Hazlehurst and divorced my mother – I don't think she ever got over it, and it ruined his career too. Iseult already had two sons, Nick and Jack, but she and Lionel did not have any children of their own – which was just as well as Lionel and Pauline had four. This wasn't an easy time for me and my brothers – Richard suffered from a chronic illness and was permanently in hospital from the age of sixteen, and Nigel had asthma.'

'But who was Iseult?'

'Her two sons have the surname Dracopoli – that was their father's name . . .'

'So she wasn't married to Hazlehurst?'

'I thought she was.'

'Another marriage?'

'Must be.'

For Pearl Brewis, this is looking back into 'another lifetime'. She had been born in 1921, the youngest of Lionel and Pauline's

children. She was twelve when they divorced, and twenty when
she married in 1940. As a trainee nurse, she had sailed with
her husband to Burma where she joined the Women's Auxiliary
Service. Bombed and machine-gunned, she somehow managed
to keep up a canteen service for troops in the front line, as
well as nursing the wounded soldiers in searing heat at primitive military hospitals. She was like the heroine of a fast-paced,
adventure-packed novel by Nevil Shute. She was to give birth
to a son in the mission hospital at Shillong following an
earthquake – with its awful trembling and roaring, and the
tremendous chasms opening in the ground, this was more
frightening than anything she had experienced in the fighting
zones, retreating just ahead of the Japanese during the Burma
campaign. Shortly after the birth news came that her husband
was dead. Her brother Nigel too, with whom she was very
close, was later killed in action. Her father also died. The reason
why I could never find his death certificate was that his body
had been lost at sea when the ship on which he was sailing on
a secret mission concerning the Allied landings on Crete was
torpedoed in the Caribbean at the end of 1942. But Pearl and
her son came through the war.

Pearl is a fighter, a survivor. She has a good, strong face,
with a firm chin, beaked nose, wide forehead. There is something Churchillian about her. She is almost eighty and suffering
from osteoporosis and arthritis. She is unable to stand without
acute pain, but she is tough and independent-minded, full of
life, and has devised a number of ingenious ways of getting
around. She uses two sticks, as she advances, her cat Tiddles
playing around them. We gossip: and she hands me a pile of
legal papers concerning her family which looks very like the legal
papers that piled up round my own family, and so many
families. 'It is a disaster,' she says, pointing at these papers,
and she laughs.

Once she was Pearl Beaumont-Thomas, and what she tells

me helps to identify the regiment of Mrs Beaumont-Thomases
I have amassed. I knew now that Nora Beaumont-Thomas had
married into the steel business and became the ambitious mother
of Lionel, and the mother of Reggie too. I knew that Germaine
Blanche Aimée Beaumont-Thomas was Reggie's first wife (a
Parisian dancing girl, according to Pearl) whom he left in France,
before marrying Agnes May. I also knew that Pauline Beaumont-
Thomas (Pearl's mother) was Lionel's first wife, and that Iseult
Beaumont-Thomas, Lionel's second wife, was, as his widow, to
evolve into the robust and unforgettable Mrs B-T of Highgate
Village, before energetically retiring to East Anglia. Finally I
knew that Vera Beaumont-Thomas was that slim and stylish
lady (ex-wife of a dentist) who, when Agnes May Beaumont-
Thomas left Reggie to pursue her further adventures, nursed
him in his wheelchair through his many affluent last years in
Brighton.

So, having seen my way through these ranks of Mrs
Beaumont-Thomases, I emerged at last. But had I gathered
enough clues to fashion a story, actually two interconnected
stories, from such a random pile of confusing facts and rumours?
Could I use these bits and pieces as sources of light, strange
stars, by which to plot a clear and explanatory narrative? This
was what I must try to do. I would begin with my Aunt
Yolande's fiancé, the elusive Hazlehurst.

His name was not Hazlehurst. When he corrected my aunt with
such decisive capital letters, he was in fact misleading her. The
change was not great, but it was enough to fool me later when
hunting for his birth. Henry Edward Haselhurst was born, not
in Ireland, but in the small town of Beverley, in north-east
Yorkshire, on 12 March 1894, the elder son of Louis Haselhurst,
a journeyman in a chemical manure works there, and his wife,
Maria Annie (née Appleton). She was the eldest daughter of a
local grocer who had died shortly before her marriage in 1890.

She had been working as a hosier's assistant at the Wednesday market (her mother was a draper) and seems to have continued working until the birth of her son. But why had she not given birth earlier in her marriage? It was most unusual. Had Henry perhaps been adopted? Not officially, of course, but privately as sometimes happened in those days. Only very few people would know the facts, especially if some grand family were involved in the transaction. In the north of England, secrecy was highly prized over such matters. And if this were true, then it would account for the sense of difference, the feeling of not belonging, that grew in the boy's imagination.

His mother, Maria Annie, being two years older than her husband, was aged thirty-three when Henry Edward was born and thirty-five at the birth of her second son, Roland Percy. He was rather a dull boy and really did seem to be an authentic child of this journeyman and hosier's assistant. But perhaps Henry had been billeted on them with an allowance which enabled them to afford a child of their own – someone not given the names of English kings as he had been given. These were the sort of speculations that could burden or enrich your life – burden it at home and enrich it whenever you escaped from home.

There were many Appletons in and around Beverley at that time, and even more Haselhursts. Louis Haselhurst seems to have been a steady enough chap. He was the third of nine children, his father William being classed as 'a labourer', sometimes described as a fireman, but more probably a foreman, at the Tigar Manure Company in Beverley. The company works stood in Grovehill Road where the Haselhurst family lived. It had been founded in 1825 by a chemist and grocer called Pennock Tigar, originally making paint, and then adding fertilisers which became its main product. Louis's two elder brothers became a commercial traveller and a clerk for a leather merchant in Beverley, his younger brother was to be the local millwright, and two of his sisters elementary school teachers there. Louis himself left school at fourteen and followed his father into the Tigar manure works, initially as a general labourer, finally as a chemist. He remained there all his working life – that is until 1923 when the manure works closed and he, at the age of sixty, retired. His was the most regular of lives. But there was one irregularity: his birth was not recorded. He was a man apparently without a birth certificate. Because, I finally discovered, his name had been entered in the index as Haselchurch.

On their marriage Louis and his wife went to live in a small house, 6 Rose Villas, in Wilbert Lane, less than a quarter of a mile west of Grovehill Road. In 1904, with their two sons, they moved again, this time a quarter of a mile south, to a rather larger house, 24 Flemingate, next to the railway line. There was room for a domestic servant, Priscella Hart, in her young teens. Henry was then aged ten and his brother Roland eight.

It was not very long after this that something unusual happened. All the Haselhurst family had been educated and employed in Beverley, but Henry was sent, not as he claimed to Eton, but to the Hull Municipal Technical College which offered an excellent five-year course in engineering. The class records have been destroyed but Henry must have successfully completed the course since he was to earn his living as a qualified mechanical and electrical engineer, and as a 'fuel technologist'. The entry age at Hull was eleven, so Henry would have gone there in 1905 and left in 1910 when, instead of returning to Beverley, he went off to join the Royal Engineers as a private soldier and was sent to Singapore. On the army records he has left blank the name of his father and mother.

Something terrible must have happened. From the age of sixteen he was never again to see his parents or his younger brother. None of them would be present at any of his weddings, and he did not go to his brother's wedding in Beverley. His mother was to die at the age of eighty in 1941. Roland is present at her death, but Henry, who is then writing letters to my Aunt Yolande, does not mention his mother dying. Neither in her will, nor later in that of her husband, is there any mention of him. When Louis Haselhurst dies the following year he is described in the *Beverley Guardian* as 'beloved husband of the late Annie and dear dad of Roland (Jim) and [daughter-]in-law Cissie'. There is no acknowledgement of his having had another son, his elder son Henry. The break is absolute on both sides for over thirty years – and then another thirty years, since the two brothers do not acknowledge each other's existence even at their deaths in the 1970s. Only on his marriage certificates is Henry obliged to own up to having a father named Louis (though he sometimes misspells the name and always gives this long-term journeyman and assistant chemist at the manure works the superior-sounding rank of 'Gentleman', which, after Louis's death, at Henry's last marriage of all, he improves with the additional words 'of independent means').

This retrospective improvement is nicely in keeping with Henry's own successful career. He was to find another way of life in the army, a life of travel and adventure, and through this activity, stretching over a dozen years, part of it abroad, he also found a new identity.

He had a good war, a very good war. At the start, having come back from Singapore, he was appointed to a commission in the King's (Liverpool) Regiment. Then, in the spring of 1915, he was posted to France with the First Battalion and promoted to a full lieutenant. He would have met no one from Beverley in his regiment, or in the Royal Welch Fusiliers to which he was later attached. The young men of Beverley were being invited to join the East Yorkshire Regiment, which Roland Haselhurst, still only nineteen, obediently did with a friend in August 1915 – two months before the Derby Scheme to encourage recruitment was introduced. Unlike his brother he was never commissioned, though he did 'see action' in Egypt, this theatre of war being the only foreign country to which he travelled all his life. At the end of the war, he left the army, still a private soldier, and returned to his parents' house in Beverley where he lived until his death over fifty years later.

How different from Henry! On some of the forms he was obliged to fill in during his life, he would put, in place of his birth, the date of his baptism (at St John's Minster, when he was five weeks old, on 14 April 1894), as if he were a child of God. This illusion was enhanced when, early in 1916, he was transferred to the Royal Flying Corps.

The Royal Flying Corps had grown from the balloon companies of the Royal Engineers which operated air observation in the Sudan and during the Boer War. By the beginning of the First World War, though it had an establishment of officers seconded from the regular army, and men from the Royal Engineers, very few of its kites and amphibians, its biplanes, airships, its great dirigibles and magical lighter-than-air machines were fit for use in war. This was partly because, though some young visionaries already saw 'men moving swiftly through the air on simple surfaces for military purposes', officials at the War Office, senior commanders, convinced that these so-called 'aeroplanes' were sheer essays in lunacy, had made almost no money available for experimentation and development.

Pilots in those early days of the war were often buccaneers, frightened of nothing except perhaps the danger of this war ending too soon (before they really got a chance to enjoy it). They were fuelled by romance, guided by a love of display, artists in aviation who, rather than rely on some scholar's finicky map, would put down, even make forced landings, to enquire of astonished pedestrians their way to a target. Their main function once they got there was to shoot film and take back their photographs of enemy movements. Occasionally, by way of encouragement, they might lob a grenade or two over the side, but when they passed German planes on their way to reconnoitre allied lines, they would hail one another with comradely salutes. It was splendid sport, and these pilots developed very affectionate relationships with their planes, naming them after their mothers or girlfriends, Susannah, Jo, Merrill, Valerie, Linda, Janet and so on. Of course it was a dangerous game they were playing, they all knew that. There were crashes and splashes and the most terrific exploits when wounded chaps flying upside down, literally hanging out of their machines, guiding the controls with their feet like marvellous performers in a circus, would somehow get themselves back to the aircraft park, dead or alive. Most exciting of all were the solo missions to land secret agents, with their flocks of pigeons (each one a trained messenger bird) far into enemy territory, leaving themselves just enough fuel to make it home.

By the time Haselhurst joined, these buccaneering days of the lone, valiant pilot, great knights of the air, had passed, though their legendary deeds still lingered in everyone's memory and imagination. The Royal Flying Corps was now a well-knit, professional group of expert aviators. At the School of Instruction, over four months, Haselhurst was taught the arts of formation flying and night flying, how to fire the new Lewis guns attached to the wings when intervening in battles on the surface, how to win freedom of movement in the air (while denying it to enemy aircraft), and how to take photos from every possible angle – even when travelling as fast as seventy or eighty miles an hour! He learnt wireless telegraphy, bombing and the dropping of propaganda leaflets, and by the second week of June 1916 he was finally made a flying officer and wore a bright new uniform.

That summer, in France, began the greatest continuous battle the world had seen: the Battle of the Somme. In later years, Haselhurst would sometimes speak of it to his stepsons, telling them how it began over rolling uplands dotted with little patches of wood, the long corridor of kites looking down in ominous silence from both sides on this vast stage of war, while hundreds of aeroplanes, buzzing like wasps, patrolled the long lines of trenches showing up starkly in the chalky earth. Then the bombardment opened, and they dodged in between the rockets and phosphorus shells, searching for the red flares of their troops. Sometimes thick clouds hung over the country, and the mist and sleet were so impenetrable that they had to fly almost into the trenches themselves, and were flung around like corks in the barrage. But they brought back amazing pictures of the ground fighting: the spouting of the earth under the bombardment (with the terrible noise of exploding shells); the thin lines of men moving erratically forward; the streams of distress flares; then the counter-barrage growing into an awful wall of fire, and the grey figures coming up from their battered dug-outs, as if resurrected from the dead only to be killed again. It seemed never-ending.

You could see too, from your seat in the sky, a new secret weapon belonging to the allies: the tank. It appeared rather a ludicrous toy as it ambled down village streets, falling into trenches and even apparently attempting to climb trees: comic stuff in the magnificent spectacle.

This was a new type of warfare, and the planes flew increasingly, without rest, as if in a dream. Though there were vivid air battles, the vast cost of blood was to be spent on the ground, and the pilots were grateful to be away from those grim infantry encounters, tense, almost motionless tugs-of-war to and fro, which they witnessed below.

For Haselhurst himself, it appears, this flying held a peculiar appeal. To escape from the solid world of fact and rise into another element, a more fantastical element, was like an evolutionary ascent, a metamorphosis. The old life at Beverley, which had clung to him so damply, was left far behind as if it never belonged to him. He had shed it like the skin of a caterpillar, a chrysalis that becomes a butterfly. He was out, out of that narrow house in Flemingate by the railway line, and could go where he liked, be what he wanted. A blue sunny sky stretched before him. He was free.

There is no record of where Haselhurst flew or what he actually did over the period of the war beyond what he afterwards told people. It is clear that he was still a lieutenant at the end of the war, and that he had been given the three medals all such surviving soldiers received: the 1914 Star, the British War Medal and the Victory Medal. Sometimes, in later years, he wore a patch over one eye, and this, he let it be known, was on account of a war wound. Was he blind in one eye?* Sometimes, literally, he was – or so he said; at other times, metaphorically perhaps, though this may have been more of a wink at the world. Then, occasionally, the patch would give way to a monocle, but that was more for evening wear.

Against so much that was blurred, a few, rock-like facts stand out. Early in 1918 he is serving as an equipment officer (3rd Class) at a School of Aeronautics, and a little later he was transferred to a junior post at the Air Ministry, formed that year shortly before the Royal Flying Corps was re-organised into the Royal Air Force. All officers were given the option of transferring to the new force or retaining their army commission. After a short delay, Haselhurst chose to rejoin the King's (Liverpool) Regiment. There were, perhaps, two reasons for his choice. Though flying was endless fun, there would probably be less time in the air for him now that he was entering his late twenties – this air cavalry was for the very young. And then, the Royal Air Force did not have the social calibre and career prospects of the army. And this was all the more important

---

*His name does not appear in *The Sky Their Battlefield*, the massive list of those wounded in the air during the First World War compiled by Trevor Henshaw (Grub Street, 1995).

now because, on 11 September 1918, two months before the armistice, he married.

Cicely Last, his bride, was nineteen, the daughter of an Indian civil servant who had recently died. They were married in Bath. Her mother and sister were at the wedding, but of course none of his family. The story he later told of their parting following a quarrelsome game of croquet on their honeymoon seems far-fetched since his wife did not actually start divorce proceedings for another six years. It is easy to see how this wartime pilot from the skies might have appeared to her like a splendid eagle. But those days were soon over. Early in the summer of 1920 he was posted with his regiment to Ireland. Here, in these violent times, he concocted his parents' deaths in a car accident. He loved speed and had taken to racing cars himself, which may have given him the idea. He also claimed, from time to time, that he had been born in Ireland. Something did die there and something else was born. At the beginning of June 1922 he retired from the army with the rank of captain, and came back to England – but not to his wife Cicely who petitioned for a divorce on the grounds of his desertion. She was impatient to start again, having fallen in love with another man, Alec Carrie. He was the very opposite of a high flyer: a submarine man, naval officer, whom she married soon after the divorce came through. The following year, he gave her what she wanted – what Haselhurst had never given her: a son, whom they christened Michael. It is sometimes difficult to understand earlier parts of our lives. Of course, she was very vulnerable so soon after her father's death. But looking back, Cicely's one-time eagle appeared little more than a sparrow. 'Husband number two was the hero,' remembers her nephew, who grew up believing Haselhurst to have been 'a great, even shameful mistake, a charmer but a bounder; a cad even. So no photos exist, as far as I know, not even a wedding photo . . .'

But for others Haselhurst was still a romantic figure. Popularly known as 'Captain Haselhurst', he set himself up as a consultant engineer – a 'senior partner' as he sometimes described it, though he appeared to be working rather cleverly for himself and he was often away in Europe. He loved travelling, leaving places and people, as he loved speeding, loved flying, racing, moving on. He kept a little biplane at Brooklands where he also kept his car. It was a mystery how he could afford such expensive toys. No one remembers how he caught up with the mysterious Iseult, or more probably she caught up with him. There was no escaping Iseult once she had you in her sights – everyone agreed on that.

Iseult's father, Oscar Bland, came from a wealthy shipping family in Ireland, and lived rather grandly with his wife at Ettington in Warwickshire. In the summer of 1914, on the very day Britain declared war on Germany, Iseult had married a man with the exotic name of Ignatius Dracopoli. He was a twenty-six-year-old, up-and-coming surveyor from Chalfont St Giles. She was nineteen and still living with her parents. But she had a mind of her own. She was eager to shed her inappropriate maiden name and get on with life. Bland she was not. No threat of a world war, nor even the eruption of war itself, was to disturb her plans. Both families were summoned to the smart wedding at Stratford, and over the next eight years Iseult had two sons, Nick and then Jack whose birth coincided with his father's early death from cancer in 1923. He had left his widow with precious little money – six or seven thousand pounds. It would not take her very long to get through that with two children to educate. What made things worse was that her father's wealth had suddenly dried up. One day while he and his wife were in Paris they found that they did not have enough money to get home. The Bland family came to the rescue, paid off his debts and shipped him off to Rhodesia where they set him up as a farmer. But when Iseult and her mother went out to visit him, they found old Bland in a bar, drunk and destitute again. He liked the country life, he explained, and was recognised everywhere as an excellent shot: unfortunately he excelled at nothing else – certainly not farming. So he was shipped back to England. But from then on he was to be nothing but a financial liability.

Iseult needed a man with money to entertain her and help with the education of her children. Captain Haselhurst appeared to be that man. He had a small but apparently prosperous engineering business of his own – and his aeroplanes, his racing car and the yacht he was talking of buying reassured her: they were the playthings surely of a rich man. He was full of charm too, got on well with her father (both fancied themselves as good shots), and liked her two boys, though he did not appear to want children of his own, which was just as well. He was a couple of years older than she was and had briefly come to rest at Hoop Cottage, a few yards down Green Lane in Little Haddam where she was temporarily living after her husband's death. She decided to marry him.

Now aged thirty, Iseult was still a good-looking woman, fair-haired, always smartly dressed and with expensive tastes. She was also an excellent cook (and much enjoyed complaining about the food in fashionable restaurants). Haselhurst was dazzled by her, caught in the headlights. It was she who made the decision to marry – she made most of the decisions. As one of her sons later observed, she could give anyone a good run for his money and never took no for an answer. So, on 12 June 1926, she married Haselhurst.

This was very good news for the boys. Before long, their new stepfather, the Captain, was taking them both to Brooklands. Jack, the younger, was fearfully sick at first in his biplane, but eventually got used to it; and Nick enjoyed whizzing round the track in his racing car. Haselhurst would tell the boys all about the amazing races he had won and his exploits in the war. He showed them his medals too. It was as if he were a boy himself.

In 1929, he joined the British Motor Boat Company, and during the early Thirties, having given up flying, would often sail along the English and northern French coasts on his yacht *Frothblower*. This was the period when my Aunt Yolande got to know him (the 'H' with which he signed his letters stood for Henry, not Hazlehurst as I had imagined). He also bought a fifteen-ton motor cruiser named *Mongoose*. Sometimes he would go off exploring the waterways of Holland, France and Belgium, and once or twice went as far south as the Mediterranean with another boat enthusiast who was moored next to him in Cubitt's Yacht Basin at Chiswick. This was the Member of Parliament Lionel Beaumont-Thomas.

My family spent several weekends on Haselhurst's yachts in the 1930s, particularly on *Llanthony* which he later borrowed from Lionel Beaumont-Thomas. Inevitably they must have come across Lionel at one time or another, and perhaps even caught sight of his enormously tall brother Reggie – the two brothers were on friendly terms and quite frequently saw each other. But the Holroyds (my father, my aunt and even my grandfather) had only walk-on parts in the unfolding drama of these boats.

It was soon apparent that the Haselhurst marriage was not turning out well. Though Iseult had been taken with her new husband at first, she soon found him to be a man of straw. He had far less money than she supposed – at any rate, he did after three or four years of marriage to her. The more she got to know him, the less substantial and manly he appeared to be. The eagle had soared: a sparrow landed. Behind all his role-playing, he was never really a confident self-possessed man – what self was there to possess? She could not make anything much of him. She knew that his claims to have won all sorts of races were false – made up probably to impress the boys, but it didn't impress her. Eventually she put him down as an amiable rogue. But like her father, she discovered, he drank. Why did men she knew take to drink? What could it be? Henry, she thought, drank to be rid of himself, perhaps to be rid of her. In which case, she decided, he must have his way. Much as he liked the look of women, he was essentially a man's man, or more precisely a child's man, happiest perhaps in the army, but drifting nowhere in particular through civilian life in his cars and boats. It was time for her to disembark ...

... and to embark perhaps on the next boat. Lionel's wife, Pauline Beaumont-Thomas, soon began to have qualms about this neighbour of theirs in Cubitt's Yacht Basin. She used to hear her sometimes calling out to her husband Lionel from *Frothblower*. 'Leo! Leo!' she would call. It made her feel curiously uneasy – though in fact it was ridiculous: no one called him Leo. He was Lionel.

Pauline was only four or five years older than Iseult, but she appeared more mature. She had classical good looks but never troubled to dress smartly. Good breeding rather than good clothes – that was her. She was a country woman who liked walking and riding: those sorts of things. Usually in Herefordshire. At Great Bampton. Mind you, she was a damned handsome woman. According to her friends she resembled Elizabeth Bowes-Lyon (later the Queen and later still the Queen Mother). She resembled her so remarkably that from a few yards off and with the light behind her, you really couldn't tell them apart. It was extraordinary. Everyone said so. But she had less staying power than the Queen. She had been married to Lionel for some twenty years and knew well enough that he had an eye for the girls. But it didn't bother her. She trusted him – trusted him, that is, not to do anything *really* silly, especially now that he had a public position to uphold. She was often away in Herefordshire, near Madley, walking, riding, those sorts of things, while he was on the river in London, and so she was mercifully out of earshot of those frenzied cries, 'Leo! Leo!', coming now from her own boat, the boat that had been named after her, *Pauline*. Nor did she realise that Haselhurst, having fallen passionately in love with Yolande Holroyd, was content to leave Iseult to her own devices – those feminine devices that were spreading round and embracing her Leo.

Pauline was astonished, as well as deeply hurt, when Lionel came and asked her for a divorce. She could hardly credit that a man now entering his forties could be so bloody stupid. He was certainly no man of steel. His weakness made a mockery of their past. Once he had secretly married her for love; now in the light of publicity she was being asked to dissolve the marriage, also, allegedly, for love. What a farce! But it was also a tragedy. She would never forgive Iseult, and it astonished her that the two men, Lionel and Henry, could remain so friendly.

Of course Lionel did the gentlemanly thing, allowing Pauline to act as petitioner, and omitting Iseult from the whole sorry business. Though his family believed he spent a night with some woman hired to provide legal proof of adultery (he registered the dissolution of the marriage in *Who's Who*), the Court Service has been unable to find any record of this divorce, which seems inexplicable – it can't have been an annulment. In any event their marriage was apparently dissolved.

Haselhurst too petitioned for a divorce in the summer of 1933 so that he could be in a position to marry my Aunt Yolande. His divorce was made absolute in January 1934, and on 5 February Lionel Beaumont-Thomas gave up his political career and married Iseult Haselhurst in Kensington.

Also living in Kensington was his brother Reggie Beaumont-Thomas who, ten days later, married my grandfather's Dulcinea, Agnes May Babb.

They had a good deal in common, Henry Edward Haselhurst and Agnes May Bickerstaff. Both were born into poor, working-class families in the north of England, and left these families early on – left them as if for dead. Travelling south, they fashioned new lives for themselves with imaginary backgrounds. In one chapter of their lives, they both careered into my family before speeding on elsewhere, out of sight. If I were a fiction writer, I would arrange for them to meet, and find out how they got on. Would they be drawn from these parallel pasts into a natural intimacy, or feel awkward and be wary of each other? Perhaps they did meet: after all, one of them married a man whose brother married the other's wife. It is an oddly close, if separated, relationship. And if they did meet, would they have recognised at what point their lives had so curiously overlapped? Possibly not: which provides the fiction writer with an intriguing game to play. 'Oh, how I sometimes yearn for the easy swing of a well-oiled novel!' But I must not cheat. I must write my story without invention – or rather, I must use the characters' inventions and not my own.

Both of them appeared to be anomalies. While most people, then as now, develop an interest in their family histories, seeing in them their own places in group pictures extending over time, Henry Haselhurst and Agnes May Bickerstaff cut out their individual images from such groups and set them in different contexts and against grander backgrounds. Others might be content to find concealed layers to their identities and a new understanding of their roles within sagas of genetic patterns – continuing patterns that seemed to confer collective immortality on them. But for these two, such narrowness and repetition were not to be endured. For are we not, every one of us, the children of countless generations? And do we not therefore command almost infinite, unseen territory over which to travel – if nature is not confined by meagre parental habits?

Henry Haselhurst and Agnes May Bickerstaff denied their origins and went their ways, moving on wings of make-believe towards an unprecedented future. Neither was gifted with deep powers of imagination or intelligence, but they had energy, initiative and the courage to take risks. Both were motivated by romantic and perhaps economic dreams. And both, having no children of their own, felt an urge to escape what others may have seen as their domestic destinies.

> There's a divinity that shapes our ends
> Rough-hew them as we will.

Early in the twentieth century, Frank Harris rewrote Shakespeare's lines thus:

> There's a divinity rough-hews our ends
> We shape it as we please.

Now, a hundred years later, the word 'divinity' might plausibly be replaced with 'biology', and the prospect of genetic engineering seen as strengthening the validity of Harris's rewritten lines. Perhaps, after all, his was a vision rather than simply a boast.

In the meantime, his biographer Philippa Pullar's life, which in no obvious way resembled the lives of her parents, may be taken as exemplifying Harris's belief in the power of the individual will and the unexpected multiplicity of choices open to us. As society in Britain, rocked by two world wars, grew more unstable, so the push of those among its poorer classes began to be more strongly felt. The adventures of Henry Haselhurst and Agnes May Bickerstaff were part of this movement, making them not so much anomalies after all, but fragments of a new social experience.

Agnes May Bickerstaff was a year younger than Haselhurst and born a hundred miles west, over the Yorkshire border in Lancashire. Both their paternal grandfathers (coincidentally given the name William) were labourers in local chemical firms.

But Agnes May's mother, Robina Laurie, came from a lowlands Scottish family and her father was a 'dyker', a man who made stone dykes along the tide-swollen land above the Solway Firth. I doubt, however, if Agnes May and my grandfather ever spoke to each other of their Scottish mothers – that past was quite remote from them both during their few years together in the West End of London. In any event, Agnes May liked to believe that her Scottish ancestors were aristocrats and that she was descended from Sir Robert Laurie whose daughter, Annie Laurie, became the subject of a famous song written by her rejected suitor, William Douglas. 'And for bonnie Annie Laurie/I'll lay me down and dee.'

On 2 January 1888, Robina had married Joseph Bickerstaff, a glass-grinder, at Toxteth. She was twenty-eight, he five years younger. No member of their families came to the wedding, and Agnes May was not born for another seven-and-a-half years. In adult life, she never mentioned these early years in the north. She appears to have been solitary. 'I thought she was an orphan,' one of her friends told me.

She lived as if she were attached to no past, but pursuing an ever-changing future. But in fact she came from a close and crowded family and was the third of four good-looking, lively sisters. The name of the eldest, Ethel Arthur Bickerstaff, suggests some gender confusion (she would later be called 'Betty'). Born in 1888, she was almost seven years older than Agnes May – and three years older than the next sister, Robina Grey (called 'Ann'). In 1900 came another extravagant name, Melville Pretoria Bickerstaff (nicknamed 'Medal'). All four sisters were born in St Helens, but each one at a different address. The Bickerstaffs moved at least five times within a dozen years, and at every house they took in lodgers – sometimes simply nephews and nieces, but increasingly apprentices at the glass company where Joseph Bickerstaff worked, as well as young men, often from the south of England (the secretary of a YMCA office in

Sussex, a chap from the railways, and so on). There were always, it seems, young men, travelling men, staying at the Bickerstaffs' home while the sisters were growing up. The rent they paid enabled the family to employ a domestic servant (a big step up from the previous generation – Joseph Bickerstaff's mother could neither read nor write).

Robina Grey Bickerstaff was the first sister to marry. She suffered from a weak chest and was sent each winter to some relatives, the Baverstocks, in Thames Ditton where the climate was warmer. In October 1912, some sixteen days short of her twenty-first birthday (she made herself twenty-one on the certificate to gain legal authority), she became Mrs Arthur Edward Pennington, the wife of a twenty-seven-year-old cashier in Thames Ditton. The marriage certificate reveals that her father had by then risen to be an assistant manager at the Pilkington Glass Works in St Helens.

This marriage seems to have been a turning point in the story of the Bickerstaff family. Within a year they had all left St Helens and gathered in Southampton where Joseph, then in his forty-seventh year, started out on a new career as landlord of the Dock Hotel in Canute Road. Into this eccentric establishment they all piled: his wife Robina, their three unmarried daughters (including the eighteen-year-old Agnes May or 'Maimie' as she was called), as well as their newly married daughter, her husband and, in December 1914, a first grandson, Arthur Gordon Grey Pennington, who was born in the hotel.

The Bickerstaff story resembles the plot of an Arnold Bennett novel: the man from the north journeying south during times of trouble and seeking to improve himself and his family in the bustling new surroundings of a modern hotel. The hotel 'is in my opinion a unique subject for a serious novel', Bennett was to write in his diary when beginning *Imperial Palace*; 'it is stuffed with human nature of extremely various kinds ... characteristic of the age ... as modern as the morning's milk'.

The Dock Hotel, though faintly oriental, was not a hotel *de luxe*. There were no thick gorgeous carpets, no temperamental barmen or chefs to unnerve you with American cocktails or French menus, no shining millionaires from the New World, no encrusted foreign royalty or, as the plot develops, no expensive and mysterious corpses. The guests do not wear faultless evening dress and never handle complicated cutlery; they are seldom oppressed by an atmosphere saturated with deference. For it is a more homely place, the Dock Hotel, made out of three houses that have been knocked together – less in line with Arnold Bennett's tremendous *Grand Babylon Hotel* than the Potwell Inn where H. G. Wells's Mr Polly ends up. It has its share, however, of 'extremely various' human nature.

Why had the Bickerstaffs made such a dramatic change? These two years leading to the war were filled with social unrest. There had been riots in the docks, a mutiny in the army, violent suffragette demonstrations, loyalist shootings in Ireland, the Marconi share scandal and strikes by miners and the transport industry that suddenly brought the country to a halt. It was worse in the north. The headlines of the *St Helens Reporter* on 29 March 1912 biblically prophesied: 'The End in Sight'. While the Coal Mines (Minimum Wage) Bill was being debated in Parliament, the miners themselves were looting coal from the Lancashire claypits and many railway services were cut. There was fighting in the streets and one man in St Helens was killed. 'Pilkington's works close. Thousands of men thrown idle. Relief agencies at work', announced the *St Helens Reporter*. Because it relied on fuel supplies, the Pilkington Glass Works was forced to shut its gates, and Joseph Bickerstaff became one of six thousand men suddenly without a job. He hung around with his wife and three unmarried daughters hoping for re-employment, but when the King and Queen came to St Helens the following year to open the new glass works at Cowley Hill, he was not taken on. He had climbed the ladder and become an assistant manager: then the ladder had been thrown to the ground. After working at Pilkington's, man and boy, for thirty years, he was left without any chance of a job for the remainder of his life. What prospects there were lay in the south. He gathered together all his savings, sold up and took his family to Southampton.

The Dock Hotel was a public house with bedrooms. It was owned by Graves, the brewers, which appointed Joseph Bickerstaff as its landlord. This was to be a completely new career for him, but for his wife Robina, now in her early fifties, it was not so very different from managing the lodging houses in which she had lived all her married life, or even looking after other families' children in St Helens as she had done before her marriage. But Southampton itself was a very different town.

In the early Victorian days it had been a seaside resort and this southern part of the town a fashionable residential quarter. The sea came up almost to where the hotel now stood and the curve of their street traced an ancient shoreline and the arc of a once-popular bathing beach. But all this was gradually obliterated during the mid-nineteenth century with the advance of the South Western Railway (two railway lines crossed Canute Road) and the building of the Southampton docks on the mudlands. Canute Road itself was at the centre of all this development, no longer part of a residential area, but a place of active commerce. At one end of the road stood a three-storeyed Italianate block with rusticated round arches: the Terminus Station (much admired later on by John Betjeman). To the east, it ended in the sand mills at Floating Bridge Road, where a steam ferry crossed the sluggish River Itchen.

It was not a beautiful place in which to live. *Kelly's Directory of Southampton* shows Canute Road to have been simply a line of shipping agents, engineering firms, trading companies, the freight departments of Cunard and White Star, emigration offices, ice storage plants, fitters, painters, clearing houses, seamen's unions. But scattered among all these business buildings were a few taverns, cafés and small hotels.

The Bickerstaffs were to be connected with the Dock Hotel for almost twenty years. During the Second World War, it was destroyed in one of the terrible bombing raids that were to damage thousands of houses and leave Southampton a ruined place, a ghost town. Another twenty years, and the architectural historian, Nikolaus Pevsner, is walking along the 'sardonically named' Canute Road on one of his celebrated 'perambulations'. He starts off from the threadbare municipal landscape of Queen's Park with its 'grotesque monument to General Gordon'. The once busy road is now largely derelict, though many of the old buildings, sometimes unoccupied, still stand, in partic-ular the monumental South Western Hotel, attached to the Terminus Station (later to become an 'Ocean Casino'). This had been Southampton's first great hotel, the sort of proud illuminated place, with its promise of perpetual gaiety, that warmed the heart of Arnold Bennett. 'The whole building very nearly convinces,' Nikolaus Pevsner concedes. He continues walking, past the 'poor neo-Wrenish' old Custom House, the stone-dressed Cunard office, and a few decayed relics from that era of confident expansion as far as the Canute Castle Hotel. This 'agreeable piece of whimsicality', which was there when the Bickerstaffs arrived, delights him. He is now only two hundred yards from where the Dock Hotel itself stood. He looks up, concludes from what he sees that 'there are no strong architectural reasons for proceeding further', and turns back.

I have been able to find no photographs of the Dock Hotel in the volumes on pre-war Southampton; but pictures of the docks themselves, with their handsome array of liners and steam yachts, gleaming with the promise of thrilling adventures as they lie, gently rocking on the languid waters, destined for Asia, Europe and the Americas, show why Joseph Bickerstaff was drawn from the wastes of St Helens to this prosperous region.

From the Dock Hotel itself you could hear on boisterous days the flapping and jangling forest of masts from the smaller vessels and see the stir of lights and flags belonging to the great ships of the main – the China Sea, the Indian Ocean and other enticing waters leading to the uttermost ends of the earth. Agnes May, however, did not find it a glamorous place in which to live. Even as a child she had thought of herself as 'superior' to her family and was teased because of this. In her fantasies she was sometimes illegitimate, sometimes adopted, sometimes American. In any event definitely not a Bickerstaff. Travelling to the soft south of England reinforced these illusions which grew and flourished like exotic flowers in a hot house. She longed, as it were, to be transplanted, to go to London and grow into someone else. At the age of nineteen she has left Canute Road and by twenty she is married to a second lieutenant in the London Regiment, and living in Surrey. On the marriage certificate she writes that her father is dead – indeed she never appears to have seen him or her mother again during the remaining twenty-five years of their lives. One of her nieces remembers how Agnes May's mother would increasingly search the newspapers for some mention of her. She felt sure that her missing daughter would one day dramatically hit the headlines. But, for good or bad, she was gone for ever.

For Agnes May's sisters, the Dock Hotel seems to have been rather an exciting place. In their teens and early twenties, they were a strikingly attractive group, these sisters, high-spirited, good-looking, fond of parties – especially fancy-dress parties. They loved dressing up and going out – and this was to be the tenor of their lives as they began speaking with new accents, becoming different people as they entered a middle-class life. It was perhaps hardest for the eldest sister to adapt to these new ways – she was already in her early twenties by the time the family arrived in Southampton. But the second sister (who had spent many winters in the south) adapted brilliantly, using these early fancy-dress parties as if they were rehearsals for her post-war career on the stage (where she was to perform using the name 'Ann Penn'). As for Agnes May, her future life may be seen as a fancy-dress affair, with many changes of role, many changes of cast and background.

One of the best features of the Dock Hotel, especially for the youngest sister, Medal, was the number of new faces you saw there. People were always coming and going – mostly men, of course, men with stories, men of all sorts: tinkers, tailors, soldiers, sailors . . .

Did any rich men, as well as poor, turn up there? In 1918, at the age of twenty-nine, the eldest sister, Ethel Arthur Bickerstaff (now definitely called Betty), married a New Zealander, a lieutenant in the Royal Navy Volunteer Reserve named Vivian Guesdon – both of them giving the Dock Hotel as their residence. The Guesdons were to be the least well-off of all the Bickerstaff sisters. She suffered an early miscarriage, following which they had no children. After leaving the navy Vivian Guesdon worked intermittently as a marine engineer. For the last twenty years or so of his life, he seems to have been partly dependent on his wife, who managed the Anchorage Hotel, a mile or so inland from the Dock Hotel, near Southampton Cemetery. They were helped financially by her youngest sister's family. When he died in 1961, Vivian Guesdon was worth little more than a thousand pounds.

But the husband of Melville Pretoria Bickerstaff, the youngest sister Medal, was minded to be rich. True, the man she chose was a divorced gentleman, probably paying alimony, when he arrived at the Dock Hotel in the early 1920s. But Albert Rogers came from a family of quite successful shipping contractors. He owns as much on his marriage certificate, but does not admit his connections with the pork butchers at Canal Walk, Rose and Rogers, 'makers of the celebrated sausages'. He was almost twice the age of his wife, who was twenty-four when he married her in 1925. The Penningtons, the Guesdons and Bickerstaffs, all their families were at the Rogers' wedding. The only sister missing is Agnes May.

By 1925 Agnes was divorced from her first husband and had married her second husband whom she would soon be leaving to become my grandfather's mistress in the West End of London. How much of all this did her family get to hear? Almost nothing, it appears. There is only one verifiable moment of contact. In the summer of 1920, on the day of Agnes May's second marriage, her younger sister Melville Pretoria, then just turned twenty and working in London, had come to the wedding in Kensington Register Office. It must have been her steadying presence that prompted Agnes May to bring her father alive again on her marriage certificate and describe him, with only slight exaggeration, as a hotel proprietor. But after this, as Agnes May's life grows more erratic and extraordinary, all contact with her sisters and her parents ends.

She did, however, visit Southampton once. She arrived with her third husband, the small-headed, immensely tall, semi-paralysed Reggie Beaumont-Thomas in the late 1930s. They hastened on board a liner at Southampton Docks, a few hundred yards from the Dock Hotel, and sailed for the United States. It was to be a pleasure cruise, but there was little pleasure in it after Reggie fell on deck (it was claimed he slipped on a banana skin), injuring himself painfully. He was never very agile, never too steady on his feet, though he blamed the shipping company for his accident. When they got back to England, he busied himself lethargically with a legal action against the company, which eventually lapsed at the beginning of the war.

There was little chance of Agnes May visiting her sisters, the nephews and nieces she had never seen, or her mother and father when embarking at Southampton because, as she had explained to Reggie, her parents were dead and she had no family. In any event, by the late 1930s, circumstances had

changed. Joseph Bickerstaff's name disappears as landlord of
the Dock Hotel in 1920 and, for the next ten years his wife
Robina becomes its landlady. Evidently something serious had
happened. In 1925 Joseph was not with the rest of the family
at his daughter Melville Pretoria's wedding. Had he left them?
It seems that his health may have failed dramatically. His
grandchildren did not know he was still alive while they were
young, and their grandmother never spoke of him. He was
admitted as a rate-aided inmate to the West End Institution
which specialised in the 'observation of mental defectives' in
the Dickensian-sounding district of Shamblehurst. Then, at the
beginning of 1942, following a pronounced 'attack of mental
illness', he was transferred to Knowle Hospital, the local 'lunatic
asylum', where he was placed next to another Bickerstaff, a
clergyman suffering from sexual delusions. He had heavy
bruising to his chest and many cuts to his body – almost certainly
the result of an air raid. After a week here, and on the very
day he was to be discharged, he died, aged seventy-five, the
immediate cause of his death being a heart attack.

Robina passed her retirement years with two of her daughters' families: the Guesdons at the Anchorage Hotel, and the
Rogers family with their teenage son and daughter outside
Southampton, at Myrtle Cottage, Brockenhurst, where she
lived during her last years. She was not able to see so much
of her eldest grandchild because the Penningtons had by then
moved to London. But in 1943, after her death at the age of
eighty-three in St Catherine's Nursing Home at Christchurch,
the family buried her next to her husband in Hollybrook
Cemetery.*

Between her father's and mother's deaths, late in 1942, Agnes

*Grave number 205 in section L12. Also buried there are their daughter Ethel
Arthur ('Betty') and son-in-law Vivian Guesdon.

May finally parted from her husband Reggie Beaumont-Thomas. Following his fall on the boat to the United States, Reggie had been largely confined to a wheelchair. It was a horribly tedious and frustrating business for her. But she bravely refused to be imprisoned by his illness. After all, it was wartime, a time (as the newspapers often reminded their readers) to keep the spirits up. To enjoy oneself became a patriotic duty, a moral necessity. One night while she was out with an admirer, their house at Bushey was burgled, the burglars attacking Reggie, overturning his wheelchair and leaving him shocked and stranded on the floor. He seemed destined for disaster: first the rumours of infantile paralysis and 'sleepy sickness'; next the fabulous accident playing 'Rugby at Eton'; then the legendary banana skin in mid-Atlantic; and now beset by burglars in his home. When Agnes May eventually returned, he ordered her to leave. He could not stand it any longer. He would settle an allowance on her (as he had on his Parisian dancing wife); he would pay her to go away and stay away (as my grandfather had done). The pattern was by now familiar.

Where did she go? Evidently not to Southampton (I can find no entry for her in the telephone books, register of electors, or any other directory there). By the end of 1943 I have again lost her.

Around this time, the figure of Henry Haselhurst begins to slide into the mists of rumour and speculation. His last letter to my Aunt Yolande was written from the north of England in 1942 soon after he joined the Cheshire Regiment. He sends her a snapshot of himself in his uniform. Of course this is not the man she met and fell in love with ten years earlier. The photo shows a full, modestly moustached, fairly unremarkable face, with a lazy eye, almost smiling, nearly anonymous. He seems to be making the best of things whatever they are, and looks quietly confident that, somehow or other, these things will get better. And he is right. But meanwhile, despite the line of medal ribbons, the 'wings' from the Great War above them, the buttons and the regimental badges decorating his collar and hat, the picture is not quite convincing. It is the officer's hat that is at fault. It tilts towards his left eye, the good eye, and looks not so much rakish, nor even racy, as simply too large. But he will grow into it. He has been given the substantive rank of major and is stationed (though not permitted to tell my aunt this) at Caldy Manor, a not uncomfortable, red-brick, Elizabethan-style mansion, much knocked about by its recent owner, a Liverpool cotton broker.

For a year Haselhurst and his regiment trained for combat in the pleasant woods and meadows nearby – and passed on their training to the newly formed Home Guard and Civil Defence Authorities. Their days were crammed with guard duty, drill, kit inspections and fatigues (mainly road-mending, trench-digging and potato-peeling). This routine, of which he some-times complained to women and children, had a rhythm that was strangely comforting. To prepare themselves for war the men handed in their rifles. They were then given sten guns and mortars which needed months of nervous tactical handling in the fields. They moved from draughty huts into draughty tents, and then back again into draughty huts. It was an uninvigorating programme. Their main enemy over all this time, this marking of time, was not the Germans but their own boredom. They longed to meet a German, even an Italian would do.

Finally, they were judged to be ready for active service. On 9 September 1943, now a temporary lieutenant-colonel and as officer in charge of the Thirtieth Battalion of the Cheshire Regiment, Haselhurst embarked with his men on the *Athlone Castle*. They were being sent to North Africa which had recently fallen to the Allies. Much that they did over the next eighteen months was then, of course, pretty well top secret. Now it can be told. From Algiers they struggled into a transit camp on the

windswept plain of Blida from where, being overwhelmed by
several unprecedented floods, they quickly moved up to Sousse
where their soldierly work could begin in earnest. From hidden
parts of their heavy baggage, deeply concealed, the Battalion
Dance Band unwrapped its armoury of musical instruments
(chiefly a piano and some drums) and struck up a wonderful
din around a huge camp fire that Haselhurst had ordered to
be prepared. During the next three weeks their morale was
continually sustained by these open-air concerts and dances
under the stars, also by drinks parties and race meetings which,
with a little light shooting in defence of their rations, 'taught the
men to be alert and self-reliant'. In short, to keep on their toes.
Altogether it was capital fun, as was a hard-fought football match
against the Irish Guards at Bizerte (though they lost 0–2).

Excitement soared even higher when, in mid-December,
battling against the weather, under darkness and in heavy rain,
they joined a convoy sailing up the Mediterranean to Taranto.
Next morning they pushed on by slow train to Salerno where,
three months earlier, the Eighth Army had begun its invasion
of Italy. They started their duties here immediately by opening
a soup kitchen which Haselhurst himself, as it were, super-
intended (you need to read this aloud for the full flavour).
There were other employments too for the Cheshires (such as
keeping a weather eye on the docks and a sharp look out for
air raids). But the single most dangerous hostility (it covered
their uniforms and instruments with an awful grey ash) was to
be the eruption of Vesuvius that March.

Eight days after the Fifth Army entered Rome, Haselhurst
led his band of Cheshires into the city. They had 'received the
compliment', the regimental history reveals, of doing garrison
duty there, parading outside Allied headquarters ('vital installations') to general applause (one general went so far as to call
them 'a bloody fine crowd'). But their time was not without
hazards. For example, Mussolini's ornate building in which

they were billeted proved 'highly dangerous', having no handrail on the stairs. Their other duties were 'heavy' but 'miscellaneous'. They raised pigs and fowls on a farm outside Rome, and helped the farmer grow his grapes, melons and tomatoes. Haselhurst's 'constructive ideas' were singled out as being of special help to the Pioneer Section which equipped one of the theatres in Rome for additional dancing. 'Constant vigilance was needed' over finding schemes to equip the men for the threat of civilian life to come. To this end they took lessons in elementary bricklaying, carpentry and motor mechanics. Everyone had to keep mentally fit too, which is why they held plenty of sports meetings. Rome, so people said, was a beautiful city, but it was also a damn warm spot, as the Cheshires discovered, in which to play cricket. Yet 'nothing pleased him [Haselhurst] more than to be present and take part in these many functions', the regiment's *Oaktree Journal* records.

The *Cheshire Regimental History of the Second World War* contains a photograph of Haselhurst sporting his Royal Flying Corps 'wings' from the First World War (their outline repeated in the smiling curve of his mouth and razor-thin moustache above a monocle suspended from his neck, like an exclamation mark dramatically cancelled by the diagonal slash of his Sam Browne). These travels with the Cheshires since leaving Blighty might not have held the escapist rapture and high romance of his air adventures, but the nail-biting football matches and tense race meetings, the continual swimming and dancing were rather terrific. He seemed to feel most at home when travelling abroad like this and treated the men of the Cheshires as if they were his own family.

He was also absorbed into an Italian family with whom he had been billeted, and this became part of his own preparation for civilian life. He had got to know the nineteen-year-old, dark-haired Palmina Abbagnano, and her younger sister Mariolina, through their aunt, who was English. The two sisters, daughters of an Italian philosopher, were greatly taken with him, especially when he came to dinner one evening with General Alexander (the Cheshires were acting as his 'flagship guards' in Rome). Haselhurst was now in his fifty-second year – almost three times Palmina's age and five years older than her mother. But he didn't look it, and they didn't know it. So where was the harm? It seemed as if the years had rolled back and those pale, indecisive episodes with Cicely, Iseult and Yolande were all cancelled. On 5 April 1945, a month before VE Day, at the military station of the Central Mediterranean Forces in Rome, he married Palmina and began a new life.

It began well. Six weeks later he was sailing back to England and then travelling up to Cheshire with his regiment and glamorous young wife. On 1 October, having exceeded the age limit for the reserves, he finally left the army. Altogether he had passed over half his adult life as a soldier and airman – almost twenty years, and they had been happy years. Military life lent him an objective and the very uniforms he wore, with their decorations and insignia, appeared to clothe him with a convincing identity. He was granted the honorary rank of lieutenant-colonel and for the rest of his life was known simply as 'the Colonel' (as he had been 'the Captain' following the First World War). He collected more medals and on his retirement was made an Officer of the British Empire (OBE). 'We have lost not only a grand commanding officer,' recorded the *Cheshire Regimental History*, 'but also a good friend.'

Fortunately the Colonel already had some good friends in Cheshire, in particular the Blond family whom he had met there in the early days of the war. Neville Blond was a wealthy textile manufacturer (a specialist in rubber clothing) who had developed an interest in the arts (he became chairman of the English Stage Company) and who was shortly to be appointed UK trade adviser to the United States. He was happy pursuing his successful career; but he was far from happy at home. His wife

Eileen had married him in 1927 on the rebound from an intense love affair, and by the time Haselhurst turned up at their large house in Cheshire, Neville had gone south to live with a girl he was to marry in 1944. There were two sons living in Cheshire with their mother, one of whom, to my surprise, I realised that I knew.

Anthony Blond was a celebrated, rather risqué London publisher at the time I began writing books in the 1960s. His authors ranged from Harold Robbins and Simon Raven to Gillian Freeman and Jean Genet. When I located Anthony, now living in France, he gave me an introduction to his brother Peter (who worked at Sotheby's) and together they helped me to understand something of Haselhurst's post-war life.

The Blond brothers' memories of Haselhurst are very similar to those of the Dracopoli boys, Iseult's children, in the 1920s. He is their hero too: a tremendously exciting, funny, adventurous man who made their days vivid with possibilities. It seemed to them as if Biggles, the ace flier and 'air detective' created by W. E. Johns, whose gripping yarns they read each month in *Modern Boy*, had come to life and entered their world. When they were out with him, listening to his exploits as they all whizzed around the country on their bicycles, they felt as if they too were caught up in strange adventures and had become Biggles's daredevil pals, Algy or Bertie or, best of all, his tough, loyal commando-companion Ginger. These had been exhilarating days for the boys.

So when Haselhurst came back from Italy and, with his wife Palmina, rented an apartment in their mother's huge and rather empty house in Cheshire, they were overjoyed. He was such a wonderful mentor, gentle, firm, informative, encouraging: a father figure. They infinitely preferred him to their remote, real father Neville Blond whom, to their delight, Haselhurst nick-named 'the Bullfrog'.

Hasel did everything the boys expected of him. He got a

fast car, an Allard, and he fitted up and restored one of his
pre-war boats for more adventuring at sea. It was not the
motor yacht *Llanthony* which he shared with Lionel Beaumont-
Thomas in the 1930s (on to which he had invited my Aunt
Yolande and even my father for weekends). *Llanthony* had
been acquired by the government in 1939 and became one of
the famous fleet of 'little ships' – mud-hoppers, sailing yachts
and pleasure steamers – that ferried their way under heavy
German bombardment back and forth between the English
coast and Dunkirk, rescuing British soldiers from the beach
(*Llanthony* took back 280 soldiers). Then, after the war she
was given back to Lionel's widow, Iseult Beaumont-Thomas,
who sold her to Lord Astor, raising exotic fantasies of her
future use by his most enticing and notorious guest, Christine
Keeler.*

---

*Llanthony was commandeered during the Dunkirk evacuation by Rear-
Admiral Robert Timbrell of the Royal Canadian Navy. He had been surprised
to find that she was a gentleman's yacht, ill-equipped for naval duty, her only
weapon the 1914 Colt on Timbrell's leather belt. With a crew of two civilian
diesel engineers from London Transport and six lumberjacks from
Newfoundland, she set course for Dunkirk with orders to anchor off the beach
and take on as many troops as possible. 'It was a very shallow beach,' Admiral
Timbrell remembered, 'and at low tide, the water went out a long way. We
were being shelled by the Germans [and] the town was in flames . . . We could
take about 120 on each trip and our instructions were to return as soon as we
were loaded. We did that for a couple of trips. Then, on the third or fourth trip,
we got bombed . . . We were hit on the fo'c'sle. I lost about five of our crew and
both my anchors snapped . . . the fuel pipes were severed so that both engines
died. We drifted on to the beach. It was a sunny afternoon and there were
shells falling all the way down the beach with thousands of soldiers asking to
be taken back to England. It was day four of the evacuation and a stream of
ships were going in and out. We drove some trucks into the water to form a
small jetty. Then, at high tide, we could go alongside the trucks and men could
walk on top of them and jump aboard . . .

Such images, even if false, would not have amused Colonel Haselhurst. For all his free and easy ways, he was something of a puritan. Though he had never mentioned her in his letters to my aunt, he had become rather specially fond of Eileen, Neville Blond's divorced wife. She was an Italian, like his wife, which was convenient. But he couldn't hide his disapproval of her love affairs – nor of her remarriage after the war – indeed he was inclined to blame Eileen for her bad influence on Palmina.

As they grew up, the Blond brothers, Anthony and Peter, began looking at Hasel in a new way. Although he remained a generous friend to them during their adolescence (taking them both to France on his yacht and letting them 'bugger up the boat' without too much fuss), he did not seem to have any close and lasting friends among the adults. He was gregarious, but also somewhat solitary. Sometimes he gave the impression of being proud, even cold or at least distant,

---

'[A sergeant] asked if he could help and I told him to get a Bren-gun carrier and drive it out as far as he could in the water until the engine stopped so that I could use it to anchor by. That is what he did and my two civilian diesel engineers repaired the fuel pipes, got the capstan going and winched us off . . . and we sailed back to England . . .

'Our last trip was the tightest. The Germans had started to enter the town and to close a ring round Dunkirk. There was no way we could return any more. Back in Portsmouth I had a job to find anyone who would take over *Llanthony* from me. She was beaten up with bullet holes in her funnels.'

In 1952 she was bought from Lord Astor by Baron Kronacher's Société pour l'Exportation du Sucre, registered in Antwerp, and eighteen years later passed on to the Yvomarcos Shipping Company. From 1985 to 1993, renamed the *Golden Era*, she cruised between Greece and Turkey as a charter yacht. In 1995 she was discovered lying in Rhodes Harbour in a dilapidated state, and put to sail on one engine by Ms Nicola McGrail who took her to the Netsel Marina at Marmaris in Turkey where, after extensive renovation, she became a showpiece. She returned to British waters, with all her original fittings, for the Diamond Anniversary of Dunkirk Little Ships in June 2000.

and beneath his cheerful demeanour, they noticed, lay a film of bitterness and resentment. This usually came to the surface when he spoke about women. He was curiously censorious, even rude, about his wife when speaking to the boys. He had married Palmina, he told them, in order 'to have a fuck'; and she had married him, he added, as a way of getting to England.

In 1948, after three years of marriage, he began divorce proceedings against Palmina on the grounds of her adultery. It was difficult sometimes to understand his attitude. Often he appeared to be the complaisant husband, but then would suddenly come out with bursts of hostility. Indeed he had little good to say about any of his wives. Yolande he never mentioned. She was one of his secrets, like his parents and the first sixteen years of his life which he still embroidered with grand fantasies. Once, coming nearer to the truth perhaps, he remarked that, having successfully escaped the 'love' of his elderly mother, he had no wish to be 'possessed' by any woman. So, in a sense, his divorce from Palmina, which was made absolute at the beginning of 1949, was a relief. He resumed friendly relations with her family and was best man at her sister's wedding. Palmina herself went on to marry an estate agent and have two sons whom she named Peter and Anthony, after the Blond brothers. She was, in her own right, a rich woman, and perhaps this was the source of Haselhurst's resentment. He was no longer a gentleman 'of independent means' as he claimed his father had been, as he wished his father had been.

He returned to London and moved into Dolphin Square, a ten-storeyed, red-brick apartment block in Pimlico that features in the novels of C. P. Snow. Also moving in at the same time was the novelist Angus Wilson. His biographer describes Dolphin Square as being 'the height of chic'.

It occupied over seven acres, had its own private
gardens and some fine river views. The furnishings were
Art Deco, there was a restaurant with an orchestra and
a view of the swimming pool, and each room had a
radio with a Bakelite control which could be switched
to the Home, Light or Third Programme. The décor
reminded Angus pleasantly of his sea-voyage to South
Africa, and the nautical theme was echoed in the names
of the houses: Grenville, Beatty, Howard, Hood ...

It was and is inhabited by a wide range of
characters – diplomats, politicians, con men, artists, spies,
call girls, minor royals and many others with good
reason to wish for trouble-free, well-run anonymity.

Angus Wilson and Henry Haselhurst both courted anonymity,
its peace and independence, having cut free from their families
and being known now by surnames that differed from those
of their parents. But, within the same building, they occupied
very different worlds. Angus Wilson's flat looked inwards on
to the private gardens where he sat creating extravagant,
macabre scenes. Haselhurst's flats, first in Drake House then
in Nelson House, both looked out along the river where his
auxiliary schooner, *Black Pearl*, lying at anchor nearby, could
carry him away, anytime, anywhere, like one of the characters,
Swallow or Amazon, in Arthur Ransome's adventures.

He used Dolphin House as an office as well as his home
and employed a widow, the devoted Mary Gardner, who was
twenty-one years younger than himself, as his secretary. After
bumping into him in the street one day his ex-stepson Jack
Dracopoli, recently demobbed from the RAF, went to work
for Haselhurst and noticed what a clever engineer he was.
During the long fuel crisis after the war, he introduced himself
to several laundries, rearranging their systems of burners so
that they operated more efficiently – he was paid a percentage

of what they saved in fuel costs. Later he designed the drums for the 'four-hour cleaner' which was popular with house-wives during the 1950s. But he took little pride in his engineering ingenuity. Listed as 'Colonel Hazlehurst OBE', he was now a member of the Royal Thames Yacht Club in Knightsbridge, the Royal Solent Yacht Club on the Isle of Wight, the Royal Motor Yacht Club at Poole in Dorset and the Royal Air Force Yacht Club. He enjoyed passing his time with these boat people, ex-officers, 'company directors' – high fliers who had no need to be tethered to land jobs.

Women still found him attractive. Even in his sixties there was still a boyish charm to his enthusiasms. He would regularly take women out to theatres and restaurants in London, and for cruises along the river and round the coast, but these relationships were flirtatious rather than sexual. He once confessed to one of the Blond boys that despite his three wives and innumerable girl-friends, he had had comparatively little sexual experience – very little in the context of 1960s mores.

On 12 March 1964 Haselhurst turned seventy. He would spend more of his time indoors during his seventies. A friend had given him a red setter called Gary with whom he played extravagant games of hide and seek in the apartment – the sort of games that he and I have been playing. When Gary died, he was given another dog, a chocolate-coloured poodle, Piper. It seems an unlikely breed of dog for the Colonel, but like my Aunt Yolande he appears to have been fond of all dogs. Putting his black patch over one eye, he would increasingly sit in the window of his apartment during the evenings watching the boats, criticising their manoeuvres and, like Dylan Thomas's Captain Cat, recall many glorious fictional episodes from past days. 'I can find no evidence that he was involved in yacht racing,' writes the archivist of the Royal Thames Yacht Club. Yet his mantelpiece and tables glittered with silver cups and medals which were continually polished up by his stories. His secretary Mary Gardner's young niece, Sally, loved being taken to Dolphin Square and listening to these stories. Once upon a time, she thought, he must have been like Little Lord Fauntleroy. He was so quick-witted, such fun; no wonder that, with his strange eccentricities (he cleaned his teeth with a pair of tweezers) he seemed like an aristocrat in an old adventure book, a far-off romance. Once he took Sally and her aunt across the Channel all the way to France. They could have got off, gone anywhere, started a new life. It was an oddly exciting game – and in some sense (though she did not know this) it was what he had done with his own life.

When I spoke to Sally Harris and outlined some of Haselhurst's background, I could hear that she found what I told her difficult to believe. She did not want to disengage herself from the spell of his long-remembered tales. He was so wonderfully convincing and made the world a more interesting place.

What made him all the more exciting was the hidden part of his life. There was something mysterious about him. He didn't like being photographed or asked direct questions by children about his own childhood. But he gave them clues sometimes. When, very occasionally, he referred to his mother, he called her 'Mama' which was obviously very upper-class. Perhaps he was illegitimate – the son of an Irish aristocrat. He had let fall one or two hints in that direction. He had, too, a gold ring with a strange Celtic seal which he never denied was his family crest. Each month, too, he received through the post a cheque from an unknown source. 'They pay him to keep away,' his secretary Mary Gardner remarked to her niece. But who did and why? He was often abroad on his boat and several times made mysterious journeys to Guernsey, visiting someone there and coming back grave-faced. Could it be that his real father lived in exile there? Or was he being sent to Guernsey on secret missions? Then there were the telephone calls, a good number of which, he acknowledged, came from his friend Field Marshal Lord Montgomery. Sally Harris and her young cousins eventually decided that he was almost certainly a spy. Such speculations created a luminous atmosphere around him. And they gained thrilling credibility when, in the 1960s, William Vassall was jailed for spying after secret documents and a miniature camera were discovered in a concealed compartment of his flat in Dolphin Square. What a nest the place was!

It transported him, too, from all those meagre connections with the Haselhursts of Beverley – until, that is, falling seriously ill in the mid-1970s, a genetic connection pulled him back to them. He discovered that he was suffering from prostate cancer, which had killed his father and, recently, his brother Roland. In the summer of 1975 he was operated on at St Philip's Hospital in Sheffield Street, near the Royal College of Surgeons. Peter Blond went to see him there. There was something special he wished to say. Mary Gardner, Haselhurst's secretary, had been with him for some thirty years, always looking after his business, sometimes looking after him. She had come to work for him in her early thirties and was now in her early sixties. Peter knew how devoted she had been to him. If Haselhurst died, she would be left without an income and without status. He must not let this happen. He must marry her as soon as possible. There had been some talk of their marriage; now there must be some action. This was what Peter Blond told him.

Lying in his bed, very weak after his operation, Haselhurst listened to this suggestion agreeably enough. 'I'll do it some time,' he promised. But it was obvious that he would do nothing – he was not well enough and also perhaps not keen enough. He had not troubled to make a will, to consider what would happen to Mary, or really anything else, after he died and the game was over. It was not quite his style. Mary herself must have realised this and in self-defence had begun saying, half as a joke, that she would never marry someone who had already been 'used' by so many women. It became clear to Peter Blond that, to do what was right, he must organise it all himself.

The marriage ceremony took place beside Haselhurst's bed in the hospital ward, with the surgeon, some nurses, and the driver of a car Peter Blond had hired to bring along the Registrar. Peter himself brought champagne for everyone, and one of the nurses lent Mary her ring. It was an oddly moving ceremony. When it came to filling in the marriage certificate, Mary gave Nelson House now as her address and revealed that her father had been a 'dining car conductor' on the trains. Haselhurst said his residence these days was St Philip's Hospital and asked the Registrar to put 'Independent Means' against his father's profession. Then it came to the signing of the certificate. They propped him up against the pillows, they put a pen in his hand, they held the certificate against a hard board for him; and he began to write his name. But he could not do it. There was what might possibly be an 'H' and then perhaps an 'a'. But after that, where the spelling of his assumed name and his family name part, his handwriting gives out. There is a faint squiggle, then it stops.

The Registrar had not been very willing to conduct this unusual ceremony. Puffed up in his brief authority, he had put all manner of bureaucratic difficulties in the way – and now he had an early train to catch. He examined his watch; he examined Haselhurst's signature; and he decided it would not do. It was inadequate. He therefore refused to pronounce them man and wife – and said he must leave with the wedding unaccomplished. He had warned them all this was highly irregular, and now concluded that it was officially impossible. Again Haselhurst tried to write – but was he really trying? Peter Blond believed he was, and told the Registrar that he would make an official complaint if he left the proceedings incomplete – indeed he would not allow the driver to take him to the railway station. He would miss his train. So the Registrar gave in, annotated the certificate twice in the margin – and everyone drank champagne.

The surgeon had already informed Mary Haselhurst that there was no possibility of her husband recovering and so, towards the end of August, she removed him from the hospital and took him to the 'Hostel of God' on the north side of Clapham Common. This was the forerunner of the hospice movement in Britain, founded by the Sisters of the Poor in the late nineteenth century and named after the Hotel Dieu in Paris. By the 1970s, it occupied four substantial eighteenth-century houses looking down on London and the Thames. It was run by the formidably autocratic, eighty-year-old Sister Magdalene and her company of nuns of the Order of St Margaret who specialised in caring for those who were dying of cancer.

In many ways this was a fitting place for Haselhurst to end his days. These houses, with their spacious gardens and conservatories, had once belonged to wealthy gentlemen and been visited by Pepys and Evelyn, Tennyson and Browning. They still retained the atmosphere of private residences. The hostel had royal patrons, too, who would sometimes pay visits when they were in the neighbourhood.

The Hostel of God had a second name: the National Free Home for the Dying.* It existed outside the National Health Service and was dependent on private donations for its free care. But the mid-1970s was not a favourable period in its history. Though the nuns were practised at alleviating the anguish of dying and at changing a patient's attitude to death, they were falling behind the times in medical treatment. 'We have done our best,' said Sister Magdalene. 'We must not

---

*It is now called Trinity Hospice.

cling to the past.' But it was not until 1977 that they were able to leave, and the hospice went on to benefit from developments in palliative care. When Haselhurst was there, the official history records, there was not enough money to buy new equipment 'and visitors were sometimes shocked by its absence'.

Haselhurst died at the Hostel of God on 12 September 1975. He was aged eighty-one. Because he had made no will and the circumstances of his marriage were so peculiar, probate took over six months to prove. But his wife, who had looked after his business for so long, managed everything very competently, and the final value of his estate at a little below £35,000 was modest – she was herself to leave four times this amount when she died some years later.

Haselhurst was cremated later that month and his ashes scattered at sea where they could move with the tides upon the living waters, with the weather and the winds, all over the world, free from the imprisoning ground of fact.

Almost the last library that invited me to speak on autobiography and family memoirs was the one my aunt and father used in Surrey. I drove down in the late afternoon, remembering the journey I had made so soon after my aunt's death, and stopped at the cemetery to look at her gravestone. It was surrounded now by other gravestones – a village of the dead – but looked good, I thought, with the evening sun lighting up its Shakespearean words of farewell. As I walked back along the green pathway towards St Mary's Church, I wondered what she would have thought of my search for Haselhurst and the discoveries I had made about this man she loved and, for so long, hoped to marry. It was impossible to know.

That evening in the library I spoke a little about my aunt and also my father. A few people in the audience had known them by sight or by eccentric reputation – even my father's dog came in for some generous comments. Towards the end of the discussion I asked, as I had so many times elsewhere, if anyone knew anything about Agnes May Beaumont-Thomas: and suddenly a woman at the back of the room stood up and said yes, she did know of her. I felt a frisson of excitement as I made plans to see her later at her home.

Sarah Constantine had married into the family of the one original Beaumont-Thomas who had fallen off my list – Lionel and Reggie's manly, almost equine sister Irene. She lived only a mile from where my aunt and father lived. And she knew Agnes May by reputation – Reggie she used to see at Brighton after they had separated. She liked him. He was a kindly uncle. But he had, she noticed, a very short attention span and would grow quickly irritable if people made demands on him. He was lazy and rather immature: his women and cars were like toys – dolls and Dinkies. He wanted an easy life and, though still well off, was becoming concerned about money (he didn't like people using his telephone). The trouble with the Beaumont-Thomases, she indicated, was the very opposite of that in my own family: they simply had too much money, many of them. She leafed through some family albums. The pictures were often filled by a curious obstruction, the people being pushed to one side by vast cars – in much the same manner as my own family albums were dominated by huge dogs. Sometimes there were no human beings to be seen at all in these Beaumont-Thomas records – just an elbow or an ankle in the margins. In other photographs they cowered inside or lurked behind these monstrous cars which were Reggie's passion.

Sarah Constantine was sure that Agnes May returned to London after leaving Reggie. So I recommenced my search by looking through London telephone directories from the early 1940s. It seemed a somewhat random trawl, inspecting these ranks of subscribers, but quite soon I caught sight of her. By 1944 she was back in the West End and living at 58 Buckingham

Palace Road, an apartment block not far from Victoria Station. The building no longer exists, but this was patently an address of high respectability. There were ladies' hairdressers, French cleaners, antique shops, confectioners and restaurants nearby – and then, perhaps more dubiously, the Central Association for Mental Welfare and the rather drastically named World Prohibition Federation. The building itself contained almost fifty flats (Agnes May lived in number 43) and they were mostly occupied by retired clergymen, high-ranking officers and foreign diplomats, with a sprinkling of well-connected widows (Mrs Bingham-Bird, the Hon. Mrs Eveleigh-de-Moleyns) and a few late-flowering debutantes from the country. In short, it was an irreproachable place.

But Agnes May does not stay there long. Before the end of the 1940s she leaves these bishops and brigadiers, these admirals and ambassadors of Buckingham Palace Road, and reappears at 37 Ennismore Gardens, in Knightsbridge – the very address at which my stepfather Edy Fainstain was meeting his mistress, Mrs Hanbury. Perhaps this odd coincidence gives a clue to Agnes May's status there. But again, she does not stay long – just a couple of years. Then she is off and I lose her once more. I cannot tell where she is heading because I do not know in what year she died and have been unable to find her will. Did she, like Haselhurst, omit to make a will or have I simply been unable to locate it? I have ploughed laboriously through twenty-five years following her separation from Reggie to see if she remarried, and checked if there is a Beaumont-Thomas in the lists of wills over this period. I abandoned my search at the time she would have reached her mid-seventies, having found nothing. But there is one person I know who might be able to turn up something.

David Sutton is a carefully bearded, eternally youthful, radically minded, softly-spoken-yet-eloquent socialist gentleman, a football and manuscripts scholar, well known in Reading (where he is chairman of the Labour Council) and in Texas. By training he is a librarian and works as director of research projects at the University of Reading Library. Two of these research projects have been sponsored by the Strachey Trust, a charity created in the early 1970s by Lytton Strachey's sister-in-law, Alix Strachey. I am one of its founder-trustees and for twenty years have watched David Sutton steer these difficult projects to success. One of them is a Location Register of English Literary Manuscripts and Letters covering the eighteenth to the twentieth century. The other is even more forbidding: an information database of copyright holders (compiled jointly with the University of Texas). Copyright in published writings persists for seventy years after the author's death and, since there is no legal requirement to register it, the identities of the living owners is all too often lost. The only sure way of tracing a copyright owner is to follow the trail through a series of wills made over these seventy posthumous years. So David Sutton and his team are often at First Avenue House in Chancery Lane where the Court Service now keeps wills, and they have become expert at digging them out of the obscure past.

I had few qualms about misusing David Sutton's time. He likes a challenge and has a good-natured passion for solving other people's problems – and he solved mine. One day he telephoned to say that he thought he had found her, under the name Agnes Thomas. Next day I went back to First Avenue House and checked the entry. She had the right initials and was the right age. It had to be her. I ordered a copy of the will.

Agnes May died in Worthing at the end of 1974. She was in her eightieth year. Her will is an unusually detailed document, an inventory of objects carefully marked out for their new owners: a candlestick for one; some carpet runners for another; a wastepaper basket for a third. There are precise sums of money, ranging from twenty-five pounds to two hundred pounds, reserved for her doctor, the porter at the apartment block where she had been living, a secretary in her solicitors' office and people she knew in the old racy days at Bushey and in London. And she makes amendments to these amounts in codicils. She, who has been a go-getter all her life and never had a job, has prepared for herself another role in death: that of the patron and benefactor. Her pages are covered with donations to charities: to an old people's home, to the Fire Service Benevolent Fund, to the Sussex Constabulary (Charitable) Fund, to the Royal Society for the Prevention of Cruelty to Animals, to the Royal National Institution for the Preservation of Life from Shipwreck, and others, several others. Her charitable gestures are flung wide. But 'I have made no provision in this my will,' she writes, 'for my Husband who is a man of Independent means and deserted me in 1942.'

In her sisters' wills there are gifts to one another and to their nephews and nieces.* But, though Worthing is only fifty miles from Southampton (and a mere ten miles from Hove where her sister 'Ann Penn' died in 1970), Agnes May has still never met these children, probably does not know their names, and makes instead a donation to the National Society for the Prevention of Cruelty to Children. Unlike her three sisters, who have worked steadily all their lives, she has taken risks, gone from one man to another, spent their money, cut her losses, gambled and lived as if there were no tomorrow. But when tomorrow came and the men left, she has found it difficult to keep up her standard of living which must have been why she moved from London. At her death her estate

---

*From these documents I was able to make the Bickerstaff family tree at the end of this book, and to locate one of Agnes May's nieces.

is valued at £14,000 – on the whole less than that of her sisters' families. But all of them, and their families, have risen above their parents' generation and are estate agents, company directors, colonels' ladies – or they have gone to the United States and made history there. They are no longer recognisable as 'working class'.*

Many people feel a reluctance to make wills – a reluctance to which Haselhurst succumbed. But Agnes May apparently enjoyed making an inventory of her acquisitions (they are like his silver cups and medals). There are over seventy items and they tell the story of her life, only part of which I can decipher. Among her mirrors and lights, the cocktail cabinet and tallboy, are those Lalique glass decorations which my grandfather gave her in the late 1920s: the vases, lamps and bowls, the ashtray with surrounding birds and 'smoke-coloured' scent bottle with apple-blossom stopper which have survived almost fifty years. But, so far as I can see, there are no family albums and nothing from her very early years – the years that she has denied. Two other items catch my attention: 'My Oil painting half length Portrait of a Lady in blue dress by Rolin [sic] Goodwin' and

---

*Agnes May's great-niece, Penelope Margaret Ann Pennington (born 1938), however, appears to have had a more adventurous life. At Corfe Castle, in 1956, embroidering her surname to Grey-Pennington and declaring herself to be an actress, she married John Alexander Cumnock Forbes-Sempill – and almost landed in the ranks of the aristocracy. Had she remained married, she would have found herself styled as Lady Forbes of Craigievar, wife to the twelfth baronet, with a family motto ('Watch'!), a coat of arms involving muzzled gules, a crest displaying 'a cock proper', and supporters that featured a bear and a lion rampant. She would also have settled with these distinctions to live in Kirkcudbrightshire, where her great-great-grandfather, Thomas Laurie, had worked as a dyker. Unfortunately, after a protracted divorce that eventually omitted co-respondents, the marriage was dissolved in 1964 and, under one name and another, she was free to pursue further adventures.

'The water colour Portrait in silver frame in my lounge'. If I can find one of these portraits I will at last see what she looked like.

There are three chief executors of her will: Mrs Vera Wall, who lived near her in Worthing; Mrs Patricia Ellegard who came from London; and Agnes May's solicitor. Each of them receives £2,000 (equivalent to ten thousand pounds at the end of the century) in addition to an assembly of gifts. I decided that I would try to find the solicitor first, hoping that his firm may have kept some files of Agnes May's papers.

It is extremely unusual for a solicitor who is appointed executor of a will and whose company charges fees for the administration of that will to receive money and gifts – indeed it would not be permitted today. The practice has changed its name and its address since Agnes May's death, but I was able to track it down. Agnes May's solicitor, though long retired, was still alive, they told me, but he lived in a nursing home now and would probably be unable to help. While one of the clerks looked in the storeroom for any lingering Agnes May files (none would be found) I wrote a letter to the solicitor's wife.

She is rather intrigued and then perhaps a little perplexed by what I tell her. I explain in my letter that Agnes May, being extremely grateful for the legal work her husband did for her in the last difficult years of her life, had left him several presents (actually six champagne glasses and fifteen red Venetian wine glasses, a Queen Anne table, a Lalique vase with thorns, a hippopotamus ashtray and so on – but I do not specify these items, suddenly aware that they might resemble a list of indictments). When we speak to each other on the telephone, she grows curious – and then somewhat incredulous. What exactly had this woman left her husband? I begin to chronicle the gifts. But she knows of no champagne glasses – has never seen them. Surely I must be mistaken. I change direction and ask whether she ever met Mrs Beaumont-Thomas herself, but she has no memory of her ('he never discussed his clients with me'), and nor, she adds, has her husband any memories – she has read him my letter. When I ask her whether, nevertheless, he might possibly remember her oil portrait in a blue dress, she answers for him, her voice rising slightly, saying that, since he never visited her apartment, he could not have seen it. I do not press her further. It is a long time ago – over a quarter of a century. So we end our conversation cheerfully enough.

To find out something of the next executor, Mrs Vera Wall, I decided to go down to Worthing. Maggie and I were spending a weekend nearby, so we started early and, a finger on the police street map which the West Sussex County Librarian had sent us, negotiated our way through roundabouts and along one-way systems to the eleventh floor of a car-park tower – then raced through cascading rain to the Worthing Reference Library. Here we took shelter and stationed ourselves for the day's work.

I am not a fluent worker. The researcher and the writer are never the same person. Their temperaments and motives are different – the writer seldom seems to know what he wants and cannot give clear instructions to the researcher. It is not an easy partnership: it is a dance in the dark. While I am tunnelling deep in my research, I dream of the writing to come as if it were an ascent into sunlight. I long to be arranging the facts I have found into coherent and imaginative patterns, telling stories, recreating worlds. But then, when I actually come to the writing, and am a stationary figure at a desk, in a bed; when those empty pages, these empty pages, confront me, I feel restless and impatient. Am I not getting slower? Is there not less time? I must get a move on. I look back nostalgically at those exciting detective days when I was on the road, in the air, off to all sorts of places, roaming the country, picking up clues and signs, making some of the discoveries I need to recreate these lost lives (and recreating, perhaps, my own life too). Why did I not relish the pursuit more at the time? Partly, I think, because these bits and pieces I call my discoveries, when I actually dig them up, present themselves as problems I may never solve. A pile of odds and ends – how can I connect them all? The connections are made in the writing, and what is unknown, even unknowable, may be, as the biographer Hilary Spurling has suggested, key elements in a biographical design, like the empty areas in lace which are part of a pattern, or like those dark holes in space which hold secrets. Until I can find a design that makes sense of everything, including what is not found, my discoveries are no more than moments of light which briefly illuminate the outlines of dark shadows. Initially I can detect nothing more than a worrying jumble of shapes. So I am an anxious worker: anxious over research, anxious within my writing – with spasms of unexpected happiness when I seem to make connections and the partnership works.

Also I am not methodical. I work by instinct. Certainly I have ends in view. But I do not know how to reach them. My plan at Worthing Reference Library was to discover when Agnes May arrived in the town, locate her addresses and go to look at them, and also find anyone who knew her, in particular Mrs Vera Wall to whom she left that half-length 'Portrait of a Lady in blue dress'.

The Worthing Reference Library has electoral registers, street directories up to 1975 (when Kelly's went bankrupt), intermittent old telephone books, microfilm copies of local newspapers – all of which may be useful. It is a well-ordered library, but all reference libraries arrange their material rather differently and as I entered and glanced round, I had the sensation of being a traveller without a compass. Maggie asked where she should go now, what I would like her to do, and I gestured vaguely towards the shelves while ordering some old telephone books from the basement. After a badly choreographed hour, we had not progressed very far. There is no notice of Agnes May's death in the *Herald* or *Gazette*, and no attention is paid to her charitable gifts, though these newspapers enjoy chastening their readers with luxurious descriptions of other people's generosity. As for Mrs Vera Wall (who lives with her son or husband Stephen Wall), she left Worthing a couple of years after Agnes May died. I already knew Agnes May's last address from her will and could see from the map that it was not far from the library. The sun was now shining and Maggie, anxious to escape from such haphazard and lacklustre work, volunteered to go in search of it and also visit the art gallery to see if Robin Goodwin's *Portrait of a Lady in a Blue Dress* was hanging on the wall.

I bent over the street directories and electoral registers plotting Agnes May's movements and did not notice the vast storm tumbling around outside – until, two hours later, a drenched, dismal and dripping figure came to a halt next to me. It was Maggie, back from her 'field trip'. I had misread the map or rather miscalculated the distances. But she was able positively to assure me, almost with a sense of triumph, that there were no Robin Goodwin pictures in the gallery. After drying out a little, she took on the most dire of jobs, what I call the 'death machine' – microfilms of all the people who died in England between 1977 and 1992 (when the parade ends). She was making an inventory of V. and S. Walls so that I could later check them out at the Family Records Centre in London to see if I could track down that portrait of a lady in a blue dress. We had not finished our work by the time the library closed that evening.

So we returned next morning to complete our lists and notes. Agnes May appeared to have spent her last ten years in Worthing. She arrived in late 1965 or early 1966 and lived in one of the maisonettes at The Towers, in Grand Avenue, West Worthing, to which we drove that afternoon. This is a

tall, ornate building next to the front with fine views of the
sea. It is a typical example of imposing sea-front architecture
and looks expensive – probably too expensive. After two or
three years, Agnes May moved to a less grand, red-brick apartment building, Downview Court in Boundary Road. These are
small, comfortable 1930s flats with well-kept gardens but no
sea views. After another two or three years, she moved again,
this time to a more modest building of the same period, Arundel
Court in Lansdowne Road, where she remained for the last
four or five years of her life. All these buildings are in the same
residential area of West Worthing, but each marks a step down-
wards. Her flat at Arundel Court is on the first floor (there is
no lift) and has a narrow balcony facing east towards the town.
It is adequate, but by no means luxurious. Agnes May was in
retreat.

At about the same time that she was moving into Arundel
Court, Vera and Stephen Wall came to live in Pembroke Avenue
a few hundred yards away. Since I had been unable to trace
where they went after Agnes May's death, I decided to walk
down Pembroke Avenue and, like a postman or milkman, knock
at everyone's door. Dogs barked at me, curtains twitched and
flapped, and I asked anyone brave enough to open the door if
he or she knew Vera or Stephen Wall. No one did, but almost
everyone thought that he or she knew someone who might –
until I came full circle empty-handed. I stopped people in the
street, went into banks, the Post Office, estate agents, undertakers, the crowded shopping centre nearby. Agnes May and
Vera Wall had left no echo or rumour of themselves, no living
memory.

After our two days in Worthing we drove back to London.
For Maggie it had been a rather dreadful glimpse into the biographer's life – so banal and disappointing, the work, a mixture
of arid drudgery in the library and pointless effrontery in the
streets. What was the value of this raw, invasive questioning

about ordinary people who never invited, never wanted, such persistent interest in them? Perhaps the motive behind this dogged pursuit, this hunt, was revenge against those who wounded my grandfather and my aunt. I felt slightly rattled by these speculations, believing my quest to be merely 'the proper study of mankind' – our appetite for discovery which is part of a natural curiosity about all life.

When we got back to London, Maggie ascended with relief into her fictional world (which uses researched facts as a runway into imaginative flight) and I went in search of Agnes May's half-length portrait in a blue dress. Because there are so many people with the name V. or S. Wall, it proved impossible to trace this picture through wills (though someone thought he'd seen it on the *Antiques Roadshow*). I decided to find out more about the artist.

Robin Goodwin is an elusive painter, though his name is familiar to me. This is because, I remember, in the late 1940s he rented Augustus John's studio in Tite Street (John, having pocketed the money, continued to turn up at the studio causing much chaos and many mixed feelings). He had begun his professional career at the end of the Second World War, taught for a time at the Slade School of Fine Art, did commissioned portraits for the money and sea pictures for love. He appears to have exhibited everywhere, from the Royal Society of Marine Artists in Greenwich to the open-air shows along Victoria Embankment, but he joined none of the painters' societies, not even the Royal Society of Portrait Painters where he exhibited a number of his paintings. Among the list of his known portraits, none appear to be of Agnes May – she is unlikely to be the subject of *Sea Urchin*, *The Third Mate* (a woman) or even *Girl with a Fringe*. Robin Goodwin almost certainly painted Agnes May in Augustus John's studio in the late 1940s or early 1950s, after which time he turned increasingly to marine subjects. The portrait, which was probably

commissioned by an admirer, is as much a signpost in her life
as her Lalique glass, but I could not find where it pointed.

Robin Goodwin died in 1999 aged ninety and his widow
has no record of his portrait commissions. He is remembered
best by his pupils, the most famous of whom, the successful
animal painter David Shepherd, describes him as 'a fully qualified, hard-working sensible artist' who 'taught me to paint (if
I had not met him I would be driving a bus)' and adds 'I owe
him everything'. But among his sitters, David Shepherd cannot
recall Agnes May. I contact several other painters whom he
taught – among them one who reminds me that she held an
exhibition of her work at Philippa Pullar's house in Barnes.
Robin Goodwin, she confirms, was a very successful society
portrait painter fifty years ago, and so it is not surprising
that no one can identify this single sitter. Somewhere perhaps
his unidentified oil painting, half-length, of a lady in blue
dress still hangs, but I have run out of clues that might lead
me to it.

So I switch my attention to the second picture, described in
Agnes May's will as a 'water colour Portrait in silver frame'.
This has been left to the third executor, Mrs Patricia Ellegard.
How can I find her?

David Sutton knew the answer. It is www.192.com, a website
called Info Disk. Its principal source material comes from the
British Telecom directories and the local electoral registers
throughout the United Kingdom, all loaded into a database
which can be searched in a variety of ways. 'This is nothing
more or less than helpful, publicly available information,' David
assured me, 'but I am always a little uneasy when I recall that
I first learnt about it from a radio programme about the likely
modus operandi of Jill Dando's murderer.'

What I was looking for was simply an address to which I
could write. Fortunately the surname Ellegard is extremely rare.
David Sutton found her in less than ten minutes, living just

outside London in the stockbroker suburbs of Middlesex – golf course and new town country.

Dear Mrs Ellegard,

    I wonder if you could help me. I am very anxious to find out some information about the late Agnes May Beaumont-Thomas who died at Worthing towards the end of 1974. She was, earlier on, a close friend of my grandfather about whom I have been writing. I have never seen a photo of her, and her life after the 1940s is rather a mystery to me. I believe you knew her over these later years and would be very grateful for any help you could give me – perhaps (if it would not be inconvenient for you) I might pay you a short visit. In any event I very much look forward to hearing from you.

I ended the letter with an apology for writing out of the blue and troubling her in this way, posted it that evening, and waited.

I waited a week. Then Mrs Ellegard telephoned while I was out and left a message. She doubted whether she could give me much help. I could not ring her back because her number had not been disclosed. I recognised that this was a delicate matter and needed diplomacy. After another fortnight I wrote again, thanking her for ringing, asking her to telephone me again and giving her various times when I would be at home. She did ring again and I invited myself to tea, promising to bring her a copy of my family memoir. She was somewhat reluctant to see me, but what persuaded her was my under-standable wish to see what my grandfather's friend, her friend too, looked like. She had a picture of her, she said – and I knew at once that this must be the 'water colour Portrait in silver frame' listed in Agnes May's will.

The following week I drove to Middlesex, arrived early, parked my car and looked around. This is a fairly expensive area of tree-lined avenues and squares, neo-houses with neat gardens, occupied, I imagine, by retiring, middle-class, successful businessmen and their families. I walk the streets until I can arrive at Mrs Ellegard's house at the polite hour. Then I ring the bell, speak into an entryphone, and stand there like a soldier. I hear the laborious sound of bolts being moved across and keys twisted: then the door opens.

Mrs Ellegard is a refined, rather nervous, white-haired lady probably in her late seventies. She lives alone in this well-protected house set in a quiet circle of differentiated yet similar houses, her husband, a 'hotel negotiator', having died three years ago (she points to his cheerful photograph in colour on the wall). I follow her into her drawing room and she offers me a cup of tea. But when I accept this offer, we find ourselves confronting the first of several difficulties that afternoon. How is she to deal with this tricky problem of tea? It is a rather awful complication. Should she leave me, a stranger, alone in the drawing room or take me with her into the kitchen, which is hardly the place for a man? Neither course strikes her as quite satisfactory, altogether correct. I consider cancelling the tea, but feel I cannot. We stand paralysed with sensitivity. Then I suggest that I can read her newspaper – a rather sensational tabloid I see lying on a chair – and sign the copy of my memoir which I have brought for her while she marshals the tea. In manly and ladylike fashions, we will, I point out, be simultaneously employed. Rather hesitantly she agrees to this solution and I am left to ponder the agonised negotiations ahead.

There are, I notice, no books in the room; nor can I see any of the items Agnes May bequeathed her friend – two silver swans, a sweet basket, the Lalique vase with thorns . . . It is a rather bare place, this room, painted hospital-white, spotlessly clean and extremely tidy – it shines with taste and the absence of life. There are a few plates on vertical display, a jug, one meagre plant on the window-sill above the discreet radiator. The atmosphere is that of a museum from which all objects of interest have been removed. What I see gives me few clues as to the owner's personality. The polished surfaces with large, immaculate spaces in between convey a sense of controlled anxiety.

Ten minutes later we are sitting at different sides of this room with our cups of tea and pieces of cake trying to make conversation. I hear myself parading my credentials. I mention the Royal Society of Literature and even my CBE. Why am I doing this? It is to establish my respectability and set my host's mind at rest. But my babbling is not noticeably successful. Mrs Ellegard may not read books, but she has an active imagination and entertains a very lively fear of the world outside her house – about which she must read each day in her newspaper. I have come from that fearful world outside and she feels apprehensive.

Our conversation over the next hour is stilted, but I do learn some interesting facts and fictions, about Agnes May. She had asked Mrs Ellegard to be one of her trustees and executors of her will because she had no family of her own, being a single child, and brought up in an orphanage. She had married once, nursed her husband when he contracted polio, and then been dreadfully hurt and shocked when he, an invalid, began an affaire with one of her friends. It did not seem natural or right. Until the 1940s, she had lived a very smart society life, but came down sadly in the world after separating from her husband, and would sometimes speak feelingly of her 'reduced circumstances' when Patricia first met her in the 1950s.

Patricia Ellegard cannot remember how they met, though it was before her own marriage. She does remember, however, being invited early in their friendship to tea in Agnes May's flat at Chelsea Cloisters in London, and being given strawberries. She had been impressed by those strawberries which were quite a rare luxury then (post-war food rationing having continued in Britain into the 1950s). 'Manita knew how to do things well,' she adds admiringly, still remembering the strawberries.

Manita is the name she gave Agnes May. Hearing her use it for the first time, the letters re-form in my mind and appear as 'Man-eater'. But of course I cannot say this. Patricia knew that some people called her 'Maimie', but she liked being called different names, new names, and this one, Manita, seemed for some reason to suit her. It stuck.

I ask her about Chelsea Cloisters and am told that Manita had an admirer who lived there, a gentleman who would escort her to parties and take her out to dinner; but Mrs Ellegard cannot remember his name (and he is not mentioned in Agnes May's will).

Our conversation stops, and I try to get it going by asking some innocuous questions. Why did Agnes May leave London? Mrs Ellegard tells me that she went to Worthing to be near her ex-husband in Brighton, Mr Beaumont-Thomas, with whom she hoped to be reunited. She was not sensible with money. The clouds were darkening, but she had not saved for a rainy day and by the mid-1960s could no longer afford her carefree strawberry life in Chelsea.

The conversation stops again. And starts again. Patricia Ellegard (or Patsy, as she was called) used to go down occasionally to Worthing where she met Manita's new friends and fellow executors, the solicitor and the Wall family, Vera and Stephen. She did not like them – and they did not like one another. The solicitor was a 'creepy' man who she felt had never looked after Manita's financial affairs as he should have done, though they saw a good deal of each other. As for Vera

Wall, she found it difficult to understand what Manita saw in her. She was a nondescript, rather common woman in her late fifties, perhaps older, who worked in the Post Office, and was probably too interested in Manita's money – what was left of it. As for Stephen Wall, he was taken out of Manita's will because she felt he was being too friendly. Perhaps he wanted the Wall family to get all her money – in any event something had gone wrong between them, though not with Vera Wall. She stayed, like a limpet. On one occasion Mrs Ellegard took her husband Neil down to Worthing to give Manita some financial advice after Mr Beaumont-Thomas had settled extra money on her, but when they arrived they found that she had already blown a good deal of it on an expensive fur coat. That was very typical of her.

We stop and start again. Usually Mrs Ellegard travelled to Worthing by herself. Manita, who owned a small car, would meet her at the station and take her to her club. 'I will introduce you as my niece,' she rather mysteriously volunteered on her first visit, and this pretence was kept up, though there were very few of these introductions. Manita appeared to be leading a reserved and isolated life, almost secret, without real friends or family, and to be suffering from some anxiety. In the last year or two, when she became ill with a heart condition, Mrs Ellegard did not see her at all. Whenever she telephoned, Vera Wall would answer – it was very off-putting. She did not go to her friend's funeral either, because the solicitor discouraged her from doing so. In her opinion, Manita had fallen into very bad company at Worthing. It was not surprising that, though she was really a vulnerable and sensitive woman, her contact with the world had also made her hard – that was, very critical of people, especially men.

This story has come out in bits and pieces, and now there is no more that Patricia Ellegard can tell me. So I ask her about the picture – the 'water colour Portrait in silver frame in my lounge' – that Agnes May had given her. It has been in Mrs Ellegard's cupboard for the best part of twenty-five years, but she has kindly found it, dusted it, in preparation for my arrival, and now brings it into the drawing room and places it in an armchair. So, for the first time, I see my grandfather's mistress, for whom he left home and almost, with the aid of many lawyers, bankrupted the family.

My first reaction is one of bewilderment. What am I looking at? Is it really a watercolour? It seems more like a coloured photograph. It is not large, about 60 by 25 centimetres, I estimate, within its silver frame. But I have no doubt that I am looking at an accurate representation of Agnes May. She is aged, I would say, about thirty – in her early thirties anyway – which is the time my grandfather knew her. She wears a soft, draped, floral-print dress of silk crêpe-de-chine. Her hands are raised as if in prayer – not quite prayer – on second thoughts the gesture is rather more winsome, almost flirtatious though not immodest, and her head is cocked slightly to one side as she eyes the artist/cameraman with a slight smile. In the lower right-hand corner there is a signature in what appears to be pencil. Mrs Ellegard and I approach the picture together, crouch and bend before it as if it were a religious icon, and try to decipher the name. 'Janet' is fairly clear, but the second name is more difficult to read – it may, we agree, be 'Evans'.

We move back and begin our negotiations. I ask whether I may borrow the picture for a few days, have a reproduction made, and return it to her within the week. But Mrs Ellegard says she would rather not do this. I ask whether, at my expense, she would hire a professional photographer herself to make a copy for me. But Mrs Ellegard replies that she would prefer to photograph it herself and, to close the matter, she goes to get her camera and, trying to avoid reflections from the glass, she begins snapping it at various distances from the chair. The film

in her camera is fairly new and it will be several weeks, she
informs me, before she can have the negative developed. 'I must
not keep you any longer,' she suddenly announces, ushering
me to the door. I have delighted her enough. Outside again, I
hear the bolts and keys being manoeuvred with a sense of relief,
and I walk back to my car.

I sit in the car making notes on what Mrs Ellegard has said,
and reflect on the implications. She has not thought to reveal
much, partly because she is on her guard (she might have
spoken more easily to another woman – as Patsy and Manita
probably spoke together) and partly because she is not given
to analysing character and describing details (she cannot recall
the oil painting left to Vera Wall). Much of what she has told
me of Manita/Agnes May might, equally, I think, apply to
herself, though she has been more cautious in her life – her
drawing room is a monument to caution. She exudes an aroma
of respectability, but beneath the acquired cultivation of her
voice runs an insinuation of scandal and unsavouriness – the
sort of drama she must spy, as through a periscope, in her
newspaper. She has conjured up in my mind a picture of Agnes
May at the centre of a small gang of people continually at
odds with one another, like a trio or quartet which cannot
find the right pitch or tempi. I begin to see them as aspects
of Agnes May's own character which, for ever inharmonious,
has carried her to this lonely and insecure conclusion of her
life. Patricia Ellegard represents a younger version of herself.
She must have been pretty when young, upwardly mobile like
Agnes May herself, but, whatever adventures she may have
had, she steered her way skilfully through the hazards. She
has come through. Agnes May could well have relived something of her youth in Patricia's company even if she could not
learn from her carefulness how to play her cards better. She
needed men around her who were married, who could give
her reassurance, protection and the prospect of a good life,

men who knew the male world of business. But there had to
be a sexual ingredient in her relationship with men, even if it
was only in play, and she could not really make friends with
them since instinctively she was always making use of them.
Even in her late seventies she dyed her white hair blonde and,
as Mrs Ellegard hinted, she may well have flirted with Stephen
Wall. Perhaps she was at her most natural with Vera Wall,
who was nearer her age than Patricia Ellegard and whose class
appears to have been similar to Agnes May's origins. There
was no need to pretend that she was a niece or any other relation, no call to take her to the smart club in Worthing. She
could relax and be her old self. Vera looked after her almost
like a domestic servant (like the domestic servant at the
Bickerstaff home when she was young). This is how I interpret what I have been told.

While waiting for Mrs Ellegard to send me the photograph
of Agnes May, I followed some of the leads she had given me.
First of all I went to the Chelsea Reference Library in the King's
Road and examined in the street directory the lists of tenants
living at Chelsea Cloisters. Agnes May appears to have moved
there in 1947 and for a couple of years she had two addresses –
her apartment at Ennismore Gardens in Knightsbridge as well
as flat number 637 in Chelsea Cloisters. By 1951 she has given
up Ennismore Gardens and transferred to flat number 911 on
the top floor of Chelsea Cloisters where her new friend Patricia
comes to tea.

I know Chelsea Cloisters. It is some three hundred yards from
Sloane Avenue Mansions where my mother lived between
husbands in the late 1940s and even nearer to Nell Gwynn
House, the block of flats where I wrote my first book in the
late 1950s. I must surely have passed Agnes May in the street
during the years we lived so close to each other. It is a tantalising
thought.

Could there be anyone there now who remembers Agnes

May? I find one tenant, a legend in the building, who has been there almost fifty years. He is eager to help. Yes, he remembers her vividly – he is almost sure he does. Isn't she the woman who was so often at Buckingham Palace? His voice cracks with amusement, with excitement. A lady-in-waiting, that's what she was, sparkling with evening jewels. What else would I like to hear? What would please me? We float in this dreamland until we are out of breath, when I fall back to earth and try to find a more solid trail of research.

Chelsea Cloisters, built in red brick during the late 1930s, is one of four large, rather forbidding but comfortable, private blocks of flats between the King's Road and Fulham Road in Sloane Avenue. It was known in the 1950s for its artist tenants, most particularly Matthew Smith, and it seems likely that it was during her early days here, probably commissioned by her gentleman admirer, that Agnes May had her portrait painted nearby in Tite Street. Robin Goodwin, unlike Augustus John, preferred middle-aged to very young sitters. This oil painting was clearly a more substantial work than the modest, silver-framed rather mysterious picture I had seen at Mrs Ellegard's house, but it must have shown Agnes May some twenty-five years after my grandfather knew her. For my purpose, the 'water colour in silver frame' is the portrait I want, and after two months of waiting I grew anxious as to whether I would ever see it again.

In early December Mrs Ellegard sent me a tasteful Christmas card and, my hopes rising, I immediately sent a card decorated with angels to her. Another month went by and my hopes began to sink once more. Then, in January, she sent me the fruits of her camerawork. Only one photograph had come out at all reasonably, but it was small and not perfectly in focus. I was immensely relieved yet slightly disappointed, and decided to write to Mrs Ellegard and argue my case for a professional reproduction.

Dear Mrs Ellegard,

    I really am most grateful to you for seeing me,
answering my questions, and taking these photographs.
It was kind of you.

    I immediately took your photos to see if they could
be professionally enlarged ... [but] though it is a very
good amateur photograph of what is evidently a
charming watercolour, I was told it would 'not meet
reproduction standards'. This puts me in some difficulty.
I am very conscious of disturbing you and have no wish
to intrude. On the other hand, here is an artist's portrait
that was painted to be seen – and would do no one any
harm by being seen. It is my belief that Agnes May
would not have kept this portrait if she had disliked
it ... I therefore have to ask whether you would mind
having it professionally reproduced at my expense ...
The larger oil painting which was left to Vera Wall has
been lost – and I consider this a great shame and not
what was intended when it was left to her. You have the
only likeness of Agnes May in her younger years.

In her reply, Mrs Ellegard wrote that 'during the few years
of my friendship with Agnes May Beaumont-Thomas, I found
her to be a rather private and sensitive person'. The disclosure
of her liaison with my grandfather, she continued, 'which was
of a relative short period of time, in her early life, would have
caused her great distress'. Therefore, she concluded, while happy
to let me have her snapshots, she was unwilling to provide any
further help that might compromise her friend's privacy.

All biographers will be familiar with these sentiments, and
many readers may find themselves in agreement. These feelings are natural and go deep. But I maintain that it is the
privacy of the living that should be protected, while the dead
no longer require it, cannot be distressed by it, are above it.

They can still, however, contribute through their posthumous disclosures to our understanding of the living world.

I was sure that Mrs Ellegard would not change her mind, but felt I must make one more appeal. So I wrote again, explaining that I was not seeking scandalous gossip, not attacking the privacy of Agnes May's late years, simply trying to obtain the best possible likeness of her in her youth. 'An artist painted her portrait,' I wrote, 'she sat for it. You have had it for many years in a cupboard which has helped to preserve its freshness. But may I suggest, without any disrespect, that this is taking privacy too far? I believe it deserves to be seen – that is why it was painted – that is why Agnes May kept it. When one receives a gift from a friend like this, one also receives a responsibility. One day, if we are not careful, no one will know who it is.'

I noticed a slightly pompous, bullying tone beginning to enter my letter, and sought to soften this by offering to show Mrs Ellegard anything I might eventually write about Agnes May. Then I signed off with an apology for invading her own privacy. To this letter I never received an answer.

So I had to content myself with investigating what I had. Mrs Ellegard remembered that Agnes May had told her the artist 'was highly thought of and much in demand during the 1920s'. But nowhere could I find a watercolourist or photographer named Janet Evans, and nor could the curator of the Twentieth Century Collection at the National Portrait Gallery, Honor Clerk. I had worked with her before on exhibitions at the gallery and she had recently helped me with my search for the elusive Robin Goodwin. She is an encyclopaedia of knowledge, and if she had never heard of Janet Evans then I felt confident that no such professional photographer existed. For, having shown Mrs Ellegard's snapshot to several experts, I was now convinced that this portrait was a hand-painted or over-painted version of a studio photograph.

Honor Clerk has not merely encyclopaedic knowledge, she

is an ingenious lateral thinker, and soon came up with a new idea. In the mid-1920s, she told me, a camerawoman called Peg Jevons defected from Dorothy Wilding's celebrated photographic studio and set up in business with another woman photographer, Janet Tyrell, creating a firm in Mayfair named Janet Jevons. There are a dozen or so of their prints in the National Portrait Gallery, and I examine the signatures on the lower right-hand corner. I recognise them at once as the same signature before which Mrs Ellegard and I bowed down in her drawing room before intoning the wrong name. The Janet Jevons studio was very close to the apartment in Piccadilly which my grandfather bought for Agnes May, and I have no doubt that this picture, showing what she looked like soon after they met, was his gift to her. This is an accurate portrait and a memento of the woman for whom my grandfather left home.

Agnes May was to enjoy another twenty years of high living after this likeness was made and before the downward spiral of her life began. Then, over a further twenty years or more, a slow decline: from Knightsbridge into Chelsea, and from London off to Worthing, one of the most genteel of English seaside resorts. She would achieve some spirited moments during this retreat – the oil portrait painted in Augustus John's old studio surely marking one of them. Even in her early seventies she was making a dramatic stand, accompanied by her solicitor on the steps of the High Court, waving a doctor's certificate as she intervened in a case which her husband, Reggie Beaumont-Thomas, was bringing to Chancery – had been bringing to Chancery for the last several years.*

---

*Soon after the Variation of Trusts Act 1958 became law the Beaumont-Thomas family hatched a scheme to reduce the duty to be paid on the Trusts set up in the will of Reggie's father. The plan, which involved Agnes May as a 'reversionary annuitant', required Reggie to take out an insurance policy against his death.

She was to die of heart failure at the Berkeley Lodge
Nursing and Convalescent Home, next to Worthing Hospital,
on 12 December 1974. The instructions in her will were clear.
'I desire that there should be no mourners and no flowers.'
There was little to celebrate now and she must have dreaded

The case was barely in its sixth or eighth year when Agnes May, claiming
that the anxiety of waiting was making her ill, staged her dramatic intervention 'with the result that we heard on Monday that the case was coming on
today [18 July 1967]', wrote one of the platoon of solicitors and insurance
agents. 'This took us completely by surprise . . . I would like to say that this is
the end of the matter, but unfortunately it is not, because at the last minute the
Order that we were asking for had to be varied because of a condition made
by Mrs Beaumont-Thomas . . . now we have to go back to the Court of
Protection.'

Eventually Agnes May received a lump sum of £6,000 plus an annual
income of £2,000 which was to continue until her death even if Reggie died
first – all this (in addition to the settlement Reggie had made) came from the
will of a father-in-law whom she never met and who had died almost twenty
years before her marriage to his son.

The significance of this to me is it suggests that had the Holroyd family
discovered the Variation of Trusts Act 1958, it might have broken their own
ruinous family Trust set up by my grandfather to secure funds for his family
after he absconded with Agnes May (a trust that in due course almost
bankrupted the family).

Despite his ill-health, Reggie Beaumont-Thomas outlived Agnes May. He
died at Brighton in 1982 leaving approximately £650,000, a rather trivial
sum by his family's standards. But part of his plan had been to ensure that
his common-law wife Vera Thomas had enough money following his death.
In this he appears to have been successful. On her death in 1991 she left a
respectable two-and-a-half million pounds.

One curious happening which arose following Reggie's death was the
reappearance of his first wife, the Parisian dancing girl Germaine Blanche
Aimée Dubor from whom he had been divorced in 1933. The French government instituted proceedings to have the annuity Reggie had been paying her
for the past fifty years continued after his death and paid out of his estate.
This ingeniously argued case eventually failed, and the French government
was obliged to pay for her care in a home.

the possibility of so many contradictory parts of her life coming together at her death: the Bickerstaffs and Beaumont-Thomases, her sisters' and husband's families – and even, a final horror, her previous husbands.*

Nor did she want a gravestone to perpetuate and repeat her names and dates: her stories with their many beginnings and endings. At the very end she seems to have wanted simply to make what haste she could and be gone. 'I desire that my body may be cremated and my ashes scattered.' While Vera Wall cleared out her flat at Arundel Court (which mysteriously remained empty for several years), the solicitor took charge of the ashes. But no one now knows where they were deposited or released into the air.

Somewhere perhaps, hanging in someone's home or at a gallery, an oil painting 'half-length Portrait of a Lady in blue dress', still exists. It will have Robin Goodwin's signature on it, but no mention of the sitter who, in middle age, has finally lost her identity as she always wished to do, though without gaining another permanent name or recognition for herself.

---

* Though she almost certainly did not know this, her first two husbands had married again and were dead. William Lisle, who had informed Agnes May that his father was a solicitor (he was actually a clerk in a solicitor's office) and that he was a man of money, an accountant (though he too was a solicitor's clerk), married Lily Matthews, the daughter of a postmaster, in 1924 and died in 1936 leaving £450. Thomas Babb worked for a short time as an electrical engineer in the same Royal Air Force office as Henry Haselhurst and was awarded the CBE. He married a divorcée, Marie Louise Welter (née Vermière) in 1934 but, like Agnes May, she left him. He went back to live with his mother for several years in Minehead and died in 1957 only two or three miles from my father and aunt in Surrey, looked after by a lady from London. His mother's estate had been valued in 1951 at approximately £10,000, but he left only £800 six years later.

But I have the reproduction of the hand-coloured photograph, originally commissioned by my grandfather. I have had it enhanced and have restored her name to it. For nearly a quarter of a century it has lain in the dark. This is Agnes May in her adult prime, as she appeared soon after my grandfather met her during the General Strike of 1926, the woman who serenaded him from home, setting off all manner of emotional and financial shock waves that ended seventy years later with my aunt and myself.

I feel my quest is over. I have found her. She is here.

The End.

The Beaumont-Thomas Family

Richard Beaumont-Thomas = Nora Anderson
m. 1888

Pauline Grace Marriott (1) = Lionel = (2) Iseuit Marjorie Haselhurst
marriage dissolved 1934 b. 1893 [formerly Dracopoli
  m. (1) 1913 née Bland]
  m. (2) 1934 b. 1896, d. 1987
  d. 1942

Richard Nigel Paul Pearl

Irene Muriel = Joseph Strensham Oldham
b. 1894
m. 1918
d. 1975

Wilton Joseph David Anthony
b. 1919 b. 1921
d. 1987 d. 1981

Reginald Alexander = (1) Germaine Blanche Aimée Dubor
b. 1903 *divorced 1933*
m. (1) 1925
m. (2) 1934 (2) Agnes May Babb
d. 1982 [formerly Lisle née Bickerstaff]
  separated 1942
[liaison with Vera Thomas
d. 1991]

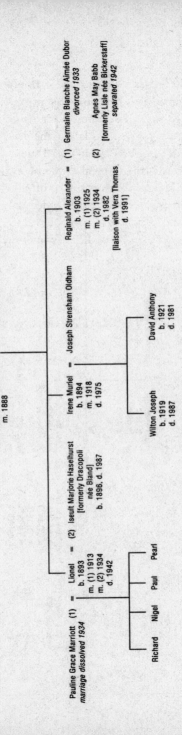

The Haselhurst Family

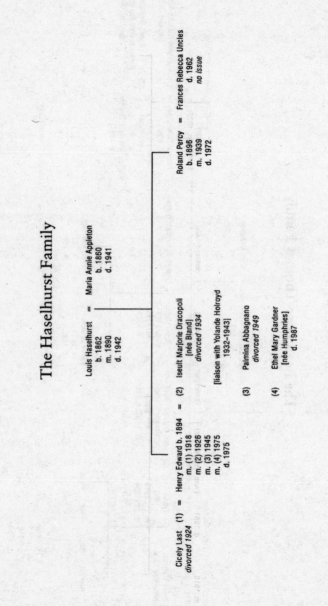

Louis Haselhurst = Maria Annie Appleton
b. 1862   b. 1860
m. 1890   d. 1941
d. 1942

Cicely Last (1) = Henry Edward b. 1894 = (2) Iseult Marjorie Dracopoli   Roland Percy = Frances Rebecca Uncles
divorced 1924   m. (1) 1918   [née Bland]   b. 1896   d. 1962
                     m. (2) 1926   *divorced 1934*   m. 1939   *no issue*
                     m. (3) 1945   d. 1972
                     m. (4) 1975   [liaison with Yolande Holroyd
                     d. 1975   1932–1943]

                                      (3) Palmina Abbagnano
                                          divorced 1949

                                      (4) Ethel Mary Gardner
                                          [née Humphries]
                                          d. 1987

The Bickerstaff Family

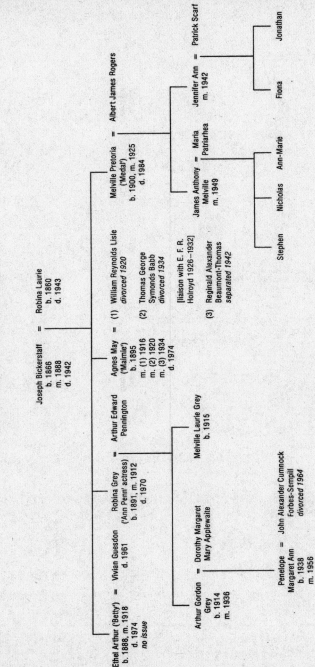

Lytton Strachey

When Michael Holroyd's life of Lytton Strachey first appeared in 1967, it was hailed as a landmark in contemporary biography. In this edition he draws on new material, published and unpublished, to completely revise and rewrite his masterwork to tell the full story of this complex man as could not be told while many of Strachey's friends and lovers were still alive. At the heart of the story is the poignant liaison between Strachey and the painter Dora Carrington.

A panorama of the social, literary, political and sexual life of a generation, *Lytton Strachey* reverberates in the mind like a great novel.

'Michael Holroyd's revised biography of Lytton Strachey is masterly: full of new insights on Strachey, including his strange love affair with Dora Carrington. She becomes the heroine of the book, and her death at the end brings tears to the eyes'
Gerald Kaufman, *Sunday Express*

'You will be won over by Strachey's originality, independence and humanity; by his hatred of humbug and prudery; by his life-saving gift for comedy'
Richard Shone, *Evening Standard*

'Holroyd's prose, in this second version, is as elegant as ever. He is also one of the few biographers who has retained a pronounced sense of humour'
Peter Ackroyd, *The Times*

VINTAGE BOOKS
London

Bernard Shaw

This is the definitive Shaw for the general reader and the student. It has verve and pace, the light and shade of his life are emphasized, digressions cut, and Shaw comes over just as much larger than life as he always was, just as contrary, and even more sympathetically and movingly portrayed. This is a dazzling portrait of the man and his age.

'A flamboyant new landmark in modern English life-writing'
Richard Holmes, *The Times*

'This elegant volume is a conglomerate of four detailed volumes and gives the quintessence of Shaw ... it will serve admirably for the millennium and do justice to a great Irishman'
Irish Independent

'A man whose art rested as much upon the exercise of intelligence could not have chosen a more intelligent biographer ... The pursuit of Bernard Shaw has grown, and turned into the pursuit of the whole 20th century'
The Times

'A masterly exercise in biographical magic'
Spectator

VINTAGE BOOKS
London

Augustus John

This revised and updated biography of the British painter, drawing on the mass of new material which has come to light since Holroyd's first edition in 1974, reveals the complete story of John and his circle. Using new material, new correspondence and drawing on numerous new studies of Gwen John, Epstein and others, Michael Holroyd can now tell the full and true stories behind the life of this archetypal bohemian and artist-reprobate. Proto-feminist subplots involving Gwen, Ida and Dorelia John bring the book thoroughly up to date for the modern reader.

'Wonderfully engrossing and even moving'
Daily Telegraph

'Holroyd has discovered more about John's family, especially his relations with his sister, the formerly enigmatic Gwen ... There is a wonderful *divertissement* on John and contraception and some superb new quotations'
Observer

'An entertaining, essentially comic story – although one's heart goes out to some of the women, Ida particularly. Holroyd tells it with great skill and intelligence'
Sunday Telegraph

'Here, reissued in a substantially revised form 20 years after its first appearance, is one of the most entertaining lives ever written ... Holroyd depicts his subject with great sympathy and understanding ... Very funny ... thought-provoking'
Philip Hensher, *Mail on Sunday*

VINTAGE BOOKS
London

A Strange Eventful History

Henry Irving – a merchant's clerk who became the saviour of British theatre – and Ellen Terry, who made her first theatre appearance as soon as she could walk, were the king and queen of the Victorian stage. Creatively interdependent, they founded a power-house of arts at the Lyceum Theatre, with Bram Stoker as business manager, where they recast Shakespeare's plays on an epic scale and took the company on lucrative and exhilarating international tours. In his masterly biography, award-winning writer Michael Holroyd explores their public and private lives, showing how their artistic legacy and their brilliant but troubled children came to influence the modern world.

'Magnificent – not just as a fascinating exercise in group biography, but as a masterpiece of comic writing. I can think of no higher compliment that to say that I think Proust would have been addicted to it . . . such *joie de vivre*'
Paul Taylor, *New Statesman*

'Holroyd has a wonderful eye for detail . . . an entirely captivating biography'
Richard Eyre, *Guardian*

'This has all the tumbling narrative, spicy detail and easy empathy that determine his midas touch . . . shows Holroyd yet again pushing the biographer's art to new imaginative planes'
Jackie Wullschlager, *Financial Times*

'Michael Holroyd has once again triumphed over a seemingly impossible subject. For so capacious is this tale of two great actors and their descendants that he has written a sweeping social history of theatre in late 19th- and early 20th-century England . . . deftly plotted, with an infectious verve that springs from his delight in the waywardness of human nature'
Frances Spalding, *Independent*

VINTAGE BOOKS
London

For Yvonne

FOREWORD

THIS book was written to do two things: to provide a condensation of the two-volume *Faulkner: A Biography* so as to make its essence available to a wider audience, and to bring that account up to date by incorporating material from the enormous outpouring since then of scholarship, criticism, and other writings, including posthumously published Faulkner works.

For a fuller account of various aspects of William Faulkner's life and work, the reader is referred to the two-volume version of 1974[1] and to two other books: *Uncollected Stories of William Faulkner*, primarily for the stories but also for the notes, which treat in detail the changes in the various versions, and *Selected Letters of William Faulkner*, which supplies the full texts of some letters quoted in part here.[2]

The notes to this book provide references to all material quoted from published sources and to all interviews conducted since 1974. For the names and dates of earlier interviews that were also used in the two-volume edition, scholars and other interested readers are referred to that edition, where all such data are provided in full and may be located chronologically in both the text and the notes.

This edition has afforded the opportunity to correct earlier errors, and where it differs, should be regarded as presenting the best information now available. It is not just different from its predecessor of a decade ago; it is to some extent a new book. Almost all of it has been rewritten, and though it, too, generally follows chronological order, it does so less rigorously. In the intervening years four works by Faulkner have appeared: *The Marionettes, Mayday, Sanctuary: The Original Text*,[3] and *Helen: A Courtship and Mississippi Poems*, all in carefully edited scholarly editions. There have been a number of memoirs of varying lengths and forms. Jill Faulkner provided new insights into her father's personality and art in her part of the television documentary film *William Faulkner: A Life on Paper*. A journal kept by Murry Falkner, his father, came to light. His stepson, Malcolm A. Franklin, published *Bitterweeds: Life at Rowan Oak with William Faulkner*, and his niece, Dean Faulkner Wells, wrote *The Ghosts of Rowan Oak: William Faulkner's Ghost Stories for Children*,[4] and completed a biography of her father, Dean Faulkner, as her M.A. thesis—which changed my view of him, based though it had been on interviews with a number of friends and relatives. Joan Williams published an essay on her relationship with Faulkner, and Susan Snell completed a full and careful doctoral dissertation in the form of a biography of Phil Stone. Meta Carpenter Wilde, who had declined to be interviewed when I was doing the research for *Faulkner*, wrote, with Orin Borsten, *A Loving Gentleman*, and has kindly permitted me to quote from it.

New collections of Faulkner letters became available in the Tulane University Library and the New York Public Library. Three new catalogues of the contents of rich Faulkner collections appeared. Two complete bibliographies of Faulkner criticism were published, as well as many books of criticism, including several on individual Faulkner novels. As I was finishing this book, I read (through the kindness of their publishers) two new studies then in proof. The annual Faulkner number of *The Mississippi Quarterly* continued, to be joined as a fixture in the Faulkner research field by the publication in book form of papers given at the Faulkner Symposium held each summer at the University of Mississippi. All of these materials became available, some demanding to be used in this new book. The authors quoted are all identified in the notes. I should mention at least one new interview. I finally was able to see William Faulkner's Aunt Sue, the wife of John Wesley Thompson Falkner, Jr. She had been sick during the times when I was working on *Faulkner*, and on one of my later visits to Oxford, my friend Jimmy Faulkner took me to see her. So that went into this book too.

To some extent I have used *Faulkner* as I had hoped others would use it, and have used it, in books on William Faulkner published since 1974. There is proportionally more criticism, mine and other people's, in this book. Some of it will serve, perhaps, to balance the assessments of Faulkner works as they were made during his life, assessments often short-sighted and downright wrong, but presented here to show what his career was like as he strove to perfect his art, and make a living. As he said of his characters in his Foreword to *The Mansion*, so I trust I can say of his life and work, that now I know them better than I did when I wrote *Faulkner*. And now, twenty-five years after I first met him, I see some things differently—and, perhaps, more clearly.

I have tried to avoid the limitations of one angle of vision where I could, by drawing on all the resources that went into the writing of *Faulkner* and the new ones I have enumerated. William Faulkner was one of those most keenly aware of the difficulty of seeing things clearly and whole. As he said of his work—that he thought he would be aware of many more discrepancies among the three volumes of the Snopes trilogy than the reader would—so I can say of my awareness of shortcomings in this book. But I am consoled to know that others, too, have despaired of presenting what the biographer seeks and many readers demand: the very heart and kernel of their subjects' genius clearly and absolutely revealed. Two other biographers felt something like this during their work on another great Southerner. "In my youthful presumptuousness," wrote Dumas Malone, "I flattered myself that sometime I would fully comprehend and encompass him. I do not claim that I have yet done so, and I do not believe that I or any other single person can." He was talking about Jefferson. Twenty years later Merrill Peterson wrote, "Of all his great contemporaries Jefferson is perhaps the least self-revealing and the hardest to sound to the depths of being. It is a mortifying confession, but he remains for me, finally, an impenetrable man."[5] I think that this is likely to be the case for most biographers when they approach the lives and works of transcendent geniuses. But they continue to try.

I hope that this book will be useful to the general reader and to the specialist. It is offered for the purpose of throwing more light on that life and that work, on that man of whom, I think, many others would also say, as I did in the Foreword to the two-volume *Faulkner*: I cannot hope to look upon his like again.

Joseph Blotner

CONTENTS

LIST OF ILLUSTRATIONS